THE
MERCHANTS

THE MERCHANTS

The Big Business Families of Saudi Arabia and the Gulf States

MICHAEL FIELD

The Overlook Press
Woodstock, New York

To Davina

First published in 1985 by
The Overlook Press
Lewis Hollow Road
Woodstock, New York 12498

Copyright © 1984 by Michael Field

Library of Congress Cataloging in Publication Data

Field, Michael, 1949 –
    The merchants: the big business families
    of Saudi Arabia and the Gulf States.

    1. Businessmen—Arabia.   2. Arabia—Social conditions.
I. Title.
HC415.3.F54   1985   380.1'0953   85-4386
ISBN 0-87951-971-1 (cloth)
ISBN 0-87951-226-1 (paper)

Contents

Illustrations

Maps

Family Trees

(A shortened family tree of Al Saud will be found in Appendix 4.)

Preface and Acknowledgements

This book stems directly from my last, *A Hundred Million Dollars a Day*, which dealt with petrodollars and was published in 1975. In the reviews of that book, in readers' letters and in the remarks made to me by other journalists and friends involved in the Middle East, it was often observed that the most interesting parts of the book were those in which I had written about some of the famous Arabian families. Encouraged by these comments, I decided to write a new book on a few great merchant families in Saudi Arabia and the Gulf states. After enormous troubles and trials, mainly concerning publishers whose views on what was important in Arabian society disagreed with my own, this is what I have produced.

My intention is to describe Arabian society for those interested in it and to help businessmen who visit the Arabian Peninsula. The merchants are important to anyone who does business in Arabia, on several grounds. First, it is the law in Saudi Arabia and in all the Gulf states that anyone exporting to the area or running any type of contracting, financial or service operation in the countries must have a local agent, sponsor or partner. Second, personalities are much more important in Arabia than institutions or rules and regulations – as anyone who visits the area rapidly discovers. Thirdly, the stories of the merchants, through the insights they allow into the workings of Arabian society, give some indication of how stable are the Arabian states. Since the revolution in Iran, which was a disaster for the West, this subject has become a major concern of businessmen in the industrialised countries. Much of the consultancy work I do now for European, American and Japanese companies and government institutions concerns political and social matters and the assessment of political risks.

The merchant families featured in this book were chosen on the basis of the size of their companies and how well-known they were. In one or two cases I chose to write about families whom I knew already. I also tried to arrange a reasonable variation between Arabian states, and regions within Saudi Arabia, and in the types of businesses in which the families specialised. Here and there I was biased towards families whom I thought might have a good story. I know very well that Arabians will say to me: 'Why did you not choose so and so?' or, 'Surely so and so is as big and as important – or bigger and even more important – than some of the families you have chosen.' My answer is that I have not tried to pick a 'Top Nine' and I agree entirely that there are twenty or thirty more families who would qualify for the book just as well as those who have been included. In effect the choice has depended on the luck of the draw.

I would like to stress that none of the families has sponsored the book in any way. They have not paid my expenses. I have not showed them the text before publication. They have not undertaken to buy copies. When I asked for their help in telling me their stories I only promised that I would not say highly personal, embarrassing things about their members. Such things would certainly have been entertaining, but they would not have been important. On the other hand, where I have discovered dramatic material which has thrown light on the reasons for the families' rise to fame and fortune I have included it, regardless of whether the families will approve of it or not.

I ought also to explain the reason for the division of the book into two parts. It is simply that the families in Part I have more or less self-explanatory stories, whereas those in Part II all have stories rooted on the eastern Arabian coast in the first fifty years of this century. It seemed that the second group of stories would be more interesting if they came after some background chapters on modern Arabian social history. I decided that a major division in the middle of the book would separate these family stories from the first group and would emphasise that the two history chapters (9 and 10) represented a new departure.

During the course of research on this book I was helped by two or three hundred people. I would like to thank most of all the members of the nine merchant families for trusting me. I would also like to thank many of their employees, a number of Arabians from other families, who were prepared to talk about their memories of Arabia before oil and occasionally make comments on the nine families themselves, and many Western expatriates who knew my families thirty, forty or fifty years ago and were prepared to talk very frankly about them. A great many of my sources in all categories said to me that it would be better if I did not mention their names, so in the end I have decided not to mention any of them. This does not diminish my gratitude.

Unpublished Crown Copyright material in the India Office Library and in the Public Record Office transcribed here appears by permission of the Controller of Her Majesty's Stationery Office. This material, which makes engrossing reading, has been a major source for the second part of the book.

Finally, I must say that I immensely enjoyed researching this book. Talking to the nine families took me into a new Arabian world, which foreigners in the region seldom encounter. I hope that those who read this book will have a little of the same experience.

1st August 1983

PART ONE

On a warm, humid morning in November, about a year after I had begun researching this book, I was summoned to the office of Shaikh Ahmed Alireza in Jeddah. I had contacted the Alireza family during a visit to Saudi Arabia six months before and spoken to Ahmed's younger brother, Mahmoud. He had agreed that if I wanted to write about his family, he and the other senior members would be willing to talk to me. Since returning to Jeddah I had met Mahmoud again and had spoken briefly to Ahmed, who had given a very short sketch of his family's history. He had begun by mentioning, in a slightly ritual manner, that the Alirezas traced their descent from Amr ibn al Aasi, one of the lieutenants of the Prophet Mohammad and the man who had won Egypt for Islam in AD 640.

Today it was intended that we should have a long, detailed conversation about the Alirezas' history. I arrived at the building of Haji Abdullah Alireza & Co. and went into the room outside Ahmed's office. This served as a company post room and the office of Ahmed's secretary, a greying Englishman of near retirement age. The secretary explained that Ahmed was certainly expecting me, but that ten minutes earlier a Saudi friend had called. This type of occurrence is one of the ordinary hazards faced by anyone who tries to do business in the Middle East. Whoever the visitor may be, and whoever may be waiting in the ante-room, good manners dictate that the host must welcome his visitor properly and give him as much time as he wants. This is far more important than trying to keep to the day's schedule.

Eventually the visitor left and I was ushered into Shaikh Ahmed's office. We exchanged greetings. Shaikh Ahmed was severe and rather sharp in his manner. He had an austere face, not unlike King Faisal's in his later years: a hooked nose, a grey goatee beard and an ascetic, almost sour look. An occasional twinkle in his eye suggested a warmer, more humorous person underneath. He apologised for keeping me waiting, ordered some coffee and asked me to sit in a chair in front of his desk. We then started to work steadily through his family's history, beginning not with Amr ibn al Aasi but with Ahmed's great-grandfather, Alireza himself. Our conversation was interrupted by several telephone calls, a telex brought in by the secretary, and another caller who stayed for only a few minutes.

Then, after about an hour and a half, something rather unexpected happened. We had reached the career of Ahmed's uncle, Mohammad Ali, who had been one of the most successful Arabian pearl dealers in Bombay and Paris before the First World War and in the 1920s; it was Mohammad Ali who had introduced the family to the jewellery business, which still contributes a minor part of its income. Ahmed was explaining how Mohammad Ali had switched from pearls to other types of jewellery after the bottom had fallen out of the pearl market in the 1930s; suddenly he got up and said: 'I think I ought to show you something.' He looked into a drawer in his desk, found a bunch of keys, and led the way through a door at the back of his office. It opened into a short corridor. A little way down he stopped at a small safe on the floor. He unlocked this and began picking out a succession of black velvet trays of bracelets which he handed up to me. I stacked them on my hand, one above the other, until I had a pile of six or seven, worth about a million dollars. The bracelet on top was a spectacular ruby and diamond specimen. The rubies were the size of small olive stones, each gem surrounded by an oval ring of diamonds, and each cluster joined to the next by links of white gold. This was the bracelet for which Ahmed had been looking. He took it and held it to the light. He then explained that the bracelet was an unusually fine specimen because the rubies in it were of the colour known as 'pigeon's blood'. He went back into his office to find a reference book on precious stones – an old volume with a faded blue cover. He peered at this through half-moon spectacles and read out several paragraphs on the different chemical processes that could give rubies their colour. Before he put the bracelets back into the safe, Ahmed commented that he and the rest of the family looked upon jewellery more as an enjoyable pastime than a business. Dealing with such beautiful things as precious stones could not fail to be a pleasure.

Anyone who has never been there might imagine that in Saudi Arabia the sight of million-dollar piles of jewellery would be commonplace. The idea of old shaikhs discussing the finer points of large rubies matches Arabia's reputation as a land of fabulous riches. The Western assumption is that if Saudi Arabia and the Gulf states[1] have small populations and oil revenues running to over $100 billion a year, then everyone must be rich and their wealth must be highly visible. In fact episodes such as my encounter with Shaikh Ahmed's rubies are very untypical. Compared with Western cities, the cities of Arabia do not display much of the wealth of their inhabitants. There are few smart shops; people's houses are surrounded by high walls; the richer classes, and especially the richer women, can seldom be seen in public. In Saudi Arabia visitors say that they are aware of being in a very rich country because they hear from time to time of people making $10 million bank deposits and see an extraordinary number of jewellery advertisements in the glossy Arabian magazines; but they find that they hardly ever come face to face with great quantities of personal wealth.

The Alireza family in particular dislikes showing off its wealth. It prefers to be thought of as important and well established rather than very rich. The old offices of Haji Abdullah Alireza & Co., in which Ahmed showed me the rubies, were built in the 1950s. They are dark, with rather dated fittings, drab paintwork and stone corridors. Their main positive feature is that they are extremely solid and clearly built to last, which is in contrast to most of the more recent building in the Kingdom. The offices sum up the company that built them – conservative, reliable, but lacking the aggression and innovative flair of newer merchant firms. The company's character did not change when it moved into a new glass and concrete tower block just behind the old building in 1979.

Shaikh Ahmed's own office in the original building conveyed much the same impression as the Alireza establishment as a whole, except that it was enhanced by rows of interesting photographs. These have now been transferred to his new office in the tower block. Most of the pictures on the wall are sepia tinted. There is a photograph of Ahmed's father, Yusuf, greeting Prince Faisal bin Abdel-Aziz (later King Faisal), and a portrait of Ahmed's grandfather, Zainal, in about 1920. Zainal is shown as a serious old gentleman with a white beard and a white turban. Then there is a group photograph of a delegation from the Ottoman parliament in Constantinople visiting the British parliament

1. The Gulf states are Kuwait, Bahrain, Qatar (pronounced 'Catter') and the United Arab Emirates. The two leading members of the UAE are Abu Dhabi and Dubai. Apart from Saudi Arabia, the only other oil-producing state in the Arabian Peninsula is Oman.

at Westminster in 1908. In the second row, behind Lord Curzon, is Kassem Alireza, the Ottoman parliament's member for Jeddah. Kassem spoke seven languages and was known as the best-educated and most widely travelled man in Jeddah in the first thirty years of this century.

Further along the wall there is a picture of greater political importance. It shows Ahmed's great-uncle, Haji Abdullah, the governor of Jeddah, drinking coffee with Ibn Saud[2] on the day he surrendered Jeddah in December 1925. This was a momentous event, which established Ibn Saud's authority over the biggest city in Arabia and left him unchallenged as the major power in the land he was about to turn into the Saudi Kingdom. Unfortunately the picture tells nothing of the emotions of either man seated at the table; their faces are half in the shade, frozen and impassive for an official photographer.

Finally, there are two relatively modern pictures of Haji Abdullah's sons, Mohammad and Ali, in official diplomatic dress. Shaikh Mohammad, who died in 1982, was once Saudi ambassador in Cairo and Paris, and Shaikh Ali was Saudi ambassador in Washington until early 1979. It was these two, together with Ahmed, who were mainly responsible for the Alireza company's development as a modern business during the 1950s, 1960s and 1970s.

Haji Abdullah Alireza & Co. (HAACO) is now a diversified trading and contracting company. The big profit earners during the later 1970s were a joint company with Mobil which sold aviation spirit at Jeddah airport, and an air-traffic control telecommunications contract. This involved ITT, which the Alirezas represent in Saudi Arabia, as a subcontractor, working under Lockheed. Other HAACO operations included insurance, shipping agencies, aircraft handling and ticket sales – the company has the general sales agencies for KLM and Air Algerie. In contracting, the firm has joined with two British companies to form Laing Wimpey Alireza, which won some profitable military airfield contracts in the late 1960s, and in October 1981 signed contracts for two hospitals in the Qassim province north of Riyadh. Most valuable of all are the family's holdings of real estate, part owned by the company and

2. Ibn Saud, who was known as King Abdel-Aziz after the conquest of Jeddah, built the Saudi kingdom in stages between 1902, when he reconquered his family home of Riyadh, and 1934, when he consolidated his control of the south-western corner of his domains. He ruled until 1953. He has been followed by four of his many sons: Saud bin Abdel-Aziz (1953–64), Faisal (1964–75), Khaled (1975–82) and Fahd.

part owned by family members privately. Unexpectedly in a country of limitless space and small population, Saudi real estate commands prices that can compare with the highest in London and Manhattan.

The Alirezas are one of thirty or forty big, highly diversified merchant families in the Arabian Peninsula. This book will deal with the Alirezas and eight similar families, all of them well known and all with high-profile businesses. Where possible I have chosen the families with the biggest turnovers in their states or regions. There is no question that the Juffalis of Saudi Arabia have the highest turnover of any family company in the Arabian Peninsula. Likewise the Alghanims and Kanoos own the biggest companies in Kuwait and Bahrain, and the Sultan family's company, W.J. Towell, has as high a turnover as any other merchant group in Oman. Suliman Olayan has probably the third biggest Arabian private business, and Ahmed Hamad Algosaibi is certainly the biggest of the Saudi Eastern Province merchants. These are a group of half a dozen major businessmen whose operations are closely bound up with the work of the Arabian American Oil Company (Aramco) and who still do almost all of their business in the oil-bearing part of the Kingdom.

The family of Algosaibi, of whom Ahmed Hamad Algosaibi is probably a distant relation, is not dissimilar to the house of Alireza. The two families' fame comes from the role they played in the creation of the Saudi state in the 1920s and 1930s. In Qatar the Darwish family was an important influence – in fact the dominant influence – in the state's affairs in the early days of oil in the late 1940s and the 1950s.

The merchant houses make up most of the private sectors of the Arabian oil-state economies. Their activities cover contracting, the import of all types of goods from instant coffee to bulldozers, shipping and travel agencies, exchange dealing, insurance broking, real estate development, hotels and light manufacturing. Unlike Western businesses, which are mostly fairly specialised, most of the Arabian merchant houses have diversified into almost all of these activities. Where possible they try to ensure that their operations complement each other. A merchant who has a string of shipping agencies and a normal run of other businesses will make sure that the shipping lines he represents will buy fuel from his bunkering service, air-tickets for relief crews through his travel agency, and will have their ships unloaded by his stevedoring company. Where possible, cargoes will be insured through the merchant's insurance business. Any of the crew who have to spend a night or so ashore before flying home will be likely to find themselves booked into the merchant's hotel.

The best-known and by far the most visible of the merchants' activities is importing. The Arabian oil states are classic single-product economies, which means that almost everything they need for their development programmes and their people's consumption has to be imported. Together with contracting, importing has been the obvious area of operations for the Arabian entrepreneur, and over the past thirty years, since oil production began, it has become the merchants' business *par excellence*. It is relatively safe and highly profitable. Like a lot of trade within the Western world it is based on importers having agency agreements with manufacturers, but contrary to the practice elsewhere, agencies in the Arabian Peninsula are almost always exclusive.

The merchants are favoured by Arabian commercial law. In every oil state of the Arabian Peninsula it is the law that foreign companies may sell their products only through local agents; they may not set up their own sales branches. They are obliged to have a local businessman as a sponsor or partner if they want to bid for government or private construction contracts. Most states insist that foreign companies should also take merchant partners if they want to establish manufacturing or service operations. Exceptions to these rules are few, and companies are discouraged from taking advantage of them.

Foreign companies without Arabian partners find it difficult to deal with the local bureaucracy. Personalities – and the relations of influential people with each other – are more important in Arabia than institutions and regulations. People dominate the bureaucracy, not vice versa. Even the most important decisions at the top of government are influenced at least as much by personal factors as by objective considerations; if the King or a senior prince is anxious that a particular person should be awarded a contract, that person will get the contract regardless of whether or not his bid is the best. At a lower level bureaucratic obstacles are removed, permits are issued, accommodation for foreign employees is obtained mainly through personal influence. Inevitably personalities are a prominent topic of conversation among both Arabians and foreigners. The irony is that the strong Arabian sense of what is proper to be made public means that virtually nothing on personalities is ever published in Arabia.

The most successful merchants have become extremely valuable to the companies they represent. Many merchant houses are the biggest export customers for their principals. Yusuf Ahmed Alghanim & Sons in Kuwait in the late 1970s was the biggest overseas distributor for General Motors. In Saudi Arabia E.A. Juffali & Brothers sells more than $600 million worth of Daimler Benz (Mercedes) trucks every year. The company is not only by far the world's biggest Daimler Benz agent; on its own it imports more Daimler Benz trucks than any other country.

Juffali represents about sixty other major Western manufacturers, including IBM, L.M. Ericsson, Siemens and Michelin. The company's turnover is now estimated to be running at well over $1 billion a year. Yusuf Ahmed Alghanim & Sons in 1982 had revenues of some $400 million, which put it at number five in the league of the biggest Arabian merchant companies. There are perhaps fifteen other merchant companies with turnovers of $200 million or more and maybe a further twenty with turnovers between $50 million and $200 million. These include Haji Abdullah Alireza & Co., which is estimated to have a turnover of $80–90 million a year. All of these figures are impressive by the normal standards of family-owned companies. Juffali and a few other companies stand comparison with all but the biggest public companies in the West. Juffali claims that if it were an American company it would be well into the list of the *Fortune* 500.

It is difficult to judge the size of the merchants' personal fortunes. One cannot put a market value on their companies when there is no proper stock exchange in any Arabian state except Kuwait. Even in Kuwait no merchant company has ever thought seriously of offering shares to the public, and so nobody has ever thought in detail about how much money it might be able to raise. Further complications stem from the difficulty of valuing land in Arabia and from the merchants' preoccupation with keeping the size of their foreign assets secret. It is probably fair to say that the six or seven richest merchant families (who include some bankers and exchange dealers) are billionaires. This puts them on a par with the very richest Americans – in the Daniel Ludwig and Paul Getty class – and with the richest members of the Arabian ruling families.

The size of their companies and their personal fortunes are beginning to push the merchants into playing more prominent roles in international business. In the eyes of major companies and government agencies in the West and in Japan, the merchants represent huge export opportunities. Since the 1973–4 oil crisis Saudi Arabia has become one of the biggest export markets for all the industrialised countries. During the recession which began in 1979, when much of the world trade was stagnant, the Arabian Peninsula was one of the few markets that continued to grow. Most of the imports of Saudi Arabia and the other oil states pass through the hands of the merchant companies, making the merchants people to be courted. The Juffalis alone must account for more than a billion Deutsche Marks of German exports a year.

As the merchants' foreign investments expand, Western financial institutions are beginning to see them as a force in the stock markets. Companies in which they have bought large shareholdings consult them on developing business in the Middle East; in a few cases companies have talked to Arabian shareholders about their taking seats on their boards. Suliman Olayan has assets in Europe and America estimated at about $300 million. He has become the biggest shareholder in Chase Manhattan after David Rockefeller. He is a member of the board of Mobil and he represents the Saudi private sector on the US–Saudi Joint Economic Commission.

It is easy for Westerners to see the big Arabian merchants only as international businessmen. When journalists meet them in Europe and America the merchants are in Western dress working in their companies' liaison offices or in their private apartments, talking about their foreign investments or their theories on management or marketing. They are seen against a Western background. Journalists write about the merchants' houses and their investments because these are aspects of their lives which are easily understood by Western readers. Unconsciously they present the merchants as a new breed of tycoon – Arab in nationality, but in every other respect Western. They also imply that the merchants are important to Westerners mainly because of the lives they live in the West and the investments they own there.

An American journalist once referred to Kutayba Alghanim, the young chief executive of Yusuf Ahmed Alghanim & Sons (YAAS) and Alghanim Industries, as '. . . the Arab multinational businessman of the future – now . . . [The owner of] a modern, multinational corporate structure in an embryo stage, poised to expand throughout the Middle East and around the world . . . a cosmopolite, as much a citizen of the world as of Kuwait.' At the time this was published, in 1978, Kutayba was running his company on half modern and half traditional, Middle Eastern lines; he was being given most praise in Kuwait for having tried to create a modern company before anyone else had taken the plunge. Kutayba was preoccupied with rival Kuwaiti importers of General Motors cars and a very Arabian family wrangle. YAAS was making rather small profits and was thought likely to move into deficit (see chapters 5 and 15). The dynamic, international appearance of the company and its owner stemmed from Kutayba's American education, his flair for explaining his ideas for the development of his company, and good public relations.

The merchants are judged best against an Arabian background. They are important to the Western world because of what they have achieved in their own countries. They have made their fortunes in Arabia and they wield their commercial and political power there.

The merchant families are part of the Arabian establishment. They dominate Arabian commercial life and they have been responsible for as many economic innovations as the governments. They have established most of the new Arabian investment banks, light industries and high-technology service companies. In the Gulf states, which have a tradition as trading communities, the merchants are the most valued constituents of the ruling families; their senior members are consulted on most important domestic political issues. In both Saudi Arabia and the Gulf states the merchants serve the ruling families in government. Kutayba Alghanim's elder brother, Abdullah, until recently was Kuwaiti Minister of Water and Power; Abdullah Mohammad Alireza, the eldest son of the former Saudi Ambassador in Paris, is the deputy minister in charge of economic affairs in the Saudi Foreign Ministry. In this capacity he heads the Anglo-Saudi Economic Commission, which was established in 1975 to promote British involvement in Saudi development projects.

The merchant families' histories during this century have been entwined with the political and economic histories of their countries. Their changing fortunes reflect the big economic watersheds – the collapse of pearling, the disastrous years of the Second World War, the opportunities presented by the arrival of the oil companies in the later 1940s, the boom of the 1970s. They show the sources of strain in Arabian society and the relations between the various communities of the Peninsula. They also show how the merchants and other sections of society are bound to the Arabian ruling families: the nature of people's loyalities in Arabia is very different from that in the Western world.

This book is not meant to be a social or political history, still less to make any political forecast. It is a collection of family stories which it is hoped will add up to more than the sum of its parts, and so give an insight into the workings of Arabian society.

1

The House of Alireza

Big companies in Arabia are as susceptible to changes in fashion and business practice as the corporations they trade with in Europe and America. To be *modern* in Arabia a company needs a computer; it needs to develop its own autonomous 'in house' service departments for advertising, public relations, market research, personnel, sales and maintenance training, hire-purchase finance. It must also adopt the latest Western ideas on planning employees' careers by setting 'performance objectives and personal development goals' – the jargon comes from Alghanim in Kuwait. In practice only a few merchant companies have gone for modernisation in this way, and in many of those which have, the modernisation is more a matter of appearances than substance. In very few Arabian merchant firms does anyone outside the ranks of the family carry authority to make decisions or spend sums of money above a few hundred dollars.

In less important and more visible areas modern business practices have taken firmer root. Adnan Khashoggi, the Saudi international entrepreneur, has held an 'in-group' employees' conference so that managers in different branches of his empire can get to know each other. Suliman Olayan's company issues its managers with a little black personnel directory, with telephone numbers and addresses of group subsidiaries. Half a dozen companies have brought out glossy group brochures in English. The first to do so was Juffali, followed by Alghanim, the Kuwait branch of the Alireza family and Suliman Olayan. The procedure has been to sign up a British, American or Lebanese public relations firm. The firm sends out a writer and a photographer, who are shown round all departments of the business and then produce about two pages on each aspect of the company: container cargo handling and haulage, heavy transport, plant hire and contracting, trading. The pictures, which are much the same from brochure to brochure, show warehouse racks bulging with spare parts, mechanics being trained in the company garage (Arabian companies are notably weak on spares and service), heavy trucks thundering across rugged terrain, and the in-house advertising team gathered round a table, looking with intelligence and enthusiasm at a mock-up of a new ad. The text between the pictures is crammed with modern business jargon.

Inevitably it was decided that Haji Abdullah Alireza & Co. ought to have one of these brochures on itself. 'Keeping up with the march of time', was how one of the directors put it with a classic Alireza turn of phrase. A London public relations company was duly commissioned to do the work, and it sent out the usual team of writer and photographer to begin research on what became *The House of Alireza*, an attractive production with a golden palm tree embossed on a chocolate-brown cover. Naturally enough the Alirezas wanted to emphasise how long they had been in business in Jeddah, so the first item in the brochure was headed 'One Hundred and Thirty Years', not a page title which any of the other merchant companies had been able to use. However, this desire to emphasise the firm's antiquity led the people working on the brochure to a rather interesting discovery. The family brought out an ancient and yellowing company ledger dated 1867. The entries were written in the old form of Turkish, using Arabic rather than Roman script, and contained many obscure and archaic expressions applied only in commerce. The ledger was encased in an expensive green and gold leather binder, apparently to be produced on appropriate occasions and shown to interested Western business associates.

The public relations men were genuinely interested: they commented appreciatively on the ledger, photographed it and put a picture of it at the top of page 2. But what was remarkable was that nobody had bothered to discover what the ledger actually said. It was known in broad terms that it dealt with the amounts of goods supplied by the firm to customers; but as to what the goods were, what they cost and who bought them, nobody had the faintest idea.

The early parts of the Alireza story have a somewhat legendary flavour. The family is delighted with the prestige it gains in Western eyes from having been in Jeddah for 130 years, but, like all Saudi families, it is much less interested in discovering accurate details about its past. The world of pre-oil Arabia is regarded as too poor and too monotonous to deserve serious study.

The broad outline of the Alirezas' early history is not disputed. The family's business was started by Zainal bin Alireza, who arrived in Jeddah from Iran in the 1840s when he was a boy of about twelve. Zainal's departure from Iran, however, is one of the more hazy events in the story – an episode which has more than one version. The most detailed account runs as follows: Zainal's father, Alireza, lived in a town in southern Iran, a few miles from the port of Lingeh, near the entrance of the Gulf. Alireza was a man of some substance. He owned a caravan of camels, which transported goods from the coast into the interior, and he was a cousin of the governor of the region. His prestige in his town had been enhanced by his marrying the governor's daughter. Unfortunately both Alireza and the governor were fractious, hot-tempered men. They quarrelled so badly over some political or religious matter that the governor took one of Alireza's family as a hostage. He seized young Zainal, clapped him in irons and threw him into prison. The enraged father dug a tunnel under the walls and into the prison courtyard, released his son and escaped with him to Lingeh. Here, by a happy chance, he met a member of a family called Zahid, who had come from the same part of Iran as Alireza and had moved to Jeddah some years before; Alireza had met members of the family when he had been through Jeddah while on a pilgrimage to Mecca. The Zahids were now prosperous merchants and dhow owners, plying the Persian export trade in carpets and tobacco. Alireza asked his friend if he would take his son with him to safety, the friend agreed, and so Zainal sailed to Jeddah.

When he arrived in his new home Zainal was taken into the Zahid household and began work for the family's business. A few years later he went into business on his own as a food and cloth importer, and in due course he took one of the Zahid daughters as his bride. The bond forged between the Alirezas and the Zahids by these events has been strong ever since. It has been maintained by numerous marriages and a considerable amount of commercial co-operation. In the late 1940s, a century after Zainal arrived in Jeddah, the Alirezas gave the Zahids the Western Province agency for General Motors.

The Jeddah in which Zainal lived was a walled city backed by a range of mountains. It had only one tree, which still stands outside the house of the Nasif family. It was extremely hot and humid; the air carried an oppressive, sickly, salt smell of decaying rubbish and dead fish. The

Alireza Family Tree – Zainal Branch

Excluding some of the youngest members, who are still children

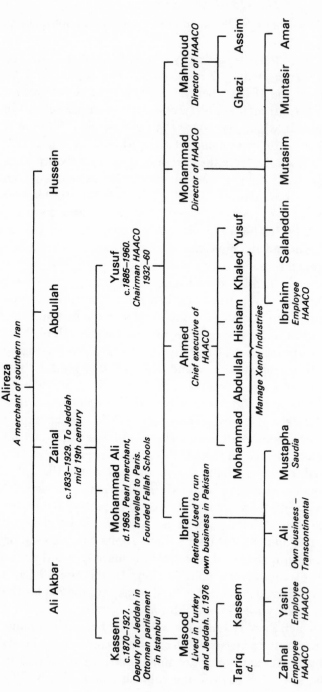

Alireza
A merchant of southern Iran

Ali Akbar Zainal Abdullah Hussein
c.1833–1929. To Jeddah mid 19th century

Kassem
c.1870–1927. Deputy for Jeddah in Ottoman parliament in Istanbul

Mohammad Ali
d. 1969. Pearl merchant, travelled to Paris. Founded Fallah Schools

Yusuf
c.1885–1960. Chairman HAACO 1932–60

Masood
Lived in Turkey and Jeddah. d.1976

Ibrahim
Retired. Used to run own business in Pakistan

Ahmed
Chief executive of HAACO

Mohammad
Director of HAACO

Mahmoud
Director of HAACO

Tariq
d.

Kassem

Zainal
Employee HAACO

Yasin
Employee HAACO

Ali
Own business – Transcontinental

Mustapha
Saudia

Mohammad Abdullah Hisham Khaled Yusuf
Manage Xenel Industries

Ibrahim
Employee HAACO

Salaheddin Mutasim Muntasir Amar

Ghazi Assim

NOTES

1. Haji Abdullah Alireza & Co (HAACO) is owned by most of the male and female descendants of Zainal and Abdullah. Exceptions are the male descendants of Kassem, the descendants of some of the daughters of the family, and children who have not been issued with shares.

2. Before 1948 there were two companies owned by the Zainal and Abdullah branches of the Alireza family. These were Haji Zainal Alireza in Jeddah and Haji Abdullah Alireza in Bombay and Calcutta. After the independence of India, restrictions imposed on foreign businesses made it impracticable for the family to continue running the Bombay and Calcutta offices. The whole Indian business was given to Ibrahim Zainal, and its name, Haji Abdullah, was transferred to the Jeddah operation. In due course Ibrahim Zainal gave the Indian business to his head clerk. He moved to Pakistan, where he established a new business of his own. Ibrahim has now closed this business and retired to Jeddah.

3. Xenel Industries Ltd is managed by the four senior sons of Ahmed Yusuf Zainal Alireza – namely Mohammad, Abdullah, Hisham and Khaled. These four hold the majority of the company's shares. The other shareholders are their younger brother, Yusuf, their sister, Mariam, Zainal Ibrahim Yusuf Zainal, Abdullah Omar Agil, Ibrahim Mohammad Yusuf Zainal, and Ghazi Mahmoud Yusuf Zainal. The company invests mainly in joint-venture service and manufacturing businesses. These include the Saudi Cable Co.

Alireza Family Tree – Ali Akbar Branch

Showing all sons of Ali Akbar, but otherwise much shortened

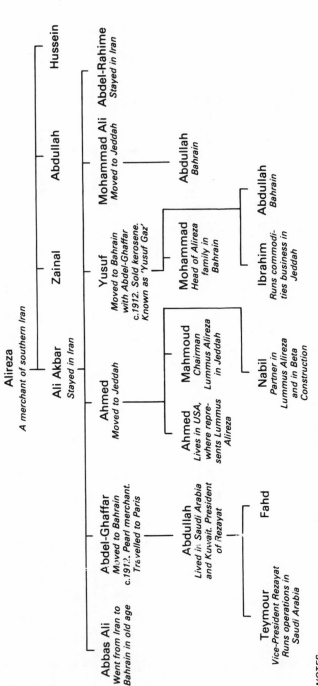

Alireza
A merchant of southern Iran

Ali Akbar — *Stayed in Iran* | **Zainal** | **Abdullah** | **Mohammad Ali** *Moved to Jeddah* | **Abdel-Rahime** *Stayed in Iran* | **Hussein**

Abbas Ali — *Went from Iran to Bahrain in old age*

Abdel-Ghaffar — *Moved to Bahrain c.1912. Pearl merchant. Travelled to Paris*

Ahmed — *Moved to Jeddah*

Yusuf — *Moved to Bahrain with Abdel-Ghaffar c.1912. Sold kerosene. Known as 'Yusuf Gaz'*

Abdullah — *Lived in Saudi Arabia and in Kuwait. President of Rezayat*

Ahmed — *Lives in USA, where represents Lummus Alireza*

Mahmoud — *Chairman Lummus Alireza in Jeddah*

Mohammad — *Head of Alireza family in Bahrain*

Abdullah — *Bahrain*

Fahd

Nabil — *Partner in Lummus Alireza and in Beta Construction*

Ibrahim — *Runs commodities business in Jeddah*

Abdullah — *Bahrain*

Teymour — *Vice-President Rezayat Runs operations in Saudi Arabia*

NOTES

1. The Rezayat Group, based in Kuwait, is owned and managed by Abdullah Abdel-Ghaffar Alireza and his son Teymour. Lummus Alireza, a joint-venture involving the Lummus process engineering company of the USA, is owned and managed by Mahmoud Ahmed Ali Akbar and Nabil Ahmed Ali Akbar. Nabil also holds an interest in the Beta Construction Company, which is run by the Zaidan family.

ALIREZA FAMILY TREE – ABDULLAH AND HUSSEIN BRANCHES
Excluding some of the youngest members, who are still children

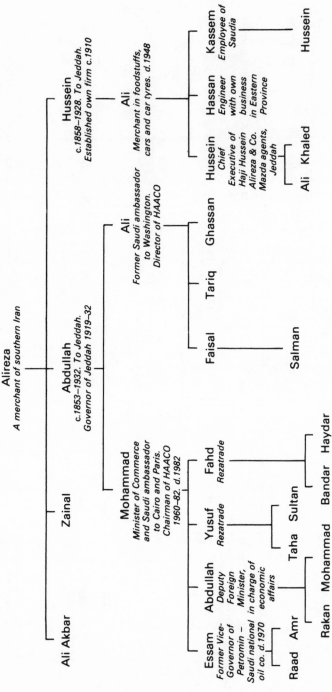

NOTES

1. For ownership of Haji Abdullah Alireza and Company (HAACO) and comments on the company see notes below Zainal branch family tree.

2. Haji Hussein Alireza & Co., the Saudi importer of Mazda cars, is owned by Hussein Ali Alireza, his brothers, Hassan and Kassem, and their aunt.

3. The Rezatrade Group is owned by all the living sons of Mohammad Abdullah Alireza and Ali Abdullah Alireza. Like Xenel Industries, the company invests mainly in joint-venture service and manufacturing businesses. It has a paint factory which is run in partnership with ICI.

houses were tall, coral brick buildings, with many carved wooden shutters and ornate balconies, which jutted over the streets below. The windows, the floors inside the houses, even the walls sloped. The dark alleyways between the houses were floored with damp, matted sand.[1]

The northern, southern and eastern sides of the town were surrounded by walls; on the western side was the port, which was the source of all Jeddah's prosperity. Jeddah had been a trading city for centuries. Its merchants bought goods in India, Africa, Egypt and Syria. Some of the goods were re-exported to Egypt and Yemen, most of what they bought was sold to the tribes of western Arabia and to the towns and villages of the Hijaz. This was the coastal region of Arabia running from the northern end of the Red Sea to the borders of Asir, about 200 miles south of Jeddah. In the nineteenth century it was part of the decaying Ottoman Empire, though the most important magnate in the region, the Governor of Mecca, enjoyed some independence. In accordance with a tradition that stretched back a thousand years, all governors of Mecca were chosen from the house of Hashim, the family of the Prophet Mohammad. At times the Hashemites had ruled all of the Hijaz.

The main source of income of the Hijaz was the annual influx of pilgrims (*hajis*), who came to the holy cities of Mecca and Medina from all parts of the Muslim world. One of the most numerous and richest contingents came from central Asia, others came from India, the East Indies, Turkey, Egypt, Syria, Iran and West Africa. The people of Jeddah and Mecca made money out of selling provisions to the *hajis*, and they benefited indirectly from a head tax of £30 in gold levied on each *haji* by the Governor of Mecca. In the late nineteenth and early twentieth centuries, when about 100,000 Muslims were making the pilgrimage every year, this tax brought the government an annual revenue of some £3 million. The Hijazi merchants earned another £4–5 million from the *hajis*' spending on food and transport, sacrificial sheep, and guides to instruct them on the rites and rituals of the pilgrimage. The merchants were none too scrupulous about the prices they charged, and it was known that the pilgrims themselves, approaching the supreme spiritual moment of their lives, were not over-worried about what they paid. Most of the *hajis* in the years before mass transport were much richer than the men and women who make the pilgrimage today.

1. See the famous description of Jeddah in *The Seven Pillars of Wisdom* by T.E. Lawrence, Jonathan Cape, 1935, pp. 72–3.

The total income of some £7–8 million derived from the Haj does not seem very impressive by the standards of the 1980s, but at the beginning of this century it made Jeddah and Mecca almost the richest towns in Arabia. The only richer town was Aden, which was a British colony and a major port on the shipping lanes between Europe and India. Bahrain, the home of the Gulf pearling industry and the biggest trading centre on the eastern side of the Arabian Peninsula, earned less than £2 million of foreign exchange a year. The Hijaz towns, furthermore, gained an intangible human benefit from the pilgrims they received. The pilgrims increased the Hijazis' contact with the outside world. A few of the more learned and devout stayed behind after completing their religious rites and became teachers in the mosques; many more established trading businesses, dealing with the countries from which they had come. The foreign cultural influence made the Hijazis a relatively tolerant, easy-going people. Despite their proximity to Mecca and Medina, they were not especially strict in their religious observances.

The Hijazis were totally different from the people of the Arabian interior. The central Arabians, most of whom lived on the upland plateau around Riyadh, known as the Nejd, were a mixture of bedouin and townsmen. The bedouin sold horses and camels to the towns and villages, and the oasis dwellers supplied the bedouin with dates and a few manufactured goods which they had bought from merchants coming from Kuwait, Bahrain or the Hijaz. Trade was regularly interrupted by bedouin raids on the oases.

Both the townsmen and the bedouin of the Nejd were desperately poor. The houses in the villages were built entirely of mud brick; the people were ignorant, superstitious and hungry. Hand in hand with these harsh conditions went a strong, puritan faith. The Nejdis had adopted the fundamentalist interpretation of Islam, commonly known as Wahabism (see chapter 3), and were only too willing to believe that the austerity of their lives made them more virtuous than the peoples of the richer regions that surrounded them. The Wahabis, or *Muwahidin*[2] as they called themselves, prohibited alcohol and tobacco, insisted on a strict regime of prayer and despised foreign influences. One of their early phobias was of domes. These structures were manifestly foreign, they were associated with the veneration of the tombs of saints (which

2. *Muwahidin* means Unitarian – a reference to the Wahabis' adherence to the Muslim principle that only God (*Allah*) is holy. The Wahabis abhor all practices that seem to venerate the Prophet Mohammad himself, or members of his family.

the Wahabis regarded as being idolatrous) and they were architecturally far too sophisticated for the central Arabians themselves to build. The Wahabis regarded them with outrage and bewilderment; the destruction of domes punctuated the story of early Wahabi conquests in the eighteenth and nineteenth centuries. The intolerance and xenophobia of the Wahabis, symbolised by their attitude towards domes, was undiluted by contact with the outside world. By the 1840s, at the time Zainal Alireza arrived in Jeddah, only five Europeans were known to have penetrated to the central Nejd. Sixty years later the number had still not risen above ten. The contrast between the austere culture of the Nejd and the relative sophistication of the Hijaz is still significant in Saudi Arabia today. It has played a vital role in the history of the Alireza family.

The Alireza business emerged as a force in Jeddah trade in the 1860s. By this time Zainal was in his thirties. He was being assisted by his much younger brother, Abdullah, whom he had brought over from Iran at the age of ten or twelve to work with him as an apprentice. Very little is known about the brothers' activities during the next twenty years, except that Abdullah followed Zainal's example by marrying into the Zahid family. His bride was the younger sister of Zainal's wife. Some years later the brothers repeated the procedure of both marrying girls from the same family. When Zainal's wife died and Abdullah divorced his wife, the two men took wives from the Nasifs, the family with Jeddah's only tree outside its house.[3]

The most important development for the Alirezas' business in the later nineteenth century took place in the 1880s. When Abdullah grew up he was sent by Zainal to India to open purchasing offices for the family company in Bombay and Calcutta. The purpose of these offices was to give the Alirezas a foothold in the Indian commodities market and enable them to buy cheaper than their Arabian competitors, whose contact with the subcontinent was confined to occasional visits. The Indian offices had other unexpected benefits. In 1893 Abdullah signed the family's first 'modern' contract in Bombay. He arranged for the

3. Muslims are allowed to take up to four wives at one time and to divorce them at will. This practice leads to there being large gaps in age between men's children; there were twenty years between Zainal and Abdullah. It also makes for very large families. Abdullah had eleven children – nine daughters and then two sons.

Alirezas to become the Jeddah agents of the Mogul Line, which held a monopoly of the pilgrim traffic between India and Jeddah. The agency contract involved the Alirezas arranging the disembarkation of pilgrims and the reprovisioning of the company's steamers when they called at Jeddah. In a less material sense also, India benefited the Alirezas by introducing them to the modern industrialised world. In succession Abdullah and all of Zainal's sons, Kassem, Mohammad Ali and Yusuf, served in the offices in Calcutta and Bombay. Apart from the influence of Zainal, who seems to have been a man of great foresight and strength of character, it must have been their exposure to British India at a young age that made these members of the Alireza family so much more enterprising than their contemporaries in Jeddah.

When they returned from India all of the Alirezas carved out remarkable careers for themselves. Kassem, Zainal's eldest son, grew up a liberal man; he was 'born fifty years ahead of his time' the family says today. In India and Jeddah he had given himself the broadest possible education. He had learnt no less than seven languages – Persian, Turkish, Arabic, English, French, Urdu and Amharic. When the Young Turks staged their revolution in Istanbul in 1908 and convened a parliament, Kassem was elected as deputy for Jeddah. He became an active member of the reform movement in Turkey, and within months of his election was chosen as one of the Turkish delegation which paid an official visit to the British parliament at Westminster. He lobbied the Turkish government for an early type of coal-fired sea-water distillation plant to be provided for Jeddah – and, more remarkably, got it built. After the collapse of the Turkish Empire in the First World War, Kassem lived permanently in Jeddah. In the last decade of his rather short life he remained one of the leaders of the Jeddah community – though he held no formal post. He was a popular dinner-party guest of the small corps of foreign consuls and businessmen who lived in the town. They regarded Kassem as by far the most sophisticated and cultured of Jeddah's citizens and a good source of news about local politics.

Still more unusual was the career of Kassem's brother Mohammad Ali. As with the story of Zainal's escape from Iran, there is a somewhat legendary flavour about Mohammad Ali's early life, and of course the only source of detailed information is the Alireza family itself; it is not possible to corroborate the story from documents. From boyhood it seems that Mohammad Ali had always been deeply religious. During his teens he was seen to be bringing the poor people of Jeddah into his family's house and inviting teachers to instruct them in reading and writing. His father and uncle had no objection to these activities but they did nothing to encourage Mohammad Ali to continue his good work. As part of the normal course of running the family's business they arranged for him to go to India to help Abdullah manage the Bombay purchasing office.

After some months in Bombay, Mohammad Ali decided that he was not happy with his job. He considered it tedious and of no benefit to anyone except his increasingly rich relations, and in 1901 or 1902 he ran away to Egypt. There are two versions of what happened next. One has it that Abdullah took ship after him and the other says that quite by chance he met his father, Zainal, who was visiting Egypt on business, on the quayside at Suez; in any event one relation or the other stopped his flight soon after he arrived in Egypt. The conversation that took place at the meeting, as recounted by members of the Alireza family today, has acquired an attractive simplicity with the passing of time: 'What are you doing here?' demanded Zainal or Abdullah. 'I am going to Cairo to join Al Azhar [the great theological college of the Arab world] because I want to become a teacher, to preach and to educate the people,' replied Mohammad Ali. 'Ah,' said Zainal or Abdullah, showing a sudden change of heart, 'if you come back to Jeddah the family will give you the money to found a school so that you can educate many teachers, but on your own you will be just one.'

So Mohammad Ali returned to Jeddah. He was given some capital by his father, and with characteristic single-mindedness he sold his wife's jewellery. With these funds in 1903 he started his first school, which he called *Fallah* – 'Success'. This he followed after two years with a school in Mecca, and later he opened further schools in Bombay, Bahrain and Dubai, though the last three in due course were closed by the British, who objected to the modern, nationalist tone of the teachers Mohammad Ali employed. In the Gulf the teachers were Egyptians, mostly from Al Azhar; in Jeddah and Mecca they were Turks, employed because Turkish was still the language of commerce and government in the Hijaz. In his own town Mohammad Ali was known to go through the streets in the morning with a bag of silver piastres, which he would give to children to encourage them to go to school.

Once his schools were properly established Mohammad Ali was anxious that they should have a regular source of income, preferably one which would be independent of his family's company. He knew from his travels that the only business in Arabia which could make a man really rich was pearl dealing, and so he resolved to become a pearl merchant himself and to allocate his profits to his schools. Once again he prevailed on the generosity of Zainal and Abdullah – who by now may not have been unaware of the goodwill that Mohammad Ali's work was winning for the family. With the funds he was given he returned to Bombay, contacted his old business acquaintances and gradually established himself in pearls. Bombay was the processing centre of the pearl industry. It was fed by the market in Bahrain, which Mohammad Ali used to visit every autumn at the end of the Gulf pearling season. In Bombay the biggest pearls were polished and drilled for export to Europe; the ordinary seed pearls were used in India to sew on garments. The very smallest specimens had an alternative, more exotic use: they were bought by maharajas to be crushed, mixed with food and eaten as an aphrodisiac.

As he gained experience in his profession, Mohammad Ali decided to eliminate the Bombay exporters and deal directly with the big European jewellery houses. In 1920 he went to Paris for the first time. Drawing on the help of business friends, he opened an office at 62 rue La Fayette, on the edge of the main shopping area of Paris. In the building he chose were the offices of at least one of the big European pearl dealers. From the early 1920s, Mohammad Ali made it his habit to spend several months at a stretch in Paris each year – he bought a house on the Champs Elysées. In keeping with the normal practice of the Alireza family, in which each generation makes a point of handing down its experience to its children, he would sometimes take with him Abdullah's son Mohammad, who was later to become Saudi Arabian ambassador in Paris. It was this type of work – as well as his philanthropy – that made Mohammad Ali so valuable to his family. During the height of his career in pearls, in the 1920s, he lived almost permanently in Bombay and Paris; he had little to do with the family's business or with the development of its political standing at home in Jeddah.

The man who dominated the Alireza family's fortunes during the first thirty years of this century was Haji Abdullah. It was Abdullah who brought the Alirezas close to the centre of power in Arabia and in so doing put them in a position from which they would later be able to take the best advantage of the business boom that came with oil production.

Abdullah returned permanently from India to Jeddah in about 1905. He found himself the *de facto* head of his family – Zainal by this time was in his seventies – and one of the richest and best-respected merchants in the Hijaz. The other merchants of Jeddah acknowledged his importance by electing him president of the town's chamber of commerce. His period in office saw the First World War and the Arab Revolt, in which the Hashemite Governor of Mecca, the Sherif Hussein,[4] rebelled against Turkish rule and declared himself king of an independent Hijaz. With British financial backing and the leadership of T.E. Lawrence, Hussein's armies evicted the Turks from Western Arabia and advanced to Damascus. After the fighting ended, Hussein laid claim to the rest of the Arabian Peninsula and declared himself to be Caliph of the entire Muslim world. While he schemed to fulfil his vaunting ambition, he set about ruling his new kingdom. One of his early decisions was to appoint Haji Abdullah to the post of Governor of Jeddah.

Hussein was not an easy man to serve. He was conceited, suspicious and dictatorial. Those who had to deal with him found him a hard worker and intelligent in some respects, but they quickly became exasperated by his blind obstinacy and utter lack of practicality. His difficult qualities showed in numerous small incidents. One day he ordered that a bi-plane about to take off from the airstrip at Jeddah should be loaded with sacks of grain. When he was told that there was not enough room for the sacks in the plane, he commanded that they be stowed on the wings. Not wanting to kill himself on take-off, the Italian pilot of the plane promptly resigned.[5] On another occasion the Sherif was talking on the telephone to Sir Ronald Storrs, a British envoy in Jeddah, when his conversation was interrupted by a crossed line. To his surprise, Storrs heard the Sherif suddenly address the operator at the exchange and order him to cut off every other telephone in the Hijaz for half an hour. Abdullah Alireza suffered as badly as any of the capricious monarch's other subjects; he was for ever being obliged to try to comply with impossible commands or having his own decisions overruled.

Not the least of the trials that Hussein's rule inflicted on his subjects was a war with the Sultan of the Nejd, Ibn Saud. This war might have happened regardless of who had been King of the Hijaz – the Nejdi

4. Sherif is a title which may be used by all direct descendants of the Prophet Mohammad.
5. See *The Camels Must Go* by Sir Reader Bullard, Faber, 1961, p. 124.

ruler had long been anxious to establish his hold over all Arabia – but there is no doubt that Hussein's arrogance provoked Ibn Saud. At the same time it lost him the support of the British and the loyalty of the Hijazi people. In September 1924 Taif, a hill town about a hundred miles from the coast, fell to the Nejdi forces almost without a shot, and was the scene of an ugly massacre. On hearing the news, most of the inhabitants of Mecca, at the foot of the mountains, fled to Jeddah. Preparations for the defence of Jeddah itself seemed hopeless – and were characterised by strong elements of comic opera. The armoured cars, purchased for the government by its Lebanese ambassador in Italy, turned out to be war-surplus lorries covered with thin metal sheeting; and the Russian pilots of the Royal Hijazi Air Force, who were paid a bottle of whisky per day, crashed or immobilised all of their aircraft without inflicting damage on the Nejdis. In the circumstances Haji Abdullah Alireza called a meeting of 140 of the leading citizens of Jeddah on 3 October, and proposed that the Sherif should be asked to abdicate in favour of Ali, his pleasant but rather ineffective son. The Sherif had mentioned once or twice already that he might abdicate, but he had been thought to be bluffing and the Jeddah notables had been afraid to put him to the test. On this occasion the assembly whole-heartedly endorsed Abdullah's proposal, and gave Ali bin Hussein the unenviable task of conveying its decision to his father. Much to everybody's surprise, Hussein readily agreed to the idea and left Jeddah within a matter of days. He took with him the entire treasury of his government – some £800,000 in gold sovereigns, the profits of sixteen years' pilgrimage tax – locked in a large number of specially sealed petrol cans.

The siege of Jeddah began immediately after the Sherif's departure. Ibn Saud could easily have stormed the city, but he held back his troops from the thin barbed-wire defences and contented himself with having his artillery lob a few shells into the town. He knew that Jeddah was to be by far his most important conquest – the only major town in the territory he was about to turn into the Kingdom of Saudi Arabia – and he did not want to incur the everlasting hatred of its inhabitants. The people of Jeddah, of course, were unaware of his decision, and in the early stages of the siege there were great fears that a Wahabi attack would lead to a massacre, as it had done at Taif. Haji Abdullah was as worried as everybody else and had all the female and the young Alirezas packed into a Mogul Line steamer and sent to join Yusuf and Mohammad Ali in Bombay. When the initial terror subsided, however, there emerged a strong pacifist movement, which grew to include the majority of the city's population. At the radical end of this movement there was a small but important clique which was definitely defeatist in outlook and desired the triumph of Ibn Saud, or at least the collapse and disappearance of the Hashemite dynasty, in whose continuance it saw no spark of hope for the future.

Haji Abdullah himself made it clear that in his actions the interests of the people would take precedence over those of the ruling family, and if the *sine qua non* condition of peace was the departure of Ali bin Hussein, he would favour such a course. His nephew, Kassem Zainal, was much more extreme. Kassem rapidly became the acknowledged leader of the defeatists and lost no time in establishing intelligence links with the enemy. The government could hardly fail to find out about his activities. Within a few months after the beginning of the siege, the government discovered the identity of one of Kassem's messengers and sent a scout to follow him through the lines. The scout caught up with the messenger and obtained the letter that Kassem had been sending to the Nejdi camp, by the simple device of paying the messenger more than the £10 that he had received from Kassem. Kassem and two others were arrested, tried and sentenced to death. Immediately after the sentence had been passed, however, all three conspirators were reprieved and set free. It was never announced why the Sherif Ali had decided to be lenient at the eleventh hour, but it was widely believed in Jeddah that the convicted men had each made a 'voluntary' £2,000 contribution to the Hashemite defence fund. Kassem was quite unperturbed by his narrow escape. A few weeks after the incident he went to dinner with Harry St John Philby[6] and stated openly that the departure of Ali was 'indispensable to the salvation of Jeddah'.

After fourteen months of siege the citizens of Jeddah began to feel that they had had enough. Food and water supplies were running low, the government was bankrupt and its army and civil servants were going unpaid. What funds the government had been able to muster had been

6. Harry St John Philby went first to Arabia in 1917 as a representative of the British government. From that time on he spent most of his life in Arabia as an explorer, part-time (and unsuccessful) businessman, and great personal friend of King Ibn Saud. He became a Muslim and made the pilgrimage – he was known to the Arabs as Haji Abdullah Philby. His son Kim was the notorious Soviet double agent. Philby describes the siege of Jeddah and the attitudes of the Alireza family in one of his books: *Forty Years in the Wilderness*, Robert Hale, 1957, pp. 110–42. The quotation is from page 136.

lent to it reluctantly by the Alirezas and some of the other richest merchants. Matters had clearly reached a desperate state when the British consul discovered that one of Ali's secretaries had tried to raise a loan of £10 from a merchant, and had been refused.

In early December 1925 the city heard the news that Medina had surrendered to the Nejdis. Most of the senior members of the Hashemite government packed their bags and took ship to Egypt. The Sherif Ali cabled his younger brother, Faisal, who had been made King of Iraq by the British soon after the First World War, and arranged to take refuge with him in Baghdad. On 20 December he quietly boarded a British ship, HMS *Cornflower*. According to members of the Alireza family today, he was actually on board the vessel before he let it be known to Haji Abdullah, who had come to say his last farewells, that he had no funds for his journey to Iraq; he offered the Governor his gold dagger in exchange for some money. Haji Abdullah naturally refused the offer – it would have been inconceivable in Arabia at that time (or even today) for a merchant to have accepted direct payment for a service he had rendered to his monarch. Instead of taking the dagger, Haji Abdullah gave Ali 500 gold Sovereigns, and ordered that Yusuf and Mohammad Ali in Bombay, where HMS *Cornflower* was sailing, should pay all of Ali's expenses until he departed for Iraq.[7]

Even before his final conversation with Ali on board the British warship, Haji Abdullah had begun negotiations with Ibn Saud. On 17 December 1925 he had ridden ten kilometres down the road towards Mecca at the head of a small party of notables, which included the British representative in Jeddah. After six days of early-morning meetings terms for a surrender were agreed. Among other matters it was accepted by Ibn Saud that all the civil servants of the Hashemite government should be kept in their posts – though to obtain this concession Haji Abdullah had once again to dip into his coffers to lend the new government £6,000.

The final act was the surrender itself. Ibn Saud was invited to come to a pavilion which had been put up in a garden just outside the walls of Jeddah. (On this site today is the Kandara Palace Hotel, well known to visiting businessmen and journalists as a hugely expensive establish-

7. After their eviction from the Hijaz, the Hashemites ruled Kingdoms in Iraq and Jordan, which had been created by the British from parts of the former Turkish Empire. The Iraqi monarchy was overthrown in 1958. The present Jordanian monarch is Hussein bin Talal bin Abdullah bin Hussein – the Sherif Hussein's great-grandson.

ment of mediocre quality.) Here the leading citizens of Jeddah came to greet their new ruler and pledge their loyalty to him. When the simple ceremony was finished, Haji Abdullah formally handed Ibn Saud the keys of the city and proffered his own resignation as Governor. This Ibn Saud refused to accept. He stated immediately and bluntly that he wanted the careworn Abdullah to remain at his post to reassure the citizens of Jeddah and to lend continuity to the life of the city under the new government. It was not a request which Abdullah would have been allowed to refuse. As soon as their conversation was finished the two men drank a cup of coffee and posed for the famous surrender photograph which now hangs in Shaikh Ahmed Yusuf Zainal Alireza's office. There is a symbolic element in the photograph which seems to have presaged the type of regime which was to come. It is quite clear in the picture that both the future King of Saudi Arabia and Haji Abdullah were drinking the thick, sweet Turkish coffee of the Hijaz, out of small Turkish coffee cups, and not the bitter coffee of the Nejd, which is served in little bowls. The promise implied in this simple gesture was fulfilled. Two days after the surrender, at a council (*majlis*) in the house of the Nasif family, Ibn Saud agreed to the proposal of Haji Abdullah and other important citizens that the Hijaz should not be incorporated into the Sultanate of Nejd, but should be part of a new state, the Kingdom of Nejd and Hijaz. Ibn Saud became known as King Abdel-Aziz and seven years later, in 1932, the name of the state was changed to the Kingdom of Saudi Arabia.

The Alirezas emerged from the siege of Jeddah with their already great prestige enhanced. They had helped guide the citizens of Jeddah through a difficult period, and under King Ali had been the mainstay of the government's treasury. They were now to play exactly the same roles under the Saudi regime.

Not much changed in Jeddah after the conquest. The Wahabi armies were promptly withdrawn to the Nejd. A stricter routine of prayer was enforced, and smoking in the street and the cultivation of tobacco were banned. The last of these restrictions had much to do with the fact that the government levied a tax on tobacco imports. The most serious material disadvantage of Saudi rule was that the Hijaz had to share the pilgrimage tax with the rest of the Kingdom. The transfer of this tax to the new regime represented a huge augmentation of the revenues of

Abdel-Aziz. The King had previously survived on the customs dues of the Hasa ports (on the eastern side of his territories), a few oil-concession rental payments, British subsidies, and loans from Hassawi and Bahraini merchants. For the Hijazis, however, the new arrangements meant that their own government became as impoverished as the Nejd government.

Politically, the worst effect of the conquest was that the Hijazis became the subjects of an alien ruler, whose people regarded them as degenerate and not quite Arabian. The Hijazis were much better educated than the Nejdis. Over the thirty years after 1925 they came to run the commerce and administration of the Kingdom, and so began to erode the austere Wahabi culture of the Nejd. This radically altered the character of Nejdi society, but it did not lead to the Hijazis being accepted as equals. To this day the Nejdis regard the Hijazis as second-class citizens.

The man appointed Viceroy of the Hijaz was the King's third son, Prince Faisal bin Abdel-Aziz – the future King Faisal. As both prince and king, Faisal was always mindful of the need to foster national unity. While he administered the Hijaz he did what he could to prevent his subjects becoming resentful of Nejdi rule. He made it part of his policy to seek out the friendship of the Alirezas and other leading Jeddah merchants. These families had a wealth of contacts and a web of influence in the Hijaz; they were rich and therefore powerful, and Faisal thought that their money and the influence that went with it would be a barrier against the return of the Hashemites or pro-Hashemite sympathies. It was also necessary for the prince and his father to draw on the merchants for 'loans'. These were seldom repaid, but they earned the lenders the favour of the Sauds.

Prince Faisal had a particular regard for the Alirezas, and formed a lifelong friendship with the family. The Alirezas were important to him mainly because one of their number was Governor of Jeddah and another had given the Hijaz its only modern schools – thus gaining the enormous goodwill of the Jeddah and Mecca townsmen. The respect in which the family was held was shown when two of its members died during the early years of Saudi rule. Kassem died in 1927, and Zainal, his father, in 1929.[8] On the death of Zainal, who had been widely loved

8. It is agreed among members of the Alireza family that Zainal was well into his nineties when he died, though his exact age was unknown. Even today many people of middle age and older in Arabia do not know their dates of birth.

as a devout and charitable man, so many people came to pay their respects that the family had to arrange for them to 'sit' in turns. The normal procedure was for people to come to the house of the dead man and to sit for an hour or so between sunset and the evening prayer to listen to readings from the Koran. On this occasion they were allowed to sit for only a few minutes before being moved on to make way for others.

A few years after Zainal's death the family's good standing was demonstrated again when Mohammad Ali's financing of the Fallah schools ran into trouble. In the early 1930s, when pearl prices crashed under the impact of the Depression and the introduction of cultured pearls by the Japanese, Mohammad Ali found that his pearl-dealing income fell far below the level demanded by his schools. There was no question of his turning to the government, whose income from the pilgrimage tax was also being destroyed by the Depression. His brother, Yusuf, and Abdullah's elder son, Mohammad, therefore gathered the support of other merchant families in Jeddah and asked the government to allow them to collect a special Fallah schools tax. They persuaded Abdullah Suliman, the King's Finance Minister, to authorise a new customs duty of one piastre to be levied on every sack, case or barrel of goods landed at Jeddah port. From that time the Fallah schools of Jeddah and Mecca, which now have over 3,000 pupils, have continued to be financed mainly by public money. Their incomes are supplemented by substantial trust funds accumulated from the gifts of members of the Alireza family, various other charitable Jeddah merchants and former teachers of the schools.

The year 1932 saw the death of Haji Abdullah, worn out, so it was said, by his official duties. The leadership of the family in Jeddah was taken over by Yusuf Zainal, who was already in his fifties. Yusuf ran the family firm for about ten years and then moved into semi-retirement, becoming a somewhat patriarchal figure, mainly concerned with the formalities of business. The members of the family who ran the business on his behalf were his son Ahmed and Mohammad Abdullah. Both of these men were roughly contemporaries of Prince Faisal, and it was they who cemented the family's ties with the prince. In the later 1930s and 1940s they were as useful to Faisal as their elders had been – though their help was given in different ways. By this time the prince had been made Foreign Minister as well as Viceroy of the Hijaz. The young Alirezas' value lay in their sophistication, fluent English, and experience of the world outside Arabia. They had travelled widely in

India, Egypt, the Levant and Europe; in the 1940s they arranged family holidays for their wives and children in Lebanon and Ethiopia. The prince was able to use them to deliver messages and carry out odd diplomatic assignments when they went abroad. At home they could be used to look after foreign diplomats – whom the Saudi government always dealt with through Jeddah.

This did not prevent the young Alirezas, and particularly Mohammad, from expressing strong anti-government opinions when they disagreed with anything that the Sauds were doing. Mohammad was outspoken and impulsive. At a party at a foreign legation in 1938 he told a British diplomat that he thought that the central government was exploiting the Hijaz financially and that he had become a member of a society called 'The Friends of the Hijaz', which was going to meet in Egypt to 'see what could be done'. Reporting this piece of intelligence to his superiors in London, the British consul in Jeddah, Sir Reader Bullard, cited Mohammad as one of a small group of educated Saudis who 'sighed for the cinema and stronger drinks than pink lemonade'. He added that Mohammad had a personal grievance because he believed that King Abdel-Aziz had shortened his father's life by insisting that he should retain the post of Governor of Jeddah when his father had been anxious to resign. Bullard said that he had some sympathy with Mohammad on this score, because Haji Abdullah had held the same position, under compulsion, under King Hussein, and his own memories went back to the trials the Governor had suffered under 'that monument of unreason and unaccountability'.[9]

None of Mohammad's indiscretions had the slightest effect on the Alirezas' standing with Prince Faisal. The Nejdis themselves were a blunt people, and the prince probably admired Mohammad for expressing his views in the way he did. As more foreigners began to arrive in Jeddah, the prince began to use the Alirezas to entertain guests on his behalf. He felt that they would give newcomers a good impression of the Kingdom.

There was no doubt that the Alirezas' house was extremely comfortable by Jeddah standards at that time – everyone who went there in the 1930s and early 1940s seems to have remembered it. The house was a huge, tall building with big rooms, rough floors covered with Persian carpets, kerosene lamps hanging from the ceilings, and rows of sofas

9. See India Office Library, London, reference L/Pe5/12/2082.

and cushions arranged around the edge of the rooms next to the walls.[10] It had a large number of very expensive *objéts*, such as Sèvres vases, spread through the house. In one room in a corner was a more conventional Middle Eastern possession – a big samovar of tea, kept brewing throughout the day by servants. These were men and women whom the family had bought as slaves and set free.

The upper part of the house was a maze of rooms and apartments on different levels and half levels. Husbands and wives had apartments to themselves. If they wished, members of the family could pursue their own lives as if they had households of their own. Steta Fatma, one of Abdullah's daughters, whose childless marriage ended early in divorce, would take orphans into the house, raising them as her own and making arrangements for their future. For a boy she would give help in setting up a business, for a girl she would negotiate a suitable marriage. The lower part of the house was divided between the women's quarters and the men's quarters – with a few rooms where the whole family would meet occasionally for meals or for entertaining close friends and relations.

Guests at dinner were struck by the Alirezas' habit of cooking ten times more food than they needed and then distributing it to the Jeddah poor. As they left the house at the end of the evening they would see the poor lined up outside, patient and expectant, clutching their bowls. In the daytime most Americans and Europeans calling on the Alirezas would be coming to see the family about business, and would be ushered into the offices of the Alireza company, which were on the ground floor of the house. It they wanted to see Yusuf they would go upstairs for a short conversation before getting down to business with the other members of the family. This was the procedure normally followed by Bill Sands, an American diplomat (now at the Middle East Institute in Washington DC) who came to Jeddah in 1944. 'I used to visit Yusuf,' he explained to me in a conversation in Washington in 1978, 'partly out of good manners and partly because I liked spending an entertaining half hour with the old man. Like all the rest of the family he had great charm. I remember him sitting there dressed in the old Hijazi style, with a conical hat bound round with a white turban. He'd be stroking his beautiful white beard and reading Persian poetry. He

10. Much of this description of the Alireza house has been taken from *At the Drop of a Veil* by Marianne Alireza, published by Houghton Mifflin in 1971. Marianne Alireza was a Californian girl who married Ali Abdullah and was taken to Jeddah in 1946.

used to say that he wished to spend the rest of his days 'in contemplation of the good and the beautiful'. He would give the impression that of all things in life commerce was the least important to him, but I think that behind closed doors he would be as shrewd and as cunning as anyone else. As soon as any business visitor had finished talking to the other members of the family, I think that Yusuf would have been keenly interested to hear what had transpired.'

The big Alireza household of the first half of this century was part of the old Arabian world, and in the mid-1940s that world began to change. It was a sign of the times when, in 1945, Mohammad Abdullah moved his branch of the family from the old house into a revolutionary new type of mansion, with glass windows and courtyards with fountains. The source of all the Alirezas' modern commercial success has been the family's ability to see what was happening better than the other merchants, while being uniquely well qualified to take advantage of the change. All the older members had been educated in India or Egypt. In the early 1940s the family arranged for Haji Abdullah's second son, Ali, to go to the University of California at Berkeley – making him the first Saudi to receive a university education in the West. The timing was no accident; oil had been discovered just before the Second World War and the first significant production began in 1946. To the Alirezas the message was clear. Oil revenues would mean spending by the King on development projects and more gifts to the tribes, the princes and the members of the royal retinue which acted as a government. For the first time Saudis would have enough money to buy more than food and clothes.

Mohammad Ali Alireza, typically, responded to the new opportunities in his own way. Immediately after the war he closed his office in Paris and left the Gulf pearl business, which by this time was on the point of extinction. He vigorously began to diversify into other forms of jewellery. Using his old contacts, he began to learn about precious stones, particularly rubies and diamonds, which he bought in India and had cut in his own workshop in Bombay. As everyone who knew him predicted, he proved to be as clever with precious stones as he had been with pearls, and by the mid-1950s he had been elected President of the All India Jewellery Association. He became known in the trade as 'the King of Diamonds'. In the process of transferring his area of expertise he moved from being an exporter, supplying Gulf pearls to Europe, to being an importer, bringing Indian and European jewellery to Saudi Arabia. Among European jewellers he developed his best connections with Van Cleef and Arples and Cartier. His business legacy to his family became the jewellery department of Haji Abdullah Alireza & Co., which trades under the name of The Golden Palm.

The other members of the family were more conventional. Ali Abdullah on his return from California became a special adviser to Prince Faisal. This included accompanying the prince on a series of diplomatic assignments which ranged from the 1945 United Nations conference in San Francisco to the Non-Aligned meeting at Bandung ten years later (see chapter 4).

Ali's brother, Mohammad, and Ahmed Yusuf concentrated on expanding the business in Jeddah. Despite the hesitation of Yusuf, who had spent all his career as a foodstuffs trader, they decided to diversify into machinery. Sometimes they went abroad to win agencies, on other occasions they were sought out in Jeddah by Western manufacturers' regional representatives. Their education and the fact that they and their Indian clerks spoke English made them the obvious choice for anyone seeking to introduce new business into the Kingdom. Every time a salesman arrived in Jeddah, his embassy or the banks (of which there were already two or three in the early 1950s) would direct him to the Alireza offices. Mohammad and Ahmed signed up Westinghouse, Goodyear, Dunlop, ITT and Pepsi-Cola. They built Arabia's first Pepsi-Cola bottling plant and won ITT a contract to build the first broadcasting station. They were offered Mercedes and Siemens but referred them to other merchants. In 1948 they expanded their shipping–agency operations. They already represented Mogul and the Hansa Line (won in the 1930s), and at the end of the war it occurred to Mohammad and Ahmed that they would do well to add an American company to their list. They realised that if most of the world's best manufacturing capacity was in the United States – Europe and Japan being bombed out or bankrupt – it would be the US that would be supplying most of Saudi Arabia's new imports, and these would be bound to come in American ships. They therefore persuaded the Isthmian Line to terminate its agency with the British trading firm Gellatly Hankey and switch to their own company. The reasoning that lay behind this deal put the Alirezas in a different category from their competitors in Jeddah. None of the other established firms at this time had the same understanding of how the world economy was evolving outside Saudi Arabia and what it might mean in terms of business opportunities.

The most famous new Alireza agency, Ford, was won early on, in 1940. The deal stemmed directly from Mohammad's realisation that the company's existing agent was ineffective. This was Haji Philby, the British writer and explorer, who ran his business to finance his travels and to support the pleasant life he led when he returned to London on leave. He was a man who enjoyed having lunch at the Athenaeum and watching cricket at Lords. Commerce for its own sake meant nothing to him: 'Money making is a very dull business,' he confided in a letter to his wife in England, 'and I hate the sight and sound of motor cars.'[11] Neither of these views is often heard in Saudi Arabia today, and they did not impress Ford in 1940. The company shared Mohammad Alireza's view of their agent's performance, particularly as the eccentric Philby had been somewhat irregular in his payments – though this was less the fault of his accounting than of the King's chronically impoverished treasury. Ford was unsympathetic, however, and its disillusionment showed in the quota of just four trucks that it allocated to Saudi Arabia in 1940. When Mohammad visited Ford's regional headquarters in Alexandria in that year he had little difficulty in persuading the company to cancel Philby's monopoly and to transfer its agency to the Alirezas. Within a short time the family had built a new showroom. There it installed a gleaming new four-door Ford sedan, protected from the dust by big glass windows and illuminated by Arabia's first neon lights. In a city where most business was still carried out in hole-in-the-wall shops in the souk, the showroom in itself caused a minor sensation.

A few years after his success with the Ford agency Mohammad pulled off much the same deal for the General Motors agency, this time at the expense once more of Gellatly Hankey. In this instance the British firm had recently taken one of the Alirezas' staff, so Mohammad's action was one of retaliation. Mohammad admits that he was 'very aggressive' in those days. In the event, having prised GM loose from Gellatly Hankey, the Alirezas decided that they had too good a relationship with Ford to take GM as well, and referred the company to their relations, the Zahids. The Zahids have since become famous as the agents for Caterpillar and now own one of the biggest merchant houses in the Arabian Peninsula. One of the most interesting aspects of the Ford and

11. See *Philby of Arabia* by Elizabeth Monroe, Faber, 1974, p. 211.

GM affairs is that Mohammad admits that he would never have poached the agencies from another Saudi.

Mohammad did not remain in business for very long after his commercial coups of the 1940s. In the early 1950s he embarked on a political career, which was to continue intermittently for nearly twenty-five years and was to bring him the same prestige that his father had enjoyed. In 1978, a few years after he had retired, Mohammad described to me in detail how his career had developed. The story tells much of the very personal nature of relations between a king and his subjects in Arabia.

'I had been elected President of the Union of Saudi Chambers of Commerce, which gave me quite a big political influence in Jeddah. It also made me the logical choice for the job of Minister of Commerce when the government was reorganised when King Saud came to the throne in 1953 – after Abdullah Suliman I was the first person who was not a member of the royal family to be appointed to the Council of Ministers . . . An interesting thing happened while I was in this post, which was to have quite a profound influence on the rest of my career. In 1956 I found myself on holiday in Egypt when the Suez crisis erupted. As an Arab I naturally couldn't help getting caught up in the general passion of the moment. I sent a telegram resigning my post and joined the Liberation Army . . . By one of those odd chances, the day I was to go to Suez the crisis ended. For the time being that was the end of the matter.

'I went back to Saudi Arabia and carried on my work as a minister. Then in 1958 I resigned from the Ministry of Commerce. This was much against the wishes of Prince Faisal, who by this time had become the main power in the country. We'd been friends for many years, but over several months relations between us had been getting very bad. There's always been a bit of a rebel streak in me, and I couldn't agree with some of the decisions Prince Faisal was taking in the government. I left Riyadh without saying goodbye . . . Then in 1962 there was a lot of anti-Saudi propaganda from Cairo, with parachute drops of arms north of Jeddah, and Cairo Radio saying that we Saudis were unhappy with our government.[12] So Prince Faisal and I agreed to freeze our differ-

12. The latter part of the reign of King Saud bin Abdel-Aziz (1953–64) was marked by great turbulence in Saudi Arabia, and in the rest of the Arab world. In 1962 one of the King's brothers, Talal bin Abdel-Aziz, and three pilots of the Saudi Air Force defected to Egypt. Talal declared himself a socialist and broadcast anti-Saudi propaganda on Cairo Radio – though he has since recanted and been allowed to return to the Kingdom. These political problems, coupled with the King's overspending, led to the abdication of King Saud and his replacement by Prince Faisal in 1964.

ences – and then I suddenly had the idea that I ought to organise a demonstration in Jeddah in favour of the government. Of course, I had to ask the Prince for permission: after all, it's not usual in our country to have a demonstration of any kind. Prince Faisal said he wouldn't interfere. So we held the demonstration with about 20,000 people. I made a speech in reply to the Egyptians and I handed Prince Faisal a golden key to Jeddah.

'It was not long after this, in 1963, that my involvement in Suez became important again. The point about my enlisting in the Liberation Army was that it had served to introduce me to Nasser. The resignation of a minister of another Arab country, and that minister joining his army, had been a big moral triumph for him. In its way it had been one more factor helping Nasser establish his role as a leader of the Arab nation. So when in 1963 Nasser sent a delegation – including Anwar Sadat – to Saudi Arabia to request that we establish diplomatic relations with him, I was the man the prince thought of first. He sent me a letter in his own handwriting by a messenger from Riyadh asking me if I would be ambassador in Cairo. Of course I said yes. It turned out to be a very difficult job. Our relations with Cairo had been getting worse since the Egyptians had intervened in the Yemen civil war at the end of 1962 – and once I was in Cairo I found that my personal relations with Nasser deteriorated dramatically. He was alternately trying to frighten me by making threats or offering me personal inducements – things got to a point where I simply refused to meet him. This went on for several years, until 1967, when Egypt was disastrously defeated in the Six Day War. After that war I had the pleasure of arranging the repatriation of the Egyptian army from Yemen, which was done on Saudi Arabia's account. My relations with Nasser did not get any better. I stayed on officially as ambassador until two months after Nasser's death in 1970 – but for most of this time I was not in Cairo – I feared for my life. At last I was thankful to retire to Jeddah. I thought this would be a final retirement, so you can imagine my surprise when I heard on the radio one day that I had been appointed ambassador to Paris. I was amazed – I called the King and asked what had happened. He told me that he thought that France was going to become important to Saudi Arabia – at that time President Pompidou had emerged as the leader of the Common Market and he had just agreed with Edward Heath that Britain should join. The King knew that I had spent some time in France because he remembered that I had been there with Mohammad Ali when I was young. So, once more I became an ambassador, and I didn't retire again until 1975 . . .'

Mohammad's long absences from Jeddah were a mixed blessing for Haji Abdullah Alireza & Co. He and his brother Ali never took any pay for the work they did for the government. They earned their company the goodwill of the royal family, but they left it without their services at a time when its business was becoming much bigger and more complex. For nearly fifteen years, from the mid-1940s to the late 1950s, Haji Abdullah Alireza & Co. was unchallenged as the leading merchant house in the Kingdom. Thereafter it began a gradual decline. Under pressure from energetic young merchants who had only started in business since the Second World War, it lost Westinghouse and most of its other agencies. Where it retained an agency the manufacturer often requested that it entered a partnership or joint-venture so that the manufacturer could itself participate in marketing its products. The Alirezas set up an unsuccessful branch in Libya and lost money on a contract to deepen Jeddah harbour, which against expectations involved blasting coral rock. Worst of all Ford fell foul of the Arab Boycott. Under the Boycott Office rules a company may normally export to both Israel and the Arabs, as long as it is not supplying Israel with goods of strategic importance, but it may not buy Israeli exports, carry out construction contracts, sell patents or invest in Israel. Ford had given offence by setting up a vehicle-assembly plant, apparently imagining that its agents in the Arab world would help it break the boycott. In this it was underestimating the strength of most Arabs' personal commitment to their nation's struggle against Israel, for in the event the Alirezas did not even contemplate taking up Ford's case. Quite apart from personal sentiments, it would have been politically impossible for the family to have helped Ford at a time when Mohammad was serving as his country's ambassador in Cairo.

A more fundamental weakness was the family's failure to diversify properly out of the Hijaz. The Alirezas have never felt at home in the Nejd and even today the elder members seldom travel there. In the 1960s not only did the family miss a business opportunity in the development of the central and eastern regions, it left itself without a presence in Riyadh at a time when Nejdis were becoming better educated, more confident and more influential in the day-to-day commerce and administration of the Kingdom.

While King Faisal was alive the Alirezas' lack of presence in the Nejd was partly offset by the old King's long-standing affection for the family. This relationship, begun when Faisal had been Viceroy of the Hijaz, had been strengthened by the personal friendship he had built with Ali Abdullah during the diplomatic assignments they had carried out together in the forties and fifties. In those days Faisal had been much less austere than he was to become in later life; on his travels he had been known as a humorous, exuberant person and a player of practical jokes. For their part, the senior members of the Alireza family – who in the 1960s were Mohammad, Ahmed and Ali – were very aware of the importance of their friendship with the King and were anxious to see that it continued into the next generation. Before their sons went abroad, and whenever they returned to the Kingdom, the older Alirezas made sure that they paid courtesy calls on the King, so that he would grow to know them and look well on them in the future. The friendship paid off in business. In the 1960s, when the King knew that the family's company was not prospering, he awarded Haji Abdullah Alireza & Co. several military-construction contracts (carried out by Laing Wimpey Alireza) and an extremely valuable contract for refuelling aircraft at Jeddah airport.

The assassination of King Faisal by a mentally deranged nephew in March 1975 was a great personal and political blow for the Alirezas. Faisal's sons, naturally enough, have inherited much of their father's affection for the family, but the core of the present ruling establishment is distrustful of Hijazis, and has no bond with the Alirezas. King Khaled and the brothers who were closest to him were much more orientated to the Nejd, whose people had always been their family's principal constituents. Although it is known that King Fahd has some personal liking for the Hijaz, in the latter part of 1982 the practical effects of this had yet to show themselves.

It was noticeable in the later 1970s that Laing Wimpey Alireza went through a very quiet period, during which it won contracts for only one big project – the Abha airport in the south-western corner of the Kingdom. At the same time the Alirezas, in common with some other merchants, were embarrassed by some trouble-fraught dealings with younger members of the royal family, several of whom had taken to forcing themselves on to the merchants as unwelcome joint-venture partners.

The outcome of the Alirezas' Hijazi orientation and the firm's various misfortunes has been that in recent years Haji Abdullah Alireza & Co.

has grown more slowly than its competitors – though the refuelling contract and some of its real estate interests must be earning impressive sums. It was only in 1980 and 1981 that there were signs of a major upswing in the company's business. The most important new contract to be signed in 1981 was for the construction by Laing Wimpey Alireza of two 100-bed hospitals, costing $75 million, in the central Nejd.

The older generation of Alirezas does not much care for throwing itself into the hurly-burly of bidding and wheeler-dealing in Riyadh. Its members do not feel at ease with the influence-broking that surrounds the award of contracts in Saudi Arabia and they seem to be in two minds about how much they want to get involved. Now that they are reaching retirement age they are not particularly interested in making money for its own sake; or, to be more accurate, they are less preoccupied with this goal than other Saudis. They have entered the realms of the world's conservative, multi-millionaire aristocracy, with the smartest houses and friends at the top of the American and European establishments, people they have met and grown to know during their diplomatic postings. Drawing parallels is difficult, because Saudi society is very different from Western society, but it would probably be fair to see the Alirezas as a Saudi version of the Rockefellers or Barings. All three families have distinguished themselves in government as well as being well established and very rich.

In common with old families elsewhere, the Alirezas are conscious of their reputation. This is something that concerns the whole family, from the oldest to the youngest. Faisal Ali, the eldest son of Ali Abdullah and Marianne Alireza, in a conversation with me in 1977 described reputation as the most precious asset that a family can have: 'You can't buy it overnight, but you can destroy it overnight.' What is striking about the Alirezas is that this concern with reputation, coupled with the knowledge that the family's past makes it unique in Arabia, pervades all aspects of the family's thinking. The older members are most concerned to know what is said and written about them. They spend not a little time projecting 'the Alireza image', particularly in the diplomatic community in Jeddah.

At the same time all members of the family are unusually conscious of having an 'Alireza philosophy': a code of principles for success. They believe in the careful instruction of their children at home, a foreign education starting at an early age, and foreign travel to broaden the mind. Being firm believers in the value of prestige, they attach great importance to being seen to be serving the royal family in government. They make a practice always of noticing where power lies and then trying to get close to it, which in Arabia is probably the most important principle for commercial advancement. If they succeed, as they did with Prince Faisal, they prosper; if they fail they withdraw from the limelight and wait and watch for times to improve. This is what they were doing in the later 1970s.

At all times the family will defer to the decisions of its most senior member or to the chief executive of the family company. It will always rally to the support of any member of the family who finds himself in dispute with an outsider – either another Saudi or a foreigner. What the head of the family says to the same member in private may be another matter.

Most of these principles would apply to the other established merchant families, along with a more general rule under which different branches of a family often try to co-operate or at least not to compete with each other in business. One would think that this principle would be of major importance – especially as ties within a large family are often reinforced by the marriage of cousins – but in practice Arabians seem to be fairly casual in dealings with their more distant relations, even though they observe all the social formalities. In the Alirezas' case the descendants of Zainal and Abdullah are close to the Hussein branch of the family but fairly distant from the Ali Akbar branch (see family tree), even to the extent of being unable to name more than a few of its members. The important point about the Alirezas, though, is not so much that they are typical of Arabian merchant families – in many ways their long history makes them very untypical – it is that all members of the family are unusually articulate in expounding their philosophy. They do not like to discuss the more Machiavellian aspects, such as the need to be near the centre of power, but their conversation does provide an insight into how the family instils into its children from the earliest age the most fundamental of the principles for success. The Alirezas are ideal for a case study of the ways in which an Arabian merchant family seeks to maintain its fortunes from one generation to the next.

The Alirezas set great store by classic values: honesty, charity, hard work, discipline, good manners and a good education. The quality most often referred to by the family is honesty, through which a man may win trust in business, and there are many anecdotes which the family tells to illustrate the point. A particular favourite comes from the 1920s and 1930s. At that time the Alirezas and their Indian employees were the only people in Jeddah who spoke English, apart from the staff of Gellatly Hankey, the British consul, Philby and a handful of other foreigners. So if another merchant received a telegram in English he would take it to the Alirezas to be translated by an Indian clerk in the shipping office. Abdullah and Yusuf never asked to see the contents; in fact they told the clerks that if they divulged the contents to anyone other than the recipient of the telegram they would be fired.

Most members of the Alirezas and other merchant families assume a distinctly pious manner when they refer to stories of this type, looking serious and responsible and gazing at the ceiling. At these moments their tone is such as to make one wonder whether they are seriously interested in business at all. Certainly the tone is in stark contrast to the ruthless opportunism which is the normal code of Arabian business. However, Shaikh Mohammad, who was an open and practical character, was not so given to idealistic flights of fancy. Once, after telling the telegram story to me, he paused, smiled and remarked in a down-to-earth way: 'Well, to be frank, I'm not sure that a lot of trust in business doesn't come from you selling at 69 cents and the other man at 70 cents, and the customer finding that your product is as good.'

The younger members of the Alirezas absorb their family's philosophy through being brought up in large family compounds – one for the Zainal branch and one for the Abdullah branch. In these compounds the numerous members of the younger generation are in everyday contact with fathers, uncles, grandfathers and great-uncles, and are all the time being taught by instruction and example. In the evenings, if a senior member of the family is present, all the adults and older teenagers in a compound may congregate for dinner in the main dining room; otherwise a small group will meet in the house of one of the young married couples. Here even young children are allowed to stay up quite late, while their relations play games with them and read them stories, spending hours doting and being entertained. This happens in all Arabian households; the children are only sent to bed just before dinner arrives, which may be as late as ten or eleven o'clock.

In the mornings the older Alirezas, when they are in Jeddah but not at the office, are 'at home' in their studies. Between his retirement in 1975 and his death in 1982, the person most often at home in the

Abdullah compound was Shaikh Mohammad, a tall, distinguished figure with a wise face, who was the head of the family but was not involved in the day-to-day running of the firm. His study was a large, homely room full of odds and ends, with comfortable old chairs and the smell of pipe tobacco. Visitors went there to pay their respects or exchange some news, while children filed in and out with their various requests and minor problems.

It was in everyday circumstances such as these that Shaikh Mohammad brought his influence to bear. In the course of a conversation I had with him in his study one day a twelve-year-old nephew came into the room eating a sweet. 'What is that you have got in your mouth?' demanded Mohammad. 'Go out of the room and throw it away and don't let me see you with sweets in here again.' The reprimand was in English because the conversation we were having was in English. English was also the language which the child would have to speak when he went abroad to school or university and when he went into business or government later on.

On another occasion Shaikh Ahmed, during a business discussion with some American executives from ITT, asked his visitors whether they would mind if he called in some of the children so that they could listen, and learn from what he was saying.

There is also a more formal side to the upbringing of the young Alirezas. It has always been the policy of the family to give its children the best possible education. Members of the younger generation who started in business of their own in the 1970s go out of their way to explain how their time spent in schools in the West has been an advantage in the joint-venture manufacturing and service industries they have set up with foreign partners. In the simplest sense their education has helped them to understand engineering technicalities; more important, it has enabled them to bridge the cultural gap between themselves and the Western technicians who build and operate their projects.

Until the 1940s the Alirezas used to send their children to school in India, after a primary education at the Fallah school in Jeddah. Since Ali Abdullah went to Victoria College, the English public school in Alexandria, and then to California, the pattern has changed. The girls in the family go to private schools in Switzerland to get a good grounding in languages, which it is felt are an asset for travel and for the diplomatic social life in Jeddah. With the boys the usual practice now is to give a basic education in Saudi Arabia and then send them to one or two boarding schools in Britain (a public school and possibly a preparatory school as well) before they go on to university in the United States. Britain is preferred for their schooling partly because it is closer for visiting during term time and for the children to return to Jeddah during the holidays, and partly because the family feels that there is greater emphasis on discipline and hard work in the English educational system during the teenage years. There is also a preference for public schools that are in the countryside. According to Mahmoud Yusuf, the youngest brother of Shaikh Ahmed, 'the advantage is the rural environment, there are fewer distractions than in the towns.' This spartan approach does not always suit the younger generation. One of them, on discovering what his parents had in store for him, let it be known to a friend of the family that he would prefer somewhere warm and sunny, preferably in California, where he would not have to do too much work.

The way their education has given the older Alirezas and a handful of others like them an advantage over most of the rest of the older generation in Saudi Arabia is illustrated in an indirect way in a story told to me by Ali Abdullah, the stout and avuncular member of the family who used to be the Saudi ambassador in Washington: 'It was in Beirut in 1968. I was walking down one of the big streets – it may have been Hamra – and who should I see but my old housemaster from Victoria College? You won't believe this, but he hadn't changed a bit – not a bit. So I went up to him and introduced myself. I said, 'Do you remember me? A.A. Alireza, sir?' Well, he did remember me. So we got into conversation: it turned out that he'd retired and gone back to England, because of course the English teachers were all thrown out in Nasser's time. Anyway, we went back to the hotel where one or other of us was staying to have a drink, and I suggested that he should come to Saudi Arabia. We arranged the visit, and some months later he came to Jeddah. He arrived at the airport and when he came down the steps of the plane two old boys greeted him on the tarmac. They took him into the VIP lounge where all the lights were off. Then we switched on the lights, and there were fifty Old Victorians assembled, who began to sing 'For He's a Jolly Good Fellow'.

There is nothing very remarkable about this story – except that it is totally un-Arabian and is told by somebody who went to Victoria College forty years ago. That is the point of the story. It shows that the Saudis who went to the College entered a completely new world – Ali Abdullah even played cricket while he was there – and this experience later enabled him to deal with Westerners, in business and government, on Western terms.[13] If the story had been told by a Saudi who went to an English public school ten years ago it would not have been unusual; but, as Shaikh Ali says, the Saudi Old Victorians who were at school more than thirty years ago, who include Hisham Nazer, the Minister of Planning, and Adnan Khashoggi, are few in number and very much a closed circle – more so than people who went to Eton or Oxford or Harvard could possibly be. The binding forces are the very unusual nature of their education and the special advantage they gained from it.

Today the members of the younger generation who are about to become the driving force in the Alireza family's future will have spent a third of their lives at schools abroad by the time they graduate in their early twenties. In this they are no different from other Saudis with rich parents, and like other Saudis, when they leave university they do not continue to live abroad but return home and begin careers in Saudi Arabia. This is a much-noted characteristic of young Arabians. The conventional explanations are that they are remarkably conformist and only feel completely at home within Arabian society, but it may also be that in Arabia the opportunities are greater than elsewhere for making large sums of tax-free money.

Some of the young Alirezas on their return to the Kingdom have gone to work for the family company or government institutions; more of them have set up businesses on their own. Their elders have not always supported them in breaking away. In the mid-1970s there was a strong preference on the part of the directors of Haji Abdullah Alireza & Co. for their sons to join the firm, but several of the young were unwilling to become part of a conservative institution in which they would not have been given much authority. Their feeling was that their backgrounds and styles of work were too different from those of their elders. Certainly in managing their own companies since, the young Alirezas have shown themselves to be aggressive and more prepared than their elders to involve themselves actively in winning contracts.

The young Alirezas of the Zainal and Abdullah branches – both sons and daughters – have capital of their own through their shareholdings in the family company, worth between about $500,000 and $80,000 in

13. The Alirezas' interest in cricket has been maintained by younger members of the family who have been to public school in England. On 20 November 1980 the *Saudi Gazette* ran a story under the unlikely headline: 'Rain-soaked pitch delays Alireza Cricket League'.

December 1979, depending on how many shares their fathers had been prepared to allocate to them. (The firm's total capital at that time was $23 million.) All of those who have begun their own businesses have started by saving their dividends, which have probably been a lot bigger than most dividends from the same value of shares declared in London or New York. Then they have borrowed to the hilt from the banks and tried to keep their overheads to a minimum until they have got a down payment on their first contract or cleared their first batch of stock. The two biggest companies to have emerged from this process have been Xenel Industries, in which most of the shares are owned by the sons of Shaikh Ahmed, and Rezatrade, which is owned by all the sons of Shaikh Mohammad and Shaikh Ali. These companies are involved in a whole range of joint-venture service, manufacturing and contracting activities, ranging from the conversion of old containers into instant housing for contractors' labour to the manufacture of electric cable.

There are also a number of (much smaller) boutiques established by the sisters of the Alireza entrepreneurs – boutiques being regarded in Arabia as thoroughly respectable ventures for young ladies of good breeding. In Jeddah some of Shaikh Ahmed's nieces are partners in Yellow Rose. In Bahrain, Samira, the daughter of Mohammad Yusuf of the Ali Akbar branch of the family, has not only set up her own boutique but has shaken the island by becoming the first woman member of the Chamber of Commerce. Three years after this sensational event, during a lunch to which she and I had been invited by some friends, she declared: 'I'm tired of the rag trade, I must find a more important business to run.'

2

Saudi Arabia and the Gulf States

People who have never been there suppose, naturally enough, that all the Arabian oil states must be much the same as each other. Broadly speaking this is true. They share the same Arabian culture, albeit with regional differences; they are very rich by the standards of other states in the Organisation of Petroleum Exporting Countries (OPEC); all, except Bahrain and Dubai, are almost entirely dependent on oil revenues. It goes without saying that they are all preoccupied with developing and diversifying their economies in preparation for the day when their oil revenues become inadequate to finance all their spending.

The answer to the question that journalists are asked so often, namely: 'Are *they* spending their money for the benefit of their people?' (as opposed to spending it on solid gold Cadillacs, mountains of jewels and hundreds of concubines) is, 'Of course – or at least that is what they are trying to do even if their spending programmes do not always produce the desired results.' For obvious reasons of self-respect it is the ambition of all underdeveloped countries to develop their economies to a point where they will eventually compete with the Western industrial powers. In Arabia so far this has meant developing the banking business, capital-intensive export industries, such as refining, petrochemicals, fertilisers, liquified gases and aluminium, and import substitute light industries, mostly producing building materials and foods. At the same time, to different degrees in different states, it has been the policy of governments to enrich their own citizens through land purchases, paying high salaries in government and creating lavish welfare states – taking care at all times to exclude immigrants from most of these benefits. Whether this rule of 'Absolute Welfare' and the industrial diversification programmes are the right policies for the oil states may be open to question, but in the Arabian circumstances of great wealth and dependence on a single commodity they are probably inevitable.

If they are similar in the general sense, one of the things that strikes the first time visitor to the Arabian oil states most forcibly is how different they all are in character and in the stages of development they have reached. Obviously to describe each state in any detail would take more than a single chapter, but a fairly good impression of the differences can be given through comparing Saudi Arabia with the Gulf states, and then Kuwait and Bahrain with Qatar, the United Arab Emirates and Oman.

What makes Saudi Arabia so different is its size. It is as big as the United States east of the Mississippi and has a population of some 7 or 8 million, against 1.5 million in Kuwait, the most populous of the Gulf states. It also has by far the biggest oil reserves, some 160 billion barrels, or a quarter of the world's total reserves. This compares with 65 billion barrels in Kuwait, 30 billion barrels in Abu Dhabi, some 20 billion barrels proven in the North Sea by 1982, and 27 billion barrels in the USA.[1] With these reserves it goes without saying that Saudi Arabia in the last ten years has been by far the biggest oil producer and revenue earner in OPEC. In 1981 it received some $130 billion in foreign exchange, including income from gas sales, the Pilgrimage and financial assets invested abroad.[2] Yet because of its relatively large population most of its people are not as well off individually as the citizens of the Gulf states. Indeed, the Kingdom's whole development profile is markedly different from that of its small neighbours. By virtue of the numbers of its population and the fact that oil production started in 1939, and then restarted in 1946, which is fairly early by Arabian standards, the Kingdom has many more well-trained, able and sophisticated administrators than the Gulf states – albeit nowhere near as many as it needs. On the other hand physically it has the appearance of being more backward than the Gulf states because it received no more revenues in total before the beginning of the 1970s than Kuwait, while its size and population (and the fact that it squandered huge sums in the 1950s) meant that its money had to be spread more thinly. Even now it takes much longer to complete Saudi Arabia's massive development

1. 1 barrel = 35 imperial gallons, 42 US gallons or 159 litres.
2. Saudi revenues in 1982 and 1983 were much lower because of the oil glut and the cut in OPEC prices. Here and later in this chapter the figures quoted for Arabian revenues apply to 1981, because the 1981 figures give a better impression of the norm in the 1979–81 period.

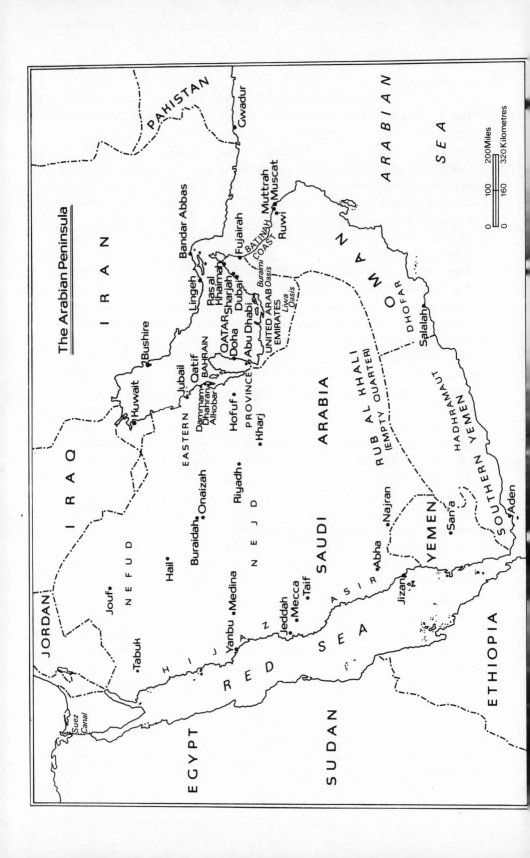

The Arabian Peninsula

projects – many of them involving the biggest contracts of their type ever awarded – than it does to complete equivalent projects in the Gulf.

As befits the leading power in OPEC, Saudi Arabia's international perspective is much broader than that of the Gulf states. Its ministers, when interviewed, are likely to talk of global issues, whereas in the Gulf, with the partial exception of Kuwait, the attention of government, newspapers and the foreign business community is focused mainly on local matters.

The other aspect of Saudi Arabia which makes a big impression on Westerners is its austerity. Alcohol is absolutely illegal, women are forbidden to work or drive cars, cinemas, clubs and theatres are banned, and the courts enforce the capital and corporal punishments that are prescribed in the Koran for murder, rape, adultery and theft. Trafficking in alcohol is also punishable by flogging. Combined with the network of close family and community links, which is still the foundation of society and which involves everyone in a neighbourhood noticing a stranger and knowing what he is doing, these punishments make Saudi Arabia a relatively crime-free society. Until the last four or five years, during which there has been an increase in immigrant crime, nobody hesitated to leave his key under the doormat, or thought of locking his car or bolting his windows against break-ins.

These are the more obvious comments which expatriates make to back up their descriptions of the rather disciplined, austere life of Saudi Arabia. Whether or not they are conscious of it, their impression of the Kingdom must also be moulded in part by the ruling family's devotion to a definite free enterprise philosophy, involving less state capitalism than is practised in the Gulf and a more limited version of the Gulf's welfare states. There were some telling remarks in the Second Five Year Plan, published in 1975. In this document the government said that its principal social objective was to assure all Saudis '. . . an adequate, dignified minimum standard of living. Levels above this minimum will continue to be the reward of individual effort and achievement.' Since the first oil-price explosion of 1973–4 gave it the money to spend on social programmes, Saudi Arabia has moved closer to the Gulf states' policies. It has increased salaries, subsidised basic foods and electric power and given interest-free loans for citizens to build their own homes or apartments for letting. But it is still some way from the Kuwaiti system, under which the transfer of oil revenues to the public has been virtually the main purpose of government for the last thirty years. For example, Saudi Arabia is not likely to follow Kuwait in contriving to buy land at inflated prices or baling out private businessmen from unsuccessful industrial ventures.

It has always been the Saudi government's intention to preserve the country's Islamic values and restrain the pace of social change, whereas the Gulf states have embraced the modern world without inhibitions. The royal family's motives in this have been partly idealistic and partly pragmatic. Over-rapid change would be liable to erode the fabric of family life, which is the cornerstone of Islamic society, and destroy the Saudi vision of creating a new type of society in which Islam will eventually be melded with modern industrial life. It would also pose a threat to the network of family and tribal loyalties and the endorsement of the *ulema*, the religious leaders, which have been two of the foundations of the Saud family's rule. Traditionally the fear has been that any of these developments might lead, at the worst, to a socialist revolution, or more likely to irresistible demands for popular participation in a government that has always been an absolute monarchy. Recently the fear has been of religious opposition from extreme conservatives.

During King Faisal's reign, from 1964 to 1975, the impact of the modern world on Saudi Arabia was limited by keeping as many as possible of the Western expatriate community out of Riyadh and the Nejd heartland. 'The vexatious foreigner', as a British diplomat described him, was encouraged to remain in Dhahran, the oil-company town in the Eastern Province, or Jeddah. Jeddah, the commercial capital, contained most of the big merchant houses, almost all of the foreign banks, the central bank (the Saudi Arabian Monetary Agency), the Foreign Ministry and the embassies. It was only in the late 1970s that SAMA and the foreign banks, by then partly Saudi-owned, were allowed to establish themselves in Riyadh. The embassies remained in Jeddah.

Another characteristic of King Faisal's rule was his habit of taking a big step forward and then compensating by taking a smaller step back. He might introduce girls' education, for example, or television broadcasting, thus arousing the misgivings of the *ulema*, and then take a comparatively trivial step to reassure them by banning the sale of the infidel immigrants' Christmas trees in the Kingdom or repeating the ordinance that prohibited women from travelling unaccompanied by their husbands.

Since the oil-price explosion the most important regulator of the

Kingdom's social development has been the rate of government spending. A higher rate of spending brings in more foreigners: visiting businessmen and, much more socially disturbing, contractors, military-training personnel and technical advisers, who come out as temporary residents, many of them bringing their wives and families. High spending also pumps money faster into the hands of Saudis. It accelerates the drift from the countryside to the towns, encourages people to change their jobs, and gives citizens higher incomes, opportunities for travel, and western material and social aspirations. The flow of money is felt immediately by a whole range of people who are not government employees. If government spending rises, causing a new building boom, the Riyadh taxi driver, who has been living a relatively traditional, independent life, plying his trade by day and at night going back to a taxi drivers' camp in the desert, may decide to chance his luck as a contractor. Most probably he will begin by providing some minor service to an established contractor working on a government project or building houses or apartment blocks. In due course he will move permanently into the big city. He will get an interest-free government loan with which to build his own home and will bring his relatives in from the country to join him. Before long he may find himself accompanying his aged mother who is being sent for special medical treatment in London. If the government wants to slow down this sort of change and dampen the rate of inflation, which is as socially destabilising in Arabia as it is anywhere else, it scales down some projects or delays awarding contracts. It does not rewrite the national plan or make any formal announcements of postponements or rearranged priorities, it simply instructs its ministries not to sign any contracts until further notice. On occasions this has involved a moratorium on new contracts lasting for several months.

The Saud family's concern about the social evolution of its Kingdom has had its effect. One notices that the Kingdom is much more assertively Arabian than the Gulf states. The business visitor certainly finds himself talking to Americans, Europeans and Palestinians, but for the most part he does business with Saudis. In the Gulf, with the partial exception of Kuwait, he is likely to do business with Palestinians, Egyptians, Englishmen or Americans, or possibly even Indians. In Qatar, the UAE and Oman it would be possible to spend several weeks and not meet more than two or three nationals (apart from taxi drivers) either socially or in business.

The Gulf states have geared themselves to allowing their Western expatriate communities to live comfortable lives – letting them wrap themselves in a sort of suburban cosiness. Western expatriates in the Gulf, always known as 'expats', have greater freedom to form their own clubs and pursue their own sports; in some states they are subject to different drink laws from the rest of the population. In Bahrain, which is by far the most Western influenced, there is even a special beach, the Ruler's Beach, which is reserved for expatriates. The life of the Western community in the Gulf may be located in Arabia geographically, but culturally it is somewhere on the fringes of Greater London. As a journalist in Bahrain put it, 'It's Croydon with palm trees.' In Saudi Arabia, Dhahran, the Aramco town, is definitely in Texas – women may even take jobs and drive cars in the compound. In all other Saudi cities the Arabian culture is dominant.

The Gulf states' more liberal attitude towards foreigners stems from their less austere religious traditions and their having had longer contact with the outside world than any part of Saudi Arabia except the Hijaz. Leaving aside Dubai, which is a phenomenon unlike any other in Arabia, the most outward-looking states are Kuwait and Bahrain. These were big trading and pearling centres in the early days of this century, when Qatar and Abu Dhabi were nothing more than tiny coastal settlements. Kuwait and Bahrain have also had the advantages of having rather liberal ruling families and having had oil revenues for much longer that the states further south in the Gulf. Bahrain saw the first oil discovery in the Arabian Peninsula, in the early 1930s, but ironically this field proved both to be very small by Arabian standards and to be the only one that has ever been found on the island. Kuwait's first strike, the Burgan field, was made a few years later and could not be brought on stream until 1946, after the Second World War. But as the oil company appraised its find it realised that it had discovered a giant. Burgan is now known to be the world's second biggest field, still holding reserves nearly twice as big as the total reserves of the USA, including Alaska. (The biggest field is Ghawar in Saudi Arabia.)

The decisive influence on the subsequent histories of Bahrain and Kuwait has been not just the widely different sizes of their oil reserves but the fact that their early discovery enabled them to embark on serious development decades before the lower Gulf states. Consequently they are much the most diversified of the Gulf states. Kuwait has a wide range of well-established industries, running from car batteries to cement asbestos pipes. It has a big oil tanker and dry cargo shipping fleet and a sophisticated international banking and foreign investment business, without the presence of foreign banks in the state. Bahrain's diversification has been aimed more at turning the island into the Arabian service centre: a regional base for foreign companies, the hub of the Gulf's air communications, an offshore financial centre providing a link between the Saudi banking system and international markets, and a place to which other Arabians can go to enjoy themselves. Most of Bahrain's neighbours have been only too happy to allow it to collect the spin-off from their much greater wealth, reasoning that it saves them giving Bahrain more aid and keeps the Bharaini populace prosperous, and therefore politically stable.

The proof of Bahrain's success can be seen in recent budgets, in which oil (including the island's half share in the revenues from a small offshore Saudi field) has accounted for only 70 per cent of the state's total revenues. Much of the rest comes directly or indirectly from the offshore banks, an aluminium smelter, the Arab dry dock and Gulf Air, the last two of which are owned by groups of Arab governments and based in Bahrain.

The other similarity given to Kuwait and Bahrain by their early discovery of oil and their trading background is their well-educated and sophisticated population. Bahrain, as its inhabitants never tire of telling Western visitors and their Arabian neighbours, opened its first modern school in 1919. It began girls' education ten years later. (Someone who helped overcome the opposition of the religious leaders and the more conservative fathers to this horrifyingly radical innovation, with its limitless potential for encouraging girls to neglect their domestic duties and question their parents' commands, was Mohammad Ali Alireza, the pearl dealer and founder of the Fallah schools.)

It is when one starts to examine what education has meant in terms of the careers followed by Kuwaitis and Bahrainis, that the effects of the states' vastly different scales of oil revenues become obvious. Bahrain's oil revenues in 1981 amounted to about $1.25 billion, for a population of 350,000, whereas Kuwait's oil revenues and investment income amounted to some $22 billion. Kuwait, furthermore, has received a very high level of oil revenues since the early 1950s and the government has made a conscious effort (by methods described in chapter 4) to enrich its citizens. In the course of thirty years this has meant that its people have become the richest in the world. Over 70 per cent of Kuwaiti families have their own private incomes from letting accommodation to Western, Indian or other Arab expatriates. (These immigrants are not allowed to take Kuwaiti citizenship, except in the most unusual cases, and are therefore barred from buying property of their own.) Kuwaitis also benefit from the government's policy of over-staffing its establishments and paying huge salaries for civil service jobs, which often require only perfunctory attendance and symbolic effort.

The ease with which they can earn a good income has meant that Kuwaitis can afford to be selective about what jobs they are prepared to do. The members of the elite, among whom there are a fair number of impressively able and energetic people who run the state, are in the government and state corporations, banking and financial services and other businesses. Below this level there are any number of Kuwaitis in civil service grades going down to drivers, doormen and tea boys. Outside government employment there is a preference for driving taxis and taking very simple jobs, such as multi-storey car-park attendant, which involve handling cash without expending more than a minimum of energy. The bedouin of the Kuwait hinterland, who can qualify for a second-grade citizen status, serve in the army and the police.

In Bahrain, in contrast, the government has been unable to provide more than the basic amenities of a welfare state, so its citizens have had to be prepared to do genuinely productive jobs. There has even been the necessity, familiar to the rest of the world but unheard of in the other Arabian oil states, of building new industries with the specific intention of providing citizens with job opportunities. This is what led to the construction of the Aluminium Bahrain (Alba) smelter in the late 1960s. Bahrainis account for over three-quarters of Alba's workforce, which would be an unthinkable proportion elsewhere in the Gulf. They work as clerks in the civil service and trading businesses, in banks and in airline offices. There are Bahrainis in medicine and the other professions, which is rare among citizens of the oil states. There are even Bahraini teachers working in Saudi Arabia and in the other Gulf states.

Westerners in Arabia tend to work on the principle that all those in the long white *thobe*, known in Kuwait and Bahrain as a *dishdasha*, are 'citizens', whereas those who are obviously Arabs but wearing shirts and trousers must be Egyptians, Palestinians or other Arabs from Iraq or the Levant. In Kuwait, where the *dishdasha* has become a sort of national uniform, so anxious are citizens to set themselves apart from foreigners, this rule is almost always correct. The more affluent classes keep their *dishdashas* immaculately laundered and change them two or three times a day. But Bahrain is the one place in Arabia, outside the Aramco headquarters at Dhahran, where an important part of the indigenous population has forsaken the *dishdasha* for Western dress. During the working day it has been found that Western dress is more practical.

Qatar, Oman and the United Arab Emirates[3] are better off in their oil incomes than Bahrain, but, with the exception of Abu Dhabi, they lack the vast incomes of Kuwait or Saudi Arabia. None of them has anything to compare with the freak Burgan field or Saudi Arabia's Ghawar, which stretches for 150 miles and contains 60 or 70 billion barrels. Abu Dhabi in 1981 had a combined oil and investment income of some $17 billion, which was more than three-quarters of the Kuwaiti figure, but Qatar received only $7 billion, Dubai and Oman about $4 billion each, and Sharjah a nominal $60 million. Like earlier revenue estimates, these figures are extremely rough, designed just to give an impression of order of magnitude.

It also happens, for a combination of historical and geological reasons, that oil revenues are a rather recent phenomenon in the lower Gulf. Sharjah only began oil production in the early 1970s, while Abu Dhabi, Oman and Dubai started in the 1960s. Then in Abu Dhabi and Oman the spending of oil revenues on a significant scale was delayed for several years by the intense caution and conservatism, not to say eccentricity, of the two states' rulers. One of these, Shaikh Shakbut of Abu Dhabi, ventured the unusual opinion that the oil companies needed the money more than he did. The hiatus was embarrassing to the British, who then had a semi-colonial role in the lower Gulf, and frustrating to the other members of the ruling families and those few members of the populations for whom the British had sponsored a foreign education. Eventually it was arranged for more enlightened relations to take over. Qatar faced a similar problem, albeit in a less clear-cut form. It received its first revenue cheque in 1950 and its rulers

3. The UAE's membrs are Abu Dhabi, Dubai, Sharjah, Ras al Khaimah, Ajman, Umm al Qaiwain and Fujairah.

did embark on some small-scale development straight away, but change was slow. It was not until the coup of the present ruler, Shaikh Khalifa bin Hamad al Thani, in 1972 that anyone took steps to curb the proportion of revenues going into the ruling family's pockets and accelerate the pace of development spending.

The result of this later start has been that the lower Gulf states are less economically diversified or socially evolved than their northern neighbours, but that since development spending has got under way the rate of change has been more hectic. The states have had the advantage of being able to see what Kuwait and Bahrain have done and learn from some of their mistakes. This has enabled them to press ahead faster. Inevitably they have entered a race to catch up. After fifteen years of development, superficially Abu Dhabi town does not look different from Kuwait after thirty-five years, and it is way ahead of what Kuwait was in 1960. In its social and industrial development Abu Dhabi has gained on Kuwait but is far from catching up.

The effects of fast development are all the more striking in that before oil there was almost nothing to Abu Dhabi, or to its neighbour, Qatar. These two are *the* archetypal oil states: little history, tiny populations (450,000 in Abu Dhabi and 250,000 in Qatar), no resources other than oil and gas, and not much to their geography except flat desert. Qatar and Abu Dhabi are the places where it really is true to talk of bedouin having jumped from camels to Datsuns.

The modern rulers of Qatar and Abu Dhabi are extremely generous to their people – and Abu Dhabi's standards of welfare are extended to the other six members of the UAE through the federal ministries of Education, Housing, Social Affairs and Health, all of which are financed by Abu Dhabi. Both the UAE and Qatar governments have copied, and expanded, the Kuwaiti welfare state. More people than in Kuwait and Saudi Arabia seem to qualify for free housing. Both states seem very willing to send patients for medical treatment abroad, accompanied by a member of their families, without whom, it is felt, they would be bound to feel lost and recover more slowly. The health ministries are perfectly aware that there is more than meets the eye to the sudden deterioration that afflicts so many people's health as the hot season sets in. The official feeling is that a trip to London or Vienna, with hospital fees, travel and a living allowance for the family paid by the state, helps broaden the minds of the people. For this purpose the governments of all the Arabian oil states maintain medical offices, attached to their London embassies, for providing interpreters and drivers, arranging and paying for private treatment, and handing out the families' allowances. Qatar and the UAE are exceptional only in so far as they are reputed to be the most generous of the oil states in financing foreign medical trips.

The major difference in character between Abu Dhabi and Qatar is that Abu Dhabi seems to be more confident in its headlong modernisation. Qatar has recently become more aware than the other oil states of its past as a fishing and pearl-diving community, and certainly it has kept itself from becoming such a cosmopolitan place as Abu Dhabi. This is partly a reflection of its modest revenues, its relatively small diplomatic role in Arab affairs and the state of its oil reserves, which are declining and are very unlikely to be supplemented by new finds. Abu Dhabi in its confidence is a liberal place, where immigrants probably feel more welcome, or less unwelcome, than they do elsewhere.

The Ruler of Abu Dhabi, Shaikh Zayed bin Sultan al Nahayan, is President of the UAE, or 'the Emirates' as it is generally known. This is a rather loose federation of seven shaikhdoms, put together by Britain when it withdrew from its colonial role at the end of 1971. At that stage there existed only the barest bones of a federation. Since then Shaikh Zayed and the other more Union-minded rulers have been striving to create something which better resembles the normal federal systems found in the United States or Australia. On paper they appeared to have reached this stage by 1980. The welfare services had been united, and so had foreign affairs, information, the police and justice, telecommunications, roads and defence. However, many of the ministries were less 'federalised' than they appeared to be. Likewise the unification of the emirates' various private armies, which had been agreed only in 1976, had remained distinctly theoretical for two years and had caused a federal crisis in 1978, when three of the rulers challenged Shaikh Zayed's appointment of a commander-in-chief. A cynic would say that most of the unified ministries involved functions on which the poorer states were happy to see Abu Dhabi's money being spent for their benefit. Not federalised were oil, the investment of oil revenue surpluses (which only affects Abu Dhabi), development planning and industrialisation.

With its half-federalised administration, the outstanding territorial disputes between its members and the periodic crises over petty issues, the UAE has often seemed in danger of breaking up. Yet its rulers are a pragmatic group. They are obviously not separated by differences in ideology, so they do not take stands on issues of principle. When they find themselves disagreeing they withdraw from the brink, and more often than not go hunting while they let their passions cool. In most instances the 'northern emirates', Sharjah, Ajman, Umm al Qaiwain, Ras al Khaimah and Fujairah, have co-operated with the federation better than Dubai has done. Their rulers have not had their own oil, except for Sharjah's minute field, and have needed Abu Dhabi's money for development and for keeping themselves in the style to which they feel they ought to become accustomed.

In Dubai, the least federally minded of all the emirates, lack of interest in the union has stemmed from varied causes: the old rivalry with Abu Dhabi, a clash of personalities between the Ruler, Shaikh Rashid bin Said al Maktum, and Shaikh Zayed, and Dubai's self-interest in remaining a *laissez-faire* entrepôt, unhampered by federal regulations. Shaikh Zayed is completely committed to the Federation, he accepts bureaucracy and he believes in the welfare state. Shaikh Rashid abhors these attitudes. Under his supervision Dubai pulled itself up by its own bootstraps, without any oil revenues until 1969, to become the most dynamic trading centre in the Arabian Peninsula. Rashid developed an intensely personal style of rule. Until very recently Dubai was not so much a state as a diversified industrial, banking and trading enterprise, headed by Rashid as chairman of the holding company. In this corporation, as in any other, there was a sensible emphasis on keeping down costs and making departments pay their own way. This meant doing without a government in the conventional sense and relying on a few long-serving and trusted lieutenants to oversee particular bits of the affairs of state.

The foundation of Dubai's prosperity has been trade – which makes it quite different from any other oil state in the Arabian Peninsula. The state's rise has been mainly at the expense of Sharjah. In the early years of this century Sharjah did not have able rulers. It was intolerant of foreigners and it suffered from the gradual silting of the creek that provided an anchorage for its dhows. Dubai, under the much shrewder rule of the Maktum family, made a point of welcoming foreigners. In the 1920s it received an influx of Persian merchants from Lingeh, which in turn encouraged Arab traders, including the famous Owais family, to move down from Sharjah. The Owais were big pearl merchants, who had already accumulated a capital equivalent to $600,000 by 1946, according to a bank representative who went to Dubai in that year to negotiate a concession for the Imperial Bank of Iran (now the British Bank of the Middle East). The real breakthrough, however, came in the later 1950s. Shaikh Rashid embarked on a series of schemes to deepen the creek that winds through the centre of his town and improve the wharfs beside it. He also stabilised the creek's entrance by building a breakwater to prevent the formation of sand bars, and with his characteristic eye for a profit made the scheme pay for itself by selling the land that was reclaimed behind the breakwater. The first of these projects was completed in 1963 with money borrowed from the Kuwaitis, at just the time when Sharjah's creek finally became unusable.

The trade that blossomed under Shaikh Rashid's enterprising rule was gold smuggling. When the business reached its peak in 1970, the flow of gold through Dubai totalled 259 tons. This accounted for slightly more than 20 per cent of the non-Communist world's new gold supply that year and represented some five kilos for every man, woman and child in the emirate. From the point of view of the government of India, whose people bought the gold as an essential part of every bride's dowry, the trade was a nuisance. But because most of the gold was paid for by a flow of silver back to Dubai, much of it in the form of coin dating back to East India Company days or ornaments said to have been looted from temples, the trade did not cost India too much of its precious foreign exchange. The government also reasoned that if the flow via Dubai was stopped some other channel would be opened up, so vital was gold to the prestige of simple Indian families. So it was not until the early 1970s that it took serious steps to arrest the traffic. This was not an easy task. To all outward appearances the smuggling dhows looked exactly like any other dhows of the Arabian Sea. They were indistinguishable from the fishing fleets with which they mingled off Bombay in the early hours of the morning while they transferred their cargoes to the dhows of the smugglers' Indian agents. The big gold merchants of Dubai used sometimes to challenge Western guests or business associates to say which of a group of dhows tied up beside the creek might be the smuggling vessel. Anyone who got the right answer did so by pure luck, and anyway the merchants would never confirm whether the guess was right or not. It goes without saying that beneath the waterline and in the engine room the smuggling dhows were not ordinary at all. As the Indian authorities became more efficient the dhows were built to sail faster: the best could outpace any coastguard cutter. Rivalry in speed led to rivalry in fire-power. After 1970 there were reports of running battles, and dhows started coming home riddled with bullet holes. There were occasions when dhows had to throw their cargoes overboard – and there was also a mutiny when a crew seized its cargo and disappeared.

These mishaps did not affect the trade too badly. For the London and Zurich gold markets, the airlines that freighted the gold into Dubai – where it landed and was re-exported perfectly legitimately – and for the Dubaian smugglers the business continued to be extremely profitable. Practically the whole merchant community was involved: the long-established Ghurair family, who are reckoned to be the biggest real estate owners among the Dubai merchants, Juma al Majid, Mohammad al Gaz, the Owais family – now the doyen of the Dubai merchants, Mohammad al Mullah, Othman Sagar, a Pakistani known simply as Harun, and the Galadari brothers. The Galadaris had some of the best dhows and their fortune was probably the biggest to be made entirely out of gold. (Part of the profits of one of the Galadaris, Abdel-Wahab, can now be seen in the shape of Dubai's Hyatt Regency hotel.) Even Western expatriates went into gold. These were respectable family men with children at school and mortgages at home, whose jobs as bankers or contractors, or managers of ports or airports, had brought them to Dubai. They would simply deposit a piece of their savings with one of the smuggling syndicates and receive their dividend, together with accounts, at the end of the season.

The only well-known businessmen not to become involved were Majid Futtaim, Eassa Gurg and Nasser Abdelatif. Majid Futtaim now runs what is probably the biggest and certainly the most professionally managed importing business in the UAE, with Toyota and a clutch of Japanese electronics agencies. Being an unflamboyant man who likes to have as many as possible of the factors that affect his business within his control, in accordance with the best modern theories of Western management, Majid was not attracted by the gamble in smuggling. On the other hand he was one of those who imported gold for resale to the smuggling syndicates. The international gold market at the time was stable and likely to yield a small, but safe and fairly predictable return. A merchant could plan his corporate expansion while still being much involved in gold imports.

Unfortunately for all those involved – with the exception of the Indian coastguards – the gold business did not last. In the early 1970s gold began the first of its dramatic series of price rises from $35 an ounce, and it quickly moved beyond the reach of the ordinary Indian buyer, no matter how fearful he might have been of losing face in his village. At the same time Mrs Ghandi, the Indian Prime Minister, imprisoned many of the smugglers' Bombay agents. Dubai's turnover dropped steadily, until in the disastrous month of June 1973 imports of gold hit zero. Although there was a minor revival of imports in the late 1970s, much of the metal going to make jewellery for sale to foreigners passing through Dubai, the smuggling never really recovered. It was not the end of the merchants though. While doing best out of gold they had built up a flourishing business in other types of contraband – particularly cloth and cigarettes to southern Iran and Pakistan.

They had also developed a legitimate re-export trade. This trade has continued. In the last few years the merchants have described it as taking four distinct forms. There are capital goods, cars and foodstuffs which are imported through Dubai to be sold in other members of the UAE and are no longer officially regarded as re-exports; there are legitimate (and illegitimate) re-exports of consumer goods of all types to the south Asian countries from Iran eastwards – though the smugglers are no longer the Dubai merchants themselves but natives of the recipient countries doing their purchasing in Dubai; and there are consumer durable exports to Mecca, Jeddah and Medina, where there is a big seasonal demand at the time of the Haj. By far the most unusual trade, however, involves more than $100 million a year of consumer durable goods – watches, sound recorders, etc. – that are sold over the counters of shops within the UAE, and are taken out by the purchasers. It is reckoned that this trade accounts for three-quarters of all the consumer durable goods brought into Dubai.

It is consumer goods that have brought the Futtaims and a few others like them into their own in the past six or seven years. Some of the buyers are visiting businessmen; most are immigrant labourers, clerks, teachers, mechanics. The development boom has brought to Arabia hundreds of thousands of immigrants from south Asia and the poorer Arab countries, where imports of the best Western consumer goods are restricted. Each of these immigrants aspires to become the owner of some of these luxuries, which will bestow on him great prestige when he returns home. In fact many of the immigrants not only buy radios and TVs for their own use, but during their time in the Gulf will make several trips home and on each trip will take a TV which can be sold on the black market. With luck the profit will be big enough to pay for the entire holiday. One sees the most obvious evidence of the immigrant market at the airports just before the departure of flights of Air India or Pakistan International. Always there are masses of huddled workers, the poorer ones with painted tin trunks, bundles wrapped in blankets and tied with rope, plastic sandals, baggy pyjama trousers and the perpetual air of bewilderment and slight fear that these people carry with them in Arabia. In every person's hands is an object which seems to belong to a completely different world – a TV or cassette-player and sound recorder.

The scene is rather pathetic and hardly seems a plausible foundation for much of the prosperity enjoyed by Dubai since the end of gold smuggling. Yet the volumes of goods involved are staggering. In 1977, which was in no sense an exceptional year, over eighty tons of watches were landed, which worked out at nine watches for every man, woman and child in the state. In the same year Dubai imported four transistor radios and three radios-cum-sound-recorders per head, one television for every two people, and the better part of a gallon of perfume for every adult female. It was these figures which prompted Enver Masood, the Pakistani manager of Majid Futtaim's electronics sales operation, to say that he thought of the goods he sold not so much as 'products' but as 'produce', like bulk grain or soya beans.

Everyone when asked to explain Dubai's extraordinary success over the last quarter century gives most of the credit to Shaikh Rashid, who was no small merchant in his own right and is always thought to have had a big hand in gold smuggling operations. Since he began to improve the creek in the 1950s, Shaikh Rashid has worked on the maxim that 'what is good for my merchants is good for Dubai'. Although he had to rely on the customs for his revenues before 1969, he imposed only very small duties. To encourage the business climate he issued liberal commercial regulations, which gave foreigners much more freedom to set up their own businesses than they enjoyed in other states. He also kept bureaucracy to an absolute minimum. Many of the activities which in other Gulf states or the Western world are regarded as functions of government in Dubai are handled by private enterprise. This is the case with the airport, the port and the state's heavy industries. The industries are allowed more or less to run themselves without any industry ministry to oversee them.

This at least is the conventional picture of Dubai: the businessman's paradise and the last place on earth to be holding out against the invasion of red tape. In practice the picture is not quite so simple, and there are contradictory elements within it. Not all of the private enterprise services have made profits; the telephone company and the electricity company have had to be taken over by the federal and state budgets. More damaging to Dubai's image have been the questionable commercial prospects overhanging its dry dock (for million-ton tankers) and the new industrial port at Jebel Ali. In the early 1970s Shaikh Rashid overinvested in his first major port and airport developments, only to be saved by the 1973–4 oil-price explosion. This was an event entirely unforeseen and beyond his own control, which through great good luck filled the port and airport and caused everyone to praise the Ruler's foresight. Now his second generation of development schemes has been saved by a new-found (and possibly temporary) enthusiasm for the Federation, which since 1979 has involved a certain amount of Abu Dhabi money being injected into the state. Equally important has been another set of oil-price rises – once again unforeseen and beyond Shaikh Rashid's control.

Anyone who goes to Oman after visiting the Gulf oil producers realises immediately that he has arrived in a different part of the Middle East with a different culture. The coastline around Muscat and Muttrah, the twin towns that serve as capital and commercial centre, is a spectacle of craggy red cliffs tumbling into the sea, very different from the white salt flats of the Gulf coast. Wherever there is a settlement, built underneath the cliffs on the shore of a little bay, there seems to be a castle, probably begun by the Portuguese in the sixteenth century but then taken over and modified by successive Iranian and Omani chiefs. This in itself sets Oman apart from the Gulf. Whereas the Gulf and the Arabian interior until the last century were nearly as cut off from the mainstream of European and Asian history as it was possible to be, Oman at times ruled a small Indian Ocean empire.

Oman is far bigger than any of the Gulf states. Like Saudi Arabia it has distinctive regions. In the north, inland, is Oman proper: a mountainous region, historically often independent from the Sultanate of Muscat on the coast, with a tribal population engaged in arable farming and livestock rearing. The area used to be a big producer of dates and dried limes, used to flavour tea, which were Oman's major exports in the nineteenth century. In the centre of the country is a flat empty region, and in the south is the province of Dhofar, divided between a narrow coastal plain and a high grassland plateau, both of which catch the tail end of the monsoon. Just as Oman is separate from the Gulf, Dhofar is seen as being separate from Oman, cut off from the rest of the Sultanate by 400 miles of wilderness. Its people are regarded by Omanis as foreigners – though the old Sultan, Said bin Taimur, had an affection for the greenness of Salalah, the Dhofari capital, and in his later years never left the place. Few Omanis have ever had much contact with Dhofaris. One reason for this is that in the early 1970s the province was the scene of a Communist insurgency, backed by southern Yemen. It remains an area which one can visit only with government permission.

The modern centre of Oman is the northern coastal region. This contains the largest part of the country's population, reckoned to be about 850,000 or rather less than the total population of the UAE. On the coast one has the impression of an even stronger Indian influence than one does in the Gulf states. There is a large, long-established Indian community, and more Indian-owned stalls in the souk, filled with Indian-made artefacts and Omani items with Indian designs. The cultural connections of the Omani coast with the rest of the Arab world to the north and west are minimal; the region is orientated to the countries around the Indian Ocean. There is an extraordinarily polyglot population in the souk: Persians and tribesmen from every part of southern Iran, Pakistan and Afghanistan, most of the races of north and west India, Omanis from the interior, all of them with long beards, white turbans and curved daggers thrust into their belts, and the coastal Omani people. The Omanis of the coast look very like the Gulf Arabs, except that instead of the long white *ghotra* and *agal* headdress they wear white and gold embroidered Zanzibari caps bound round with small white turbans.

Some of the Omanis are of obvious African descent, having been brought to the Sultanate in the last century, when Oman was the centre of the thriving Arabian slave trade. This trade developed in the earlier part of the century when Zanzibar and Oman were one sultanate, ruled over by the great Sultan Said bin Sultan, who conquered a large part of the east African coast, entered into treaties with the British and exchanged presents with Queen Victoria. (He received the Queen's portrait, a four-poster bed, a state carriage and harness which he later gave to the Nizam of Hyderabad, and a silver gilt tea service.) When

Said died in 1856 his empire was divided between his sons.

From that point on, the Omani part, separated from the family's much richer East African possessions, declined. The process was accelerated in the later nineteenth century by the British navy's suppression of the slave trade and of the arms smuggling business that supplied the tribes on the north-west frontier of India. There was then a period of internal strife, followed by the extravagant rule of Sultan Taimur, during which the government got disastrously into debt, and then the reign of the eccentric Said bin Taimur, from 1932 to 1970.

Said bin Taimur was not only a recluse, who was scarcely ever seen by members of his government, let alone by his people, he also was preoccupied with avoiding spending money. He was not like Shaikh Shakbut, the Ruler of Abu Dhabi from 1928 to 1966, who had simply no understanding of how to use money and doubted whether his people would be any happier if he began pumping millions of dollars into his state.[4] Said was charming (to those few who ever met him), and he was well educated – but he was obsessed with debt. He had felt humiliated at having had to pay off his father's debts, helped by some temporary finance from Khimji Ramdas, who is still a leading member of the Hindu merchant community. He was determined never to get into a position where there was any possibility of his being in debt again. The £250,000 British subsidy he received annually he was obliged to spend, but he hoarded his own meagre revenues from the customs and the oil concession rental, for fear that by spending them he would create a need for money which he would be unable to meet if his income ever stopped. On only one occasion did Said ever explain his policy, and this was in 1968, just after the start of oil production, when he issued the only public statement of his thirty-eight-year reign, entitled: 'The Word of Sultan Said bin Taimur, Sultan of Muscat and Oman, about the history of the financial position of the Sultanate in the past and the hopes for the future, after the export of oil.' In this document, known thereafter as 'The Word', Said explained: '. . . we did not want to overburden the Sultanate's finances and weigh them down with new debts, after having paid off the old ones. Doubtless it would have been easy to obtain money in various ways, but this would only have been by a loan with interest at a set percentage rate. This amounts to usury, with which I

---

4. See *A Hundred Million Dollars a Day* by Michael Field, Sidgwick and Jackson, Praeger and Fayard, 1975, pp. 78–80.

completely disagree, and the religious prohibition of which is not unknown.' Later in 'The Word' he added a remarkable justification for his policy, referring to the five-month period between the end of his British subsidy in March 1967 and the beginning of oil exports in August: 'During this interim period we depended on such financial reserves as we had. Had it not been for our economy and for our reserves we would have been unable to bear the burden of expenditure during these months.' An incidental consequence of this cautious approach to money and Said's own isolation in Salalah was that Oman remained shut off from the world outside. Without access to the Sultan for consultation the government came to depend on a series of rigid edicts, all of which had once had a specific purpose, though that purpose had often been forgotten with time. Omanis had to wear Omani dress, Europeans were not allowed to sail boats east of Muscat harbour, everyone had to carry a lantern after dark, nobody was to smoke in public, the gates of Muscat were to be closed three hours after sunset. Hardly anybody was privileged to receive entry or exit visas.

All of this changed very suddenly. From 1967, in accordance with his undertakings in the later passages of 'The Word', Said had begun spending some modest sums on a few development projects, including government offices, a water-supply scheme, a girls' school and a hospital for Muscat. The effect was hardly noticeable and in 1970 Said's son, Qaboos, with some encouragement from the British, seized power. He sent his father into exile. In this way Oman was thrown into the twentieth century more abruptly than any other oil state. In matters of money Qaboos proved to be precisely the opposite of his father. On two occasions in the 1970s he caused his government's spending to run out of control. This was worrying in a country with very limited oil resources and a production rate which at best in the 1980s is going to be on a plateau.

In its resources other than oil Oman is fortunate. It has agricultural land and minerals, though not much has been done to exploit these as yet. It has also managed to be unworried by its manpower problems. Qaboos and the ruling family have allowed much of the administration, including the army, the security forces and many of the civilian facilities such as the port and the airport to be British run, which probably makes them more efficient than they would otherwise be. British cultural and political influence is much greater in Oman than it is in Bahrain and the lower Gulf. This is ironic because the British have been bound to Oman only by treaties of friendship, never by the treaties of protection which were signed with the Gulf states. The effect is to make Muttrah, the commercial centre, and its overspill in the Ruwi valley strongly 'Brit ex-pat' and to give the administration a somewhat colonial flavour; yet the Omanis seem confident enough in themselves not to mind this. Their problem has been mitigated by their having a unique source of skilled manpower in the Zanzibari Omanis and *émigrés* who left the Sultanate or were exiled in Sultan Said's day. These people have now returned to enjoy their country's (relative) new freedom and business opportunities.

The thing that strikes visitors about all the Omanis, after talking to people elsewhere in the Arab world, is how extraordinarily frank they are with their opinions – a characteristic that endears them to journalists. It used to be possible to put this down to Oman having only just entered the modern world, but the trait has endured.

Qaboos, who lacks none of his father's charm, seems to be as open as his people – though during the early part of his rule he did not make himself easily available to them. Like previous Omani rulers, he relied heavily on his *walis*, the powerful provincial governors, for the day-to-day administration of his realm. He also showed signs of enjoying being a recluse. Having been brought up in Dhofar, and having spent most of his twenties under virtual palace arrest there, he showed the same taste as his father for taking himself away from his government and spending much of his time in Salalah. Yet he seemed no less popular with his people or less well informed about what was happening in his country as a result. It was only after the overthrow of the Shah of Iran, which reminded all the Arabian rulers about the importance of maintaining contact with their subjects, that Qaboos modified the style of his rule. In 1979 he embarked on a series of tours of his country, visiting remote places and talking to ordinary people.

3

Arabian Society

In the 1960s it used to be said in Bahrain that the old Guest Palace of the Ruler had been designed as an Indian railway station. It was a plausible suggestion. Bahrain was then still under British protection and retained a flavour of the Raj. Most of the Bahraini elite had been educated in India, traditionally almost all imports had come from India, and there was a long-established and prosperous Hindu merchant community on the island as well as a Hindu labouring class. In private houses and in hotels and restaurants one was waited on by Indians in well-creased white trousers, white shirts and plimsolls.

Today the Indian influence is still there but the emphasis is more modern. Nobody notices the Guest Palace because it is well away from the centre of town and, compared with the high-rise blocks along the sea front, no longer seems impressively large. The most striking change is in the sheer numbers of Indians and Pakistanis one sees. Indians still provide most of the hotel staff throughout the Gulf, though they now wear standard Western uniforms instead of the white trousers. Others work as clerks, tailors, mechanics, domestic servants and labourers. There are as many Indian businesses as ever – though they are not so large in relative terms as they were thirty years ago – and they still have the characteristic Indian incongruity and exaggeration about their shop names: Snow White Laundry, Universal Haircutting Salon, Paradise Restaurant. In Doha, the capital city of Qatar, there is a restaurant which may have the distinction of being the only place in the world to put curried spaghetti bolognaise on the menu.

In most of the Gulf states the indigenous population is outnumbered by immigrants – Egyptians, Palestinians, Yemenis, Iranians, Philippinos and other Far East Asians, as well as Indians and Pakistanis. The proportions vary from a high of 80 per cent in Abu Dhabi and Dubai, to 55–60 per cent in Kuwait and Qatar, down to about 20–30 per cent in

Saudi Arabia, Oman and Bahrain. Immigrants of different nationalities fill the manual labouring, technical and industrial jobs. They provide nearly all the labour in the service industries, where they work as porters, clerks, telegraph operators and hotel staff, and they account for most of the professional classes – doctors, teachers and engineers. Westerners newly arrived in the oil states say that the huge and highly visible population of immigrants makes one of their strongest and most surprising first impressions. It goes without saying that in all the states the immigrant population is a political issue of some sensitivity.

Seen beside the immigrants the Arabians themselves are a homogenous group. To the modern Western eye, looking not too closely, the citizens of Saudi Arabia and the Gulf states are indistinguishable from each other in dress, manner and lifestyle. Among the indigenous peoples of the Arabian Peninsula, only the Omanis and the Yemenis are obviously set apart by their different cultures and histories. The difference of the Yemenis, who are counted as immigrants in the oil states, is underlined by their socialist governments and their lack of oil.

As the Arabians see themselves the picture is more complicated. If one manages to look beneath the thick layer of new immigrants and tries to ignore the influence of modern national governments which have developed with oil revenues since the Second World War, one can discern an Arabia made up not of nation states but of 'communities' – and it is the divisions between communities, rather than the basic immigrant/national division that is most relevant to the family stories in this book.

The Arabia of communities is the Arabians' Arabia, where people still think of other people's characters in terms of the well-known characteristics of their places of origin. Arabians 'know', for example, that 'all' men who have come originally from the Hadhramaut, in the interior of what is now Southern Yemen, are grasping, with a flair for saving money. This is also the Arabia that the occasional traveller and the British authorities saw fifty years ago. Then people talked of Nejdis, Hassawis (from what is now the Eastern Province), Hijazis, Baharna (the unorthodox Shia Muslim community of Bahrain), Persians. The expression 'Saudi' was unheard of – the Kingdom was not named Saudi Arabia until 1932 – and the expressions 'Bahraini' and 'Qatari' were used to denote place of residence, not nationality.

In no sense were all the communities of equal standing, and nor are they today. By the consensus of Arabia's ruling classes the greatest prestige at present is enjoyed by those who have come from the Nejd. The anxiety of so many Arabians to dig up traces of Nejdi ancestry underlines the point. Only marginally less fortunate are those who have come from areas of Arabia around Nejd, who are usually thought of as being Nejdis. A tribesman on the Red Sea coast, for example, has much more in common with a Nejdi than with a townsman of Jeddah.

The bias in favour of central Arabians is founded in part on the sense of superiority felt traditionally by the bedouin, who have been the chief cultural influence on Arabian life. It has been reinforced by the political domination of the Peninsula by the Saud family and by Unitarianism (or Wahabism), the austere, rigorously orthodox interpretation of Islam espoused by the family for the past 250 years, which is now the established Saudi Arabian creed.

The Nejdis, and all other central Arabians, today are more likely to be of village than of bedouin origin; in no part of Arabia does it seem that the bedouin ever outnumbered the oasis dwellers. Those who are bedouin all belong to tribes, which gives them additional prestige and a lineage stretching back 2,000 years or so. The villagers may have either tribal or non-tribal roots. Most of the villagers and townsmen still know which tribe they came from, but a few families – including such distinguished names as the Sulimans, whose father was the Finance Minister of King Abdel-Aziz, and the Algosaibis, whose family represented the great King in Bahrain – have lost their tribal origins. Sometimes this has happened simply because the support of a tribe ceased to be relevant to a family's life after it had settled in a village, so that after two or three generations members of the family forgot to tell their children from which tribe they had come. On other occasions all the adult members of a family perished through war, disease or starvation, disasters which were not uncommon in Arabia before oil. They left children who were brought up without knowing precisely what the lineage of their parents had been. Modern Arabians are still very conscious of which families are tribal and which are not. For practical purposes the main importance of being tribal or non-tribal is in determining whom one may marry; tribal families do not like their daughters to marry into non-tribal families.

Most of the Arabians who now claim to be of Nejdi stock are no longer living in their homeland. The ruling families of Kuwait and Bahrain both came from the Anaizah tribe in the area to the north-west of Nejd and settled on the Gulf coast some 240 years ago. Like most emigrants, they were forced to leave central Arabia by drought. Other humbler men have been lured from the Nejd in the present generation by the prospect of better employment elsewhere.

The Nejd and its northern borders are the original homes of many of the most distinguished merchant families of the Arabian Peninsula. All of the oldest established merchant families of Kuwait, including the Alghanims and Alsagars, are from the north or north-western border area; the Algosaibis and Mohammad Jomaih, who has the central region agencies for General Motors and Pepsi-Cola, are from the towns of Herreimlah and Shaqra in central Nejd. An extraordinary number of the Nejdi merchant families come from the towns of Onaizah and Buraidah in the oasis region known as Qassim. Even in the last century Onaizah had a reputation as a community of hospitable, well-educated people, interested in the world outside Arabia. Prominent families in modern Saudi Arabia with their roots in Onaizah include the Juffalis and Olayans, whose stories are told in later chapters, and the Sulimans. The Rajhi brothers, the multi-billionaires who run Saudi Arabia's biggest exchange-dealing business, come from the village of Bukair-iyah, just outside Buraidah. Other prominent businessmen from Qassim are Ali Tamimi, the big Eastern Province contractor, and the Bassam family. The Bassams have dispersed themselves throughout the Middle East and India. One of their better-known ancestors was Haji Mohammad Bassam, a gold smuggler, who pioneered the trans-desert road route from Damascus to Baghdad in the 1920s.

In the eyes of Nejdis, the most acceptable communities after themselves are other Arabians of the orthodox Sunni branch of Islam, indigenous to the Gulf states. This is in accordance with a Nejdi view of Arabian society which seems to have themselves at the centre and all other communities arranged around them in a widening series of circles, spreading outwards like ripples on a pond.

The people of the Gulf, like the Nejdis themselves, are of mixed tribal and non-tribal origin. Those who are of both tribal and bedouin descent are almost impossible to separate from the central Arabians. Fifty years ago a section of a tribe that grazed its flocks partly in Qatar, for example, would frequently move inland towards the Arabian interior. Its members would spend eight months of the year looking after their sheep and camels – which they would hope to increase by raiding other tribes' flocks. For the remaining four months they would work on the pearling dhows.

The distinguishing feature of the coastal area was its maritime culture. This is still important today and accounts for many of the differences between Saudi Arabia and the Gulf states. Before oil the poorest members of the population worked as pearl divers and fishermen, the better skilled were sailors and boat builders. The richer families were merchants, trading in pearls, foodstuffs and timber, and in regular contact with India and Iran. Like the Hijazis on the other side of the Peninsula, they developed relatively outward-looking attitudes, which they passed on to the other elements of the coastal population, including the ruling families of central Arabian origin.

After the Gulf Arabs come the Hijazis, who are an exclusively urban people living in Jeddah, Mecca, Medina and Taif; what bedouin there are in the Hijaz count as central Arabians. The Hijazis are composed partly of people who have moved into the towns from the surrounding tribes, who are particularly numerous around the big oasis of Medina, and partly of people whose ancestors came on the pilgrimage and did not return home. The classic pattern was of an old man performing the pilgrimage and then deciding to live out the remainder of his days close to the holy places in the company of one of his sons. In later years other sons and daughters, and nephews and nieces, would arrive on the pilgrimage, or would be told that the original pair were prospering in Mecca, and would come to join them.

Naturally enough, communities of particular peoples grew up in particular towns. To this day Mecca has large populations of Indonesian and Indian descent, while Medina has Syrians, Turks, Egyptians and Central Asians. Jeddah, which was (and still is) the gateway to Mecca, had a partly transient population of seafarers and merchants. Individuals and families would live in Jeddah for a few years and then move on to some other part of Asia or Africa, which was not the practice of the peoples of Mecca and Medina. Those people who did stay in Jeddah included a small number of Persians and a much bigger community of Hadhramis. The members of the latter group have become money changers, food importers, small businessmen in the souk and accountants. A great number of the more traditional businesses of Jeddah have Hadhramis looking after their finances; although they are quite avaricious, the Hadhramis are regarded as being completely trustworthy and prepared to take responsibility. A Hadhrami will seize a business opportunity on behalf of his employer in his employer's absence, which a Pakistani or Egyptian would never dare to do. Most of the big Jeddah merchants whose names begin with 'Ba' or 'Bin' (where Bin is used as part of the family name rather than in the literal sense of meaning 'son of') are Hadhrami. They include the Bin Ladens, who own the Kingdom's biggest and most famous construction company, and the Bin Mahfouz, who have a majority of the National Commercial Bank, the biggest bank in the Arab world. Other well-known Hadhrami families are the food importers, Baeshen, Bassamah and Binzagr, the Barooms, who trade in building materials, and the Bugshans, who represent Komatsu, the Japanese bulldozer manufacturer.

Whereas the other peoples who make up the broad Hijazi population marry into each other's communities, the Hadhramis mostly marry Hadhramis. A few Hijazis marry central Arabians, but most Nejdi families prefer their offspring to marry their own kind. In the view of the Nejdis, who are particularly concerned with purity of breeding, the Hijazis are a distressingly mixed community.

The Hijazis merge with yet another grade of community: the non-Arabian hundred-year immigrants. These people are Hindus and Indian Muslims, Persians and Hawala – 'wanderers'. The members of the last group are Sunni Muslims who left Arabia several hundred years ago, lived in Iran and became partly Persianised and have since re-turned to the Arabian side of the Gulf. Needless to say the Hawala, who include the Kanoo, Almoayed and Fakhroo families of Bahrain, are nowadays at pains to emphasise the brevity of their stay across the water. They are regarded by all parts of the population as being very much more Arabian than the other long-standing immigrants.

Both the Indians and the Persians are well established and most of them regard the Arabian Peninsula states as their homes, but they are still liable to be classified by the Nejdis as *ajnabi* – 'foreigners'. In the case of the Indians this is quite a fair description. Most of the Indian families still speak their own tongues in preference to Arabic. In Oman and Kuwait members of the Sultan family, which owns the firm of W.J. Towell, speak Kutchi among themselves at home. They are Khojas (also known as Luwatiyas), members of an Indian Muslim sect from near Bombay, many of whom crossed to Oman some 200 years ago. Until the early 1970s the Sultans and the other Khojas in Muttrah, the main Omani port, lived in a ghetto-like quarter known as the Sur Luwatiya (literally the 'Wall of the Luwatiyas') at the end of the souk. Now the quarter is largely demolished and the Sultans have moved to a substantial Lebanese-style villa in Ruwi. This is a new urban area which has grown up inland from Muttrah.

Outside Oman the largest Indian communities in Arabia are in Dubai and Bahrain. The Jashanmals, who own Bahrain's biggest and the Gulf's first department-store chain, are Indians. In Dubai there are perhaps ten big Indian merchant families or individual merchants, some of whom have been in the state for two generations, and many of whom are worth tens – or hundreds – of millions of dollars. Unlike the Sultans in Oman and the Jashanmals in Bahrain, the Dubai Indians do not carry passports of the state in which they live. It is assumed that they have periodically renewed their Indian passports, which suggests that they intend eventually to return to their homeland.

The Persians are much better integrated into society than the Indians. It is often said by semi-knowledgeable Western expatriates, who have lived in the area for two or three years, that 'most' of the big merchants of the Gulf are Persian. This gives an indication of how difficult it is to tell Persian families from other Arabians, because in fact there are relatively few Persians among the big merchants. In Saudi Arabia the only prominent Persian names are the Alirezas and Zahids, the latter being the agents for Caterpillar and a large number of other machinery manufacturers. In Qatar the only important Persian name is Darwish and in Abu Dhabi there are no big Persian merchants. In Kuwait there are the Behbehanis, who represent Volkswagen, and in Bahrain there are the Kazroonis and Diwanis, who are Shia Muslims, and the Eshaqs and a branch of the Alireza family, who are Sunnis. (There is no doubt of the Alirezas' Sunni beliefs now, though the family's name and the names of some of its early members have a pronounced Shia flavour.) The older generation of the Bahraini Persian families still frequently speaks Persian at home.

The state in which the Persians are most obvious is Dubai: here the Persian community includes the names of Galadari, Rostamani, Naboodah, Khoory, Fikri and Eassa Gurg. Of these only the Galadari family, which has a vast range of interests in property, trade and banking, and Abdullah Rostamani, who has the immensely profitable Datsun agency, can be counted as really big merchants. (The other great names of Dubai – Owais, Futtaim and Ghurair – are Arabians.) Where the Persians are most strongly represented in Dubai is among the shopkeepers and souk store owners. It is at this level, rather than in the ranks of the big families, that the Persians have their strength in commerce in all the Gulf states. At a more menial level an extraordinary number of the bakers in the region are Persians.

The big Persian names mentioned above carry Arabian passports and consider themselves more or less Arabians. But the Persians of the small shopkeeper, baker and taxi driver class are probably more mixed in their loyalties, even though they have Arabian passports and their families may have lived on the southern side of the Gulf since early in this century. The difference in loyalties can show in quite trivial day-to-day matters, such as an incident which involved a Persian taxi driver – who would have been just an ordinary Arabian in the eyes of most Westerners – in Bahrain several years ago. The man was told to pay a minor fine for a traffic offence, by the magistrates of Manama, the Bahraini capital. On hearing the decision he flew into a rage, cursed the magistrates and told them that the Shah would come and take over the state (the Iranians had recently had a claim to the island), that the Persian flag would fly over the court house, that he would have his revenge in person and that they would all lose their jobs.

Since the revolution in Tehran there have been no demonstrations of support for the Iranian leader, Ayatollah Khomeini, by the Arabian Persians, though it is known that many of the Persian labourers who have come to work in the Gulf states in the last few years support him. The inactivity of the established Persian communities is thought to have been mainly a result of the considerable wealth their members have amassed, though in 1981 and 1982, as Iran degenerated further into chaos and bloodshed, there is no doubt that the revolution also lost any small allure it may have had originally. The basic question of loyalties remains, however. If there were to be a different regime in Iran and if the Gulf states were to become unstable at some time in the future, it is not easy to say whether the small trader class of the Persian communities would look to their Arabian rulers or to their original homeland across the water.

Below the Indians and the Persians, in a category of their own at the very bottom of Arabian society, are the Shias. These people are of Arabian descent, but they espouse an unorthodox and rather mystical form of Islam, involving the veneration of saints. In Wahabi eyes this makes them idolaters and puts them quite beyond the pale. Conservative members of the Nejdi establishment say that the Shias' beliefs run totally counter to what they have been taught is right, and that because no person can be selective in which aspects of a religion he accepts and which he rejects, the Shias are not true Muslims. They also suggest that the Shias probably feel a stronger natural loyalty to the religious regime of their fellow Shia, the Ayatollah Khomeini, in Iran than to the Saud family or the ruling Khalifa family of Bahrain.

The schism between the Sunnis and the Shias is of great political and social significance in the Middle East today, and is therefore worth discussing in some detail. It dates from the very earliest years of Islam, just after the death of the Prophet Mohammad in AD 632 and the early Arab conquests in Egypt, and Levant and Persia. The origins of the schism lay in a dispute between two of the main families of Mecca, the Beni Hashim and the Beni Umaiya,[1] over who should succeed to the Caliphate – the leadership of the Muslim community. The Beni Hashim, who were the Prophet's own family, argued that the succession should go to a relative of the Prophet's; the Beni Umaiya said, in the time-honoured way of the Arabs, that it should go to whoever was deemed most suited to be Caliph.

Almost from the beginning the quarrel acquired a broad social significance. The family that won the dispute was Beni Umaiya. Its leaders established the Caliphate in Damascus and rapidly became devoted to a Graeco-Syrian life of luxury. The losers, the Beni Hashim, did not give up the struggle. They continued to press their claim, and gained the support of those of the original God-fearing and puritan Arab armies who were not relations of the Umaiyids and who resented the material extravagance and the nepotism which characterised Umaiyid rule. These people became known as the Shias, strictly speaking the *Shia Ali*, 'the Party of Ali' – the Prophet's cousin and the leader of the Hashemites. Ali organised the first rebellion against Umaiyid rule, and was later murdered. The Umaiyid faction meanwhile became known as Sunnis, after the word *sunna* – 'tradition' – because of their belief that the Caliph should be somebody who reflected the tradition of the Prophet's rule. In practice, though, they were hypocritical in this matter. The first Umaiyid Caliph was elected by a committee of Muslim elders, but thereafter for a hundred years control of the Caliphate stayed with the Umaiyid family. Often the position was passed from father to eldest son.

In 680 the Shias acquired a martyr. Hussein, the second son of Ali, together with his family and retainers, was killed by the Umaiyids in the

1. Literally the Sons of Hashim and the Sons of Umaiya, or the Hashemite and Umaiyid families.

most brutal and pathetic circumstances at Kerbela in Iraq. The martyrdom served only to strengthen the association of the Shias with the
underprivileged and oppressed. Increasingly at this time these were
non-Arab Muslims – Syrians, Palestinians, Greeks and Persians – who
had been converted to Islam after the conquests. In theory these people
were supposed to be equal to all other Muslims, but in practice in the
early days they remained subjects of the Arabs and continued to pay the
taxes which were supposed to be the lot only of infidels. The foreigners
adopted Arab speech and dress, but they introduced into the Shias'
Islam elements of their own previous religions and so transmuted it into
a more mystical shape. Messianic notions of a Mahdi, a God-guided
deliverer, became established, saints were created and places of pilgrimage (above all Kerbela) appeared – all of which was anathema to the
legalistic and purist Sunnis. Thus within a century Shiism evolved from
a family political party into a distinctive religion with a strong anti-
establishment bias.

The Shias' leaders, the Imams, remained (or were supposed to be)
direct descendants of Ali, until the late ninth century AD. At this point
the twelfth of their line, a semi-mythical figure who happened to be
called Mahdi, went into hiding, where he is supposed to remain to this
day. Other elements of the Hashemite family achieved power in the year
750. They overthrew the Umaiyids and established the Abbasid
Caliphate in Baghdad – named after their ancestor Abbas, an uncle of
the Prophet. These men were not closely related to Ali and not con-
nected with the Imams. They won their victory over the Umaiyids with
Shia support, but thereafter turned on the Shias and suppressed their
frequent rebellions. From that time onwards the Hashemites have not
been associated with the Shias, and the branch of that family which now
rules in Jordan is strongly orthodox Sunni. Only in Iran has Shiism
been made the religion of the establishment. This was a conscious
political act by the Safavid Shahs in the sixteenth century. The Shahs
forced the conversion of the majority of their subjects who were not
Shia, with the specific intention of generating a stronger Iranian
national consciousness and feeling of separateness from the neighbouring Turks and Arabs.

In theory there are only two fundamental differences between the
Sunnis and the Shias. One is that the Shias invest their *ulema* (religious
leaders) with a spiritual authority, whereas the Sunni *ulema* are distinguished from the rest of their community only by their superior

learning. The other remains the matter of the succession to the Caliphate in the seventh century; technically all one needs to do to change from being a Shia into a Sunni is to revise one's opinions, in the privacy of one's own conscience, about the right of Ali to that succession. This means that there are people in the Muslim world occupying responsible positions in the establishments of their countries who are secretly Shias but who have found it expedient and possible to present themselves outwardly as Sunnis – dissimulation having become an early part of the Shia cult. In practice most Shias are quite open in showing their beliefs. Their mosques are much more ornate than Sunni mosques, they pray at the tombs of their saints and some of their richer members buy grave plots in Iraq. They also often give their children names with Shia connotations – such as Hussein or Ali Akbar (Ali the Great).

Most spectacularly, during Moharram, the first month of the Muslim year, the Shias commemorate publicly the martyrdoms of Ali, Hussein and Hussein's elder brother, Hassan. This is a time of great emotional tension. Processions of mourners troop through the streets of Shia towns with chest beaters and back flagellants, shouting *Ya Ali*, 'Oh Ali', and scourging themselves in unison, bringing steel whips tipped with razor blades down on their bare backs. The mourners carry in their midst a moving passion play representing the events that took place in Kerbela 1,300 years ago: there are horses with their trappings smeared with red paint to simulate blood, 'corpses' carried upright in their biers, so that the bodies are clearly visible to the onlookers, Hussein on a white horse, bedizened with finery. When the processions pause preachers repeat the tale of the martyrdom.

Often the preachers are visitors, men of passionate eloquence who travel from the great Shia centres of Iran and southern Iraq as professional sermonisers. They tell how Hussein's little party is surrounded by thousands of its Sunni enemies. Entreaties for mercy to be shown to the women and children fall on deaf ears, and so Hussein draws up his seventy-two retainers for battle. The Sunnis stand back and shoot down the whole party with arrows until finally there is only Hussein left, wounded and exhausted, cradling his little son dead in his arms. He sinks down beside his tent to drink some water, and in the act of drinking he is shot through the mouth by an arrow. As they hear this heart-rending tale, punctuated by the preachers' calling on God to bless the souls of Hussein and his relatives, the listeners weep at the pity of it. As Molly Izzard says in her book *The Gulf*: '. . . the sight of blood, the groans and fervour, produce an effect far removed from the cool, modern analysis of political and economic motive to which the Muslim world is increasingly subject, and which treats it from a purely secular point of view.' [2]

The ritualised flagellations, bloodletting and chest-beating of Moharram are often seen as a reaffirmation by the Shias of their status as a subject population, culturally alienated from their rulers. Everywhere in the Muslim world, except in Iran, Shiism, with its emphasis on the pathetic, suffering and millennial aspects of religion, remains a cult associated with the underprivileged. In Iraq the Shias form a majority of the population but they are much poorer than the Sunni establishment and they have been seen as a threat by successive governments. In Lebanon the Shias are the poorest of all communities, living in near-slums in Beirut and in the barren, war-torn south of the country. It was an attempt by the Shias to organise a political movement to improve their lot that was one of the triggers of the Lebanese civil war. In Bahrain Shias make up almost all of the island's original inhabitants, but for most of the last 200 years they have been oppressed by the Khalifa family. Today relations between Sunnis and Shias in Bahrain are not exactly relaxed, but they are not bad either – there are five Shia ministers in the government and the ruler has attended the weddings of important Shia families. The Shias say, however, that they do not believe that they are treated as well as the Sunnis by the government. They find it more difficult than other Bahrainis to get government jobs and they tend to congregate in ministries and other state agencies that are headed by fellow Shias.

In Saudi Arabia, where they are thought to number about 380,000, the Shias constitute a little over a third of the non-immigrant population of the Eastern Province. The oasis towns of Qatif, Seihat and Safwa have always been entirely Shia and the great Hasa oasis near the town of Hofuf is thought to be about half Shia. Traditionally relations between the Shias and the indigenous Eastern Province Saudis, most of whom must once have come from the Nejd, have been quite good. There are strong Sunni–Shia friendships and Sunni–Shia business partnerships. The well-known Sunni merchants Abdullah Fouad and Ali Tamimi

2. Molly Izzard's book *The Gulf: Arabia's Western Approaches* was published in 1979 by John Murray. Part of the description of Shiism and the Moharram processions here has been taken from this book (pages 36–79), as has some of the description of Arabian domestic life later in this chapter.

built part of their business with a Shia, Ali Seihati, who died in 1980. Sunnis employ large numbers of Shias, and the more enlightened employers give them days off in Moharram and have contributed to one of the Shia self-help organisations, the Seihat Society for Social Services. In the distant past it seems that there have even been conversions from Sunni beliefs to Shiism. What happened in these cases is that Sunnis found themselves living in predominantly Shia villages in Hasa, began celebrating Shia feasts and attending Shia mosques and gradually accepted Shia doctrine. A member of the Ajaji family, which has both Sunni and Shia members spread between Bahrain and the Eastern Province, recently told a Saudi friend that he assumed that it was in this way that the religious division in his own family had occurred.

The people of Saudi Arabia who distrust and abhor the Shias are the members of the Nejdi establishment who are either still living in the Nejd or who have arrived in the Eastern Province since the Sauds conquered the area in 1913. The Nejdis believe the Shias to be mad. A Saudi prince, referring to the Moharram processions, once remarked to me that the Shias did not need to feel guilty about the deaths of Ali and his relations because, after all, the events took place long before they were born. For their part the Shias are terrified of the Nejdis. The two communities' attitudes towards each other are conditioned by a host of irrational fears.

A story which illustrates these attitudes in the most graphic terms is told by an American consultant. In early 1981 the consultant took a flight from Dhahran to Riyadh, and found himself sitting beside a well-dressed, affluent but extremely nervous Saudi. As they talked it emerged that the Saudi was a Shia from Hofuf, a gold merchant by trade. He had to go to Riyadh to see a client. He said that this was the third occasion on which he had come to Dhahran to take the flight, but that on the previous two occasions he had been so frightened that at the last minute he had turned round and gone home. He then explained that when he was in Riyadh he would be all the time in the company of friends and that whatever happened he would fly back to Dhahran before nightfall, even if he had not completed his business. The consultant left the Shia at Riyadh airport and did not see him again. However, that evening, or a day later, he recounted his experience to a member of the Saudi royal family who was known as a young technocrat with enlightened views. The prince immediately claimed that the royal family was now doing a lot for the Shias, but he hastened to explain that even so, most of them were totally unemployable. They were quite mad, he stated in a wholly unargumentative manner: 'If you take them on as office boys,' he said, 'they will urinate in your tea and spit in your coffee.'

For most of the period since the Saudi conquest the Shias in the Eastern Province have been oppressed. Until recent years Moharram processions were banned, and even now only very modest affairs are permitted, without distasteful flagellations. The Shias have been excluded from the armed forces and the government; in the whole Kingdom in 1982 only two senior officials were Shias. There are relatively few Shia businessmen. The only Shia to have a fairly high-profile business in the Eastern Province is Abdullah Matrood, who owns a big dairy farm, an automatic bakery and a laundry.

Apart from Hofuf and other settlements in the Hasa oasis, Shia towns and villages have been at the end of the queue for schools, health care and municipal services. The community's main benefactor has been Aramco, which has employed Shias in large numbers because the company operates in Shia areas and Shias have been willing to work for it.

Inevitably the Shias have been prey to the heady propaganda of Ayatollah Khomeini, whose radio stations have urged them to overthrow their Nejdi masters. In late 1979 and early 1980 there were severe riots in Qatif, which marked the most serious open, repeated opposition that the Saud family has faced since before the beginning of oil production. A year or two before the riots the authorities had at last begun spending significant sums of money on Qatif, and disbursements were increased after the troubles. In 1982 Qatif did not look very different from any other Saudi provincial town.

The relationship between the different communities of Arabia – the Nejdis, the other Sunni Arabians, the long-established foreign groups and the Shias – suggests that it is better not to think of Arabian society in terms of half a dozen pyramids, one in each nation state. It is a single regional pyramid, which happens to be under the authority of several different rulers. Each community layer in the pyramid as a matter of course mixes horizontally across national boundaries, but less often mixes with the layers above it or below it in the same state. One sees this most obviously in marriages. A tribal Nejdi family in Riyadh, for example, is more likely to arrange a union for a son or daughter with distant central Arabian relations in Kuwait than with a Hijazi family from Saudi Arabia. The family's view of the matter will probably be reinforced by the common Arabian preference for unions with relations. This in itself means that its children are almost bound to marry within their community.

Often it is difficult to discover what nationality an Arabian sees himself as being, or what passport he carries. The Alirezas have Saudi, Kuwaiti and Bahraini nationals in their different branches, and a history of nationality being changed from grandfather to father to son to suit each person's place of business. For example, Abdel-Ghaffar, a pearl merchant in the Ali Akbar branch of the family, which did not go to Jeddah, was a Bahraini; his son Abdullah (see Chapter 10), who has lived in Bahrain, India, Jeddah, the Eastern Province, Iran and Kuwait, is Kuwaiti; and his grandson, Teymour, who has expanded his family's business into the Eastern Province, is Saudi. The Algosaibis have both Saudi and Bahraini members, occupying important positions in both governments, but they see themselves principally as expatriate Nejdis long-established on the Gulf coast. The Kanoos have Bahraini and Saudi passport carriers, though they remain definitely Bahraini-Hawala in everyone's eyes.

For all the importance of community – which re-emerged as a major force in Saudi Arabia in the early years of King Khaled's reign – the concept of nationality is not entirely alien to Arabians. There is a growing awareness of nationality that co-exists with the traditional awareness of community, particularly in the Gulf states and among the younger technocrat generation. Before oil and the beginning of development programmes there was no reason for there to be any national consciousness. The individual states had only come into being as separate political entities in the previous 100 or 200 years, as a result of the consolidation of the rule of particular families over particular bits of territory, and then the endorsement of this rule by the guarantee of British protection. Now the states are slowly turning into separate nations through the social differences that emerge from individual government's spending policies and differences in the scales of their oil revenues.

The Kuwaitis are aware of their enormous personal wealth setting them apart. They also feel themselves to be more sophisticated and economically advanced than their neighbours. They like to suggest that the lower Gulf states today are where Kuwait was ten years ago. The Bahrainis are conscious of their superior educational tradition and of the fact that they have had to work harder than other Arabians. A few years ago a Bahraini remarked to me that his country played Avis to Kuwait's Hertz.

In all the oil states people are starting to become aware that they have a past of which they should be proud, and that there are different cultural traditions in their different states. The Kuwaitis were renowned as the best boatbuilders and the bravest seafarers in the Gulf, which they feel makes it appropriate for them to develop a big modern merchant fleet. The Bahrainis remember that their island was the pearl market of the Gulf in the early years of this century, and that its greenness and fresh-water springs have attracted traders since the beginning of civilisation in the Middle East. Going back still further, there have been discoveries of prehistoric graveyards on the island. Today the public relations men of the Bahrain government are delighted to mention that the authors of the Bible may have thought of Bahrain as the site of the Garden of Eden.

Within the growing ranks of the Arabian middle classes – the business-men and civil servants who come from all the communities – there are extraordinary contrasts in lifestyles. Taking just the richest elements, one finds the Alghanims, Bin Ladens and Alirezas living the lives of international millionaires. Kutayba Alghanim has a private jet, a yacht and houses in New York, London and St Moritz. He had his children taught to ski while they were still only three and six. Salem Bin Laden, the eldest son of the man who founded the Bin Laden contracting company, has a consuming passion for flying his own aircraft. Shaikh Ahmed Yusef Alireza, who is thirty years older than Kutayba and Salem, entertains his guests to tea with chocolate cake and cucumber sandwiches, crusts cut off. He has been heard to complain about the difficulties of having provisions flown from London.

At the other end of the spectrum there are people who are equally rich but who live relatively simple, traditional Arabian lives. Most of them are members of the older generation. The Rajhi brothers, members of a Nejdi family and owners of a huge foreign-exchange business, are thought to be the richest Saudis outside the ranks of the royal family. A few years ago Suliman, the brother in charge of the Jeddah operation, could still be found sitting at a simple metal desk with a glass top in a small office in the souk. The floor of his office was made of stone-chip tiles, the furniture was plastic covered. The Riyadh office he inhabits today is not much smarter. In Western eyes Suliman does not conform at all to the image expected of a billionaire banker; but in the eyes of Arabians he carries as much social prestige as those who have become sophisticated in the European or American sense.

Inevitably lifestyles are reflected in homes – and the decoration of the merchants' houses shows the same range of contrasts. The smart houses seem to fall into two categories – Updated-Oriental and Italian. The Oriental style, favoured also by the princes and several ministers, has crenellated arches reminiscent of Morocco, and marble columns, Persian carpets, wooden filigree screens and hand-painted or wood-inlaid panelling imported from Damascus. There are carved doors (traditional Arabian), courtyards in the middle of the buildings open to the sky and little fountains in star-shaped brown and white marble pools. Throughout the houses there is a mass of greenery – potted palms, creepers, rubber trees. The same goes for the Italian style, which is roughly what Ahmed Juffali has adopted for his mansion in Jeddah. Here, the greenery is interspersed with wicker chairs, long couches with colourful pillows, fish tanks, mirrors, big pieces of sculpture. Floors and courtyards again are marble. What sets apart the best of the Oriental and Italian homes is that they are mostly not the creations of the owners themselves, put together bit by bit over the years, inspired by exhausting hours spent traipsing through department stores and numerous visits to European houses or the palaces of Damascus and Fez. Except where the owners have Western or Western-educated wives with a bent for interior décor, the houses have been handed over to architects and designers, with a commission to look after every detail down to the cushion covers.

Houses less inspired than these are best described as 'grandiose suburban with Lebanese touches'. The same superb Persian carpets are there, but the other furnishings are less impressive. The armchairs are covered in the same velvety material as the more luxurious types of car seats, there are rough-hewn interior stone walls of the sort sometimes seen above fireplaces in modern houses on the outskirts of London. The flowers are plastic, the paintings cheap original oils of sunsets or Swiss mountain scenes such as one can buy on Saturday afternoons along the railings beside Piccadilly and Green Park in London. Dotted around the rooms on occasional tables are objects beloved of Arabians of all classes: boxes of coloured tissues fitted into special brass holders.

In the most sophisticated as well as the plainer households social life revolves around the family and close relations. The families are very self-sufficient; they have their own particular favourite pastimes. In Bahrain the Zayanis fish, the Almoayeds play tennis, Hussein Yateem cultivates his flowers and vegetables and grafts his own roses. In Jeddah the Alirezas go for picnics at their beach house on the creek north of the city.

A few families still live in compounds, where each couple has its own house but if it wishes can share a central kitchen and dining room. There are obvious advantages for women and children in this arrangement, especially in Saudi Arabia where the women may not drive; but the main argument advanced in favour of compound living is that at a time when all Arabia's traditional institutions are under threat from encroaching Western values, it provides a formal way of making sure that families stay together. The emphasis in this argument is on the degree of cohesion, because no families in Arabia split up into widely dispersed, independent households of husband, wife and children, as are the norm in the West. Usually relations live close to each other and in large households containing unmarried adult sons and daughters, grandparents and possibly old aunts and uncles.

Within the home, when there are no visitors present, the male and female members of the family mix naturally together. The women greet the men when they return from the office, fuss over them, bring them coffee and tea. They eat together, play with the children together and watch television and video tapes together. What men and women do not do together are things that involve appearing in public – except going to the airport to greet other members of their families. Nor do men and women meet in the home in the presence of visitors other than close relations. Women do not appear much in public on their own. If they go shopping they go in pairs. It would be almost unthinkable for them to eat together in restaurants, or even take tea in the most respectable hotels. Only in Bahrain and Kuwait are a few of the bolder members of the younger generation to be seen having tea in little female groups.

The most important part of women's social lives consists of paying calls – just as it was in Europe and America in Victorian times. Whether the occasion is a morning coffee party with piles of sweet biscuits, lunch, dinner or a big family gathering with the men in the evening, the ladies dress formally and perfectly. One of the main pastimes of Arabian women when abroad is choosing clothes which they can show off to other Arabian women. At home they may spend a whole morning before a lunch party making up their minds about what to wear.

For the male Western visitor to Saudi Arabia and the Gulf, it is extraordinary and tantalising to have a vague impression of this women's world existing around him, but never actually see it. In the evenings, as he kills time by going for a walk, he may see a large car draw up outside a house, a group of women get out swathed in black shawls but with a hint of silk dresses and a glint of gold underneath, an open door, a babble of voices exchanging greetings, a brief glimpse of warm yellow light inside. Then a servant closes the door and the chauffeur goes to sleep in the car. What more substantial impressions he may gain of Arabian women's society will come from a few Western wives who are lucky enough to be invited occasionally to parties or to the amateur dress shows which are such a popular entertainment among young Arabian women.

It is only with the most sophisticated families – encompassing a few of the big merchants and a handful of ministers and senior civil servants – that Western visitors will ever find themselves mixing with men and women together, on the rare occasions when they may be invited to a meal. These families are exceptional in giving mixed parties among themselves including couples who are not relations. In many cases the wives in this exclusive circle are European, American or from some other part of the Arab world. Virtually all of the merchant families mentioned in this book have members with non-Arabian wives.

If most women's social lives are separate from the social lives of their men, this does not mean that they are in an inferior position within the household. If a husband has a quarrel with his wife, he must contend not only with her but with her sisters, his sisters, their aunts, their mothers, and if by any chance he has taken a second wife, she will generally side with the first wife against him. This gives husbands some incentive to live their own lives away from the presence of their women. There are one or two rooms in each house that are reserved for themselves and for conversations and meals with other Arab men and foreign visitors. They spend a lot of time in their offices and occasionally they will meet with friends in hotels or restaurants – though for the most part restaurants in Saudi Arabia and the Gulf states are the domain of foreign businessmen.

An Arabian's relationship with his wife is normally based not so much on a strong emotional bond, as it would be in the Western world, but on mutual respect and affection, and the approval of society. Sometimes in an arranged marriage there is a successful courtship after the wedding, but most women anticipate their greatest happiness coming from the possession of children and the companionship of other women in the household. The few women who are prepared to talk about Arabian family life say that the boredom of part of their day-to-day existence is compensated for by the joys of living in an extended family, with the protection and support that this affords to any member who is in difficulties, divorced or bereaved. If a woman is divorced the normal practice is for her to move back into the household of her parents.

It is partly the desire of families to be able to protect the interests of their daughters after marriage that makes them encourage marriage to a relation, who will be within the orbit of their influence. Contrary to common Western belief, daughters are loved and cherished by their families, the objects of protective care on the part of their male relatives. In a society where divorce is easy, and sometimes casual, there is great concern to see that a girl's husband is someone whom the family believes will look after her. This is more important than that a son should choose an appropriate wife. Other considerations favouring marriage to a relation are the desire to keep capital within the family and concern that the daughter should remain close to the parents, brothers and sisters she has known all her life. In the past this was best achieved by marriages arranged by agreement between fathers, and the results were often more romantic than one might expect. A successful Arabian businessman remarked to me a few years ago that his mother had once said to him that when she was told whom she was going to marry – somebody she had never met – she knew that she would love him when she saw him. Nowadays there are more conventional love matches, though the circle within which young men and girls can find a partner they love is always confined. Few couples would ever be prepared to flout their parents' wishes.

But the attitudes of parents to how they must prepare their daughters for marriage are changing. In the last ten years young men who have been educated in the West, and have possibly found girlfriends there, have been looking for something more akin to the companionship of Western marriages when they return home. They want wives more experienced in the world and less dependent on their families. So to escape the unattractive possibility of foreign wives marrying men that their own daughters might be expected to marry, families have become concerned to have their daughters well educated. Because of the limited scope for other activities, Arabian girls have always done better than boys at school; now there is growing enthusiasm for having them follow up their success at home by going on to university abroad. They are even supported by fathers and brothers if they want to set up their own businesses – often boutiques or picture galleries. In the Gulf states, where girls are not prohibited from working as they are in Saudi Arabia, they are encouraged to train for the professions or go into the government service. Much pride is taken in the girls' new achievements – but it is not intended that this academic and professional independence should lead to social freedom. When their work is finished in the evening it is still expected that the girls should return to the protection of the family.

The older members of the Arabian merchant families are deeply conservative. They are men in their fifties and sixties who have passed in their lifetimes from the traditional culture to modern life. The coming of the first motor car and the cinema, their first business trips to London and America are landmarks in their recollections. Most of them are rather quiet and soft-spoken, cautious and questioning with visitors, outwardly modest – though as one gets to know them better one realises that they are intensely proud of what they have achieved and are not averse to letting the world know about it. Their pride is uncomplicated by any need to justify their wealth, in the way that successful Western entrepreneurs feel obliged to pretend that their profits are not as big as they appear to be. The merchants believe in hard work, honesty, self-discipline and starting at the bottom. They are very demanding of their employees, though generous in granting compassionate leave for family reasons.

A few anecdotes and quotations illustrate these points. In the 1940s Yusef Almoayed, who is now the Datsun agent in Bahrain, ran an ironmongery business, which he expanded into a local buying contract for the small Royal Air Force base on the island. Asked what he regards as the best stroke of business he ever did, he replies that it was to return a cheque for 3,000 rupees ($900 at the time) which the RAF by mistake had issued twice. By this he acquired such a reputation for honesty that increasing use was made of his services, and by the end of the war he was worth about $200,000. 'For fifteen years I worked sixteen hours a day and took no rest,' he told Molly Izzard. 'It's important not to waste time in youth – that's what I tell the young men nowadays, you've got to run about, seek your opportunity, be straight with your clients.' [3]

Another revealing remark was made by Hussein Alireza who is the Saudi importer of Mazda cars and owns a company which must have a turnover of over $200 million. On this occasion the merchant was talking to his English general manager and the subject was what to do with money once one had it. 'Having had a lot of money from the time I was born,' Hussein said, 'I have learnt something which I shall pass on to you. Never spend because you have the money – only spend if it is necessary.' Despite being extremely rich, for many years Hussein drove a slightly battered Mazda. His offices in Jeddah are unpretentious to the point of being scruffy. Like the other merchants, Hussein had a disciplined and unsentimental upbringing. He once explained to me that in his teens he was sent away to Victoria College, the English public school in Egypt, regardless of the fact that this was in the middle of the Second World War and that it seemed unlikely he would see his parents again for a year or two.

A comment on a rather different theme, which relates to the merchants' attitudes to making money, was made to me by Haji Ahmed Sultan, one of the brothers of the Omani commodity-trading family which owns W.J. Towell. Haji Ahmed was talking about the company's early rice deals at the beginning of the 1960s; when he got to the deal that marked the family's breakthrough his face lit up and he added: 'Do you know, this was the first deal on which our profit – our net, net, net profit –' he emphasised, 'came to over one million dollars.'

The merchants are unashamed of large profits; it would be fair to say that they have no qualms whatever about making as much money as they possibly can out of every deal, without regard to what anyone else might regard as a 'reasonable' profit. If the market will pay a certain price, the merchants reason, then there can be no conceivable objection to their charging that price. A sidelight on this ruthless philosophy is provided by a small incident which occurred in the 1930s, when Sir Charles Belgrave, adviser to the Ruler of Bahrain and virtual chief executive of the government, was acting as a magistrate in the island's

3. See *The Gulf: Arabia's Western Approaches*, p. 115.

court. On a certain occasion he demanded a fine from a dhow captain who had been cheating his pearl divers. 'You are more like a shark than a man,' Belgrave declared; and to his astonishment he discovered later that the captain had taken the description as a compliment and had gone to the souk to tell his friends about it.[4] Recently the merchants' rapacity has been best seen in the property market, where landlords have had no compunction about pushing up rents to levels unheard of in London or New York.

The merchants' philosophy is best summed up as 'buyer beware'. The attitude is that if a buyer pays too much, then the more fool he. This applies as much to the payment of a multi-million dollar commission to an agent for securing a big contract as it does to a taxi fare. The moral responsibility for setting the right price is seen as resting with the buyer, as does responsibility for the ethical considerations of the deal. Although no payment is expected if no service is rendered, there is no restriction on asking for one. This might apply where a middleman who is involved on the sidelines of a deal, but who is not in practice going to play any decisive role, asks a foreign bidder to promise to pay him a percentage if it wins the contract.[5] Likewise, as explained in detail in the next chapter, there is a whole series of transactions where in Western eyes the payments made to agents would be regarded as corrupt, but in the Arabian Peninsula are seen as means of spreading the oil money among the establishment or giving people the income that is due to them on account of their social position. The important point is that such payments are never made as direct bribes. In every case the recipient is being *paid* for a *service*, however overpaid or morally questionable that service may be. The concept of conflict of interest, as it is known in the West, is weak. Arabian political figures are commonly owners of Arabian business enterprises – for instance, Shaikh Nasser bin Khaled al Thani, the Qatari Minister of Commerce, is agent for Mercedes and a major contractor and real estate owner.

Within this rather liberal, free-wheeling business context the Arabians are generally scrupulously honest. A man's word is still regarded as his bond, and one almost never hears of an Arabian businessman going back on his word once given, regardless of legal technicalities.

4. See Sir Charles Belgrave's autobiography, *Personal Column*, Hutchinson, 1960, p. 33.
5. See *Saudi Arabia* by David E. Long, no. 39 of *The Washington Papers*, published by the Centre for Strategic and International Studies at Georgetown University pp. 54–5.

Where, to the Western mind, Arabian businessmen can be less straightforward is in their reluctance to make firm commitments. This is a problem which Western businessmen can find extremely frustrating, to the extent of being tempted to brand their Arabian opposite numbers as being disingenuous. Often a Western visitor will come away from a meeting with a positive or negative impression, but without having had the merchant explain much of the reasoning behind his attitude. At home he would expect the executive with whom he was dealing to explain – or at least appear to explain – his company's position, even if he had not been able to make a definite decision at the time. Arabians dislike saying no, or arguing out an issue on which there is disagreement. They may pretend that a particular letter/conversation/decision never existed; there are certain awkward things that are never alluded to.

Arabian businessmen, like all other Arabians, are very different from their Western counterparts. The more Westerners get to know them the more convinced of this they become.

There are some similarities – in the importance they attach to hard work and the simple pride they take in financial success – between the modern Arabian merchants and the newly rich American and European industrialists of the nineteenth century. Also, in a modern material sense the Arabians have all the superficial trappings of Westernisation. They live in a technological environment of high-rise office blocks, industrial estates and pocket calculators. Almost all the elite of the younger generation speak excellent English. This leads first-time visitors to see them unconsciously as Westerners in fancy dress, and to analyse them in terms of Western stereotypes: thrusting young executives, technocrats, tycoons, international playboys. The parallels are helpful if one is seeing Arabians in a Western context – either visiting Europe or America or pursuing some purely Western activity in their own countries – but they are useless if one is looking at them against the background of their own society. The symbols which give rise to the parallels are deceptive. This was explained in early 1978 by Zaki Nusseibeh, the special adviser of Shaikh Zayed, the Ruler of Abu Dhabi, in a conversation with the British journalist Jonathan Raban.[6] '. . . don't get taken in by the vertical architecture,' he said, referring to a panorama of Abu Dhabi city. 'The real city is lateral. It's the hardest

6. See *Arabia through the Looking Glass* by Jonathan Raban, Collins, 1979, p. 153.

thing for a visitor to see that Abu Dhabi is really a bedu town. You look at the way people visit each other, who they marry – the way they actually use the buildings. The secret infrastructure of this place is pure bedu. And you'll never really see it, because it's something that no one but an Arab can. The best you can do is to know that it's there. Everything you see here is a kind of optical illusion – it makes you see one kind of society while what you're looking for is really quite another. It's much, much more foreign than it looks.'

Arabia is as family and community orientated with cars and apartment blocks as it was with camels and dhows. Arabians never say it, but all the objects and ideas imported into their lives often seem like windows opening on to empty rooms. They are rather indifferent to the miracle baggage suddenly given to them by their wealth. It is fun and useful – each new piece of technology is something which they take in their stride – but at the same time it is abstract, impersonal and unrelated to anything that really matters to them. The priorities of Arabians are very different from those of Westerners.[7]

The Arabians' lives are permeated by Islam. In some ways this is visible and obvious. One can be having a conversation with a senior civil servant and find that he breaks off in the middle to say his prayers. On Friday in Saudi Arabia the towns are filled with the deafening noise of competing sermons broadcast by loudspeaker from the minarets of the mosques; every day, five times a day in all the towns of Arabia, as in the rest of the Muslim world, the minarets issue the call to prayer.

Other manifestations of the pervasive influence of Islam are more subtle. Islam draws no distinction between the religious and the secular, which means that it conditions *all* of a man's attitudes. It teaches that God is the creator of all things and ultimately responsible for all actions. This has imbued Muslims with a profound sense of the inevitability of events. When a Saudi says that he will meet one tomorrow or that the repairs on his car will be finished tomorrow, *Inshallah*, 'God Willing', he really does mean 'God Willing' because he knows that whatever he intends or whatever the statistical probability, if God does not will it, it simply cannot happen.

Many of the principles of Islam are linked to the enormous importance that Arabians attach to family life. Much of Shariah Law is

7. See Peter Iseman's article 'The Arabian Ethos', in *Harper's* magazine, February 1978.

constructed around the objective of protecting the family unit. Arabians have much more confidence in the correctness of their family-orientated society than Westerners have in their own more open society. They show great respect towards their elders. One of the Saudi merchants in this book, a man in his forties at the head of a company with a turnover numbered in hundreds of millions of dollars, gave me an example of this: 'I know that it is illogical, but after dinner I always retire with the younger members of the family to smoke. My uncle smokes, and he asks us to stay and smoke with him. But somehow I feel that I cannot smoke in front of him.'

The family in turn is the foundation of the intensely personal view of the world that Arabians have. One characteristic is that they like to personalise institutions, inanimate objects and the minor routines of everyday life. It is as if everything with which they come into contact has to be equated to relationships they have known within their families or tribes.

People – individuals and families – are much more real to Arabians than institutions. The Saudis and the other Arabs of the Gulf do not think in institutional terms about the government departments that affect their lives; they focus their thoughts on the people with whom they deal within these institutions. A government department is seen not as an impersonal machine, but as being within the realm of influence of the uncle or cousin or friend of the family who happens to work there. An approach to the Ministry of Health for a medical trip to London will be made through uncle Abdullah; a request for customs clearance for a cargo of canned food will start with a friend, Mr Ahmed, even if the friend does not work in the department of the customs which will issue the clearance.

The same principle applies to commercial dealings with foreigners. Every Western company selling to the Arabian Peninsula comes to realise sooner or later that its customers see themselves as dealing with the individual local sales representative rather than with the corporation. This, at least, is the case if the customers are relatively small merchants rather than giants on the Alghanim or Juffali scale. If the exporting company is wise it responds by keeping the same salesman attached to the area for as long as possible, so that he can become a friend of all of his customers. If he achieves this the company's products are likely to receive much more active promotion than they would otherwise. Conversely, for a company to try to boost its sales through occasionally sending the managing director may be a waste of time. It can be useful in giving him some personal experience of the conditions under which his salesmen are operating, but it can also be counter-productive if it leads the customer to expect frequent visits from him thereafter.

The Arabians' highly personalised view of institutions extends to their view of society as a whole. Arabians do not see society as a vast, impersonal mass of people containing a few individuals whom they will meet at various times in their lives and with whom they will form business or personal relationships. Rather, their world is made up of a web of communities, tribes and families – some they know personally, but all they know of. It is no exaggeration to say that in the Gulf states the old men in all families know something about, or at least are aware of, every other indigenous family in their state. In Saudi Arabia, Nejdis will know all the main families from their part of the Nejd, Jeddawis will know all the important families of Jeddah.

Arabians are not free, as Westerners are, to evolve whatever relationships they like with whomever they like. Their relations with other members of society are largely determined for them. There are certain people whom they may or may not marry, people and families with whom they must be on cordial terms, people with whom they could not form friendships without shocking their own families. Arabians are not particularly interested in history for its own sake, but in practice the pattern of their social lives is determined not by their own efforts but by the circumstances of their families' past.

4

Merchants and Rulers

Nobody in Saudi Arabia or the Gulf states owns an oil well. It comes as a disappointment to cartoonists and inventors of jokes to hear that there is no such person as an 'oil shaikh' in the sense that in the West there are steel magnates and property tycoons – men who have actually made their money out of steel and property. In the Arabian Peninsula, as everywhere else in the world except the United States, minerals under the ground are the property of the state. The oil companies buying Arabian oil make their payments into the New York and London accounts of the central banks and finance ministries.

The finance ministries in turn disburse funds to various spending ministries, in accordance with the states' ordinary and development budgets. These funds are channelled into a myriad of uses – salaries for public-sector employees, subsidised housing programmes, industrial and civil construction projects, sea-water desalination, food subsidies, land purchases. From here the money filters through society. Government spending generates numerous employment and business opportunities. The merchants (and many of the shaikhs and princes of the ruling families) share in the profits of contractors, with whom they have entered partnerships and won government contracts. They also profit from selling contractors materials and equipment ranging from cement to bulldozers. The bulldozer driver receives his wages from the contractor and spends them on food, clothes and simple luxuries such as a transistor radio. If he works hard and saves his money it will be perfectly possible for him to buy his own car, a house and even his own bulldozer. The individual's spending benefits everyone from the souk importer of cloth and rice, to the agent for Japanese radios, to the mechanic who will work on his car. To sum up: Middle East oil revenues move from the state treasuries into the hands of the population entirely through the spending of the rulers and the governments.

The governments back up the effects of their development programmes with regulations designed to ensure that most of the profits
made from their spending stay with their own citizens. In all states it has
been decreed that import agencies should be vested solely in nationals,
that only nationals may own real estate and that foreign contractors
should enter some sort of association with a national, who will act as
their partner or sponsor. As the economies have become more sophisticated the governments have decided that shares in public companies
should be reserved for nationals, and in Kuwait and most of the other
Gulf states, though not in Saudi Arabia, it is the law that nationals
should own at least 51 per cent of all private companies.

Kuwait at a very early stage in its development set about creating the
ultimate welfare state for its citizens. Its oil production was increased
enormously and suddenly by the Mossadeq crisis in Iran, which
involved the nationalisation of the Anglo-Iranian Oil Company (which
became BP) and the company's diversion of its main production effort
to Kuwait. The state had enormous reserves which were close to the sea
and very easy to produce. The government's (or Ruler's) income
jumped from $18 million in 1951 to $56 million in 1952, and in the
following year, when Kuwait became the biggest oil producer in the
Middle East and fourth biggest in the world, its income reached $168
million. Fortunately the great surge in revenues coincided with the
accession of a new and enlightened Ruler, Shaikh Abdullah Salam al
Sabah, who made the fundamental decision that he should do everything he could to share his income. From that time until the early 1980s
the preoccupation of the Kuwait government became the enrichment of
its own citizens through numerous systems and *ad hoc* arrangements
designed to ensure that in most transactions between the state and the
individual, the state lost and the individual profited. Free education and
health services were introduced. The state undertook to send patients
needing specialist treatment to hospitals in London and committed
itself to paying for successful students to study abroad at any university
they chose which would accept them. No charge was made for local
telephone calls, water and fuel were heavily subsidised – as was housing
for the poorer Kuwaitis – and inflated salaries were paid to all government employees. It went without saying that no direct or indirect
personal or corporate taxes were levied from Kuwaitis, except in later
years through the charging of customs duties on a few items as a means
of encouraging local industries.

In the 1960s and 1970s, as their revenues increased, the other Arabian oil states followed Kuwait's example. All of the Gulf states and Saudi Arabia introduced food subsidies. The Kuwait government in 1977 went so far as to bail out its citizens from the consequences of a crash on the stock exchange, by setting intervention prices at which it guaranteed to buy distressed stocks. It even repeated this generous act in 1982, when there was a second stock market crash at a time when the government was short of revenues and was becoming anxious to accustom its people to less lavish treatment.

In all the oil states, if the rulers have wanted to make a particular individual really rich they have given him land – with the result that in the last thirty years land has become by far the most important source of personal wealth in Arabian society. The practice of land gifts began in the 1920s and 1930s. Then, the only pieces of land in the Arabian Peninsula which had specific owners were a few plots in Bahrain and Al Hasa, and urban land in the Hijaz, the Yemens and one or two towns on the Gulf coast. The rest was thought of as being more or less ownerless – though different tribes had well-established grazing rights over particular areas, and it was accepted that the ruler of each state could assign ownership of limited plots of land to any of his subjects if he wished to do so. All of the rulers were poor, so when they wanted to reward somebody the cheapest way of doing so was to give him land. This land was nearly valueless and it was sometimes given for quite minor services. Fahd Algosaibi, whose family acted as King Abdel-Aziz's purchasing agents in Bahrain, once told me that when he was in his teens he was sent on a debt-collecting mission to the oasis of Kharj, south of Riyadh. This town was a favourite residence of Abdullah Suliman, the King's minister in the 1930s and 1940s. Fahd was kept waiting for his money for some days or weeks, but when he was finally paid, Abdullah Suliman rewarded him by giving him two plots of poor land in the oasis. Fahd said that he simply forgot about the land, but discovered the title deeds at the time of the boom in the mid-1970s and sold the land for just under $1 million.

The practice that began in King Abdel-Aziz's days has continued. The Saudi monarch and the rulers of the Gulf states regularly grant land to their relations, ministers and anyone else they wish to favour. The recipients sometimes sell their land to private developers; but the biggest and most generous buyer – the buyer whom all owners hope will acquire their land – is the government. In all the oil states it is intended that governments should pay massively for land. The rulers do not give their governments more than a small part of their land requirements. Nor are governments allowed to make compulsory purchases on the tough terms that are normal in the industrialised world. In Abu Dhabi in 1980 the government actually arranged for all those who had been obliged to sell land to it in the previous ten years to have their already adequate compensation upgraded. Those who had sold in 1970 were given ten times the original amount and those who had sold in 1971 nine times the amount, and so on down to those who had disposed of their land in 1979, whose remuneration was merely doubled. At the same time as it has bought land for roads, public buildings and other purposes, the Abu Dhabi government has given each of its citizens up to three plots of land for their own use – one for a house, one for a commercial or industrial development, and one for an office or apartment block. At times in the last ten years in Abu Dhabi and in the other oil states it has been possible to recover the capital cost of building a block with two years' rent – paid in advance.

In Kuwait during the last thirty years the government has made a practice of buying land from private citizens at artificially high prices and selling them cheaper land in other parts of the city. It has then zoned and developed the land, built roads and installed electricity, and leased the land back to the private sector for uneconomically low rents.

It was not the original intention in any Arabian state that the land market should develop in this way, but in retrospect the governments have come to see land as a good way of moving large sums of oil revenues into private hands. This in turn has had a psychological effect. Land is obviously not in short supply in Arabia but people expect to make their fortunes out of it; they know that the governments do not drive too hard a bargain, and so they speculate. The market has been given an upward push by the very rapid economic growth of the oil states in the last few years, which has meant that demand for development land has outstripped the rate at which services – roads, water and electricity – can be provided for new areas outside the towns. In the early 1980s the price of urban land in Arabia is on a par with the most expensive urban land anywhere.

The biggest land holders are some of the Saudi princes and members of the Gulf ruling families. These people form by far the richest group of Arabian citizens.

In Saudi Arabia most of the princes have acquired their land by the simple expedient of asking the King for it. Some members of the house of Saud now have land holdings worth a billion or two billion dollars. In Kuwait in the early 1950s many of the ruling Sabah family simply took the land they wanted. As soon as they realised that land was about to become valuable they drove into the desert at night and marked out the plots of land they were awarding themselves. They used oil drums painted white and marked with their names in red. Unless they had the connivance of the Ruler or some other powerful shaikh none of the merchants or other humbler Kuwaiti citizens dared to grab land in this way.

Land is the most common and most important source of the shaikhs' and princes' fortunes – but it is not the only source. There are two other major sources of ruling-family wealth – and several more general, minor sources.

The most usual of the minor sources are stipends. These are paid to members of most of the Arabian ruling families, though the sums are not especially large. In 1980 senior princes of the Saud family, the sons of King Abdel-Aziz, received \$200,000 a year, which was deemed to include their salaries if they worked in government. Thereafter the amounts descended on a sliding scale, determined by the princes' ages and the numbers of their children, which involved the most junior members of the royal blood receiving \$20,000 a year. In 1982 a prince in his early thirties who had a responsible job in government and was quite closely related to the King told me that he received about \$48,000 a year and that he considered himself to be a 'poor to moderately well off' member of the royal family. At this relatively junior level princes draw salaries if they have jobs in government. They can also ask for presents of cash (or land) from the King: in fact the most junior members of Al Saud, who do not receive government salaries and are not in business on their own, are completely dependent on the goodwill of the King or other senior members of their family for all but their most basic spending money. A few of the more fortunate young princes, and many of the richest shaikhs in the Gulf states, have inherited the fortunes of former rulers.

If a prince heads a ministry or some other government department it is accepted in Saudi Arabia, though not in most of the Gulf states, that he is entitled to draw on the budget of that department, or take a share of its spending on major projects. This is not regarded in any sense as being corrupt (though the practice is increasingly controversial in the eyes of the Saudi bourgeoisie) and it certainly does not imply that foreign contractors can influence the award of contracts by paying bribes to princes. The ethics and politics of the practice were described by Adnan Khashoggi, the defence contractors' agent and international entrepreneur, to a group of officials in the US Defence Department in 1973. An employee of Northrop (represented in Saudi Arabia by Khashoggi) who attended the meeting wrote afterwards that Khashoggi explained that for a commoner to pay a Saudi prince would be impossible: 'Prince Sultan bin Abdel-Aziz', he said with reference to the Saudi Defence Minister, 'does not need an Adnan Khashoggi. If he wants $10 million, all he has to do is take it from the government since he is an essential part of the government and it is his to take. If Adnan Khashoggi or anyone else tried to buy a decision from Prince Sultan, they would only insult hi.a, and to insult him is not only stupid, it is dangerous.' [1] Khashoggi could have added that just as the Kingdom is seen by the Saud family as its own property, so are some parts of the government regarded as the personal domains of individual princes. It is assumed in Saudi Arabia that the Ministry of Defence and Aviation is one of the main sources of Prince Sultan's fortune and that the National Guard is a major source of the fortune of Prince Abdullah bin Abdel-Aziz, the Guard commander and Crown Prince.

A final category of royal wealth comes from business. Princes are major investors in Saudi industrial and service companies, they represent foreign companies bidding for government contracts – an activity which earned them some enormous commissions in the 1970s – and in 1980 and 1981 a few of them made huge sums from being given entitlements to state oil, which they were able to sell on the open market. At this time official Saudi prices were running at $2–$4 a barrel below OPEC prices for oil of similar quality. Most of the princes' businesses have developed in the last ten years and they are discussed in detail later in this chapter in the context of the changing relations of merchants and rulers.

It is impossible to put a figure on the personal assets of any senior member of the Arabian ruling families. To a great extent a prince of the

---

1. See *America for Sale* by Kenneth C. Crowe, Doubleday, 1978, p. 59.

house of Saud can make himself as rich as he wants to be. There are full brothers of equal prestige in the Saudi royal family who have radically different sized fortunes. The reason for the disparity is simply that one asked the King for land or took the trouble to establish a business while the other was not interested. It would probably be fair to say that in 1982 the richest members of the Saud family – excluding the King, who has title to all unallocated land and can pay himself what he likes – are worth a few billions of dollars. A plausible range for fortunes in this bracket would be $1 billion to $4 billion. Among the very richest princes are Sultan, Mohammad bin Abdel-Aziz – a full brother of the late King and the oldest living son of Ibn Saud; Mitab bin Abdel-Aziz – the Minister of Housing; and Mitab's full brother, Mishaal, a former Governor of Mecca and Minister of Defence. Below this exalted level royal fortunes fall away steadily, and descend to a point where some of the junior princes are in a state of permanent moderate indebtedness.

The princes have a mixture of motives for accumulating fortunes on a vast scale. A few of them are motivated by sheer pathological greed. Boredom is a big factor; some princes seem anxious to acquire ever larger incomes for the simple satisfaction of seeing their bank balances grow. Several of the senior princes spend colossal sums of money. They may have well over a dozen palaces in Saudi Arabia, each with a full staff of servants and a fleet of cars, often including a fair number of Rolls Royces. They may also have half a dozen palaces abroad, in such places as Morocco, Switzerland and Spain. Their hunting expeditions in the desert sometimes involve parties of up to a thousand, mostly retainers and bedouin who have attached themselves to the princes' camps.

Above all, vast sums are given away in the princes' *majles*, the council chambers of public reception rooms in which they receive their subjects. Most of the senior Saudi princes and all of the Kingdom's fourteen provincial governors, hold *majles* every day. The people who attend them are mostly ordinary Saudi citizens – especially Nejdis, who feel a closer bond with the royal family than do members of other communities. Any ordinary Saudi who walks into a prince's *majlis* will expect, at the very least, a good meal, a bed for the night if he wants it, and an opportunity to express his views on the topics of the day. More often than not he will come with a specific request. He may want some financial help with debts or bills, or a car or a pick-up truck, or some money to give as his daughter's dowry, or medical treatment in London for one of his family. Some of this assistance might be available from the state, but people from the country areas often feel that the immigrant Arab bureaucrats or the Hijazis in the ministries do not respect their tribal origins and do not properly understand them. They feel that it is more natural for them to take their worries to a prince than to a government official.

Princes who help large numbers of people at their *majles* are bound to increase the weight they carry in family councils. They also win honour for themselves and for the Saud family as a whole. To the Western mind this may sound a rather nebulous motive, and an implausible excuse for the acquisition of billion-dollar fortunes, but to Arabians it is extremely important. The ordinary people of Arabia expect princes to be rich. One of the younger princes remarked to me in 1982 that the bedouin would come into his *majlis*, and on being told, for example, that he could not afford to build a farm in their area, would reply that he should take the money from the government department where he worked.

The most generous princes are some of the richest. Abdullah bin Abdel-Aziz and Sultan bin Abdel-Aziz may receive and feed a hundred or so men at a sitting and disburse many tens of millions of dollars every year. They draw large numbers to their *majles* because they travel widely in the Kingdom, which strengthens their links with the tribes, and have a reputation for being generous. They also have jobs at the head of the armed forces and the National Guard which give them many relatively poor Saudis as their constituents. Since 1962, when he was appointed to his post, Abdullah's life has been completely bound to the National Guard. Sultan, who became Minister of Defence at the same time, has been almost as closely associated with the conventional armed forces. In the eyes of the troops, the forces' commands and the persons of the two princes are viewed as the same thing.

In a financial respect the position of Abdullah and Sultan is not unlike that of the provincial governors, among whom Sultan's full brother, Salman, the governor of the Riyadh province, has a reputation for exceptional generosity. Both the governors and the defence-force commanders disburse money to constituents from their personal and official funds, and it is sometimes difficult to define which type of gift is financed from which source. In this area of government in Saudi Arabia there is often little distinction between the spending of the prince and the spending of the government department he controls.

The blurred distinction between personal royal spending and government spending in Saudi Arabia affects relationships between the princes and all sections of Saudi society. From the point of view of the merchants it means that even today, to a certain degree, all government contracts are seen as royal favours. There may be some exaggeration in this highly personalised and very Arabian interpretation of the Kingdom's development spending, but there is no doubt that if a merchant falls foul of the King and the King decides that he should not benefit from government spending, he will not prosper. The government will not buy his land. As word of his misfortune spreads other people will avoid doing business with him.

A merchant can help his chances of winning contracts by lobbying the King and the senior princes. One of the first men to lobby the King in Saudi Arabia was Mohammad Bin Laden, a small Hadhrami contractor. It is said that whenever Mohammad was in Riyadh in the 1940s he would visit the King's *majlis* every day and sit as close as possible to him. He had begun life as a bricklayer, established his own small construction business and distinguished himself by building palaces for members of the royal family. One of his shrewdest ideas had been to build a palace for the ageing and partly paralysed King Abdel-Aziz with a ramp leading up an outside wall to his bedroom on the first floor. Through initiatives such as this and his patient attendance on the King, he put himself in a position to be awarded the contract for one of the Kingdom's first major roads, running from Jeddah to Medina. This happened in 1951, when a British company, Thomas Ward of Sheffield, asked to be released from the contract, having underestimated the difficulties of the terrain. After successfully completing the road, Bin Laden went on to win more, and more profitable, contracts, creating a construction company which was by far the biggest in Saudi Arabia and one of the biggest in the world. Although his engineers were mainly non-Saudi, he did not enter a partnership with any big Western contractor. As the scale of his operations expanded he bought an aircraft so that he could fly between his projects. One day in the early 1960s he was able to fulfil an Arabian millionaire's dream by saying his morning prayers in Jerusalem, his midday prayers in Medina and his evening prayers in Mecca – the three holiest cities of the Muslim world.

An interesting sidelight on the power of the King over all aspects of Saudi life is given by the events that followed Mohammad Bin Laden's death, when he crashed his aircraft in 1966. It was King Faisal who decided who should run the Bin Laden establishment until some of the founder's own fifty-two offspring reached an age at which they would be able to take over the business themselves. The man appointed to the job was a well-regarded engineer and manager of his own construction company, Mohammad Baharith. For about ten years after the crash the King also banned any of Bin Laden's sons from flying their own aircraft, even if they were able to obtain the normal international pilot's qualifications.

At about the same time as Mohammad Bin Laden won the Medina road contract, Salim Ahmed Bin Mahfouz used exactly the same lobbying methods to persuade King Abdel-Aziz to allow him to establish a bank. He had arrived in the Hijaz from the Hadhramaut in 1915, spent thirty-five years working in various capacities for the Kaaki family of Mecca, and in 1949 had finally entered an exchange-dealing partnership with members of the family. Almost immediately after the establishment of the business Salim decided that it would do better if it were formally reconstituted as a bank. There were in Jeddah at that time two banks, the Banque de l'Indochine and Algemene Bank Nederland, which had established its branch to serve pilgrims from the Dutch East Indies. Neither of these institutions, however, was allowed to call itself a bank, because banks were known to charge interest, and interest was condemned in the Koran as usury. The Algemene Bank called itself euphemistically the Netherlands Trading Company. Salim realised that if he was going to establish a Saudi-owned bank he would have to call it a bank in order to differentiate it from the exchange dealers, of whom there were several in the Jeddah souk. Accordingly he went to King Abdel-Aziz and began the presentation of his ideas by explaining that there were parts of the economy which were still controlled entirely by foreigners, and adding: 'The Kingdom will not be fully independent until we are independent economically.' The King asked what Salim meant, and Salim dared to use the word 'bank' – 'We want to establish a bank,' he said.

Salim added by way of explanation that only the two foreign institutions had ever been allowed to open letters of credit, which were helping to finance the growing volume of imports of manufactured goods which were flowing into the Kingdom. It is doubtful whether the King understood anything about letters of credit, but he referred Salim to his minister, Abdullah Suliman, and told him to do what the exchange dealer wanted. The bank that Salim then established was the National

Commercial, which has since become the biggest bank in the Kingdom.

The practice of lobbying the royal family has continued in the last thirty years. Even the richest and most distinguished merchants do not neglect to attend the Sauds on occasion and new young businessmen still find it useful to become part of the entourage of influential princes. An interesting case of successful modern lobbying occurred recently in one of the Gulf states. A young Dubai merchant. Ahmed Baquer, told a *Financial Times* correspondent, Kathy Evans, in 1976 that he had been attending the *majles* of the Ruler, Shaikh Rashid bin Said al Maktoum, for ten years. Shortly before the interview he had entered joint-ventures with two contractors, Costain Blankevoort Dredging and Balfour Beatty. With these companies he had persuaded the Ruler to give him some $600 million of work on the Jebel Ali industrial port being built to the south of the city. 'I get up every day at 4.30 in the morning and go and see Shaikh Rashid at his *majlis*,' he told Kathy Evans. 'Shaikh Rashid is a very secretive man, he keeps his ideas to himself until he has worked them out thoroughly in his mind. But one day when I went to his [temporary summer] camp near Jebel Ali he mentioned to me about his idea to develop the area. At this time he was thinking of making it a tourist area with a yachting marina, hotels and so on. I don't know when he changed his mind about making it into an industrial area, but a few weeks later at the *majlis* he told me. From then on I spent several weeks convincing him to give me the contract. It was a hard job because I have a relatively small company, but I did it in the end.' [2]

Another way in which merchants have won royal favour, land and contracts has been through serving their governments. In Saudi Arabia this has been part of the relationship between the merchants and the royal family since the 1930s; it has not been changed greatly by the advent of oil. The merchants' role as government servants in the Kingdom stems from the fact that King Abdel-Aziz never built a formal administration. His central government in Riyadh was composed of a group of advisers and secretaries. In the early 1930s there were about ten advisers, many of them Syrians and Egyptians, and an executive of less than a dozen. These men included a translator, an official responsible for examining petitions and pruning any of excessive length, and one or two typists.[3] The provinces were entrusted by the King to

2. *Financial Times*, 20 August 1976.
3. See *Arabia Unified, A Portrait of Ibn Saud* by Mohammad Almana, Hutchinson Benham, 1980, p. 174. Mohammad Almana was the King's translator.

strong-willed and energetic members of his own family. Any matter that came outside the orbit of regular administration was assigned to a trusted subject – more often than not a member of one of the big merchant families. The job of representing the King in neighbouring states was given to Nejdi merchants who had businesses in those states. In Cairo was Fawzan Sabgh, in Kuwait Abdullah Niffisi and in Bahrain the Algosaibi family. The Algosaibis not only had a diplomatic role, they also acted as purchasing agents for the King in Bombay. Like members of other families, they were sometimes given special tasks to perform for the King. Abdel-Rahman, the most widely travelled member of the family, was frequently sent to Europe in the 1930s. On one occasion he was given a roving commission to raise money for the King, on another he was asked to visit London to arrange for a British bank to open an office in Saudi Arabia as 'state bank' for the Kingdom. (Nobody was interested.) Other people who were frequently entrusted with diplomatic tasks were members of the Alireza family in Jeddah.

None of the families which occasionally rendered service in this way was paid a salary or given a fee for its work. One reward, instead, was prestige. Mohammad Almana, the King's former translator, who now owns a hospital in Alkhobar, remarked to me in 1980: 'This [prestige] is much more important than it sounds. Our society is not so impersonal as yours and prestige is much more valuable to a man.' Apart from gratifying the person's pride, and enhancing his standing in society, the prestige of working for the monarch gave the servant an advantage in his dealings with other Arabians. The huge fortune made by the Algosaibis in Bahrain in the 1920s was based partly on their being able to corner the carrying trade between Bahrain and the mainland. The family was also allowed to make a profit on the purchases it made on behalf of the King in India.

The other, equally important, rewards received by all the King's servants – those who were established members of his court as well as those who undertook occasional assignments – were gifts of land and opportunities to make money from the award of contracts and concessions. Among numerous other gifts, Abdullah Suliman in the late 1940s was granted the cement franchise for the Hijaz. This has yielded great profits for his son, Abdel-Aziz, who now owns part of the Saudi agency for Datsun and is one of the richest merchants in the Kingdom. The King's rewards were not always given in return for individual acts of service. The King would make a gift when he felt like doing so or when he decided that his servant had gone some time without receiving anything and deserved something more.

In the last thirty years or so the Sauds have continued to draft members of the merchant families into their government – often at only a few days' notice. This practice has produced a group of men who have rendered considerable service to the state, but who have never had full-time careers in government in the recognised European sense. Ali Alireza, who was recently Saudi ambassador in Washington, was at the University of California at Berkeley when Prince Faisal wanted to form a delegation for the United Nations conference at San Francisco in 1945. He was one of the few Saudis the prince knew who had any experience of the Western world, and so he was obliged to enter the government's service. The prince simply sent him a telegram addressed 'Ali Alireza, USA', which told him to grow a beard and prepare to receive the Saudi delegation. Over the next ten years he held a series of diplomatic posts – adviser to the prince, Minister Plenipotentiary, delegate to the UN and Minister of State. In between assignments he went back to working for the family firm.

In the 1970s and early 1980s members of the Algosaibi family had similar careers. Dr Ghazi Abdel-Rahman and his cousin, Khaled, were asked to serve, one after the other, as directors general of the Saudi railroad. In 1975 Dr Ghazi was asked to head the new Ministry of Industry and Electricity, which has become one of the most important spending agencies in the government; then Khaled was appointed deputy governor of the Saudi Arabian Monetary Agency (SAMA), a post from which he retired in 1980. In the same government reorganisation Abdel-Aziz Quraishi, whose family owns a big trading business in Jeddah, was appointed governor of SAMA.

In many posts of this type the King's servants still go unpaid; even if they do accept a salary it will not be particularly generous and will be unimportant compared with the royal gifts they receive. The Alirezas refused pay in their posts under King Faisal, but in the 1950s and 1960s their company benefited enormously from government supply and construction contracts. In the early 1960s, when Haji Abdullah Alireza & Co. was going through a temporary period of weakness, the King arranged for it to be given half of the aircraft refuelling business at Jeddah airport. This was divided between the Alireza-Mobil partnership (known as APSCO – the Arabian Petroleum Supply Company) and a similar operation owned by Shell and the Jeddah merchant Mohammad

Ashmawi. The workings of the contracts showed that the two partnerships were intended to maximise their profits from the King's goodwill.
When the Jeddah refinery, owned by the Saudi state oil corporation,
Petromin, was brought on stream a few years after the contracts had
been awarded, the government took no steps to transfer the refuelling
business to its own company. Instead it arranged to sell the Alireza and
Ashmawi partnerships the fuel they needed at a relatively cheap price
and permitted the two companies to resell it at a much higher price at
the airport. About half of the sales went to the state airline, Saudia.
Even by normal Saudi standards the refuelling contracts were reckoned
to be highly profitable.

A further expression of King Faisal's gratitude came when
Mohammad Abdullah Alireza, Ali's elder brother, was serving as Saudi
ambassador in Cairo during the fraught 1960s – which saw Nasser's
intervention on the republican side in the Yemen civil war and the
Arabs' humiliation by the Israelis in the Six Day War. Beginning in
1968 the Alirezas' contracting joint-venture, Laing Wimpey Alireza,
was awarded a series of large and profitable defence contracts. Most of
these involved bases for the Saudi air force.

Contracts given as expressions of royal gratitude over the past twenty
years have usually been small to medium-sized ones, and they have not
been awarded unless the King has been satisfied that the recipient's
performance will be as good as that of any other merchant.

There are any number of ways in which the royal family has been able
to arrange for particular merchants to be favoured. On construction
projects a contract can be awarded to a particular company without
competitors even being asked to bid. A famous, and unusually large,
example of this was the 400-mile Jizan–Jeddah road contract, which was
given to the Bin Laden contracting company in the early 1970s. The
same may happen with supply contracts, which normally involve building materials, construction equipment or provisions for the armed
forces. Where bidding is involved, both construction and supply contracts often go to people who have not put in the lowest bids. The
government reasons that even if their prices are not the best their
workmanship and materials will probably be as good as their competitors'.

In awarding these contracts the King and the older princes are
influenced by very personal factors. It is only occasionally, as when a
contract is given to save an important Saudi company from financial

embarrassment, that broad policy considerations come into play. King Faisal was known to favour certain families but seemed to make a point of not discriminating between people on the basis of the regions from which they came. On the other hand his successors, until about 1980 or 1981, appeared to be unusually well disposed towards Nejdis. In some cases friendship has been the major influence: Adnan Khashoggi's defence contracts of the late 1960s and early 1970s were built on his friendship with Prince Sultan, the Minister of Defence. In other cases the King has considered whether the merchant has been relatively public spirited in his business operations. Other things being equal, the man who has invested in Saudi industry has a better chance of winning contracts than the man who has launched highly publicised, controversial take-over bids for foreign banks.

At the same time as they have received contracts and land the merchants have made their own gifts to the royal family. Mohammad Abdullah Alireza in the 1940s gave his new house, the finest and most modern in Jeddah, to Prince Faisal. He then built a duplicate. Mohammad Jomaih, the central region agent for General Motors, has built roads to link his home town of Shaqra with the main highways to Riyadh and Jeddah. Deeds such as these not only win for the donor the respect of the public; in a country where there is little distinction between the concept of the state and the person of the monarch, they count as gifts to the King.

In 1973 Adnan Khashoggi, explaining the relations of rulers and businessmen to officials at the Pentagon, described how on different occasions he had been told by members of the royal family to provide books for a bedouin school and to give twelve trucks to a small tribal chief near the Yemen border, who wanted to be able to carry goats from one oasis to another. Khashoggi commented that in the West people would consider this to be acquiring improper influence, but that in Saudi Arabia it was regarded simply as loyalty to the royal family.

The main recent change in relations between the ruling family and the merchants in Saudi Arabia has come about as a result of princes going into business. When Abdel-Aziz was King it used to be the rule that no member of the house of Saud should engage in trade. The old King believed firmly that it was the job of his family to be generous to its subjects, not to make money from them. He felt that for the princes to try to compete with the merchants to earn money would be dishonourable and liable to cause trouble.

Abdel-Aziz's policy began to be changed in the early 1970s, in the later days of the reign of King Faisal. By this time the royal family had grown in numbers and it was felt that if all the princes were paid stipends that would enable them to live like princes they would be a heavy and unpopular burden on the state. In Abdel-Aziz's day most of the adult princes had played some role in government; by the beginning of the 1970s there were large numbers of them who were simply unemployed. Gradually Faisal let it be known that the princes could, if they wished, engage in business – though it was assumed that they would be reasonably discreet in the matter. They were not supposed to develop businesses which would involve their names, or their companies' names, being used on the fronts of offices or in advertisements alongside the names of the big merchant houses.

One of the first people to take advantage of the new dispensation was King Faisal's eldest son, Abdullah, who has since developed a considerable range of interests in manufacturing. Abdullah is not himself regarded as a particularly modern-minded businessman, but he has been a founder of some of the most successful Saudi industries. These include the Amiantit cement-asbestos company and Saudi Plastic Products (SAPPCO), both of which produce pipes.

Another early investor was Prince Khaled bin Abdullah bin Abdel-Rahman, a son of one of King Abdel-Aziz's younger brothers, Abdullah bin Abdel-Rahman, who was an elder statesman of the royal family in King Faisal's reign. Khaled was involved in some of the Saudi arms contracts in King Faisal's reign, and, like Abdullah Faisal, he has invested in some of the longest-standing and most successful industrial ventures. He is now rated as perhaps the most solidly professional of the royal businessmen. Much of his foreign and some of his domestic business he does in partnership with Suliman Olayan, another businessman with a reputation for professionalism. The two men have interests in the highly profitable Saudi Chemical Company, which manufactures explosives, an egg-production plant at Kharj, and several other Saudi industries. They are also partners in Competrol, an investment business operating in Athens, New York and London, and Arab Commercial Enterprises, one of the biggest Saudi insurance brokers. The friendship between the two men developed entirely outside the traditional prince–government servant or prince–petitioner context.

Suliman and Prince Khaled met through some friends in Jeddah in the mid-1960s and they went into business together because they found that they thought on the same lines and admired each other's judgement. Suliman once told me that Khaled has a reputation as a prompt payer – which makes him unusual in Saudi Arabia. He is also a well-regarded and influential member of the royal family. Through his marriage to one of the four full sisters of King Fahd he is included in the Fahd kinship group.

Since 1973 Khaled bin Abdullah bin Abdel-Rahman and Abdullah Faisal have been joined by a large number of other royal entrepreneurs. Prince Talal bin Abdel-Aziz, a major figure in the Kingdom's politics in the early 1960s and the present, extremely generous Saudi representative of UNESCO, has established himself quietly as an industrialist and representative of foreign contractors. His brothers Nawwaf and Mishaal also run low-profile businesses, as does Sultan, the Minister of Defence. Sultan is the Saudi sponsor of the hugely successful German contractor Philipp Holzmann.

Prince Mohammad bin Abdel-Aziz, the eldest living son of King Abdel-Aziz, has been involved in some extremely big commission deals, involving oil and construction contracts, but is not normally thought of as a professional businessman with a permanent business organisation. It is known that many of the transactions in which he has been involved have been purely for the benefit of friends and followers. In effect he has been lending his name to others.

All of the five sons of King Fahd have established their own separate businesses. They are Faisal, Mohammad, Saud, Sultan and, most recently, Khaled, who in 1982 had just left university and for the time being was working closely with his brother Mohammad. Of the same generation are Saud bin Naif, a son of the Interior Minister, who was making a name for himself in 1981 and 1982, and Bandar bin Khaled, a son of the late King. Prince Bandar was in partnership with the Dutch contractor, Ballast Nedam, which in 1981 won the contract to build the Saudi Arabia–Bahrain causeway. He operates extremely discreetly and leaves the running of his companies to others.

As King Faisal wished, the princes have avoided pushing the names of their businesses before the public. Most of them have concentrated on investing in industrial and service companies, which is regarded as an entirely public-spirited and uncontroversial activity.

In some cases their activities have been less popular. In one or two

well-publicised instances in the later 1970s princes invited themselves
into companies already set up by other people. At a conference on Gulf
security in November 1979, Richard Johns, who was then the Middle
East editor of the *Financial Times*, spoke of '. . . princes with a glazed
look in their eyes sidling up to unfortunate members of the merchant
community and demanding large percentages of the equity of their
projects'. In a few instances princes seemed to be happy to take their
share of profits without bothering to pay up any capital. At other times
the technique was for the prince to obstruct the award of a big contract
to a merchant-foreign company joint-venture and then explain to the
merchant that if he took him on as a partner the prince would be able to
use his influence to see if matters could be moved ahead faster.

One prince who was well known to have invited himself into other
people's companies at this time was Mohammad Fahd. Most of his
business was conducted through Al Bilad, 'the Nation'. This company
managed a few agencies, represented foreign contractors, and
administered the prince's interests in several private companies, including some originally established by other people. One of the ventures in
which the prince had acquired a stake was the Saudi Maritime Company
(SAMARCO), an oil-tanker operation set up by Haji Abdullah Alireza,
Mobil and Fairfield Maxwell of the USA. The prince had also become a
partner of Suliman Olayan in the Arabian Bechtel Company, which was
project manager for the new Riyadh airport and the vast Jubail industrial city. It was thought that the prince's purpose in requesting a share
in this operation was not only the prospect of the dividend from his
shareholding (of some 10 per cent), but also his interest in putting
himself in a position where he might hope to influence the choice of
sub-contractors. Whatever the motive, Olayan was furious at the intru-
sion.

Prince Mohammad and several other princes caused an equal amount
of comment through their activities as contract brokers. This attracted
far more attention in Saudi Arabia and abroad than any of the princes'
other business activities under the post-1970 dispensation. It involved
the princes setting themselves up as representatives of companies
bidding for major government contracts. The companies concerned
normally had well-established merchant partners, but they felt that they
needed princes as special bidding agents when they were competing for
contracts in the $100 million plus range.

The role of the contract broker in these cases was as follows. The prince was first of all retained by the contractor or his merchant partner – after either they had approached him or he had offered his services to them. He then made it his business to help with introductions, where he had an obvious special advantage, to cut through bureaucratic obstacles when necessary, and, most important, to keep the good qualities of the contractor's bid in front of the attention of the people who would be awarding the contract. In the $100 million plus range these people were the King, the Crown Prince and some of the other elder sons of King Abdel-Aziz. This group would listen to the advice of the minister and other technocrats at the top of the agency that had asked for tenders, and the technocrats in turn would draw on the expertise of foreign consultants. (The Saudi technocrats, rewarded for their services with gifts of land, were generally not bribable, but some of the consultants were.) All the bidders on the most important contracts retained princes, so almost invariably, if the companies followed up their bids with equal energy, the contracts eventually went to those who had put in the best and/or lowest bids. The fear of every contractor was that if he did not retain a prince his bid might just have been overtaken by the second-best bid, which on a highly technical contract would have been quite difficult to discern even for the technocrats, let alone the King.

The total commissions paid by successful bidders on a few occasions reached 20 per cent of the contract price. This led contractors into the habit of building massive elements of commission into their bids. Payments included several layers of commission – to the regular agents or partners of each company in the bidding consortium, to a host of *wakeels* or go-betweens, and to one, or maybe two, princes, who took by far the biggest slices. On the $4 billion telecommunications contract of 1978, was by a Philips–L.M. Ericsson-Bell Canada consortium, Mohammad Fahd was reported to have received anything up to $600 million. The princes' *wakeels*, the often illiterate but millionaire messengers who ironed out minor problems for their masters, could be paid by several parties at once. If the prince happened to be representing more than one contractor bidding for the same contract – a practice which did occur – the *wakeel* sometimes received an additional direct payment from one of the contractors, or the contractor's merchant partner, to make sure that the prince handled that contractor's bid more energetically than the bids of competitors.

Meanwhile the merchant who was the formal sponsor or partner of the contractor would be mainly concerned with providing the back-up for the contractor before and after the award of the contract. This involved arranging visas and providing office facilities for the bidders, and then helping them with the block visas and accommodation for the work-force. The merchant's commission on the contract was often minimal compared with the prince's. Even though the prince would have been paid lavishly by the contractor, merchants sometimes found themselves having to hand over part of their income to the prince in return for the help the prince claimed he had given *them*. On these occasions the princes argued that as they had won the contract on behalf of the merchant *and* the contractor it was only fair that they should be paid by both parties.

The relatively meagre income of the merchant could be supplemented by the normal profit on equipment sales if he was agent for some of the equipment used. Similarly, if the merchant had his own contracting company and won some of the sub-contracting work, he would make a normal profit on this work. For example, E.A. Juffali and Brothers, the agent for L.M. Ericsson, made very little money on the actual award of the big telecommunications contract, but later received a commission on some of the equipment it sold. Juffali also owned half of Saudi-Ericsson, which carried out part of the installation work.

The merchant community resented the profits made by the princes on deals such as the telecommunications contract of 1978 and felt that some of them had abused their position. One very distinguished merchant remarked to me in 1981 that the princes who lived mainly off commissions were 'hated', although those who invested in the development of their country were admired. Another businessman, a partner of one of the smaller royal entrepreneurs, told me a year later that some of the princes' incomes were earned not 'by effort, but by name and influence, which does not make it a fair competition'. Mohammad Fahd's activities were criticised in the late 1970s and early 1980s by some of the older businessmen within the royal family.

In response to the wave of criticism it seems that instructions have gone out to some of the younger and more aggressive princes, including Mohammad Fahd, to scale down their activities – though it is not known how strong these instructions were and in 1982 it was not yet clear how much effect they had had. Certainly the rate of commissions had been dropping – more as a result of increasing competition than the statutory 5 per cent limit decreed in 1979. There are also signs, now that making vast sums within Saudi Arabia has become less easy, that princes are developing longer-term professional operations, aimed partly at building up portfolios abroad.

Saudi merchants and foreign contractors for their part are using princes less in bidding for government contracts. Since the late 1970s they have learnt more about how decisions are made on the award of major contracts, and have seen that the princes' tangible contributions to their winning contracts have not been very great. They have now worked out their own contract-winning strategies and built up their own bidding teams. In future many of the biggest merchant houses are saying that they will not be using princes.

Whatever some businessmen may feel about the 'unfair competition' they have suffered at the hands of the princes, the Arabian merchants as a group have prospered mightily since the oil-price explosion of 1973–4. The fortunes of the richest merchants are almost as big as the fortunes of the richer princes, but it is just as difficult to attach figures to their wealth. Occasionally one comes across tantalising pieces of information. For example, when the directors of Haji Abdullah Alireza & Co. applied for their gold American Express cards they all answered the question about their incomes by writing 'in excess of $1 million a year'. These details are colourful, but they contribute nothing to working out a person's assets.

The people whom Westerners assume are the richest Arabian businessmen are the 'deal fixers' and international entrepreneurs, who are shown on the covers of European and American magazines billed as the Arab businessmen of the future or the emerging Arabian Rockefellers. This group includes Adnan Khashoggi, Ghaith Pharaon, Ghassan Shaker, Akram Ojjeh, Mahdi Tajir – the former special adviser to Shaikh Rashid of Dubai, and a few others like them. All of these men have conducted much of their business outside Arabia and have been involved in some spectacular deals. Akram Ojjeh once paid $17 million for the transatlantic liner *France*, which he hoped to turn into a floating hotel; Adnan Khashoggi and Ghaith Pharaon have both been involved in controversial bank purchases in America. The very nature of these transactions has meant that the men behind them have attracted publicity in the Western press; in the view of other Arabians they have even revelled in publicity. Mahdi Tajir once suggested in an interview that he might be the richest man in the world. This type of behaviour is regarded in Arabia as extremely undignified. It is put down to the fact that virtually every one of the deal fixers is of non-Arabian ancestry. Khashoggi is of Turko-Syrian origin, Pharaon is Syrian; both of their fathers were royal doctors. Mahdi Tajir is Persian, the Shaker family was originally Turkish.

In their own countries most of the entrepreneurs are not very visible on the ground. The exception is Ghaith Pharaon, who has some substantial hotel and contracting investments, which include a partnership with Ralph M. Parsons, the project manager for the Yanbu industrial city on the Red Sea coast. Most of the wealth of Khashoggi, Mahdi Tajir and Ghassan Shaker has come from winning contracts for foreign companies. Khashoggi in the 1960s and early 1970s won a series of famous arms contracts. He has some agencies and a few industrial and service company investments in Arabia, but nothing which would put him alongside the biggest Saudi merchants. Khashoggi admitted once that only one in five of his projects ever came to fruition. The same could be said for Pharaon, who in 1976 announced that he was going to invest or arrange investments in Syria, worth $1 billion. A year later the Syrian Minister of the Economy admitted ruefully to me that not one of the mooted projects was still under consideration. One effect of these attempted deals has been to make the promoters appear much bigger than they really are.

Most of the entrepreneurs' businesses have relatively low and irregular revenues and small overheads. In proportion to their revenues they have at times made enormous profits and paid their owners huge dividends. Khashoggi, in particular, must have spent a great deal of his income on running a yacht and an aircraft and living a jet-set life, which is not typical of Arabian merchants. Most probably he is now worth a sum in the low hundreds of millions of dollars. He is certainly not worth the $5 billion that his ex-wife and her Californian lawyer said he was worth in 1979, when they began a legal action against him, claiming half his fortune. It was thought that their ridiculously inflated estimate was announced as a ploy for publicity. Ghaith Pharaon and Mahdi Tajir are probably richer than Adnan Khashoggi, though they may not be billionaires. Ghaith Pharaon was once asked by Yusuf Ibrahim of the *New York Times* how much he was worth, and he replied with masterly understatement: 'I really haven't sat down to calculate. Let's just say, thank God, that we have no problems with money.' [4]

Within Arabia the merchants who seem richest are those with the big public front and famous agencies. For the purpose of this analysis these merchants form a distinct second category. The most conspicuous names in the group are the big car, truck and machinery importers: Ahmed Juffali, Abdul-Latif Jameel – the Saudi agent for Toyota, Majid Futtaim – who has the agency for Toyota and a host of Japanese electronics companies in the UAE, Mohammad Jomaih, Suliman Olayan, and the Alghanim family – who represent General Motors in Kuwait. The companies owned by these people undoubtedly have the biggest turnovers of any merchant companies in Arabia, but unavoidably they also have large staffs and high overheads. They operate in markets which by Arabian standards are competitive, and they have to have ploughed back into them a large part of their profits. A big drain on their funds recently has been the need for their companies to modernise back-up facilities – garages, spare-parts warehouses, advertising departments. These problems affect most of the families in this book. Their effect has been to give the big merchant families net assets in the hundreds of millions of dollars but to make only a few families or individuals billionaires. It is suggested in Arabia that the Juffalis and Suliman Olayan may be worth more than $1 billion, but the individuals themselves are sceptical about the estimates.

The men who are really enormously rich are those whose businesses Westerners in Arabia see least. They are the big property investors bulk-food importers, bankers and exchange dealers. The common feature of many of these people is that they have low overheads and little front. The headquarters of the Al Rajhi Company for Currency Exchange and Commerce, which has some 160 branch offices and is as big as any bank in Saudi Arabia, is an inconspicuous block in the business district of Riyadh. In 1982 it had a rather large hole in the wall above the doorway, flimsy glass and aluminium partitioning between the offices inside, and threadbare carpets. The other Saudi exchange dealers' offices are no more impressive.

It happens that the exchange dealers are the one category of merchant whose fortunes can be estimated reasonably accurately. This is because they all have lines of credit at the banks and have shown the bankers assets to back the credit. Gradually the financial community has produced consensus estimates of their worth. Abdel-Aziz Kaaki in Jeddah is believed to have a fortune of about $100 million attributable to his

4. *New York Times*, 25 November 1979.

exchange-dealing activities – though his family has a separate and probably bigger fortune attributable to its 48 per cent holding in the National Commercial Bank. Abdel-Aziz Suliman Mukairen, a Riyadh-based dealer whose family comes from Qassim, is thought to have assets of about $300 million. Mohammad and Abdullah Subai are rather bigger: their net worth is about $700 million.

By far the richest exchange dealers are four brothers, Salih, Abdullah, Suliman and Mohammad bin Abdel-Aziz Rajhi, who own the Al Rajhi Company for Currency Exchange and Commerce. In the autumn of 1982 these men were thought collectively to be worth some 24 billion Saudi Riyals, or $7 billion. Of this vast total just under $3 billion was attributable to Suliman, who held 42 per cent of the company. The sum made him possibly the richest man in the world outside the ranks of kings and princes.

5

Alghanim – the Biggest GM Dealer

In early 1979 I flew with Kutayba Yusuf Alghanim in his private jet from London to St Moritz. There were four of us – Kutayba, a rich Palestinian friend called Jeanot Khayyat, Kutayba's wife, Najla, and myself. We had had lunch and were flying over eastern France. Kutayba and Jeanot were discussing the various friends they had left in St Moritz ten days before and speculating who might still be there: it was the beginning of March and the season was a bit past its peak. Then suddenly Jeanot brought out of his pocket a small, flat, solid silver object. It was pear shaped and about half a centimetre thick, with one surface slightly hollow. He asked everyone in the aircraft to guess what it was. We all made suggestions but none of us got anywhere near the right answer. The object was even sent up to the pilot for his opinion, but he too failed. At last Jeanot relented. He explained that he had been given the object for Christmas, and that it was a special gadget for very rich people to keep in their pockets. One held it between the thumb and forefinger and ran one's thumb across the side with the hollow. This apparently gave one the feeling of counting out coins. Kutayba was delighted. His face lit up in a big enthusiastic smile. 'Ah,' he said, 'I know, another present for the man who has everything.' Then he went on to explain about an electronic match-extinguisher bellows. One lit one's cigar, held the match in front of the bellows and pressed a button . . .

The Alghanim establishment in St Moritz, to which Kutayba was flying when this conversation took place, is a medium-sized house. It has some five bedrooms, a large dining room, a huge sitting room, servants' quarters and a balcony. It is perched on a mountain side about two miles to the east of the town; technically it is in the village of Suvretta. This is a small community occupied by rich European industrialists. Kutayba's neighbours include Heineken, the Dutch beer magnate, Rossi of Martini and Rossi vermouth, the tanker-owners Niarchos, Livanos and Christina Onassis, Agnelli of Fiat, and the German steel-maker Thyssen. The most famous personality to have had a house in Suvretta was the Shah of Iran. His was a large mansion – a dark, sinister, well-defended place, bristling with radio aerials. He had come to Suvretta some time before Kutayba, which meant that Kutayba had had to build his own house half a mile further up the mountain side. This may not have pleased the Shah, but Kutayba was delighted to be able to look down on him from a great height.

For forty years Kutayba's grandfather, Haji Ahmed, was a captain at sea with his own dhow. Like the other dhow owners of Kuwait he plied the Basra–Bombay route, occasionally going to East Africa on the return journey. The season began after the end of the Indian monsoon in June. Haji Ahmed would go to Iraq where he bought dates, mostly from the date gardens of the Sabah family, who had very large plantations near Basra, and then he would sail across the Arabian sea to Bombay, sell the dates, buy food, cloth and timber from the Malabar coast, and return to Kuwait. It was not an easy living, but it was regarded as the right occupation for a member of an important family. Kuwait was the centre of the ocean-going dhow trade and much the biggest shipbuilding port of the Gulf. Most of the families that had come from central Arabia with the Sabah in the early eighteenth century made their living from dhows; Kuwaitis say that it would not have been considered proper for them to have set themselves up beside the Indian and Persian shopkeepers in the souk.

One day in June 1925 disaster struck Haji Ahmed. His brother-in-law was sailing the dhow to Basra when a storm broke. Yusuf, Haji Ahmed's son, told me that the boat had been left on the shore since the previous September and that as the hull had dried cracks had appeared between the timbers. Before the boat put to sea again nobody had bothered to renew the caulking; consequently the boat has already taken on some water before the wind began to rise, and when it was hit by big waves it capsized and sank. Ahmed's brother-in-law, who might have managed to prevent the disaster had he been a more experienced sailor, was rescued by another dhow nearby.

The sinking marked a turning point in the history of the Alghanims, because both Ahmed and his son Yusuf, who was then about eighteen,

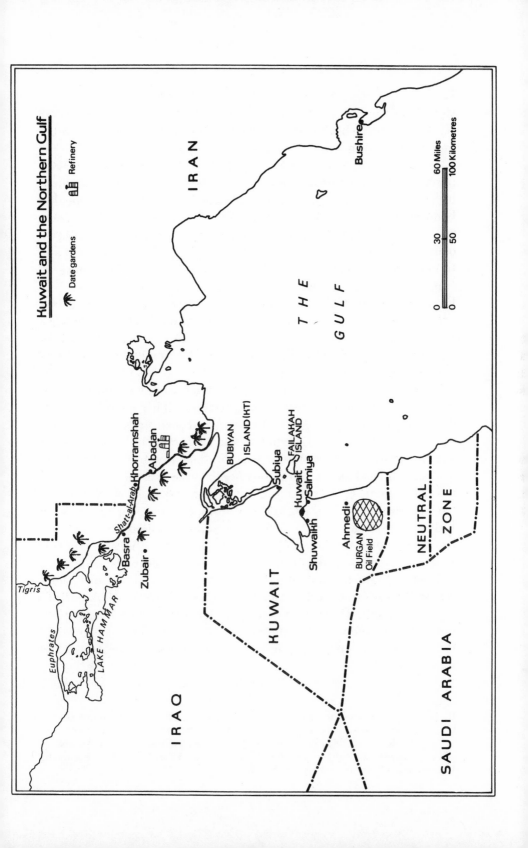

Kuwait and the Northern Gulf

🌴 Date gardens   🏭 Refinery

IRAN

THE GULF

Bushire

60 Miles
0   30
0   50   100 Kilometres

Tigris

Euphrates

LAKE HAMMAR

Zubair

Basra

Shatt-al-Arab

Khorramshah

Abadan

BUBIYAN ISLAND (KT)

Subiya

FAILAKAH ISLAND

Kuwait

Salmiya

Shuwaikh

Ahmedi

BURGAN Oil Field

IRAQ

KUWAIT

NEUTRAL ZONE

SAUDI ARABIA

were forced to embark on new careers. Ahmed did not have enough capital to replace his dhow. Instead he went into business as a timber merchant, buying wood from the dhow captains and selling it to the boat-building yards. He became a specialist in the difficult and dangerous business of organising launchings. Ahmed also served his community as a pharmacist, working on the basis of a rudimentary medical knowledge he had picked up from Indians, and preparing his own medicines. He became a well-loved and greatly respected member of the community, and when he died at the venerable age of a hundred and five huge crowds went with his family to the graveyard. The great age of Haji Ahmed, like the age of Zainal Alireza, may be exaggerated by Kuwaitis, but one of the early managers of the British Bank of the Middle East in Kuwait, who remembers Ahmed calling at Yusuf's office every morning in the early 1950s, estimates that he was then already over ninety. In the last five years of his immensely long life he lived mainly on dates and butter.

Yusuf, who had recently returned from school in Karachi when the sinking of the dhow occurred, established himself in a minor part of his father's trade, selling kerosene. His father had been given the agency for the Anglo-Persian Oil Company[1] at the suggestion of the Ruler soon after the end of the First World War, but he had shown no interest in kerosene and had delegated the job of selling it to a servant. Yusuf, with a flair for spotting the coming thing, which was to mark most of his business dealings over the next thirty years, took over the servant's job and began to sell kerosene seriously. Inevitably he found himself mixing with the English employees of APOC – he had learnt English during his time in Karachi – and in due course he was asked to provide some informal back-up for the company in the negotiations for an oil concession in Kuwait. In the early stages he was commissioned to take soundings on how APOC's bids stood with the Ruler. Later, when the company sent out permanent representatives of its own, Yusuf was concerned mainly with arranging transport and accommodation for geologists and surveyors.

A more important spin-off from the kerosene agency was Yusuf's

1. The Anglo-Persian Oil Company, which was established in 1909 to operate the Persian oil concession, changed its name to the Anglo-Iranian Oil Company in 1935 and British Petroleum in 1954, after its concession had been nationalised by Dr Mossadeq. The company supplied all of the Gulf states and the Saudi Eastern Province during the interwar years from its refinery at Abadan.

entry into the quarrying business. APOC needed gravel for making concrete, which it was using in large quantities as it built up production from its Persian oil fields, and it had found that the local gravel was too saline to be suitable. The company employed some Iraqi contractors to supply gravel from Kuwait but it soon found that deliveries were falling. While giving a general review of his career Yusuf once explained to me how he became involved: 'It is a difficult business this gravel – identifying the seams – and the Iraqis said that their seams were running thin. I went with the company's surveyors, who were looking into the problem to see whether there really was a shortage, whether what the Iraqis said was true or not. They thought that maybe they just wanted to raise the price. After some time APOC suggested that I should go into this business because I had got to know it pretty well. Then I had no money, so I didn't say yes, but I thought about it. I went to Basra, where I met three Jews, of a good family, who borrowed from a bank and in turn lent the money to me. But I had to bid to get the APOC contract, undercut the competitors. Then I began buying barges and tugs every year. I had one or two steel barges built in Iraq, but mostly I bought them from the British army who had some barges left from their Mesopotamian campaign in the First World War. The tugs had diesel engines, they towed the barges, which needed to have flat bottoms because there is shallow water between Kuwait and Abadan. I also chartered 200 dhows – they carried just 60 or 80 tons.

'By this time, the early 1930s, we were delivering 20,000 or 25,000 tons a month. We had no mechanical systems for digging; I had about 6,000 workers at Subiya for the gravel, and for the sand from Shuwaikh I had 500 people working [see map]. There were no jetties. They waded out a hundred feet from the shore and handed it up in baskets which they carried over their shoulders. This was up to 1940 when the business stopped because of the war. By then I had fifteen barges and three tugs.'

Yusuf had begun to branch out into other types of business before the gravel deliveries came to an end. He had taken the agencies for Imperial Airways (now British Airways) and Hudson cars in 1936. Two years later, in the uneasy period just before the Second World War, the oil company invited him to visit Britain, the first Kuwaiti after the Ruler to do so. The pretext for the visit was the Glasgow Exhibition. This was a trade fair with an emphasis on engineering, and exhibits and cultural shows from all over the Empire. Yusuf was shown the Clyde shipyards,

Alghanim Family Tree

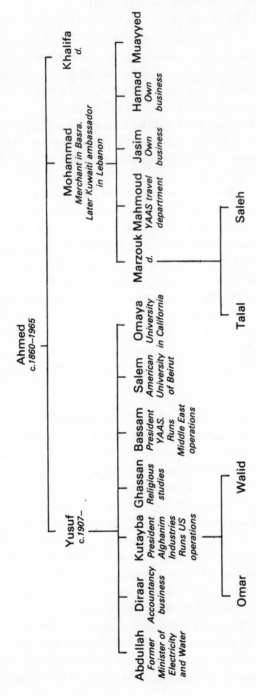

Ahmed
c.1860–1965

Yusuf
c.1907–

Abdullah
Former Minister of Electricity and Water

Diraar
Accountancy business

Kutayba
President Alghanim Industries Runs US operations

Ghassan
Religious studies

Bassam
President YAAS. Runs Middle East operations

Salem
American University of Beirut

Omaya
University in California

Omar

Walid

Mohammad
Merchant in Basra. Later Kuwaiti ambassador in Lebanon

Marzouk
d.

Mahmoud
YAAS travel department

Jasim
Own business

Hamad
Own business

Muayyed

Khalifa
d.

Talal

Saleh

NOTES

1. Family tree includes all the male descendants of Haji Ahmed. Ahmed had four elder brothers, Abdullah, Shaheen, Ibrahim and Thunayyan, from whom all the other Alghanims are descended.

2. Alghanim Industries and Yusuf Ahmed Alghanim and Sons (YAAS) are owned by Kutayba, Bassam, Salem and Omaya. YAAS is a partnership which they took over from their father in 1971; Alghanim Industries is a holding company established five years later. Alghanim Industries owns Kirby Kuwait, Kirby USA and the major shares in two joint ventures — Gulf Trading, a food importing company established with the British firm Steel Brothers, and Alghanim Shipping, a shipping agents in which Wilhelmson of Norway holds 40 per cent. The directors of Alghanim Industries are Kutayba and Bassam. Yusuf still has private real estate interests, as do his older sons, Abdullah and Diraar.

where he saw the *Queen Elizabeth* just before her launching. He then toured part of the rest of Scotland. As a result of this Kutayba and his brothers were sent to school in Scotland; Abdullah, the former Kuwaiti Minister of Water and Power, can still sing Scottish songs with a Glaswegian accent. At the end of the visit Yusuf came south and saw a naval review, where he represented the Ruler, and joined a party visiting the new television centre at the BBC.

Yusuf says that on his return to Kuwait his mind was very much broadened. He had thought of trading opportunities on his trip and had taken many consumer goods and machinery agencies. These included Lever Brothers and Burgess & Co of Glasgow, who made marine diesel engines. He had also decided that he would be able to sell more cars in Kuwait with some agency other than Hudson. A year or so later he switched to Chrysler, though this too proved to be unsatisfactory. During the Second World War it became practically impossible for him to get cars, so Yusuf devoted his attention to chartering his dhow fleet to carry food imports. In this he was exploiting the reduction of sailings to the Gulf by the British India Line. Then after the war he ran into difficulties with the Chrysler regional dealers in Beirut, whom he suspected were not being wholly honest with him. By 1947 he was ready to drop the company. There was the prospect of a deal which was to make him one of the most successful businessmen in the Middle East.

General Motors at this time had an old and rather ineffective sub-dealer in Kuwait. In Yusuf's opinion: 'He was totally ignorant about cars, he didn't even know the difference between a nut and a bolt. Well, now there was going to be oil, GM was thinking that they would need an agent who knew something about cars. And I was a good mechanic, it was my hobby, I loved it. In 1933, you know, I converted a car engine into a marine engine to be used in a dhow – I did this myself. I used to read from the instruction manual for others who were learning to work on engines. So, the General Motors team came to Kuwait and the Ruler decided that in future the agency should be direct – well, I thought so too. Up to then the man here had been under the dealership in Baghdad, but the Ruler could not see the point in having any profit going to Iraqis, and so he told the company that they should deal direct in future, but he left them free to choose whoever they liked as agent. I was the obvious choice, but I gave the old sub-dealer a commission.'

For the next fifteen years Yusuf found himself spending almost half of his time abroad. He entered new ventures in contracting and shipping and won a host of new agencies. These included the Dutch electronics company Philips. Unlike most other Arabian merchants he met regularly with the companies he represented to discuss how he could improve his operations in Kuwait. He put most of his efforts into the General Motors agency. He got to know all aspects of the car business. Every year he travelled to all the main motor shows – Paris, Frankfurt, London and New York. This was not so much to see the new models – which he says he could do perfectly well in the showrooms – but to find out about the latest equipment and accessories for running the service part of his business. As soon as he had secured General Motors he had begun work on a garage; it had been part of his agency contract that he should undertake to provide reasonable servicing, and the garage was expanded several times in the 1950s and 1960s. This did not make Alghanim service in Kuwait as good as service in Europe and America, but until the later 1960s it put the company way ahead of any local competitors. When Yusuf started his service operations Kuwaiti friends advised him to put his money into the bank or invest it in new stock – the idea of investing in something which did not yield a direct profit was totally alien to the traditional merchant mentality.

Yusuf says that what gave him the advantage over other Kuwaiti merchants in this period was his enthusiasm for mechanical work, travelling and reading. Those who knew him well agree with this judgement. Violet Dickson, the wife of a former British political agent, who has lived in Kuwait since 1929, told me that she remembers Yusuf as a 'small, thin eager man . . . He had enormous self-confidence. It seemed to me that he was working in a different world from other Kuwaitis – he was so precise with facts and figures. He always seemed to be doing something new, something which nobody had expected to happen in Kuwait for years.' Much the same comments were made to me by a former manager of the British Bank of the Middle East: 'Yusuf had the courage to put new ideas into practice. All of the other big merchants in the late 1940s were smuggling gold to India, and a few years later they switched to real estate. I suppose the richest merchants at that time were the al Hamad brothers.[2] They had a big trade in gold, foreign exchange dealing and food imports – traditional types of business. Yusuf, though, never touched gold, and he didn't seem very interested in land. He bought an old palace and was given some land by the Ruler – but he was not at all a rich landowner by Kuwaiti standards. I don't think that gold or land appealed to his imagination.'

The one important quality that Yusuf lacked was an interest in day-to-day administration. This had the ironic consequence of causing his business to begin its decline as soon as it properly came into its own in the late 1950s and 1960s. By this time the development boom which had begun in 1952–3 had brought about the distribution of wealth to all levels of Kuwaiti society. Kuwaitis were becoming mass car-buyers. This caused an enormous expansion of all aspects of Yusuf's business, but Yusuf himself did not spend enough time in Kuwait to see that it was able to operate efficiently on the new scale. During his long and frequent trips abroad, the running of his company was left at first to his younger brother, Khalifa, and then to professional managers. In Yusuf's view there was nothing very important for these people to do; as he freely admitted to me: '. . . the management when I was away was fairly simple, just importing stocks and selling – the brains was in getting the business agencies in the first place.' This was a fundamental mistake in judgement, which Yusuf paid for in an ever more slow-moving, costly and inefficient management. It seems that he was genuinely let down by many of his employees, who did not always do their best for him. Even so he blamed them too much for the problems of his company. He attributed everything that went wrong to the incompetence of the management rather than to himself for not being there.

During the early 1960s Yusuf handed over the main responsibility for his company to his eldest son, Abdullah, who had returned from university in Scotland. But within a few years the two men fell out. There was a furious argument over how the firm should be run. This ended in 1965 with Abdullah and his brother Diraar being given some assets, splitting from Yusuf and establishing their own businesses. To this day there is little contact between them and the rest of the family.

Yusuf, after the split, resumed control of the company himself for several years – between frequent hirings of new chief executives. Then in 1971 his third son, Kutayba, a half-brother of Abdullah and Diraar,

2. The best-known member of the Hamad family today is Abdlatif Yusuf, who until September 1983 was the Kuwaiti Minister of Finance. Abdlatif is one of the most able economists in Arabia. In the 1960s he established the Kuwait Fund for Arab Economic Development, the highly successful Kuwaiti government aid-giving agency. In the later 1970s he was a member of the Brandt Commission. This commission, headed by the former West German Chancellor, Willi Brandt, reported on the need for a new commitment by the industrialised countries to the development of the Third World.

persuaded his father to give him the job. In this Kutayba was power-
fully supported by his mother, who, like many Arabian wives, had
considerable influence with her husband. Kutayba was newly graduated with a degree in business administration from the University of
California at Berkeley. He entered the company with a junior executive
job and was rapidly promoted. He immersed himself in the politics of
the organisation, fighting mainly against an Iraqi chief executive who
had once taught at Oxford. This was a battle which Kutayba was well
placed to win. The expatriate managers realised that if Kutayba was the
eldest eligible son and enjoyed the backing of his mother they would do
well to support him. Within a few months Kutayba had managed to gain
a hold on enough of the controlling aspects of the company to persuade
his father that he should take over the ownership and management
completely.

The new chief executive turned out to possess many of his father's
qualities. Like Yusuf, Kutayba is highly articulate and has great entre-
preneurial flair. He has good ideas and enjoys planning strategies to put
them into operation. Also like his father, Kutayba is not particularly
interested in the ordinary supervision of his business. Where the two
men are different is in their background and education. Yusuf views
business in fairly traditional Middle Eastern terms, whereas Kutayba,
having spent several years in America, says that he 'is sold on modern
theories of business administration'.

As soon as Kutayba took over the company he began to change it.
Kutayba told me the story with enthusiasm: 'I found a terribly run-
down and terribly centralised company. All of the operating decisions
went to the top. I remember coming into the office the first day and
seeing on my desk a pile of papers a metre high – including petty cash
vouchers for office tea. Everything had to be signed by me. My father
had never been much of an operations man . . . so he had a management
of expatriate Arabs which had never been very good and had become
particularly bad in the late 1960s . . . I decided that instead of running
the company by myself it would be better to keep the idea of professional management but to make it more modern – revolutionise it. We
had to decentralise it, move the decision-making lower down the
organisation. So first of all we had to improve the quality of the staff, to
get people who were at home in the Western business milieu. We did
this in several ways: we trained our existing people, hired specialist
expatriates and began a recruiting programme to hire Arab graduates

who were just leaving Western universities. We also founded our own company to do the consultancy work on the introduction of computer use – though now we have divested this, it does work all over the Gulf. I was against using outside consultants. I felt that they wouldn't contribute that much, they wouldn't have understood "the Middle East factor".

'Next I halved the number of agencies we carried, from about two hundred to under a hundred. Agencies were a craze in the area – people collected them like stamps. Believe me, there are people here who thumb through trade journals and whenever they see something they like they ask "Is that agency taken?" and see if they can get it. It was much better for us to be frank with people and say we couldn't deal effectively with their products. Otherwise we would have got a bad reputation internationally. You know, people would have gone around and said, "Alghanim is our agent but they sell nothing." Locally the attitude has always been "the more the merrier" though. A lot of people begged us to keep their agencies on, though in many instances we would suggest alternative names. The people at the other end were surprised, but a lot thanked us for our recommendations.'

There were further changes in the day-to-day decision making and organisation of the company. The business of YAAS was divided between operating and non-operating functions, the latter covering advertising, finance, training and other back-up roles. The operating side of the company was split into five major groups: Automotive – selling GM, Holden and Isuzu cars; Commercial – selling trucks and heavy machinery; Electronics – which holds the agencies for Philips televisions and other household electronic equipment; Engineering – selling Frigidaire freezers and washing machines and installing Hitachi central air-conditioning systems; and Travel Services – which includes the general sales agencies for British Airways, Gulf Air, Air India and Qantas.[3]

Since the reorganisation Kutayba has left the running of YAAS to his brother Bassam and a team of Arab and Western managers. Most of his own time is spent working on new projects. His biggest undertaking has been his purchase in 1975 of a company which manufactures pre-engineered steel buildings – Kirby Industries, of Houston, Texas. This

3. These paragraphs describe only the formal changes made in YAAS when Kutayba took over. How the company has been managed in practice in recent years is described in Chapter 15.

diversification stemmed from Kutayba's belief that if his company was to maintain its growth in future it should establish itself in something other than trade – something which was both in keeping with the direction of business developments in the area and orientated to the region as a whole. In 1975, industry seemed to be the answer. Kutayba established a holding company for Kirby and some of his other operations in the name of Alghanim Industries. In due course he moved his own office, the Kirby management in Kuwait, and several of the overall group functions, including public relations, into a new Alghanim Industries building. But to date Kirby remains the only industry he has established in Kuwait. Within a year of its purchase Kirby was operating a pre-engineered steel buildings plant in Kuwait, exporting its products throughout the Arabian Peninsula and making a small profit. The problem in its early years was that in spite of receiving cheap finance from the government-owned Industrial Bank, the factory in Kuwait was far less profitable than the growing number of Kirby factories in the USA. In the early 1980s Kirby Kuwait became a much bigger success, but by this time Kutayba, who was living mainly in the United States, had become more interested in foreign investment.

6

⁓⁓⁓⁓

The Arabian Consumer

In the boom years of the later 1970s Yusuf Ahmed Alghanim and Sons was the biggest General Motors dealer outside the United States. It achieved this position soon after the 1973 oil-price explosion, when Kutayba Alghanim and the company's general manager, an American named Ray Craig, foresaw that there would be an enormous growth of consumer spending and decided immediately to push GM for all it was worth. It was at this point that YAAS experienced its most rapid growth.

In 1978–82 the combined turnover of YAAS and Alghanim Industries ran at $350–400 million annually – a figure which made the group the biggest merchant enterprise in Kuwait and put it among the top half-dozen in the Arabian Peninsula.

Profits in the late 1970s were about $35 million a year – which in proportion to the companies' turnover was a small figure by Arabian standards. In 1980–81 it was widely rumoured in Kuwait that YAAS was making a loss. The main reason for the company's problems was the highly competitive nature of the car imports business. Other factors were the high salaries paid to the company's new, sophisticated management, and the cost of its enterprising marketing campaigns and its servicing facilities. In fact, the company's senior managers maintain that although profits were squeezed YAAS never actually made a loss. They say that the rumours spread so widely because of the jealousy of the company's competitors.

In most recent years General Motors cars have accounted for by far the biggest part of the Alghanim business – about 70 per cent of the turnover of YAAS. The company has tried from time to time to reduce its dependence on a single product by expanding other parts of its business, and occasionally in the later 1970s it found that it appeared to be succeeding. This was whenever car sales were going through a bad patch. Then the automotive division would launch a new advertising campaign and its contribution to turnover would go back to 70 per cent.

The problems brought to YAAS by this dependence on GM have to be seen in the context of the Kuwaiti car market as a whole. In the later 1970s the Kuwaiti market was running at about 50,000 cars a year. US manufacturers accounted for about 45 per cent and the Japanese slightly less. YAAS reckoned that its own sales of GM lines – covering Chevrolet, Pontiac, Oldsmobile and Cadillac – took about half of the sales of American cars, with the other sales being divided between Chrysler, represented by Badr Mulla and Brothers, the Buick GM line, represented by Mohammad Saleh and Mohammad Reza Yusuf Behbehani, and the so-called 'parallel importers' of Alghanim GM lines.[1]

This large American presence in the Kuwaiti market is regarded elsewhere in the Arabian Peninsula as being slightly surprising. In all the states of the lower Gulf in the 1970s the Japanese took the market by storm, pushing their sales from a nominal few per cent to between half and three-quarters of the total. Rather to everyone's surprise Kuwait stood out against the onslaught. Much of the explanation for the resilience of American cars in Kuwait has been put down to the fact that Kuwaitis are richer than the lower Gulf Arabs. The highly competitive price of Japanese cars has less appeal to them. Whereas the taxi drivers in Saudi Arabia and the lower Gulf have Datsuns, Toyotas or Mazdas, in Kuwait most of them seem to run Chevrolets. Khaled Said, the head of the YAAS Automotive Division, reckons that people are buying Japanese cars for their wives and children, but that the Kuwaiti *pater familias* still feels that he deserves the luxury of an American car. American cars make the driver feel powerful, and they give him a quiet, relaxing drive in the chaotic and noisy streets. The English secretary of Abdullah Abdel-Ghaffar Alireza, who was lent a Chrysler New Yorker by his employer, said that on many days he simply could not remember the drive into the office. This is not the experience of anyone travelling through an Arabian town in a Japanese taxi.

1. These figures and percentages exclude sales of light and medium-duty trucks made by GMC and Chevrolet. Alghanim used to have the Buick and GMC lines of General Motors. However GMC trucks covered much the same range as Chevrolet trucks, and Buick cars covered the same range as Oldsmobile, and the company found that it was Chevrolet and Oldsmobile that dominated these sections of the market in Kuwait. In 1967 GM decided that Buick and GMC would do better from being in competition with Oldsmobile and Chevrolet and transferred these agencies to Behbehani.

In the eyes of Kuwaitis American cars have the advantage of changing
their styles annually, in contrast to Mercedes, their main competitor at
the top end of the market, which changes only once in five years or so.
The Arabs seem to have a special love affair with Mercedes, which has
become *the* elite car of almost the whole Middle East – Kuwait being
something of an exception. But Mercedes cost more than the GM range,
their spare parts are expensive and in the Arabian Peninsula their
servicing costs are enormous. Where Mercedes scores over its Arabian
competitors is in standing up to the Arabian environment. In all the
Arabian Peninsula countries, dust affects cars' braking systems, paintwork, lights and windshield, heat damages the tyres, and dust and heat
together wear out the inside trim. In the lower Gulf intense saline
humidity corrodes all the moving electrical parts and rusts the body.
The result is that car lives in the Arabian Peninsula are very much
shorter than in Europe or America. A Chevrolet which might have a life
of five or six years in the United States, lasts three or four years in
Kuwait and just two or three years in the lower Gulf. Japanese cars last a
year less, which in Dubai, for example, gives them a maximum life of
only two years – more probably a year or eighteen months. Mercedes are
reckoned to survive considerably longer; in Kuwait they may last up to
seven years.

The Alghanim managers are quite pleased with their success in
holding off the challenge of Mercedes from above and the Japanese from
below. Their problems come from the importers of other American
cars. In particular it is the parallel importers, rather than the Mulla
or Behbehani companies who preoccupy the Alghanim executives.
Certainly there is more anger and irritation directed at the parallel
importers than at anyone else; the very phrase 'parallel importers' is
pronounced at YAAS as if there is something inferior or questionably
legal about their operations. In fact parallel importers are simply merchants who do not have a GM franchise but who buy cars in large
numbers from GM or GM dealers in America, import them and sell
them in Kuwait. They do not maintain glossy showrooms, or run
garages or keep large stocks of spare parts – their customers can have
their servicing done at the Alghanim garage – and so their overheads are
low. They undercut Alghanim sales, and as Khaled Said said to me in
1978: 'We have no response; you can't wage a price war against people
with no overheads.'

The YAAS managers have been forced to think of indirect ways of meeting the competition. One tactic has been to develop instalment sales on a much bigger scale than most other Arabian companies. Over 70 per cent of YAAS cars are now sold on credit. This has not been without its cost to the company. In a country where there are no hire purchase houses the credit has to be provided by YAAS itself. The company suffers from bad debts and is burdened by the cost of borrowing to finance the credit it gives. Its managers say that the whole instalment sales operation has been one of the main reasons for the company's financial problems. A Kuwaiti banker has remarked that YAAS now looks more like a finance company than a car-marketing company.

Another part of the Alghanim response has been an attempt to narrow the gap between its own prices and the parallel importers' prices to a point where buyers decide that for an extra $700 or so they might as well go to Alghanim and feel more confident of getting proper after-sales service. The Alghanim garage may not be able to turn away GM cars that have not been bought from YAAS, but it has ways of giving the parallel importers' customer a less good deal than its own customer. The parallel importers' customer might find the Alghanim garage busier than other GM drivers; he might have to wait longer to book a service for his car or discover that work on his car is given bottom priority once it has been checked into the garage.

The third and last Alghanim response has been to run good advertising campaigns. These are based on the company's own market research. YAAS tries to find out about the buying habits of the people to whom it sells, which makes it almost unique in the Arabian Peninsula. It has conducted surveys into people's brand loyalties in cars, kitchen appliances and home entertainment. The good news from these was that Kuwaitis have a quite high, 51 per cent, loyalty to the 'YAAS type of car' − in other words the YAAS lines, but not necessarily bought from YAAS.[2]

2. Update: By 1983 and 1984 it was obvious that YAAS had won its campaign against the parallel importers − their numbers had been reduced from about 70 in 1980 (importing 15,000 cars a year) to two. Meanwhile Chrysler sales had suffered dramatically from YAAS's decision in 1980 to accept trade-in cars in part exchange for new, a policy which had previously been applied only at Badr Mulla. Despite its success on these fronts, YAAS sales remained at only 10–12,000 units. The reason was the sudden huge surge of Japanese car sales in Kuwait, brought about by the introduction of bigger Japanese models and a great improvement in the cars' durability.

A dominant theme of Alghanim market research has been the differences in buying habits between Kuwaitis and the various categories of immigrants – other Arabs, Indians and Westerners. If an importer makes a mistake in this area the results can be disastrous. Several years ago the staff of the YAAS division marketing household goods, mostly non-Kuwaiti Arabs freshly graduated in the United States, seriously overestimated demand when they began selling dishwashers. The product was well within the buying power of the average Kuwaiti, and as an electronic labour-saving gadget it seemed that it would be just right for the Kuwaiti mentality. But the dishwashers did not sell. Some of the Western expatriates bought them, but the Kuwaitis themselves did not – because they do not use Western-style dishes. Instead they cook much of their food in a large pot and eat it by hand from a big dish – neither of which fitted into dishwashers. Meanwhile the small tea and coffee cups used in the Arab world would not stack properly or fell through the gaps between the racks inside the dishwashers. The final mistake was in forgetting that any Kuwaiti wife who is sophisticated enough to be interested in dishwashers is rich enough to have servants to wash the dishes for her.

There are other products which sell almost exclusively to Kuwaitis. Philips says that Kuwait – with a population of not more than one and a half million – is the biggest export market in the world for its video cassette recorders, which are still regarded as an unusual luxury in Western societies. The explanation for their popularity lies in the boredom of many Kuwaiti women, who spend much of their days watching TV, and in the domestic nature of Arabian social life, with its emphasis on providing entertainment for the family in the home rather than in cinemas or restaurants.

For most of the time product managers are concerned with less exotic aspects of the multinational market. One of these is the surprising popularity of the cheaper quality lines of household goods – in markets that have some of the world's highest per capita incomes. The reason is that Westerners who are working in the Gulf for just two years are buying goods knowing that they will be abandoning them when they leave, while the much poorer Arab and Indian immigrants are buying all the consumer electronics they can to take with them. Although this lowers the demand for high-quality, big-margin goods, it enormously increases the overall size of the market.

Given these very strong distinctions between nationalities in the Arabian market, companies find themselves wondering whether they ought not to be directing their advertising to aim particular products at particular nationalities. In practice all have decided against the idea. Aiming overtly at Indians, Palestinians or Egyptians is politically impossible, although cigarette advertisements in Hindi can be seen in the flea-pit cinemas of the Dubai backstreets. Anything more conspicuous reminds Arabian nationals of their minority status in their own countries. In Bahrain and Dubai it is now the law that all posters and newspaper advertisements must have Arabic words or type bigger than any other script. The marketers have found, anyway, that it is normally best to aim at the indigenous Arabian population, which has much the richest potential buyers. Kuwaitis buy 70 per cent of all the cars sold by Alghanim, even though they account for rather less than half the population of the state. Shawket Subjally, a senior manager of Majid Futtaim's company in Dubai, which has the UAE agency for Toyota, told me in 1978 that he felt that a product which appeared to harmonise with the local culture created broader acceptance: 'My dearest wish is to get a Dubai girl model to go in the TV commercials,' he said. 'We're trying, but so far we haven't succeeded. It will come one day. Meanwhile we use Egyptians and Lebanese as the next best thing.'

Most of the other outstanding characteristics of the Arabian consumer market revolve around its lack of sophistication. This is something that is recognised by commerce ministries, which have been mainly concerned with the inflationary effects of the public's refusal to modify its eating habits in the face of shortages of particular foods. On several occasions ministries have said that the public needs training in comparing prices and the quality of goods. In Kuwait marketers have noticed that people often have no definite motives for buying things. This is not so much because they can be persuaded that they need things for which they have little use, in the tradition of the American housewife brainwashed by TV commercials – simply for a Kuwaiti to hear that a product is new, Western and high technology is often enough to make him buy it. This lack of discrimination on the part of the customers makes life difficult for the salesman who wants to explain that his new line has technical advantages over the competition. Whereas a Western housewife buying a washing machine will ask a whole range of questions – the number of programmes, the length of the guarantee, how many kilos of laundry it will take – Arabians entering the showroom often have no idea what to ask. They do not know how to distinguish quality in the face of cheaper competitors. Marketers say that part of the problem is that unlike Westerners, Arabian husbands and wives do not go window shopping – and this makes them far less aware of the range of products from which they can choose. Nor is there much chance of window shopping becoming a habit as more Arabians come back from holidays in the West. For couples, or wives on their own, to be seen walking through the town staring through shop windows would be totally out of keeping with the very private nature of Arabian life.

The same problem of consumer education occurs at the next stage. This is when the washing machine or refrigerator has been installed and the buyer reports after a few days that it will not work. Arabians themselves freely admit that they are not patient with machines; it is not part of their mentality. Many of them are also illiterate and the great majority does not have the reading habit. Arabians will always prefer to ask a question rather than read a notice; it is part of their liking for personalising things and for having personal contact replace the institutional aspects of life. Consequently when the Juffali company, the Saudi agent for Kelvinator, sells a washing machine or drier, it always sends someone from its own workshop to demonstrate the product in the buyer's home.

With this type of background it is not surprising that the Arabians are extremely brand conscious. In the Western industrialised world many people have adopted the habit of calling a product by the name of the leading brand in the market, but they apply it to only a few very well-known items, such as Sanka, the leading American decaffeinated coffee, or Hoover, the best-known make of vacuum cleaner in Britain. In Arabia the habit has gone much further and the list is endless: in Kuwait toothpaste is Kolynos, any type of washing powder is Tide, all electric shavers are Philishaves; in Saudi Arabia powdered milk is Nido, until recently pens were Parkers and sewing machines were Singers (pronounced Singe-ers), all tanker trucks are Whites. (This last example is atypical because it derives from the make of the first tankers to be brought into the Kingdom, not from the present trucks, which are nearly all Mercedes.) As with the preference for asking questions rather than reading instructions, this brand consciousness comes from the Arabians' passion for personalising things. They like to give a proper name to any modern product used in everyday life, rather than to try to think of it in the abstract and refer to it in general terms. The name gives the product a stronger identity, it even bestows affection on it. Better still is to give the product its own Arab name. This happened in Saudi Arabia during the 1950s and 1960s when transistor radios were known as Ahmed Saids, after the ranting political commentator on Cairo Radio.[3] More recently in Qatar, Rothmans king-size cigarettes have become known as Ali bin Alis, after the name of the local agent.

Most of the manufacturers who have been lucky enough to have their brand name adopted as the name of a product are those who arrived in the Arabian Peninsula early – in the 1950s and 1960s – and who had products that were relatively simple to maintain. They also had the good fortune to enter a market where most of the customers had none of the Westerner's desire to buy an unusual brand for the sake of being different or individualistic. Except among a small, well-travelled elite, this is still true today. The fact that other people are all buying the same brand only serves to endorse it as being the *right* brand in the eyes of most Arabians. There is even a snowball effect, where the popularity of a particular make of product leads to a shortage and so creates the impression that there is something especially desirable about that make. A few years ago this happened in Saudi Arabia with Mercedes trucks, which command 90 per cent of the independent truck owners' market. Despite the high price of Mercedes and the long waiting list there was virtually no evidence of a switch to other trucks; instead the Juffali managers say that hopeful buyers would try to bring influence to bear on the sub-dealers.

Helped by this extreme brand loyalty, various manufacturers in the 1960s were able to win market shares in Arabia which would be practically impossible in Europe or America. For years Singer, represented by Fahd Algosaibi in Saudi Arabia, outsold all other makes of sewing machines put together – despite the fact that it was not always competitive in price or quality. In Qatar in the late sixties Peugeot captured 30 per cent of the car market with just one or two models.

3. Ahmed Said was associated with much of the bombast and self-deception of Egypt and the Arab nation during the Nasser era. The Egyptians, who have a very funny and strongly self-deprecatory sense of humour, tell a joke about the emotional propagandist which has Alexander the Great, Hannibal and Napoleon meeting in heaven and reviewing their campaigns. 'If only I had another 10,000 men,' says Alexander, 'I would have conquered all Asia and the history of civilisation would have been different.' 'Ah,' replies Hannibal, 'and if I had had 100 more elephants I would have destroyed Rome.' 'Yes I know,' says Napoleon, 'and if I had had Ahmed Said nobody would have known that I lost Waterloo.'

In the last six or seven years several factors – mainly the influx of non-brand-conscious expatriates, and the spread of wealth that has brought the lower echelons of Arabian society within reach of buying consumer durables – have combined to erode the dominant position of the traditional brands. The establishment of improved service facilities to back new brands and the huge efforts to gain a share of the Arabian market made by companies in all the industrialised countries have had the same effect. Yet marketers say that in the Arabian Peninsula it is still more difficult than elsewhere to break into the market with a new brand in competition with the established favourite; and in some cases, as with the independent truckers and Mercedes trucks, scarcely anybody tries.

Summing up the character of his market the average Arabian agent would describe it as: multiracial, very conservative with strong brand loyalties and uneducated in the way it treats machinery. His problem then is how best to promote his product in this society.

First of all he is bound to advertise in newspapers and on billboards and television – but one feature that all these types of advertising have in common in the Arabian Peninsula is that they are much less effective than in the Western world. This is part of the reason why old brand loyalties remain so firmly entrenched. Managers in the Alghanim, Juffali and Futtaim companies have all said that people simply do not notice advertisements; the consumer society is too new for them to have learnt to respond to what they see on TV commercials or billboards. It seems they do not connect what they are told in ads with possessions they think they might need. The problem is made worse by the laughably bad quality of most advertisements produced in Arabia. There is a dearth of good advertising copywriters in the region, probably because people have not been brought up with continual sight of advertisements from the day they could read – or watch television. Another factor, suggested by Bakh Malak, the advertising manager for Alghanim, may be the emphasis placed by Arab schools on technical and scientific education at the expense of the arts and social sciences.

An alternative to having locally produced ads is to import campaigns from Europe and America, but these are often so out of tune with Arabian culture that they are ridiculed or ignored totally. Sometimes the pitfalls in imported campaigns can be quite subtle, as Kutayba

Alghanim explained with a hypothetical example, which he put in an article he wrote for *Management Review* in August 1976:

> Let's say you develop an ad campaign for a line of automobiles. You show a beautiful woman in a long white gown standing in front of a Southern-type mansion. Now that might represent an American dream and as such do what advertising is supposed to do: appeal to basic motivations in terms of desires and aspirations. But would it work in Kuwait? I don't think so – for the simple reason that while Kuwaitis might like the woman, they would not find the house particularly appealing . . . The question of values is fundamental to all marketing operations. It takes much preparation to properly identify local needs and to figure out how to appeal to basic motivations. And while you can influence and direct values, you cannot do so abruptly. If you try you're likely to fall flat on your face.

In accordance with these ideas the management of Yusuf Ahmed Alghanim and Sons probably has put more effort into working out ways of applying modern marketing to Arabian society than any other company in the region. It certainly has a reputation for much more imaginative marketing than any of its competitors. The company has established its own 'in-house' agency, which does all the creative work on its TV commercials and print ads in Arabic and English, and adapts American and English campaigns for use in Kuwait.

The agency has also launched a series of special promotions, which in a society that is not advertisement-minded have the built-in advantage of causing a stir and being talked about. Kuwait and all the other Arabian cities are notoriously gossip-prone; even today there is much more news conveyed by word of mouth than read in newspapers. One of the Alghanim campaigns gave car buyers a year's free insurance, and another, the 'Buy and Fly' campaign, gave air tickets to desirable holiday centres. The bigger the car the further the buyer was flown – Cairo, Paris, London, the Far East. Earlier there was an 'Every Customer a Salesman' campaign, in which buyers were given two coupons worth 50 dinars ($180) each, and promised that if they introduced one or two new buyers the company would exchange one or both of the coupons for cash. To the company's amazement it discovered within a few days of launching the campaign that a discount market for the coupons had sprung up in the souk. The incident was typical of the extremely mercantile mentality of Kuwaitis.

More successful still was a promotion in which every buyer was given a number. At the end of each week six numbers – one for the sales of each day – were drawn from a box, and those whose numbers came up got their cars free. From the moment the campaign was announced it made an impact. Within a matter of hours eighty-one Chevrolets were sold. Then in the following weeks it had a rather different but even better effect in encouraging people to go for the more expensive cars in the GM range. Every Thursday (the Muslim equivalent of the Western Saturday) the company would assemble the week's buyers for the draw, and because the occasion had at least as much natural drama as any TV lottery or sale programme, the television and newspapers would send teams to cover the event – thus giving YAAS huge additional publicity. There was great excitement, with embraces and interviews with the jubilant winners. Once somebody won a Cadillac and on another occasion a buyer won two pick-up trucks two weeks in succession.

Of all the Alghanim campaigns the most conventional in Western terms involved the company bringing in a team of beautiful girls to lure the public into its showrooms. Unlike the models at motor shows in the Western world, the girls were fully dressed – 'but they looked nice', as Khaled Said, the car division manager, put it. They moved around the showroom talking about the cars' performance and demonstrating some of the new electronic gadgets. The older generation, Kuwaitis in their fifties and sixties, did not approve; the next generation, those who had travelled and been educated abroad, accepted it; and the youngest age group got extremely excited. The promotion was a big success in that it got a big flow of people through the showrooms, but at the end of it all Khaled Said told me that the company was not sure what impact it had had in terms of sales or the group's image.

This is a concern one notices in all conversations with YAAS marketing men. The company is confident that overall its campaigns have helped it maintain the market for GM cars – but it is not always sure how successful one campaign has been compared with another, or how effective advertising has been compared with special promotions. Competitors take a more cynical view, suggesting that in launching its campaigns the company has been mainly concerned to be modern for the sake of impressing the market and giving itself a smart image. They argue that YAAS sales have not been much increased by the campaigns and that the whole exercise has given the company huge unnecessary overheads. The Alghanim reply is that as markets become more difficult after the boom years of the 1970s other companies will have to incur bigger overheads in bringing their marketing up to date, and that having started the process first Alghanim will then be better placed than the rest. Similarly it is argued that there is no reason why Arabians should remain permanently insensitive to advertisements. They will gradually become more advertisement-conscious and any company that makes the effort to produce better advertisements can speed the process to its own advantage. The suggestion is that for the time being the adoption of modern marketing practices has been something of an act of faith. Alghanim and any other company that introduces new methods has to admit that it is walking on untested ground.

7

⚜

Juffali and the Truckers

Everyone who visits Saudi Arabia is impressed by the numbers of heavy trucks he sees on the roads. They are driven fast, often in convoys. They carry loads of cement, rocks, steel bars, bricks, pieces of machinery, gasoline, water, sheep, goats, crates of food. The drivers range from boys in their teens to quite old men. All of them dress the same, in rather shabby white *thobes* with their heads wrapped in red and white checkered *ghotras*; they all overload their trucks, and they are all prepared to drive their trucks over almost any type of rock or desert terrain. The same heavy trucks, grey-green in colour, can be seen in every village, on patches of waste ground in the middle of towns, and in huge parks on the outskirts of the cities.

In Saudi Arabia people talk of trucking as a major part of the economy. Trucks are the physical link between the fast-developing urban centres of Riyadh, Jeddah and the Dammam–Dhahran sprawl and the traditional world of the small towns and villages. They provide one of the most important sources of employment for people leaving their old lives in the desert and moving into the modern economy financed by oil. What every visitor notices sooner or later about the trucks he sees is that they are almost all the same: they are slightly out of date, six-wheeler and four-wheeler Mercedes.[1]

Saudi Arabia is the trucking country *par excellence*. It has a huge area, a quarter the size of the United States, and a scattered population – and it has been undergoing the biggest building boom in history. Almost everything the Kingdom consumes is imported. Not only construction

1. The material in this chapter will no doubt be good publicity for Daimler Benz. I would like to stress therefore, that I have not written this chapter at the instigation of Daimler Benz, nor in consultation with the company; during the course of research I did not meet any Daimler Benz employees. The material here comes partly from Juffali managers and partly from employees of other Arabian merchant groups.

materials, but virtually all of its durable goods, consumer products and foodstuffs have to be trucked inland from the ports of Jeddah and Dammam. The industrial plants and agricultural projects in the Kingdom likewise are dependent on a large truck fleet to link them with their markets. Any new plant finds itself supplying a market spread over a huge area; gearing the plant to a smaller area and a smaller population would make it unable to take advantage of economies of scale and render it uneconomic. There is even a need to transport water by truck. Many communities that have an inadequate water supply are too small to justify the laying of a pipeline from a bigger oasis or desalination plant.

There is no prospect of trucks becoming less important in the near future. Saudi Arabia has only one railway, built from Dammam to Riyadh in the early 1950s, and although there are plans to build more lines and reopen the old Hijaz railway running from Damascus, nothing is likely to be in operation until the later 1980s. It may even be that the railway plans will never go ahead. Like the development of a comprehensive bus service they would damage the livelihood of the independent Nejdi truck and taxi owners. These are important subjects of the royal family.

During the 1980s the number of trucks in Saudi Arabia will continue to grow. Already the Kingdom has as many heavy trucks as Britain, which gives it the biggest truck population per capita in the world. Of this market Daimler Benz, the manufacturers of Mercedes, and their Saudi agents, E.A. Juffali and Brothers, have about 70 per cent. The figure used to be higher, but the growth of truck fleets operated by modern transport companies and foreign contractors has recently reduced the Mercedes hold. The contractors have mostly bought whatever trucks they have been used to operating at home, which in the last ten years, as Far Eastern companies have entered the market, has given a big opportunity to Japanese manufacturers. Notwithstanding this minor setback Daimler Benz still finds that Juffali is the biggest market for its commercial vehicles outside Germany.

The basis of Juffali's performance is its success among the independent truck-owners, where nobody questions that the company still has a market share of 95 per cent. In many country areas one sees no trucks at all except Mercedes. The Juffali dominance of this part of the market is so complete and has been as it is for so long that competitors say that it is not even worth their trying to break in. Because they are not attempting to compete, their Western employees have come to take a detached professional interest in the Juffali truck business. They admire the company for achieving what must be one of the most spectacular marketing successes of the century, and they look upon the truckers themselves as an interesting and possibly unique social phenomenon.

The typical Saudi trucker is a bedouin or villager, usually from central Arabia. He comes in from the desert wanting to remain as independent as possible, and he chooses one of three very similar jobs – driving taxis, trucks or construction equipment. If he opts for trucks he enters employment with a relation or a man from his tribe who already owns several trucks, or he might work with a contracting company with its own fleet. He saves his wages and supplements his income by using his employer's vehicle at night to undertake private commissions of his own. (It is because the drivers work too long hours and get too little sleep that there are so many accidents involving trucks in Saudi Arabia.) After a time the new driver accumulates enough money to buy a truck in partnership with his brothers or cousins. Eventually he has the money to make a down payment on his own truck. He goes into the offices of a Juffali sub-dealer, hitches up his *thobe*, and produces a dirty bundle of 50,000 riyals ($15,000) in large, blue SR100 notes, dangling from a string tied to a belt around his waist. This represents 20 per cent of the SR250,000 needed to buy the cheapest of the heavy Mercedes trucks. He dumps the cash on the table, watches the dealer's clerk count it, and then takes his truck and drives away.

With their own trucks the drivers used to assemble every morning in the truck park, which lies on a plot of litter-strewn waste ground on the outskirts of every Saudi town. This park acted as the truck market. In a corner was the tent of the broker. This man was simply a driver with a more forceful and enterprising personality than his fellows or the owner of two or three more trucks. He happened to have built up a good range of contacts with builders and traders, and whenever these people needed some trucks for a few days they sent word to him. As in every other market the hire rates fluctuated day by day according to demand.

Now there is still some business done in the truck parks but they are less important than they used to be. Owner drivers are fewer. The new fashion is for owners to buy two or three trucks as quickly as possible and manage them. The drivers employed by these small capitalists are not badly paid – they make a minimum of SR 5,000 ($1,500) a month, which is as much as a junior executive in Saudi Arabia.

If they are near their base, at night the truckers drive a little way into the desert and make their own encampments, sleeping between their trucks and the camp fire. They have great affection for their trucks. When a Daimler Benz team came out to Saudi Arabia to do a survey to determine what size of truck might be best suited to the market in future, it wrote in its report that the bedouin called their trucks *umm al awlad* – mother of their children. If they are general-purpose trucks with wooden bodies, as opposed to tippers or tankers, the drivers paint the wooden frames a bright bluish green, with geometrical patterns in red and yellow. The cab is left the usual grey-green, but other metal parts and the tool boxes underneath the bodies have unlikely pastoral scenes painted on them. A favourite design is an Alpine lake picture, with yachts, lakeside villas with brilliant pink roofs, poplar trees, and snow-covered peaks in the distance. Presumably the pictures, always done in the most lurid colours, represent an Arabian's dream of a cool, green ideal land.

In mechanical matters the truckers are more practical and conservative. There are several reasons why they like Mercedes. The trucks are fast, easy to repair by the standards of most trucks, and very high off the ground, which makes them suitable for cross-desert work. They are also extremely strong. Juffali has its trucks fitted with all the conventional tropical modifications, such as a bigger radiator, but also has Daimler Benz provide some special features, including stronger suspension, a reinforced rear-axle case and a stronger chassis. This enables the drivers to load their trucks with up to double the specified weight without their showing too obvious strain.

Above all the bedouin choose Mercedes because everybody else has them. In their eyes it is simply the piece of equipment a man buys when he goes into the trucking business. Furthermore the Mercedes has to be grey-green, and it has to have the conventional bonnet protruding at the front. This, the drivers feel, gives them something solid between them and their victim in the event of an accident. In effect the truck has to be built in the old 1960s style. Doubts exist as to whether any other model in any other colour is a genuine Mercedes.

Ahmed Juffali, who presides over E.A. Juffali and Brothers, is a small, clean-shaven man in his mid-fifties, with little outward appearance of great authority or force of character. His most conspicuous qualities are a quiet charm and considerable intelligence. He is not a man of extremes; he is known as being neither especially generous nor especially mean, he is hospitable, but not spectacularly so. The qualities that have helped him build the biggest merchant business in the Arabian Peninsula are determination, hard work and good luck, together with a willingness to delegate and a talent for choosing good subordinates – both of which are most unusual qualities in Arabia. He has also been willing to take the initiative in introducing new ideas before other Saudi businessmen – though he has always thought long and hard before doing so. He is extremely cautious, almost reluctant in taking decisions. Jafar Ma'an Askari, his finance manager and one of the two or three key figures in the organisation, once said to me: 'Ahmed makes up his mind slowly, rather like King Faisal used to do' – which in Saudi Arabian terms is a considerable compliment.

Ahmed started in business in the early 1940s, when he was still in his teens. His father, who had moved from Onaizah to Mecca in the early years of this century, had died when Ahmed and his brother Ali were still children. From that time they had been brought up by their elder brother, Ibrahim. In 1940 the family had begun general trading, but it was only when Ahmed won the agency for GEC, the British electronics company, and a concession for the electricity supply of Taif in 1946, that the family firm began its development as a modern company.

With the Taif contract the Juffalis were breaking entirely new ground. They had no previous experience of electricity generation, no idea of what the town's consumption might be, not even any population figures. They had to go round the bakeries of Taif and work out a rough census on the basis of the number of loaves baked daily. Then, when they brought their plant on stream in 1950, they found they had only 125 subscribers. They had installed a capacity of 1,200 kilowatts, but the maximum daytime consumption reached only 70 kw. People were simply unaware of what they would be able to do if they brought electricity into their houses. The company had to turn on the street lights during the day to keep its generators running and resort to various devices to bring in new subscribers. It offered ridiculously low installation costs and made a point of getting at least one subscriber in every street, in the hope that this would encourage others through a 'keep up with the Mohammads' effect.

In the next few years the Juffalis moved their base to Jeddah, where it has remained, won a concession for the Mecca electricity supply and began collecting further agencies. These were mainly for electrical and

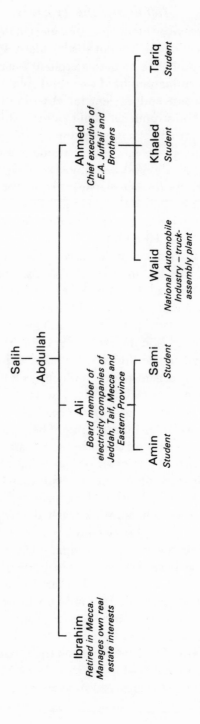

JUFFALI FAMILY TREE

Ibrahim
*Retired in Mecca.
Manages own real
estate interests*

Salih

Abdullah

Ali
*Board member of
electricity companies of
Jeddah, Taif, Mecca and
Eastern Province*

Amin
Student

Sami
Student

Ahmed
*Chief executive of
E.A. Juffali and
Brothers*

Walid
*National Automobile
Industry – truck-
assembly plant*

Khaled
Student

Tariq
Student

mechanical equipment, which they felt had potential for growth now that the government had the money to begin spending on development. Then in 1956 Ahmed made what in retrospect is seen as a masterstroke: he decided to establish a major operation in Riyadh. At that time the Saudi capital was kept shut off from the modernising influences that were felt by Jeddah and the Eastern Province, and it was neglected by Saudi and foreign businessmen. Although there were a few old Nejdi families with relatively small businesses in Riyadh, none of the leading Saudi merchants had thought it worth establishing a major presence. The fact that the Juffalis were first to break this pattern – and were Nejdis by birth – has yielded them a huge dividend in the last ten years or so. During this time Riyadh has been the centre of the fastest changing region of the Kingdom.

The man chosen to manage the Riyadh office was Omar Aggad, a Palestinian who had transferred to Ahmed Juffali from GEC in 1951. Aggad had already served two years as the manager of the Juffali office in the Eastern Province and had proved himself the company's most able manager. Once installed in Riyadh, which has been his home since 1957, he won the contract for the city's street lighting. In 1960 he followed this with the Daimler Benz agency. Ironically Ahmed was not enthusiastic about the company at the time. Daimler Benz had never done well in Saudi Arabia. Over the previous twenty years or so it had flirted with Haji Abdullah Alireza, then been taken up by Hussein Alireza, who found its cars too small and too low on the ground compared with American cars, and then switched to two other old established merchants. These were Jazar in Riyadh and Jeddah, and Haddad in the Eastern Province. Jazar, who had had to promise to buy a substantial number of vehicles in order to lure Daimler Benz away from Hussein Alireza, found the agency a complete disaster. He was able to sell only a fraction of his initial stock. It therefore took considerable force on the part of Aggad to persuade Ahmed Juffali to take on the agency for the entire Kingdom. Aggad virtually signed up the agency by himself. He says that his value to Ahmed lay in a huge personal rapport and the faith that Ahmed had in him. The independence he was given was less a matter of conscious delegation than of instinctive trust on Ahmed's part. Without it, Aggad told me in 1978, he would never have worked for Ahmed's company. Today Jafar Askari describes Aggad as 'possibly the best professional manager in the Middle East'. His qualities have been an almost perfect complement to his employer's: whereas

Ahmed provides the element of caution, Aggad is bold and impulsive, an intuitive decision-taker with a huge head for detail.

Aggad made the Mercedes agency work by producing the idea for a comprehensive network of dealers, recruited from inside the trucking business. This has been the basis of the Juffali sales operation ever since. Virtually all of the men signed up by Aggad and other managers over the past twenty years have been truckers or brokers, who have been socially and professionally on a level with their customers and can vouch for the truck they are selling. The dealers have remained rather unsophisticated men even though many of them are now millionaires many times over; one of the most successful has still never set foot outside Saudi Arabia. They have no need for glossy showrooms or smart sales talk, because there is virtually no chance of their potential customers buying any rival truck. Their sales transactions used to take place in the scruffy milieu of the truck parks and brokers' tents. Now most of the dealers have moved their operations to Riyadh, which has become the truck sales centre for the Kingdom. The dealers still maintain links with the provincial towns from which they came, but they have been encouraged to set up business in Riyadh by the increasing competition of the market. Truck buyers now come to Riyadh to shop around the different dealers to see how much credit they can get.

Having been drivers themselves and having maintained their links with the provinces, the dealers know – or can find out – whether each of their customers is a trustworthy man to whom they can give credit and be sure of being repaid. If by chance a buyer defaults, they are close enough to the gossip in the trucking business to be able to track him down. (Interestingly, debt-collecting is quite a popular profession among ordinary Saudi citizens.)

The dealers' grassroots knowledge is important because the Juffali managers reckon that credit has been as important as the dealership system in giving Mercedes its huge market share. The dealers pay for their trucks partly in cash and partly in instalments, and they sell to their customers in the same way. This spreads the burden of financing the sale between three parties – the buyer, the dealer and Juffali. The subtle part of the Juffali scheme has been to vary the credit terms according to the buoyancy of the market.

The company also made it its policy from the beginning to establish its own service and spare parts network, which runs rather against the normal practice in the Western world, where service and dealer networks are separate. The Juffali management believed rightly that if service were left to the dealers few would provide adequate facilities, the truck would gain a bad reputation and sales would be damaged. As it turned out, the relative ease of doing repair work on the Mercedes soon led to the Juffali service operation being supplemented by small private workshops. Within a few years of the establishment of the dealer network there were hundreds of garages all over the Kingdom able to do some of the repair work themselves.

Daimler Benz now accounts for about 60 per cent of the Juffali turnover, which in 1982 was estimated to be running at some $1.2–1.5 billion, though the exact figure was a closely guarded secret. Even if the lower end of the range was the more accurate, this would still have made the company the biggest merchant group in the Arabian Peninsula.

The part of the Juffali turnover that is not accounted for by Daimler Benz is made up of income from various contracting and industrial subsidiaries and some sixty sales agencies, mostly representing manufacturers of machinery. The most important of these include Siemens, L.M. Ericsson, BICC, Barber-Greene – the American manufacturer of asphalting machinery, FMC and Peiner cranes, Massey-Ferguson, Michelin, IBM, and York air conditioners made by Borg-Warner. Given the relatively undeveloped state of Saudi Arabia, the government's gigantic development programme, and the private-sector building boom – which, among its other effects, has made the Kingdom the world's third biggest market for unit air conditioners – these are an almost perfect set of agencies for a Saudi trading company. They are much more lucrative in Saudi Arabia than electronics and consumer durables agencies, which are the basis of many fortunes in the affluent Gulf states.

In industry Juffali's investments include a company with Korf Industries and other Saudi investors, which produces steel-wire mesh for building contractors, an air-conditioner manufacturing joint-venture with Borg-Warner and shares in two of the Kingdom's biggest cement plants. The company has also joined with Daimler Benz to establish a truck assembly plant just outside Jeddah. This began operations in 1977. The plant, staffed mainly by Turks who have worked as *gastarbeiter* in Daimler Benz factories in Germany, now produces all of the conventional Mercedes trucks with bonnets that are marketed in Saudi Arabia. The newer types of Mercedes, which are sold to contractors and fleet owners, Juffali continues to import.

In contracting, the biggest Juffali operation is a joint venture with Fluor, the US oil and chemical plant engineer, which has managed the construction of the Kingdom's $20 billion gas-gathering project and two of the petrochemical plants at the Jubail industrial city. Other Juffali partners are Siemens, in an electrical contracting company, the Texan civil contractor, Henry C. Beck, which built the Riyadh Marriott Hotel, and L.M. Ericsson. The last of these companies has carried out much of the work on the government's $6 billion Telephone Expansion Project.

Omar Aggad, who played a major role in developing E.A. Juffali and Brothers in the 1950s and 1960s, is now involved with the company's operations only where he is an investor with it in manufacturing ventures. He devotes most of his time to his numerous private business interests. Like other senior Juffali managers, he used to have a profit-sharing arrangement with his employer, which made him one of the richest Saudi businessmen in his own right. In the last ten years he has become a leading promoter of Saudi private industry. His place as head of the Riyadh office has been taken by Ibrahim Touq, who works with Jafar Askari as the main day-to-day manager of the group. Askari is a rotund, genial Iraqi – a King's College, Cambridge, man – who is based on the head office in Jeddah and is the manager in most regular contact with Ahmed Juffali. Both Askari and Touq have strong commitment to the organisation for which they work, though Touq has a private business in which he employs his own professional managers. I once asked him why he did not devote his energies wholly to his own business: he replied that as he had helped build the biggest private company in Saudi Arabia he wanted to stay with it and see how it evolved.

The moral of the story of Juffali and Daimler Benz is that a rigorously thorough marketing campaign, where the salesman can get on the same level as the customer and involve himself in the details of his business, can be extremely effective in the Middle East. Apart from Juffali, there is the classic example of Almana Trading, the Peugeot agent in Qatar.

Omar Almana, a member of the oldest established merchant family in Qatar, signed up Peugeot in 1959, but he found that there was a popular objection to buying French cars at the time because the Algerian war was still in progress and the French were tarred with the brush of colonial repression. Another problem was that the market, such as it was, was dominated by Austin and Opel. After a few years, however, Omar worked out a scheme based on employing European-trained mechanics and building up a very large stock of spare parts, which he knew to be a great weakness of his competitors. He gave every purchaser a letter which said that if their Peugeot (pronounced 'Peegeot' in Qatar) broke down and was kept out of service through lack of spares in his garage he would pay them 80 riyals (about $20) a day. The competitors promptly put it about that the letters were a joke, but as cars began to break down it was seen that Almana Trading was as good as its word. To help public opinion draw the right conclusion the company arranged for a few cars to be kept in its garage, even though it had the necessary spares in stock, so that it could be seen to pay out its 80 riyals.

The whole scheme had particular appeal to taxi drivers, who then expected daily takings of no more than 20 riyals. Peugeots were a logical buy for these men. They were strong, high off the ground and fitted with a bench front seat. This enabled the driver to take two passengers beside him in the front. The company gave further encouragement to the taxi drivers by paying some of them 200 riyals a month to stay outside the hotels and the airport and 'talk about their cars', as Omar Almana put it to me, to any passenger who looked as if he might be a likely customer. The drivers were given a supply of brochures to hand out and promised that they would get a bonus on their monthly payment every time they introduced a new buyer.

In more developed and less freewheeling societies the authorities and the press would probably have taken exception to some of Almana's methods, but in Qatar in the 1960s they were entirely acceptable. They replaced the need for any other form of advertising except a few banners across the roads. By 1970 Almana and Peugeot had 30 per cent of the Qatar car market, and even though the last ten years has seen the Japanese car invasion in the Middle East, the Peugeot market share is still reckoned to be only a little below 20 per cent. Apart from remaining popular with the taxi drivers, the make is a favourite with the government's professional expatriate employees – teachers and doctors – who often buy Peugeots with the interest-free car loans they are given.

The problem now for manufacturers and agents in the Arabian Peninsula is that the days when one could mount the type of sales campaign that Juffali and Almana mounted in the 1960s are probably coming to a close. The increasing regulation of commercial life would prevent a repetition of Almana's commission arrangements with the taxi drivers, while the growing size of the markets would make it difficult for anyone to establish from scratch the type of dealer network that Juffali set up among the Saudi truckers. In the past these intensive sales methods were much more effective than Western-style advertising, but now it seems that the market has reached a transitional phase where the old methods are no longer practicable but conventional Western advertising and promotion are as yet unproven.

What is not challenged by anyone involved in selling machinery of any type in Arabia is that the most effective way of building a reputation for a product is by providing good service. This may be true anywhere in the world, but it is especially important in a highly brand-conscious market, where people buy in response to personal recommendation rather than advertisements. So far Arabian companies have been notably poor at providing service. They have found it difficult to hire good personnel, with the result that work on a car which would take a day in Europe or America, in Arabia takes a week.

Most of the more traditional-minded merchants have also been reluctant to commit capital to building workshops that not only fail to yield the very large profits that are customary in Arabian trade, but are liable to run at a loss. Their instinct has always been to put their profits into more stock, real estate or foreign investment. Manufacturers normally include in their agency contracts a requirement that their agents provide service facilities of a certain standard, but in the past Arabian agents have been so universally casual in observing these clauses that manufacturers who have been dissatisfied with their agents' performance have not felt it worthwhile to switch. Instead they have tried to provide what help they can by sending staff to establish the servicing operation, seconding some of their own mechanics and taking Indian and Arab staff for training. What they have not normally been prepared to do is commit their own capital to the operation. A company which proved to be an exception to this was Komatsu, the Japanese bulldozer manufacturer represented by the Jeddah firm of A.S. Bugshan and Brothers. On finding that its agent was not wholly enthusiastic about establishing a large service depot, it invested in a depot of its own. Its decision paid off dramatically. From being virtually unknown in Saudi Arabia in the early 1970s, Komatsu bulldozers are now number two in the market after Caterpillar.

In the last few years of quieter trading conditions the Arabian agents' attitude to service has undergone a partial change. When markets were growing by up to 50 per cent a year in the mid-1970s there were opportunities and profits for all, but now to expand sales a business has to show itself to be better than its competitors. One response to this has been the greater interest shown in advertising; another has been the attempts made by trading houses to improve their service. There has almost been something of a 'service craze' among importers. Every merchant says that of all parts of his business he is proudest of his new service facilities, or, as proof of the seriousness of his intentions, he quotes figures to show how much capital he is planning to invest in this sphere of operations. The problem is that not all of the fine words have been followed by as much investment as promised. Except among the most modern establishments there is an instinctive trader's reluctance to put vast sums of capital into something that is not going to yield a direct profit; the preference is to invest a little at a time. This approach and the flaw in it are summed up by some remarks made to me in 1978 by Ibrahim Touq: 'What often happens here is that the agent suggests to the manufacturer that he modernises his service facilities as he increases his sales. But this means that the early buyers get a bad deal, and so the product gets a bad reputation at the start. It is one of those facts that one has to install the service before selling the product – before one can tell whether the product is going to be a success. The investment is high but one has to approach it as an act of faith.'

8

⚜️

W.J. Towell – the Rice Monopolist

William Jack Towell arrived in Muscat in 1866. The Sultanate then was going through one of its more turbulent phases. In the year Towell landed, the ruling Sultan was shot in his sleep; in the following year there were two separate civil wars, Muscat was besieged and bombarded, and the new Sultan, who had murdered his father, was sent into exile.

Jack Towell, however, seems not to have been worried by these disturbances. Nobody knows much about him, except that he was an American, a sailor or possibly a ship's chandler, and that he was travelling with his wife. Haji Ali Sultan, who now runs the business he founded, suggested to me during a conversation in his office in Muttrah that there were several reasons why Towell might have stayed: 'Maybe it was because Muscat was a quiet place [sic], or because there were two other Americans in Oman, or maybe he spotted an opportunity for doing business with the US.' Haji Ali once tried to find out more about Towell, but he discovered that all but one of the papers of his grandfather, who knew Towell, had been destroyed thirty years ago.

What is known from the single surviving document, is that Towell established a trading firm and in 1881 employed Archibald McKirdy, a citizen of Rothesay on the west coast of Scotland. Three years later he took on a twenty-six-year-old assistant named Mohammad Fazil, a Khoja Indian of British nationality, who had been born in Bombay and educated at the Elphinstone High School, Bombay. This man, the grandfather of Haji Ali, had come to Muscat in 1878 and worked as a merchant on his own for several years, but whether his parents had already been established in Muscat and had simply been visiting India at the time of his birth, or whether Mohammad Fazil was the first member of his family to live in Oman, nobody knows. The reason his date of birth and place of education are known is that McKirdy on his arrival had taken on the post of United States vice-consul (there was no full consul in Oman), making Mohammad Fazil his deputy in 1893; and a few years later he had been obliged in response to a State Department circular to report on the country in which he worked, his duties and the staff of his office. A copy of this report is the surviving document possessed by Haji Ali. Part of the report, handwritten and dated 31 December 1901, has become illegible, but what can be read gives a fair impression of the business and consular work McKirdy and Mohammad did together:

> . . . Principal industries are the cultivation of dates and fisheries. Exports to the United States during the twelve months ending June 30th 1901 consisted of 20,486 boxes of dates valued at $28,857.87 US gold. Imports from the United States consisted of shooks[1] for date boxes, nails, [*word illegible*] paper and Massachusetts [*word illegible*] sheetings valued at $26,436.75 US gold . . . The mass of the people are very poor and families live on $3/- per month . . . Only one American citizen, a missionary, resides here. Amongst the wealthier Arabs and Indians the general cost of living is from $50 to 100 per month . . . My official duties concern invoices, protection of the household of the Arabian Mission, payment of visits of courtesy to the Sultan and receiving visits from the Sultan and his suite [retinue] on Independence and New Year's day. Courtesy visits are also exchanged between the British and French Consuls and occasionally between various foreign warships [*word illegible*]. Office hours 10 a.m. to 4 p.m. on week days. Volume of business small viz: 32 invoices certified, 32 supplementary bills of health[2] issued and 19 enquiries from American businessmen, during fiscal year ended 30th June 1901 . . . The only furniture in my office belonging to Government is two wooden presses [Scottish expression for book shelves] for holding books, stationery etc. These are in fair condition. Nothing is charged for office rent. The total office expenses (no salaries are paid) during past fiscal year ending June 30th 1901 amounted to $75.48.

By the time this report was written Jack Towell had left Oman,

1. A shook is a bound pack of the pieces of wood – staves and headings – required to make a barrel or box.

2. A bill of health is an official certificate given to the master of a vessel stating whether at the time of sailing any infectious disease existed in the port or on the ship.

handing over his business to McKirdy. It is thought that his departure was caused by loneliness after the death of his wife. Then in 1906 McKirdy too left, selling the business to Mohammad Fazil for 11,000 rupees (about $3,400). At this time the firm acted as agents for the British India Line, Lloyds – the London insurance market, and John D. Rockefeller's Standard Oil Company – from which it bought kerosene, produced in the United States. The export side of the business consisted of selling pomegranates to India and dates to India and the United States. In the US there was a healthy demand for Omani dates before large-scale production started in California, while in India dates were an essential part of Hindu marriage feasts.

Besides his commercial activities Mohammad Fazil continued his work as deputy US consul, taking over as vice-consul in years when there was no member of the US Consular Service in residence. He became one of the prominent members of the community, referred to as 'the wearer of glasses' and well known for his knowledge of medicines, which he gained from reading medical books, and his work as an amateur doctor and pharmacist. He participated in a scheme with the grandfather of Qais Zawawi, the present Minister of State, for laying a water pipe to Muttrah. With the money he made from trade he bought the tiny oasis village of Ayyint, between Muttrah and Shutaifi. His family would retire to the wells and date gardens of the village during the hottest summer months and whenever there was an outbreak of plague in the town.

Mohammad died in 1916, a year after the Americans had finally closed their consulate. His son, Sultan, whose name is now used as the name of the family, was more interested in medicine than business; there are still many old men in Muscat and Muttrah who remember going to his dispensary to receive prescriptions. By the later 1920s Sultan had handed over the firm to his eldest son, Abdel-Reza, but Oman during the inter-war years was falling into such a wretched condition that there was little business to be done. Ever since the division of the Sultanates of Oman and Zanzibar in the mid-nineteenth century, and the suppression of the slave and arms trades by the British, Oman had been in a state of slow decline. In the early decades of the twentieth century, when the states in the Gulf were enjoying a modest prosperity from pearling, Oman languished under the debt-ridden rule of Sultan Taimur, and for forty years from 1932 his son, Said, kept the country largely shut off from the outside world. Oman's history in this century has been completely different from that of the Gulf states. It was not affected by the decline of the pearl industry in the 1930s, nor by the arrival of oil revenues in most of the Gulf in the late 1940s. Ironically, during the Second World War, when the Gulf states' fortunes were at their very lowest, Oman enjoyed a brief respite in its decline, when the British made Muscat a depot for the distribution of food supplies in the area. After the war the Sultanate returned to isolation and poverty.

During these years the Sultan family educated its children and waited for conditions to improve. Ali and his brothers were taught English by tutors who came from India – Ali remembers using Macmillan's primers and readers. In due course he was given a Hermes typewriter and told to practise his English by copying the firm's correspondence, and then he was entrusted with the task of drafting letters, which his eldest brother, Abdel-Reza, corrected.

The decisive moment for the family came in 1947. Abdel-Reza was going on the pilgrimage to Mecca, taking the opportunity of visiting *en route* Kuwait and Iraq, where his company had established small sub-dealerships for Dunlop tyres and some tobacco companies. These it represented throughout the Gulf area. At Kuwait the merchant who acted as the Towell representative, Ahmed Zayed Sarhan, came out to Abdel-Reza's ship to pay the normal courtesy call and tell him in detail about the business opportunities that were coming from the production of oil, which had started in the previous year. Abdel-Reza was much impressed. When he returned to Oman he told his brothers about the conversation, and they promptly decided that they should establish an office in Kuwait. As the *de facto* head of the family, Abdel-Reza stayed in Muttrah, arranging for his brothers, Qamar, Ali and Ahmed to take it in turns to run the Kuwaiti operation. It became their practice to spend six or eight months at a stretch in Kuwait, leaving their wives and children at home in Oman.[3]

The new business dealt in a rag-bag collection of items – foreign exchange, films, perfumes, Castrol motor oil. For the first year the family operated without a proper shop; turnover was small. Then in 1948 there was a sudden shortage of *ghee* (cooking fat) in Kuwait at a time when the Sultans knew that there were large quantities in Muttrah

3. The Omani Sultan family in Kuwait is not to be confused with the Kuwaiti Sultan family, whose members include Fawzi Sultan, a director of the Bank of Kuwait and the Middle East and International Financial Advisers.

SULTAN FAMILY TREE

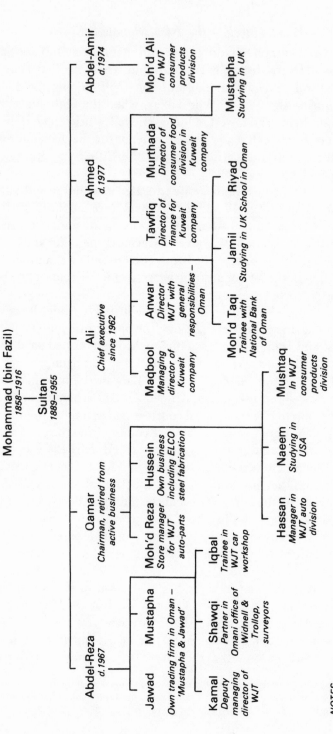

Mohammad (bin Fazil)
1858–1916

Sultan
1889–1955

Abdel-Reza
d.1967

Qamar
Chairman, retired from active business

Jawad
Own trading firm in Oman – 'Mustapha & Jawad'

Mustapha

Moh'd Reza
Store manager for WJT auto-parts

Hussein
Own business including ELCO steel fabrication

Kamal
Deputy managing director of WJT

Shawqi
Partner in Omani office of Widnell & Trollop, surveyors

Iqbal
Trainee in WJT car workshop

Hassan
Manager in WJT auto division

Naeem
Studying in USA

Ali
Chief executive since 1962

Maqbool
Managing director of Kuwait company

Anwar
Director WJT with general responsibilities – Oman

Moh'd Taqi
Trainee with National Bank of Oman

Mushtaq
In WJT consumer products division

Ahmed
d.1977

Tawfiq
Director of finance for Kuwait company

Murthada
Director of consumer food division in Kuwait company

Jamil
Studying in UK School in Oman

Riyad
Studying in UK School in Oman

Abdel-Amir
d.1974

Moh'd Ali
In WJT consumer products division

Mustapha
Studying in UK

NOTES

1. W.J. Towell is officially a limited liability company, but for practical purposes within the Sultan family it is a partnership. In the Omani operation, W.J. Towell & Co., the partners are Haji Qamar, Haji Ali, Kamal Abdel-Reza, the heirs of Haji Abdel-Amir – represented by Hussein Jawad, and the heirs of Haji Ahmed – represented by his sons Tawfiq and Murthada. The partners in the Kuwaiti operation, W.J. Towell & Co. Agencies, are the same as in Oman with the addition of Hussein Jawad, a Kuwaiti citizen, who is the son of Haji Ali's sister and son-in-law of Haji Abdel-Amir. Hussein Jawad's share of the Kuwaiti operation is 51 per cent.

2. The directors of W.J. Towell & Co. in Oman are Haji Qamar, Haji Ali, Kamal, Anwar and Maqbool. In Kuwait the directors are Maqbool, Hussein Jawad, Tawfiq and Murthada.

and Gwadur, a small enclave in Pakistan which was then still ruled by
Oman. They promptly asked the brothers in Muttrah to send 1,000 tins
of *ghee*, which they sold to a member of the Alghanim family for 100
rupees a tin. Before his death in 1977, Ahmed told me that he remembered being immensely impressed by his first sight of a 100,000-rupee
cheque. A little later the family concluded an extremely profitable
rice-importing deal, selling directly to members of the Sabah family;
and from then on for the next fifteen years, as the Kuwaiti boom began
to gather momentum causing a constant series of shortages of different
commodities, they continued to import odd batches of foodstuffs in
bulk. Sometimes it was rice, sometimes sugar or *ghee*. The quantities
were normally between 25 and 50 tons.

It was a rice deal that led to the next big breakthrough, in the early
1960s. By this time the business in Kuwait was well established and
being run by Haji Ahmed. Already Ahmed was proving himself a
brilliant trader. He had an uncanny ability for spotting opportunities
and turning unpromising situations to his own advantage. He never
missed a chance to make capital out of other people's mistakes, and if he
felt he could gain a moral advantage by exposing anything questionable
in other businessmen's dealings with him, he would do so. His coup in
the rice market, which showed all of these traits, involved his breaking
into the export business for the Pakistani rice known as basmati. For
several years the Pakistan Rice Board had been selling the export quota
of its crop of basmati through a consortium of twelve Karachi merchants led by one Hussein Murwani. Murwani was an experienced
operator but not a person whom anyone trusted – 'an absolute crook'
was how an international commodities merchant later described him to
me. He had a reputation in the trade for winning contracts by putting in
the highest bids, but then failing to pay or take delivery of his rice.
When he did intend to honour a contract, it was his practice to make a
down payment for a small proportion of the rice and give guarantees for
the rest. To market the rice he appointed foreign agents, who in 1963
included the Kuwaiti offices of Towell and the British trading house
Gray Mackenzie. It was at this point that Murwani made his mistake:
'Unfortunately he omitted to tell us that he was appointing Gray
Mackenzie,' Haji Ahmed explained to me fourteen years later. 'He also
arranged different financial terms with the British company. So there
was a long dispute. I went to Pakistan several times and I told Murwani
that unless we could settle the problem I would buy direct from the

government; to all intents and purposes Murwani was the merchant who counted, he had a majority in the partnership . . . In the end the negotiations failed; so in 1965 I went direct to the government and bought 30,000 tons, with an offer of cash which I backed up with a letter of credit.'

Once he had the contract Ahmed turned himself to making basmati the most popular rice in the Arabian Peninsula. It was not easy to cook well but had a very distinct dry, spicy flavour of its own, which made it easy to tell from the usual American or Egyptian rice. It also had the strange quality of improving with age. Ahmed decided to give his product a special image in Arabian eyes. He called it 'Peshawa' rice – an entirely new name – and advertised it on television and in the newspapers, stressing that the sole importer was W.J. Towell. The campaign worked. Peshawa sold excellently, quickly becoming the most popular type of rice in Kuwait, the lower Gulf and the Saudi Eastern Province.

Ahmed and his brothers were encouraged by the success. At the end of 1965 they decided to bid in the next year for Pakistan's entire export quota, which was scheduled to be 90,000 tons. It was announced that this rice was to be offered for tender, rather than negotiation, as had been the practice in previous years, but Haji Ahmed guessed that bribes would still be passed and that the contract might not necessarily go to the best bidder. He decided that to be safe he should go to Karachi in person. He took with him from Kuwait a draft for £1 million as a payment in advance, a further £150,000 as a deposit to be placed with the government and a letter of credit for the balance of his bid. This was much better than any of the Pakistani bidders could manage. The total amount offered by Towell was larger, and the company was able to provide an immediate substantial down payment in foreign exchange. In Kuwait the company had automatic access to any amount of foreign currencies, whereas Murwani and his consortium were operating in a country with rigid exchange controls. For the Pakistani government, which was more than usually short of foreign exchange after the war with India in the previous summer, this was the crucial consideration. The government had no hesitation in accepting the Towell bid and duly signed a contract with the company on 18 January 1966.

Murwani was disappointed and angry. He maintained that he had concluded a verbal contract with the government on 4 January and had then arranged the opening of a letter of credit and taken steps to arrange for shipment. During February and March he sought an injunction from the Pakistani High Court to restrain Towell and the Pakistan government from executing the contract, claiming that Ahmed Sultan had been well aware of his early contract. According to reports in the Pakistani newspaper *Dawn*, he also provided an affidavit of a government officer who had been present at a meeting of the Rice Board on 4 January stating 'his contention that contract with Hussein Murwani was concluded on that day'. Counsel for the respondents, Towell and the Rice Board, argued that the 4 January discussions with Murwani had constituted negotiations rather than an agreement, verbal or otherwise, and that the cancellation of the contract with Towell would entail a damaging loss of foreign exchange for the government. Mr Justice Khamisani and Mr Justice Raymond found in favour of the Rice Board and Towell.[4]

In theory Ahmed Sultan had won a monopoly of Pakistani basmati exports for the next twelve months, but towards the end of his contract 5,000 tons of rice 'leaked' out of Pakistan via commodities brokers in London into the hands of Mohammad Yusuf, the head of the Bahrain branch of the Alireza family. When Ahmed heard of this he promptly went to Pakistan with the intention of seeking an injunction to prevent shipment of the rice; but before the matter came to court he was able to work out a mutually satisfactory compromise with the Rice Board. It was agreed that Mohammad Alireza would be allowed to have his rice, while the Towell contract of 1966 would be extended for a few months. In effect the Pakistanis agreed to postpone their auction for 1967, giving Ahmed extra time in which to ship and sell the rice he had already bought. Inevitably as Ahmed delayed shipment he caused a shortage in the Gulf and the price of basmati rose; Mohammad Alireza's 5,000 tons were not enough to have a significant effect on the market. As Towell shipped the remainder of its rice its profits soared. Afterwards Ahmed was often heard to say that he was particularly proud of the deal he had done on this occasion, because he had 'turned disaster into triumph'.

In the course of 1966 and 1967 Ahmed bought a total of 113,000 tons of rice – 90,000 tons of basmati plus a further 23,000 tons of Burmese rice. His company made profits on rice sales of nearly $3.5 million. It found itself supplying most of the established commodity wholesalers in all the Arabian Peninsula countries. During the following six years Ahmed won further Pakistani contracts. He concluded a fifteen-month

4. *Dawn*, 18 February 1966, and 15, 17, 19 March 1966.

deal for 150,000 tons in 1968, bought the same quantity in 1969, and in 1971 agreed to take 210,000 tons over the two years running up to the end of 1973. As he later admitted, his company's success led to 'a general resentment'.

There was another more personal and unhappy consequence of the deals. During all of the tenders there had been any number of middlemen and brokers moving among the bidders claiming that they had the influence to 'direct' the award of the contract. In 1969 Ahmed had been approached in Pakistan by an Iraqi who said that in that year there was going to be a change from tenders back to the pre-1966 process of negotiation. He said that for a fee of £1 per ton (£150,000 in all) he would be happy to act as a go-between. Ahmed agreed to the proposition; but in practice it turned out that the Iraqi's help was superfluous. He had been wrong in his assertion of a change in the bidding procedure; the government continued its policy of inviting tenders and the actual contribution he made to Ahmed's winning the contract was nil. But the Iraqi still demanded payment, on the grounds that when it had been thought that there were to be negotiations he had rendered Ahmed some service. For the sake of an amicable settlement Ahmed gave him 'a good sum of money', and extracted from him a written acceptance stating that the sum constituted a complete satisfaction of his claim. The Iraqi, however, was a gambler. He squandered his money in Beirut and whenever he needed further funds he would write to the Sultans. The family's lawyers advised against a response and the letters were ignored. Eventually the letters stopped.

One day in January 1974, the Towell offices in Kuwait received a telex from the director of a housing company, who said that he would like to meet Ahmed to discuss a proposition to do with the development of housing in the Middle East. The telex was sent from a public booth in Beirut. The Sultans did not know the man, but they were interested in housing, which was going to be one of the major bottlenecks in all the oil state economies in the aftermath of the previous year's oil-price rises. Ahmed himself was about to go to London and could not spare the time for a meeting, but it happened that Abdel-Amir, the youngest brother, had already arranged to go to Beirut. Ahmed and he agreed that he might as well hear what the man from the housing company had to say. Abdel-Amir duly telexed back agreeing to a meeting, and the housing director suggested his room in the new Holiday Inn Hotel.

A few days later Abdel-Amir got off his plane at Beirut, but exactly what happened to him during the next three or four hours is a mystery. It is assumed that he went by taxi to the Holiday Inn, on the most affluent part of the Beirut sea front, and was invited by the man from the housing company to come up to his room. When he entered the room he was kidnapped.

Ahmed meanwhile had arrived in London and gone into the Tropical Diseases Hospital for a routine medical check. In the early afternoon of the following day, a Friday, he received a telephone call from his office in Kuwait, telling him that his brother had been kidnapped by the former Iraqi go-between and that the Iraqi was demanding that Ahmed come to Beirut with £150,000 in cash. The banks in London were about to close and Ahmed could see that it would be impossible for even a man of his resources to obtain £150,000 in cash at such short notice. He told the Kuwait office to send his 'lawyer' to Beirut 'to sort things out', but did not tell him to take £150,000 – he knew that it would be easy enough to obtain that money in Beirut should it be needed. Then Ahmed discharged himself from hospital and went to the airport.

The lawyer, who in fact was the general fixer of the Kuwait office, arrived in Beirut a matter of hours later and made preliminary contact with the kidnapper. But then something went wrong. On the following morning a chambermaid in the Commodore Hotel found the Iraqi dead in his bed, a gun in his hand and his brains blown out. On the table beside him was a suicide note, saying that at last he had had his revenge and that now he had no desire to go on living. At the bottom of the note he added that Abdel-Amir's body would be found in a room at the Holiday Inn. The police and the Sultans' lawyer went to the Holiday Inn and discovered the corpse crammed into a large polythene bag and hidden under a bed.

In the eyes of the Beirut police, who are not noted for the zeal of their investigations, the whole affair was an open-and-shut case of 'murder followed by suicide'. They promptly closed their files and refused to discuss the matter further. Meanwhile Oman's Ruler, Qaboos bin Said, banned all members of his government from visiting Beirut until further notice.

Ahmed and the rest of the Sultan family were not as easily satisfied as the Beirut police. It was obvious to anyone who thought about it that a kidnapper would not have been able to take a prisoner, hoping to guard him day and night for forty-eight hours or so, send a ransom note and negotiate with whoever came with the ransom money, if he had been acting alone. In this particular case the matter would have been made more difficult by the fact that Abdel-Amir was a youngish man of considerable size, while the Iraqi was small, rather weak and in later middle age. Ahmed Sultan immediately contacted a commodities broking friend in London and told him to call in a private detective agency and provide it with working funds of £20,000. The broker contacted Kings Investigation Bureau, who sent Mr Bollengaro, a former CID officer and one of its senior employees, to Beirut. Bollengaro agreed that the Iraqi could not have been alone. He pointed out that the murderer would not have put the body into a polythene bag unless he had intended to move it without leaving bloodstains, and that this was not compatible with the police verdict of murder followed by suicide. He also saw that there were no powder burns on the head of the dead Iraqi, as there would have been had he shot himself. Clearly the gun that killed him had been held at more than arm's length. The Iraqi too had been murdered.

Bollengaro eventually managed to obtain a photograph in Beirut of a man whom he was told had been in the company of the Iraqi at the time of the kidnapping and murders, and whom he discovered was known to be in the drugs business. He had been working as a courier for the Mafia, operating between Iraq, Turkey, Beirut and Italy, but exactly who he was Bollengaro could not discover. He suspected that the man was the son of the Iraqi, but had not been using his real name. His enquiries took him to Berlin where the man had been a student, and finally the man's former landlady was able to identify the picture. He was indeed the Iraqi's son. Why he had joined his father in the kidnapping was not clear. It could only be assumed that he had gone in for the money, but that when Abdel-Amir had been killed – by which of the partners in crime and in exactly what circumstances nobody knows – he must have decided that if his father stayed alive he would be liable to betray him. At this point Bollengaro submitted his report to Ahmed Sultan, who closed the investigation. Whether Ahmed took any steps subsequently he never said.

In the four years that followed, until his death at the end of 1977, Ahmed was gripped by a sense of remorse. He told himself that it was really he who should have been murdered. Those who knew him well say that he never recovered his former zest.

Ironically the rice contract that had come to an end just a few days before the murder was to be the last of the Sultan family's huge monopoly deals. In 1972, when rice prices had been high, the Kuwait government had asked Towell to hand over part of its stocks at a very small profit, and the company had felt that it could not refuse. The government then proceeded to sell this rice itself in competition with Towell. Haji Ahmed said that he suspected that the government had been prompted to take this action by other jealous merchants. Then in 1973 the Kuwait government established a state Supply Company with the purpose of buying and subsidising various staple foodstuffs and selling to the populace through the local co-operative societies and its own retail outlets. The foods affected were rice, sugar, barley, tuna fish, cheese, milk powder, *ghee*, tomato paste and some two dozen other items.

Within a year the oil-price rises had increased people's expectations and pushed up inflation rates, giving rise to further demands for cheaper food. The governments of Bahrain, Qatar and the United Arab Emirates followed the Kuwaiti example. The Saudi government adopted the slightly different policy of subsidising the existing merchant importers, but fixing retail prices to allow them only a small profit.

The outcome of the subsidy policies has been that in some commodities the merchants have to act mainly as buyers for the state, accepting whatever margins the government gives them. They can also supply that part of the market which does not qualify for subsidies – the hotels, the fizzy drinks companies (which are major consumers of sugar) and families who want to buy more than their ration cards will allow them. Private companies are now reckoned to have about 35 per cent of the rice market and 40 per cent of the sugar market. In other commodities, such as jam or butter, which are not such staple foods and where consumers may have preferences for particular brands, the merchants offer a wider range of choice and find themselves able to compete on fairly equal terms with the supply companies. Outside the range of the subsidies there are a few bulk foods – including coffee, tea and cardomom seeds (used for flavouring Arabian coffee) – which are still handled exclusively by the merchants.

Under the new regime the Towell commodity operation has been very much reduced. The arrival of the supply companies made it pointless for the firm to bid for any further massive basmati contracts. A little later the firm suffered a different type of setback in the sugar market. Ahmed bought a large quantity of sugar during the shortage of 1974, some of it at $1,200–1,400 a ton. In that year he sold over half of all the sugar that was brought into the Gulf and made a good profit. Like many other people Ahmed thought that the sugar shortage would continue indefinitely and he stayed in sugar too long. In the following year the price rapidly plunged to $400. By the time the market hit the bottom, Towell had sold much of its stock, but on its later contracts it made a huge loss. The Algerian government, which had signed a forward contract with Towell in late 1974, simply refused to take its sugar at the agreed price, forcing the company to negotiate a reduction. In all, Towell's losses in the sugar market ran to $24 million. Coming soon after the death of his brother, the sugar fiasco caused a further deterioration in the health of Haji Ahmed. Both Haji Ali and his eldest son, Maqbool, who were less directly involved in the disaster, say that their losses in sugar were the worst crisis they have ever known in business.

Haji Ahmed died at the end of 1977. Since then Maqbool has been the man in charge of the commodities business. All of the firm's buying is still done by the Kuwait company, even when the order is on behalf of the main Towell company in Oman. The firm now deals mainly in rice, sugar and barley for animal feed, buying partly in Pakistan and India and partly from brokers in London and Paris. Since the mid-1970s it has developed a big new business in cement and expanded its old wholesale trade in general merchandise – cigarettes, clothing, canned foods, household goods and perfumes.[5] Members of the Sultan family and their employees talk of the supply companies with a slight air of resigned disdain, as if they have spoilt the fun of the commodities business. They are sorry that the great days of the basmati monopoly have come to an end – for reasons of professional pride as much as profit – but they are philosophical: 'Commodities has always been a difficult business,'

5. Perfume importing is an enormous business in Arabia. People in the trade say that Saudi Arabia and the Gulf states must be the biggest perfume consumers per capita in the world. Manufacturers create perfumes specifically for the Saudi market; Dubai imports the equivalent of a gallon of perfume each year for every female adult resident (though much of this must be re-exported). There are even people who wash their hands in eau de cologne. The reason for this passion for perfume is partly religious: the Koran states that one should be clean and preferably sweet smelling before one prays. It also happens that however austere the regime in Arabia has been in the past, there has never been a ban on perfume; it has been one of the few sensuous substances permitted in an austere environment.

Maqbool said to me in 1977. 'You make much more money than you expect, or much less. It's not like cars, where you know what your margin will be before you import. It's not so easy to finance your trade with bank loans and you don't get facilities from the manufacturers as you do with cars. You have to put in more of your own capital and build up big reserves in case of losses. Of course the banks lend to Towell, because we are experienced, but with new companies in this business they would certainly not lend as much as they would with cars or electric goods . . . We've always got to judge the market and take the risk. This has nothing to do with the leverage that commodity dealers use – that is even more risky. We're just buying and stocking, using ordinary import finance – not dealing. We never buy without having in mind that we will receive the cargo – though possibly we may resell it if we are approached by a buyer before we see the cargo. The trouble now is that we're not just judging the market, we have to judge what the governments will do as well.'

While the Towell company in Kuwait was signing massive contracts in the international commodities markets in the 1960s, the company at home in Oman remained fairly stagnant, existing in a country that was still almost totally cut off from the world outside. At that time people in Muscat and Muttrah still had to carry lanterns after dark. The partners of Towell moved between two worlds. What this meant in practical terms became very clear to a British banker, Andrew Thompson, who in 1970 visited Haji Ali in his office on the Muttrah sea front and who described the scene to me in Riyadh ten years later: 'I went through the *godown* [Indian term for warehouse], negotiating my way through piles of sacks and bales in the dark, then up a vertical wooden ladder, then another ladder, across the roof and then into a sort of pavilion on the roof. There was Haji Ali sitting cross-legged on the floor, wearing a plain white *thobe* with his Zanzibari cap tilted forward in his usual way. We greeted each other with the usual *salaams* and so forth, and then there was a short silence while we wondered how to begin the conversation. Then suddenly he said: "I see you are wearing a Christian Dior tie." There was nothing to show that the tie was Dior, no label or anything visible, and so I asked how on earth he could possibly know. "Oh," he said, "I am the Christian Dior agent." So I thought to myself: "It never does to underestimate these people." It also showed what an impressive, detailed knowledge he had of his stock.'

Thompson's story is typical of Haji Ali – a short, chubby man, always cheerful and approachable, with a broad grin and the habit of wrinkling up his nose and tilting his Zanzibari cap down on his forehead when thinking of the answer to a question. Like his brothers he is a religious man. He does not drink or flaunt his wealth. He drives himself to work and takes exercise in moderation by walking downstairs from his office at the end of the day; to walk up the four or five flights at the beginning of the day he says would be too much work. His advice to young men starting out in business is that they should be scrupulously honest – 'this builds up people's confidence in you and makes them willing to co-operate with you. Banks always want to know your reputation before anything else.' The one side of the character of Haji Ali and the other members of his family which does not show is their toughness. Outwardly the Sultans are all charming – it is the characteristic commented on by everyone who meets them – but they cannot always be quite as amiable as they appear. Beneath the surface those who deal with them assume that there is a streak of ruthlessness, which must have come to the fore in the rice deals.

The Sultans reaped the reward of their international exposure and their success in the commodities business after 1970, when Qaboos bin Said overthrew his father and began spending Oman's new oil revenues on development. There were other Omani families which had built up capital abroad and had members working in other countries, but the Sultans had the biggest foreign business and a better base from which to expand in Oman. They had established a contracting firm with foreign partners in the mid-1960s and carried out several minor building works, including the offices of the Chartered Bank, a small power station and a house for the managing director of the oil company. The company had also continued its importing business, operated its own fizzy-drinks bottling plant, and put forward ideas for a hotel and a cement plant, both of which had been turned down by the old Sultan. It was only just before he was overthrown that the Sultan had changed his mind about the hotel, and then he stipulated that its restaurant should be barred to Omanis, and that there should be no drink and no music.

From this base, in the last ten years Towell has expanded into all the usual activities of an Arabian merchant company. It holds a variety of agencies, including Mazda, Buick and GMC, Unilever and other consumer goods companies, and a range of autoparts and building materials manufacturers. It has a contracting company, which it owns 50–50 with Taylor Woodrow, and a partnership with the supermarket group Spinney's, which owns Muttrah Cold Stores and the Muttrah Hotel. In the early 1980s the company's major new area of expansion was in Omani real estate. In 1980, the turnover of all the trading operations, subsidiaries and partnerships, along with the operation in Kuwait and the small company in Dubai, was running at about $130 million. This figure excluded the non-profit element of government supply contracts and the personal dealings of individual members of the Sultan family. Compared with most of the other bigger Arabian merchant groups the Towell turnover is prone to considerable fluctuations, caused by the big dependence on commodities in the Kuwait operation and the many one-off ventures the company enters.

In recent years Towell has been involved in activities as varied as a major building contract in Riyadh and discussions on shipping and the housing business with Spiro Agnew, the former US Vice-President. Agnew came to Kuwait as the representative of a prefabricated housing manufacturer and of some shipowners who wanted to sell some of their vessels, but he failed to do any business with the Sultans.

PART TWO

9

The Age of Pearling

In the early 1970s a young Kuwaiti film director made a film called *Bas Ya Bahr* ('Enough Oh Sea'), an emotional drama set in the days of the pearl divers. The film became famous throughout the Gulf. Audiences came out of the cinemas with tears in their eyes, purged by feelings of pity and pride. The film they had seen was about *their* past and *their* suffering. At a time when they were beginning to feel submerged by the vast inflow of foreign workers and Western materialism, here was something that was part of their own culture.

The past has since become a minor industry in the Gulf and Saudi Arabia. Just before the last old houses are pulled down, the last pearl diver dies and the old dhow building methods are forgotten, a desperate attempt is being made to preserve and record something of what is left. Sea shanties and the songs that went with all the different tasks of the pearl industry are relearnt and sung on television. Serious, Western-educated graduates from the ministries of information tape-record the reminiscences of old dhow captains and bedouin; in Qatar there is a television programme called *Bedu Corner*. Every state has built its own museum. In Jeddah more than 500 old houses have been made the subject of preservation orders.

Inevitably there is a temptation to romanticise as well as record. In Qatar the brilliantly successful play *Umm Zun* ('The Mother of Beauty' or 'The Most Beautiful') ran for fourteen nights to packed houses of 200 a time – which meant that about 12 per cent of the adult Qatari population saw it. (This would be equivalent to the most successful ever runs on Broadway or in the West End.) The play dealt with the hard but honest life in a fishing village before oil, how gradually the villagers were tempted away from the village by the prospect of work in the oil field, and how eventually the village community was dispersed and the buildings crumbled to decay. The last scene showed the villagers returning to dance among the ruins. The idealised image of the past which *Umm Ziin* portrayed is reinforced by the government public relations machines. In several of the oil states now there are British and American public relations men advising the ministries of information. They sponsor authors and publishers, produce their own glossy picture books and instruct journalists about what is and is not 'responsible' or 'necessary' to write. The image of the Gulf in the first half of this century that this machine seems to create is one of social harmony and a healthy life in the date plantations and fisheries under the benign, paternalistic government of the ruling families. To be fair, the image is created in part unwittingly, by the beautiful pictures in the glossy books; nobody of the older generation in government would want to claim that pearl diving was anything but miserable and degrading. Yet the romantic image seems to be engraining itself in the minds of Westerners. It is not uncommon to hear visitors to the Gulf suggesting that the Arabs should revive the pearl industry or that 'they were really much happier as they were'. The comment made to me a few years ago by the Saudi Minister of Industry, Dr Ghazi Algosaibi, was: 'My God, I wish sometimes that every camel could be shot.'

In reality Arabia before oil was a harsh place, desperately poor and riven by internal strife. This is the society that all the older members of the merchant families remember as the background to their childhood and their first steps in business.[1]

Charles Dalrymple Belgrave arrived in Bahrain to take up his post as adviser to the Ruler early in 1926. When he retired thirty-one years later he described his first impressions of the island in his book *Personal Column*:

> On the morning of March 31st, after a very rough night at sea, we cast anchor about three miles from the shore of a long, low island. By this time

1. The description of *Bas Ya Bahr* has been taken from Molly Izzard's book *The Gulf*: Arabia's Western Approaches, John Murray, 1979, and *Umm Ziin* from *Arabia through the Looking Glass* by Jonathan Raban, Collins, 1979. Some of the material in the rest of this chapter and in chapters 10, 11, 13 and 14 is drawn from the files of the India Office Library in London. The relevant file series are R/15/1, applying to the Bushire Residency, and R/15/2, applying to the Bahrain Agency. Other material in this and the next chapter is drawn from Sir Charles Belgrave's autobiography, *Personal Column*, Hutchinson, 1960.

the sea was calm, the sparkling water was brilliant, green, purple and aquamarine. Along the coast groves of date palms extended down to the shore, and opposite the anchorage there was a town; to the east, a few miles off, there was another town on a neighbouring island [Muharraq]. Little boats with white sails, crowded with white-robed Arabs, were skimming across the water between the islands.

When he arrived in Mahama, the town opposite the anchorage, Belgrave found rows of mud-coloured houses with no buildings of any height, no minarets and nothing green . . . 'The houses were built of coral stone, quarried from the sea-bed at low tide; few houses had more than two stories. The streets were narrow and congested, roofed with palm branch matting; the little shops, with wooden shutters, contained few European goods.'

To the south, encircling Manama in Belgrave's day, was a deep belt of palm groves. These were dark, shady forests, broken up by narrow tracks and occasional springs and streams. Water from the streams was carried every day into the town bazaar in goat skins slung from the backs of donkeys; the better the water the higher the price it fetched. Interspersed with the date gardens and along the line where the palm trees gave way to the desert were little villages, with coral-brick and palm-frond buildings and a few donkeys and camels. At night the houses were lit by kerosene lamps.

Bahrain was the most important and most cosmopolitan centre on the Arabian side of the Gulf. It was richer than the other towns. It had prosperous communities of Indian and Persian merchants; it was the main pearl market, the anchorage where the steamship lines called most regularly, the port through which most of the imports of the mainland were transshipped. The Political Agent on the island oversaw British interests throughout the lower Gulf. The other centres along the coast were Kuwait and Dubai. On a smaller scale were Jubail, Darin and Uqair (pronounced Ujair), three minor pearling anchorages and fishing villages. Darin and Uqair served as ports for the oases of Qatif and Hasa.

Inland the major town was Hofuf, at the edge of the Hasa oasis. In 1920 when Major Dickson, the Political Agent in Bahrain, visited Hasa he reported back to the British Resident in Bushire: 'I was struck with the beauty of the many date gardens. All are splendidly attended and contain an abundance of fruit trees. Water channels were numerous and

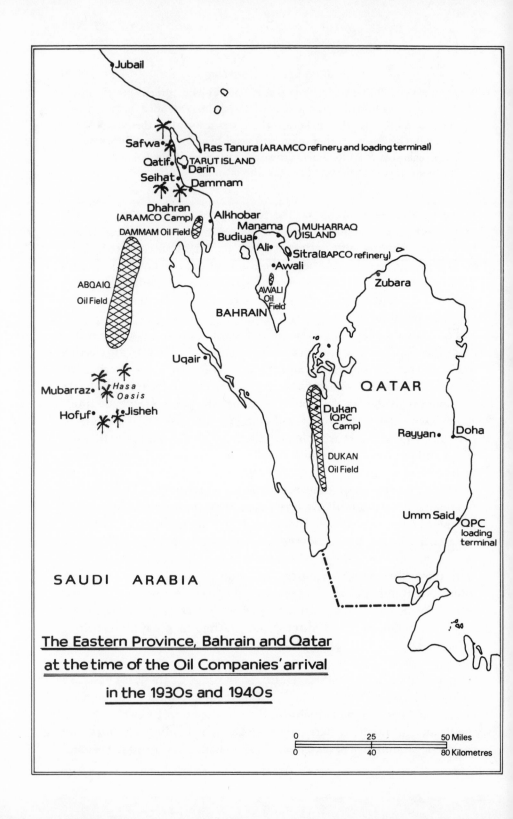

The Eastern Province, Bahrain and Qatar

at the time of the Oil Companies' arrival

in the 1930s and 1940s

in many places the roadway was built up on a raised causeway. Over the streams were good, well-built masonry bridges . . . Along the whole road to Hofuf wherever the ground was high, was to be seen brilliant green, denoting wheat cultivation.' The town of Hofuf itself was surrounded with heavy, turreted fortifications. It was famous for the manufacture of brass pots and gold embroidery, which its tailors wove along the edges of *mishlahs*, the black and brown cloaks worn by the more affluent Arabian Arabs.

In all the towns life was uneventful. Every year most of the male population sailed out to the pearl fisheries at the end of May and returned four months and ten days later at the beginning of October. In the autumn the pearl catch was sold, enabling the whole population – divers, captains, pearl merchants, boat builders, food and timber importers, date growers – to settle their accounts and buy supplies. Throughout the year there was the daily routine of catching fish, cultivating a few cereals and tending the date palms – trying to produce enough food to avoid starvation. People were undernourished and unhealthy; as many children died in infancy as lived. Most of those who survived became prematurely aged through hard, debilitating labour.

Fahd Abdel-Rahman Algosaibi, one of the eight brothers of the Saudi Minister of Industry, told me in 1977 that his main memories of his youth are discomfort and hard work: 'Childhood was different then,' he said. 'Boys would mix with the men much more – rather than staying in the home. They became men earlier, learned etiquette and traditions earlier.' His other memories illustrate the very simple tone of day-to-day life: 'The main type of construction in the villages were *barasti*, little palm-frond shacks. Another thing I remember is the elaborate wool covers that people would put over the saddles of their donkeys. They painted their donkeys red with henna, just as people decorate their trucks today.' Fahd's elder brother, Khalifa, added his comments in a conversation with me some months later: 'Almost everyone rode donkeys – except Belgrave, who rode a horse. In those days the aim in life of everyone was to accumulate enough food during the pearl market season to last twelve months – this was the main aim and object of life: to have one year's food in the cellar. Outside the pearl season little happened. For the richer people there were just continual majles – we visited each other and drank tea.'

The events which stood out in people's memories were periodic famines, when there were great emigrations from central Arabia to the coasts, visitations of plague and terrible storms. People would remember particular years by these events: 1903 and 1904 were plague years; 1925, the year in which Haji Ahmed Alghanim lost his dhow in a storm, was known as 'the year of the sinkings'. People would talk of their children being born 'in the year before the cholera year' or 'two years after the Year of Mercy'. This was a reference to 1919 when Arabia was smitten by Asian flu and the dead were said to have been spared by God the rigours of further life on earth.

Slightly more commonplace events were occasional pearl divers' riots, feuds between Sunnis and Shias, murders, raids on villages by the bedouin or by members of rival tribes or communities. Any violence of this nature would cause great excitement.

Every fortnight the political agents in Bahrain and Kuwait would send intelligence reports to the Political Resident in Bushire summing up the main events in their territories. These reports speak volumes about the monotony of life. For month after month there was hardly anything worth recording. Agents resorted to giving their superiors touches of local colour. On one occasion the Bahrain agent reported that a rumour had spread through the souk that a man who was thought to be thoroughly wicked had been turned overnight into an ass. The rumour gained enormous credence the following day when Belgrave was seen visiting a farm.

Most of the population of Bahrain, Kuwait and Hasa had some knowledge or experience of both sides of the Gulf and central Arabia. Their horizons were relatively broad by the standards of very poor societies; people did not spend all of their lives in their own towns and villages. Dhow crews, camel owners and traders went frequently between the different Gulf states, the eastern part of Ibn Saud's domains, then known as the Hasa Province, and the Nejd. Cloth, wood, rice and oats for animal feed were imported from India; charcoal, hides, sheep and goats and grain from southern Iran; a few Western manufactured goods were bought in Bombay by the merchants of Bahrain and Kuwait. Hasa, Bahrain and southern Iraq produced dates and various types of fodder – alfalfa, dried fish and date stones – all of which were used to feed donkeys and camels. The Hasa oasis raised donkeys and grew a small amount of tobacco – which under the puritan Wahabi regime of the Sauds was supposed to be illegal. All of these items were traded into central Arabia. The Nejdis financed their imports by selling sheep, goats, horses, *ghee* (cooking fat) and camels. The horses, together with dates from Hasa, Bahrain and Iraq, were exported to India. One of the major customers was the Indian army, supplied by Nejdi horse dealers in Bombay.

A person who travelled between Bahrain, Hasa, the Nejd and India for his family's firm when he was in his teens was Fahd Algosaibi: 'The worst place was Qatif, where my family had some date gardens,' he told me. 'If any visitor could possibly avoid it he would never spend a night there. It has terrible mosquitoes, very bad malaria – though the locals were immune. They were Shias, like the Baharna in Bahrain. The other place I didn't like was Riyadh, where I often had to go to collect debts from the government. It was terribly difficult, we would spend endless days there. Riyadh was horribly dirty – you cannot imagine it . . .

'People were very religious; not even cigarettes were allowed. Women were totally covered with thick black woollen veils. No gramophones or musical instruments could be imported – people would get violent if they heard music. If you wanted to have a cigarette when you visited a person you would send your servant in advance to tell your host to cook some coffee so that the smoke would disguise the smell of the cigarette. Or you would use a flit gun first. This was so that the people outside would not attack the house if they smelt the tobacco – they had a very sensitive sense of smell.'

A few people were able to break away from the poverty and monotony of life in Arabia. Several of the biggest merchant families, including the Bassams, Zamils, Alirezas and Algosaibis, had businesses in India, normally in Bombay, Calcutta or Karachi, and sent their sons to be educated there. India served as an introduction to the modern world; it brought the merchants into contact with British officials and traders, taught them English and showed them new consumer products and ways of business. The grandfather of Hussein Alireza, the present Saudi Mazda importer, at the end of the First World War launched a disastrous speculation in the Imperial Russian rouble, which he predicted would gain in value if the White Russians beat the Bolsheviks. To this day Hussein has sackfuls of old rouble notes.

After India some of the more intrepid families began to visit Lebanon and send their children to school in Beirut. Geographically Lebanon was closer to the Gulf, but in the 1920s and 1930s it was under French rule and culturally very different from the familiar British-dominated world of the Indian Ocean. It also took a hazardous cross-desert journey by taxi to get there.

Just a few people went to Europe. These were various members of the Alireza family, Abdel-Rahman Algosaibi (Fahd's father), Mohammad bin Rashid bin Hindi, and one or two of the other leading Bahraini pearl merchants. All of them are remembered as remarkable men. It took an extraordinary jump in imagination for a man such as Mohammad Ali Zainal Alireza to set up a business in Paris, albeit with help from some of the established Parisian pearl dealers, and to conceive the idea of using the profits to finance his schools. Symbolic of the contrast between their lives in Europe and their homes in Arabia are two photographs taken in Paris in the early 1930s of Abdel-Rahman Algosaibi and Abdel-Ghaffar Alireza, one of the members of the Ali Akbar branch of the family. They are studio portraits in which the two men are wearing Western dress. Their hair is tightly combed back and Abdel-Ghaffar's moustache is neatly trimmed. He is wearing a grey flannel suit, with a white handkerchief in the breast pocket and a pin through his collar underneath the knot in his tie. Both Abdel-Ghaffar and Abdel-Rahman Algosaibi look exactly like any rich visitor from southern Europe.

The main source of wealth that enabled the merchants to travel and gave ordinary people the income to spend on imported goods and foodstuffs was the pearl industry. As the pearling season approached, men came to the coast from all parts of Arabia – from the Nejd, the area of the Tuwaiq escarpment that runs down from Nejd towards Yemen, the Batinah coast of northern Oman, the Liwa oasis of Abu Dhabi on the edge of the Empty Quarter. Some parts of Arabia, including the Liwa and the Qatar peninsula, lost almost their whole male population at this time of year. In Bahrain and Kuwait and along the Trucial Coast (as the United Arab Emirates were then known) it was estimated that between one- and two-thirds of the men went to sea.

The dhow crews – divers and haulers – had a strange superstition about the pearls they hoped to find. They believed that when it rained the oysters swam up to the surface and opened their shells to receive drops of rain, which in due course turned into pearls. When they went back to the sea bed the oysters nourished the embryonic pearls by eating the mother-of-pearl in old oyster shells. Sadly, there was nothing so romantic about the lives of the divers. The diver normally made fifty dives a day, averaging one minute per dive at forty feet. He carried a weight and a bag, and if he was lucky he might be protected against jellyfish by a thin cotton overall. On the bottom he scooped as many oysters as he could into his bag. Then, when he ran out of breath, he jerked the rope that was tied to him and was hauled to the surface by the pullers.

Allowing for periodic days of rest and days when the wind made the sea too cloudy for diving, a diver could reckon to spend about fifty hours under water without air during a season. He was likely to suffer from acute fatigue or convulsive shivers even in temperatures of over 100°F; he might be taken ill with scurvy, or have the 'bends', causing joint pains or paralysis, or find that as he grew old his lungs collapsed. At sea he ate rice, fish and dates and drank stale water and tea. In the evenings he listened to his captain (*nakhoda*) reading from the Koran or visited other dhows to drink coffee and exchange news.

The oyster shells were opened at the end of the working day. They were collected into a single big pile so that nobody knew who had brought up the shells that were found to contain the most valuable pearls. In practice only a few shells had any pearls at all, and almost all of these were seed pearls. The entire fleet of the Gulf would produce the pearls for only two top-quality necklaces of exactly matching, perfectly round specimens in a season; even to find two matching tear-shaped pearls for a pair of earrings a crew would have to open tens of thousands of shells. The industry was based on there being a very large number of people – about 40,000 at the height of the industry in the first thirty years of this century – prepared to spend months at sea for a pittance. Now that pearl prices have fallen in real terms, pearl diving using modern methods in the Gulf does not begin to pay the divers' overheads. One of the sons of Khalifa Algosaibi once launched a modern pearling expedition and did not even recover the cost of the diesel fuel for his launch. In the early years of this century overheads were lower and there was no other work available. It was also said by those who knew the crews that they were born gamblers: they all dreamed of the day when they would find the giant pearl that would make them rich.

At the end of the season the captain negotiated the sale of his catch, deducted the cost of food and provisioning, and counted his profit. A large forty-man dhow operating out of Bahrain or Kuwait might expect to make a profit on an average season's catch of some 4,500–5,000

2. The main currency in all the Gulf shaikhdoms and the Hasa coast of the mainland during the first half of this century was the Indian Rupee – replaced in the Gulf states after Indian independence by the Gulf Rupee, which was at par with the Indian

rupees, about $1,350–1,500.² Of this about a fifth went to the dhow owner, who might or might not be the captain, while the rest was divided in the ratio of one and a half shares for a diver to one share for a puller. If the captain was not the owner of the dhow he would take ten or twelve shares for himself. On the basis of these rules the diver might expect to make up to 100 rupees or $30 a season.

On paper the financial terms under which the divers worked seemed quite fair, but in reality the men were almost slaves. At the beginning of each season the captains gave their divers an advance, partly so that they could leave some money at home to support their families while they were at sea. The captains in turn borrowed from money lenders and food merchants to lay in provisions for their dhows and finance their advances to the divers. On all of these transactions there were high rates of interest, of 10–20 per cent, though in symbolic deference to the Islamic prohibition of usury no interest changed hands as cash. At the end of a season a captain who had bought provisions worth, say, R 1,000 would pay the food merchant with R 1,100 or 1,200 worth of pearls. If a captain had a run of bad seasons he might go bankrupt.

The divers meanwhile were unlikely ever to be free of debt. More often than not their share of profits was insufficient to cover their advance plus interest. Once in debt a man had to hire his services to the same captain in the next season, and if he died his sons inherited his debt. If a captain wished he could transfer an indebted diver to another captain without the diver's consent, or hand him over to a shopkeeper to work off his debt onshore. Frequently captains falsified their accounts; the divers could only accept continued servitude or appeal to the notoriously corrupt Diving Court, run by the captains and merchants.

By the early 1920s the condition of the divers in Bahrain, under the ageing and ineffective rule of Shaikh Isa bin Ali al Khalifa, had become so miserable that the British decided that there would have to be reforms. In 1923 Shaikh Isa was told to make way for his son, Shaikh Hamad, the present Ruler's grandfather.

The reforms introduced over the next two or three years by Shaikh Hamad and the Political Agent, Major Daly, abolished the inheritance of debt by the sons of a diver. They imposed limits on the rates of interest to be charged and the size of advances to be given to the divers,

currency. The Gulf states changed to their own currencies at the time of the Indian devaluation in the early 1960s. Between the World Wars there were 13 rupees to £1 sterling or $4. A lakh, or 100,000 rupees, was worth nearly £8,000 or $31,000.

disbanded the Diving Court and gave divers the right to have their cases heard in the ordinary courts. They also made it illegal for a captain to demand unpaid labour from a diver ashore. It was decreed that the sale of pearls by the captains was to be witnessed by divers' representatives, that there should be a standardised system of accounts, and that every diver was to be issued with his own little book containing the details of his account with his captain. This book was to be checked by a special staff.

The divers resented these reforms. They found it difficult to understand the benefits of the account books, which they could not read, and saw only that they were getting smaller advances. The advances had always been popular on the grounds that they represented what seemed to be an attractive system of payment first and work later. At the beginning of every pearling season from 1926 to 1932 there was trouble when the government issued its proclamation on the maximum amount of advances. On two occasions, against the advice of Belgrave, the government was forced to revoke its proclamation under pressure from divers and captains, and in the other years there were demonstrations, riots and strikes. In May 1932 there was a big disturbance which resulted in several deaths. The riot was quelled and the ring leaders were arrested and beaten in public. From this time on the divers were quieter. Encouraged by the government and the religious leaders, who had abhorred the usury practised by the merchants and captains, they came gradually to see that the reforms were for their own benefit.

The people who made money out of pearls were the *tawwash*, the pearl merchants who bought from the captains. Every few days during the season the merchants would go out to the fleet in their launches to hear the gossip and try to discover which dhows had found the big pearls. Then they would go to visit the captains and see if they could negotiate some purchases before other merchants arrived to bid up the price. At the end of the summer they would congregate in Bahrain. The island acted as a clearing centre for about 90 per cent of the Gulf pearls, though there was no formal pearl market. The *tawwash* dealt with each other in their own houses and offices. They had an immense knowledge of pearls. They built their own collections, waiting years to make up matching sets for pieces of jewellery.

It was said that once he had owned a big pearl a merchant would always recognise it if he saw it again. In *Personal Column* Belgrave recounts the story of a merchant who gave two pearls to a colleague to sell: the broker tied the pearls in a corner of his *ghotra* (the shawl over his head), but while he was calling on a shop the *ghotra* came undone and the pearls were lost. The shopkeeper denied finding the pearls, and even though a search was made nothing was discovered. Several years later the merchant saw his pearls in India. He made enquiries and traced them back through a chain of dealers to the shop in Bahrain, where the owner finally admitted taking them.

The merchants sold most of their pearls in Bombay, where they were polished and drilled for stringing. A few merchants went to Paris and a group of Parisian dealers came out to Bahrain. Salem Arrayedh, a member of an old and very able Bahraini Shia family, who used to work as a translator in the courts, told me in 1978 that he remembered the most regular visitors were four Jews: David Bienenfeld, of 62 rue La Fayette, where Mohammad Ali Alireza established his offices, Victor Rosenthal, Saul Pack and Albert Habib.

As the pearls moved down the chain their prices increased. At the stage where the *tawwash* bought from the captains, the Bahrain market turned over about $1.5 million a year during the 1920s. By the time the *tawwash* and the Indian and European dealers had taken their profits the catch was priced at five or six times this amount.

The *tawwash* and the food merchants in the mid-1920s united in disgust at the reforms in the pearling industry. They saw the changes as just one of several intrusions by the Political Agent and the Shaikh into their right to conduct their businesses as they liked. During the inter-war period there was a gradual increase in the authority of both the British and the Shaikhs in the Gulf states.

Originally the British had been drawn into the Gulf by the raids of pirates on shipping bound for India. In 1819 the marines of the East India Company stormed the forts of the Qawasim shaikhs, the present ruling family of Sharjah and Ras al Khaimah. In the following decades the government of India signed several series of maritime treaties, each series in response to breaches in the previous set of treaties, culminating in the Perpetual Maritime Truce. By the mid-nineteenth century the region had been pacified. The territory which had been known as the Pirate Coast was renamed the Trucial Coast.

The Indian government's purpose in signing the treaties was defensive, but during the second half of the nineteenth century it found itself

being drawn into Gulf politics. It became involved in policing operations to suppress the arms and slave trades. More important, in the 1880s
and 1890s it began to worry about the interference of the Germans and
Russians, both of whom had designs to weaken the Indian Empire. The
Russians began investigating the possibility of opening coaling stations
in the Gulf, while the Germans at the end of the century were planning
to extend the projected Berlin to Baghdad railway to a terminal in
Kuwait. In response to these threats the Indian government signed a
further series of treaties of protection, which bound the shaikhs 'not to
cede, lease, mortgage or otherwise dispose of parts of their territories to
anyone except Her Majesty's Government, nor to enter into any relationship with a foreign power, other than Britain, without British
consent.' In return the British undertook to conduct their defence and
external relations. The first of these treaties were signed with the
Trucial States and Bahrain in 1892 and the last with Qatar in 1916. A
few years after the Qatar treaty, by which time oil exports had begun
from Iran, the British added clauses stating that oil concessions should
be granted by the shaikhs only to parties who had the approval of the
British government. At no point did the treaties give the British any
authority over the internal affairs of the shaikhdoms.

In the nineteenth century the supervision of these treaties was carried
out by the long-established British Residency at Bushire on the Iranian
coast. Then at the beginning of the twentieth century it was decided
that agencies should be established in Bahrain and Kuwait – tiny posts,
each staffed by a young army officer with a part-time Arab assistant.
The agents reported to the Resident, who was normally a colonel, and
the Resident in turn reported to the government in Delhi. Matters of
major importance were sometimes referred to London.

The people who put their names forward for the agency posts were
adventurous, self-sufficient men, often interested in exploration and
scientific pursuits. On a journey into the desert in 1911 Captain
Shakespeare, one of the early agents in Kuwait, used the last of his
whisky to pickle a dead snake. In the years before the First World War
the agents sometimes found themselves the only Europeans in their
territories. They lived arduous, lonely lives, receiving few visitors and
often not leaving their posts for eighteen months or two years at a
stretch. A Bahrain agent who visited Qatar in the early 1930s reported to
the Residency: 'It appears to be my fate to strike heat waves in Doha,
and the weather was exceptionally hot, with a *gharbi* wind blowing and

the Shaikh's house at Rayyan like a furnace. In fact I spent most of my spare time sitting in a well.' Qatar was a place which everyone dreaded having to visit. It was almost treeless and waterless, there were no Europeans living there in the 1920s and early 1930s, and the local people were devout Wahabis who frowned on material pleasures. There were none of the comfortable Western amenities that began to appear in Bahrain in the inter-war years. John Christie, the first British adviser seconded to the Shaikh of Qatar, in the late 1940s, once told me that he became the world champion player of badminton into the wind.

Officially the agents' role was quite limited. In Bahrain they were responsible for a special court – the Agency Court – which was established to hear cases involving foreigners in all states under British protection. The agents monitored developments in the tribal politics of Arabia, and advised the shaikhs in their relations with each other and with the emerging power of Ibn Saud. If disputes threatened the peace they called on the Royal Navy to send a frigate.

In all matters of security and relations between the Gulf states and Ibn Saud the policy was to be selective in the extent to which Britain became involved. If it seemed necessary to intervene the British would interpret their treaties as requiring intervention; if it was thought that it would be against their interests to be involved in a dispute they would pronounce it an internal matter – regardless of the wishes of the shaikh in question.

Events combined to make the British more inclined to intervention as the years passed. The British presence in the area was greatly expanded in 1920 by the government taking Iraq as a mandated territory. A few years later oil companies started to look for concessions along the Gulf coast, and the British became concerned that as many as possible of the concessions should go to British companies. When the shaikhs awarded their concessions the agencies became partly responsible for the security of oil-company personnel. In due course the shaikhs began employing British 'advisers', who served as members of their own staffs but were usually recruited at the shaikhs' request by the British authorities. As their interests and presence expanded, the British found themselves obliged to force reforms on some of the shaikhs; in several cases, starting with Shaikh Isa bin Ali al Khalifa in 1923, they arranged the deposition of old and ineffective shaikhs and their replacement by younger, more energetic members of their families.

The British were held in considerable awe by the Arab population.

The shaikhs and Ibn Saud generally referred to the government in India as the 'High Government' or the 'Great Government'. Although the British had an almost insignificant military presence in the area their power and influence were regarded as infinite. For their part the political agents behaved with total self-assurance. During riots in Bahrain in 1923 the agent did not hesitate to confiscate weapons personally from the rioters.

In general the British were quite sensitive to the traditions of Arabian society and politics. But there was one practice they introduced at an early stage which was totally out of keeping with the local culture. When a shaikh or one of his subjects rendered the British a service or acted in what the Resident felt was a responsible fashion in preserving the peace, he was given a medal, or even a knighthood. Agents sometimes exchanged worried despatches with the naval authorities about how many guns a particular shaikh was entitled to receive as a salute.

The British set great store by the awards they bestowed. Drawing on their experience in India, they believed that the shaikhs and people of the Gulf would be impressed by the titles. They also felt that a certain formality would preserve the necessary distance between themselves, the *de facto* rulers, and the ruled. Much of the correspondence between the agencies and the Residency was extremely patronising in its references to the Arab population; any Arab who gained some experience of Europe and treated the British on reasonably familiar terms was referred to as 'conceited'. In every way it seems that the British made a mistake in their view of Arab reactions to their formality. With few exceptions (Yusuf bin Ahmed Kanoo being an example) the titles seem to have meant little to the Arabs. The system ran against the egalitarian character of Arabian life, where men were accustomed to addressing their rulers by their first name. A normal way for a bedouin or townsman to address the shaikhs of Kuwait or Bahrain would have been 'Ya Ahmed' (Oh Ahmed) or 'Ya Hamad'.

Before the arrival of the oil companies there was little distinction between the families of the shaikhs and most of the other people of the Gulf states. A director of the Qatar Electricity Department, interviewed by Helga Graham,[3] said: 'I never regarded myself as any

3. *Arabian Time Machine — Self Portrait of an Oil State* by Helga Graham, Heinemann, 1978. The book is composed of a series of interviews with Qataris.

different from the shaikhs, neither better nor worse. The balance of power in society in earlier days was totally different . . . In fact nobody paid any attention to anyone but the Ruler, *the* Shaikh, and his son, who would help his father by acting as adviser or minister . . . But his relations only became a separate class after oil; from being quite poor they became very rich. I knew some shaikhs who used to be truck drivers, tyre repairers – anything.' In the 1940s, the present Qatari Minister of Commerce, Shaikh Nasser bin Khaled al Thani, was chief watchman.

The Shaikh's job was to mediate in disputes and to look after the security of the state. His family was expected to organise a militia of townsmen and bedouin in time of trouble and to provide commanders from its own ranks. In most of the Gulf states the shaikh's ancestors had come from within the communities they ruled; they had been chosen as leaders by the other important families of their communities, and their successors retained a special bond with these families. The bond was strongest in Kuwait, where there was a group of families – Ghanim,[4] Qatami, Sagar, Roumi/Shamlan and Badr – who had arrived under the leadership of the Sabah family in the early eighteenth century and had helped establish the state. All of them had impeccable central Arabian ancestry and it was a regular occurrence for the Sabah to take wives from them; Shaikh Ahmed Jaber al Sabah, the Shaikh from 1921 to 1950, married one of the Alghanims. The senior members of these families were treated almost as equals by the senior members of the Sabah. Other families of Kuwait, and the families of the other Gulf states, had a more distant relationship with their rulers. In most cases these people had arrived after the rulers or belonged to 'foreign' communities, including the Indians and Persians. In Bahrain there were a few families who had been on the island before it was conquered by the Khalifas in 1783, but they were Shias, who were despised by the ruling family.

There were merchants of all classes who were richer than the rulers. In all the Gulf states merchants paid taxes on their trade and were expected to lend money to the Shaikh. In return some of them – those of Sunni Arabian ancestry and a few of the Persians – were consulted on important affairs of state.

4. Elsewhere in this book this family is spelt Alghanim, meaning simply 'the Ghanim', because that is how the family spells its name today. In Kuwait, 'al' is normally put in front of all the other names on the list.

Periodically the leading families resisted the authority of the shaikhs. In Kuwait in the 1920s Hamad Abdullah al Sagar, the father of the present leader of the Kuwaiti merchant community, Abdel-Aziz al Sagar, temporarily forced the Shaikh to accept a council of advisers. Ten years later there was a similar reform movement in Dubai, led by a group of pearl merchants and some members of the junior branch of the ruling Maktoum family. The reformers, who were a mixture of genuine idealists and greedy and violent young shaikhs, established a Municipality Council, curbed the power of the Ruler, Said bin Maktoum, and took most of his revenues. Opposition to them was led by the Ruler's son, Rashid, who himself became Ruler in 1958. The two sides engaged in serious gang warfare which resulted in several deaths and the eventual flight of the reformers to Abu Dhabi and Sharjah. This type of behaviour by the shaikhs, which was very different from the image of wise paternal rule which the public relations machines now propagate, was not uncommon. In Bahrain there were frequent cases in the 1920s of petty tyrants in the Khalifa family extorting unofficial taxes from members of the island's Shia population.

The expanding British presence in the first forty years of this century started a change in relations between the shaikhs and their subjects, but did little to change the lawless behaviour of the junior members of the ruling families.

While they rested under British protection the shaikhs allowed the British to take over some of their role in settling internal disputes. They were even anxious to increase British involvement. Whenever they faced a difficult domestic problem, in which their judgement was likely to be unpopular with one section or another of their people, they were tempted to call on the help of the British. Ironically the abdication of some of their authority in favour of the British did not involve any erosion of the shaikhs' prestige. Hitherto their decisions had often been challenged and their authority brought into disrepute. Under the new regime they could draw on the support of the British, who carried more authority than the shaikhs had ever had and were known by the people to be firm backers of the shaikhs. From the time the British arrived, the shaikhs' status had been enhanced by the treaties being concluded with them personally rather than with them as representatives of their states.

An even bigger change in the authority of the shaikhs was brought about by oil revenues, which came to Bahrain in the mid-1930s and to Kuwait and Qatar in the later 1940s. Oil made the shaikhs financially independent of the merchants and gave them enormous powers of patronage. The rulers felt obliged to give stipends to the junior members of their families, which made the minor shaikhs suddenly much richer than other members of the population. They immediately became a class apart from the ordinary people of their states; from being working citizens of the community they became 'members of the ruling family'.

The change was felt even at the top of society. The last thirty years have seen a gap open up between the ruling families and the other leading families. The relationship between the two groups has acquired something of the character that it has in Saudi Arabia. Merchants have taken on the role of servants of their rulers in the hope of winning the shaikhs' favour. In the 1960s the Kanoos in Bahrain were used by the Khalifas to arrange such matters as house buying in London and foreign schooling for the younger members of their family. Mohammad Jalal, who now runs a range of auto agencies and is one of the biggest merchants on the island, was used for making travel arrangements. In a social sense too, the ruling families seem to have become more introspective and conservative; marriages between their male members and girls of the merchant families have become less common.

What has not changed so much has been the merchants' role as political supporters of the ruling families. Whereas before oil the shaikhs drew on the financial support and advice of the merchants, now the merchants are seen as the ruling families' main constituents. During the unstable period of the late 1950s and early 1960s, when Nasser's subversive propaganda was at its most virulent, the merchants' backing probably saved the ruling families from collapse. In return for this support the rulers have continued to listen to merchant opinion and seldom do anything which will seriously interfere with the merchants' pursuit of profits. In 1980 in Kuwait it was known that there was some consultation between the Sabah and the merchants over the restoration of the state's National Assembly, suspended in 1976, though how far the consultation went is uncertain.

The British presence and the arrival of oil revenues had another important consequence for the ruling families of the Gulf states. The British prevented the states from being incorporated into the realm of Ibn Saud, and oil later made them immune to Saudi political pressure.

It first became apparent that Ibn Saud (Bin Saud as he was known at the time) had designs on the Gulf states immediately after he conquered the Hasa province in 1913. Less than six months after the conquest the Political Resident wrote to the Agent in Bahrain: 'I have not a doubt that Bin Saud could eat up Qatar in a week and I am rather afraid that he may do so.' During the First World War Bin Saud received a financial subsidy from the British and held his schemes in abeyance; but when the subsidy was cancelled in the early 1920s his ambitions revived. The threat was represented in part by Abdullah bin Jiluwi, a distant cousin and trusted lieutenant of Bin Saud, who was appointed governor of Hasa.[5] Abdullah bin Jiluwi ruled his province with a rod of iron. He was backed by some settlements of the Ikhwan. This was a brotherhood of warrior farmers – Wahabis of the most austere and fanatical breed – which was established in central Arabia just before the First World War and was used by Bin Saud in his conquests of northern and western Arabia in the 1920s. Many Ikhwan settlements were established in Hasa to dilute the Shia population of the oasis. Although everyone in the province was terrified of them, it was universally admitted that the presence of the Ikhwan led to unprecedented stability, peace and respect for law.

The way Bin Jiluwi ruled Hasa was described in a despatch written to the Resident by Major Dickson, when he visited Hofuf from Bahrain in 1920. The Political Agent began with a brief sketch of the Governor: 'Bin Jiluwi adopts an untidy, dirty garb. Probably in imitation of the Ikhwan his agal was torn and his abba old and shabby . . . He struck me as a good type of the Arab strong man. He has a full black beard and a jovial, jolly countenance.' Dickson then went on to tell an anecdote which stemmed from a conversation he had had on his return journey to the coast:

> Incidentally one of the escort, Marzuk by name, was the chief exe-
> cutioner in Hasa. He told me Bin Jiluwi had fixed Thursdays for
> executions. These were done in public in the market place and the body
> left til night-fall. He himself had decapitated twenty-two men and cut off
> the hands of scores. The latter process he grimly said did not hurt, but
> what did make men cry out was putting the severed stump into boiling

5. The governorship of the Eastern Province has stayed with the family to which it was given. Abdullah was succeeded in turn by his two sons, Saud and Abdel-Mohsin. The younger son, Abdel-Mohsin, holds the post today. All members of the family, except Abdel-Mohsin, have had a reputation for strong rule, and none of them has had any liking for the Shia inhabitants of the Province.

fat. Marzuk believed the fact that executions had become rare these days was owing to the fear with which Bin Jiluwi was held. One interesting story he told me as typical of Bin Jiluwi's methods. A man came and reported to Bin Jiluwi that he had seen a bag of coffee lying on the high road between Riyadh and Hasa but within the latter's borders. Bin Jiluwi thereupon asked him how he knew it was coffee. The wretched man said: 'I kicked the bag and so knew it to be coffee.' 'Well then', said Bin Jiluwi, 'don't be curious in future and kick any more bags on the Imam's [Bin Saud's] highway. Off with his right big toe.' Marzuk did the needful.

The shaikhs of the Gulf states lived much in awe of Bin Jiluwi and Bin Saud. In the early years after the First World War Bin Saud made no secret of his belief that Kuwait and Qatar should be incorporated into his kingdom. He was given what the Kuwaiti ruling family considered to be two-thirds of its territories at the Conference of Uqair in 1922. This conference was called by Sir Percy Cox, the British High Commissioner in Baghdad, to demarcate the boundaries of Kuwait, Iraq and Nejd – as Bin Saud's kingdom was then known. Immediately after the meeting Bin Saud initiated a blockade of Kuwait in anger at the British refusal of his request for all the territory of the state.

If the British had not guaranteed to defend Kuwait, Qatar and the other shaikhdoms there is little doubt that Bin Saud would have annexed them; as it was he resorted to a policy of harassment and political pressure. He told the Shaikh of Qatar that he regarded only the towns of the Qatar peninsula as being subject to British protection; the desert, he said, was under his sovereignty. The Shaikh of Qatar, Abdullah bin Jasim al Thani, felt obliged to pay him a tribute of 100,000 rupees ($30,000) a year. At the same time Bin Jiluwi extracted taxes from the inland areas of Abu Dhabi and lent support to all absconders from the Gulf states – especially rebellious members of the Thani family. In hundreds of minor ways he sought to undermine the authority of the Gulf shaikhs. In Bahrain in 1930 there was a theft in which both the accuser and the accused were Hassawis. The accuser went to Bin Jiluwi, and the Governor immediately wrote to Shaikh Hamad bin Isa, the Shaikh of Bahrain, ordering him to have the accused sent to Hasa for trial. The Political Agent heard of the demand and stopped the Shaikh from complying. In a despatch to Bushire one of his predecessors had spoken of his irritation at the shaikhs developing 'a Bin Saud complex'.

Once again the shaikhs' position was changed by oil production. Oil brought about a much stronger British presence in the Gulf states. After the Second World War new political agencies were established in Dubai, Doha and Abu Dhabi, and the Residency was moved from Bushire to Bahrain. Military bases were set up in Bahrain and Sharjah. Hundreds more British personnel came out to the Gulf to help with development projects and setting up government administrations. In all of the Gulf states except Bahrain oil gave the governments a much greater spending power per head of population than the Saudi government had. In Kuwait for most of the 1950s and 1960s oil output was higher in absolute terms than in Saudi Arabia; the state began to generate a massive financial surplus, which after the British withdrawal in 1960 enabled it to give lavish aid to other Arab countries. This gave it an influence in the Arab world out of all proportion to its size. Meanwhile Saudi Arabia in the late 1940s and 1950s, during the latter years of King Abdel-Aziz and the reign of King Saud, slid into internal confusion. Although it pursued a claim to most of the territory of Abu Dhabi, including the Buraimi Oasis, in the early 1950s, it was not in a position to continue its attempts to weaken the rulers of the Gulf states.

It was only in the 1970s that the balance of power among the Arabian Peninsula oil states swung back in favour of Saudi Arabia. The British withdrew from Bahrain, Qatar and the Trucial States at the end of 1971, at a time when Saudi Arabia was embarking on a massive increase in the volume of its oil output. Within two years the embargo crisis and the oil-price rises made Saudi Arabia into a world power and gave its government its own huge surplus revenues.

Saudi Arabia now dominates the Gulf states; members of the Saudi royal family have spoken of their kingdom and the Gulf states as being all one country. The merchant families of the Gulf states are concentrating much of their corporate expansion in the Kingdom. Apart from being more aware of any Nejdi ancestry they may have, it is noticeable how anxious they are to establish that they had some links with King Abdel-Aziz. Now that the King has become a revered figure – more than ever alluded to by the Saudi royal family, which wants to emphasise the continuity of its rule – anyone's meeting with the monarch thirty or forty years ago has become a source of considerable pride. In the last few years families in Arabia (including many of those mentioned in this book) have been delving through their archives hoping to find a letter proving that they did some service for the great man. In the later 1970s whenever King Khaled returned to Saudi Arabia from hospital or a prolonged visit abroad, the Gulf rulers used to visit him to pay their respects. The rulers seemed to look to him not as a fellow and equal head of state, but as the tribal chief of all Arabia.

It is the behaviour of the Gulf merchants and rulers that now makes the records of fifty years ago relevant as more than background to the stories of the old merchant families. The continual references of the political agents to community divisions and the interference of the Saudis in the affairs of the Gulf states alters one's established perspective of Saudi–Gulf state relations and makes one wonder how independent the Gulf states seem today when viewed by Arabian eyes in a purely Arabian context. Should any of the Gulf states become unstable internally and begin to disintegrate in the manner of the Shah's Iran, it seems possible that people's loyalties would divide along the old community lines – with those of Nejdi and Hassawi origin looking towards Saudi Arabia. Given their earlier view of the Gulf states as a natural extension of their own territory, the Saudis would probably use any serious instability as a pretext for incorporating the states into their own Kingdom.

10

The Beginning of Modern Arabia

THERE'S GLOOM IN THE HAREM
SHEIK'S 84 WIVES ARE SAD-EYED
OFF ON HIS TRAVELS AND LEAVING THEM BEHIND
Special to 'The People'

There is gloom in the harem-house of Abdullah Ben Jasim, Sheik of Elcatar, in Eastern Arabia, staunch friend of Britain and ruler of one of the world's most romantic States.

The eyes of the 84 wives of the Sheik are clouded with trouble.

For within a few weeks the Sheik is leaving Elcatar, leaving his Arabian Nights Castle, which is watched over by stern-visaged eunuchs, and the lofty turrets of which leap upwards to the sky.

The Sheik is coming to London to be present at the Jubilee celebrations in honour of King George V. And he is leaving his wives behind him.

And while their thoughts will be with him through all the weeks that he will spend in Britain and on the Continent of Europe, they will count the hours, these beautiful Eastern damsels, until the longed-for day of his return.

GLITTERING GEMS

You may search the pages of romantic fiction and never come across so dazzling a tale as this real-life one of the 'Pearl King' of the East, whose priceless pearl fisheries yield up glittering gems which sparkle in the tiaras of duchesses, in the crowns of kings and queens, in the bracelets and necklaces of beautiful women in every corner of the world.

Thousands of negro slaves toil in the pearl fisheries owned by this picturesque ruler, whose merest word means life or death to his subjects.

'He is indeed a remarkable man, the Sheik of Elcatar', an intimate friend of the famous Arabian potentate told me, 'and a most upright, lovable personage.'

Those who have been privileged to visit his court have returned with breath-taking stories of its fabulous magnificence.

Every evening the Sheik sits in state surrounded by his ravishingly beautiful wives – he is presented by his courtiers with a new bride at every festival of Bairam, the most important ceremonial event in the Moslem calendar.

He has decided that he will not bring any of them with him to London. But he will bring one or two favourite courtiers and a vast suite of officers and officials.

This extraordinary story appeared in the *People*, a mass-circulation British Sunday newspaper, on 27 January 1935. A similar story had been published three days earlier by the *Daily Express*, which had added a patriotic note by telling its readers that the Shaikh had been made a Commander of the Order of the Indian Empire. Both papers were thought to have had the story fed to them by an American oil company involved in the bargaining for the Qatar oil concession. The culprit was believed by the British to be Standard Oil of California. The British authorities had always been sensitive to press comment on the affairs of the Gulf and at the same time were anxious to prevent American companies from winning concessions in competition with the Anglo-Iranian Oil Company (which later became BP). The logic behind the Americans planting of the story was their belief that the more international attention they could focus on the area, the harder it would be for the British to keep it as their own preserve.

The articles caused only a small ripple of interest. The British Resident in Bushire, Lt Colonel Sir Trenchard Fowle, wrote a letter to the India Office asking for copies of the press reports to be sent to the agents in Bahrain, Kuwait and Muscat 'to cheer them up'.

Someone else took the reports more seriously. A few weeks later Shaikh Abdullah bin Jasim al Thani received a strange letter from Yorkshire. It read as follows:

Honoured Sir,

By a section of our English press you have been described as fabulously wealthy, of a lovable disposition and the pearl king of the far East. Even so, I wonder whether you are really and truly happy with all this, I wonder.

In worldly goods I am probably one of the world's very poorest of men.

Yet in terms of real happiness found in the service of others I account myself one of the richest of men.

A natural born healer, I for 40 years have given of my services and spare money in the work of healing the sick poor. It is said of me that I have achieved the miraculous . . .

I would make a bargain with you. It is this. A gift of pearls in exchange for a detailed history of my remarkably successful healing methods . . .

Yours faithfully,
A.H. Woodcock, Bradford

Shaikh Abdullah seems not to have replied to the letter; in due course he passed it to the British Agency in Bahrain, which consigned it, along with its copies of the original articles, to a series of files labelled 'Qatar Miscellaneous'.

The other material that was accumulating in these files at the time gave a different picture of conditions in Qatar. On their periodic visits to the shaikhdom successive agents reported: 'Qatar is worse hit than Bahrain by the depression; the customs have dropped 50 per cent . . . The bulk of the inhabitants are on the verge of destitution, the people have sold the rafters of their houses to maintain themselves . . . There has been no rain in Qatar and the spring grazing has failed. A recently returned doctor reports that poverty is very marked, many people do not have enough to eat.' An oil-company employee who visited Qatar at about this time remembers seeing the Shaikh's eldest son, Ali bin Abdullah, who became Ruler in the 1950s, standing by the road with a sack of flour waiting for someone to lend him a donkey.

At the beginning of the 1930s the precarious economy of the Gulf was struck by disaster. The Japanese invented cultured pearls. These were made either by putting into the oyster a tiny bit of the shell of another oyster, which would then form the nucleus of a pearl, or by inserting a bigger round piece of glass, which the oyster would cover with a thin layer of pearl material. The first method produced something which looked very like a real pearl, though if the cultured specimen was cut through the middle it could be seen to have a series of rings like an onion, whereas real pearls had a consistent appearance right through. Sir Charles Belgrave said that he never knew a pearl merchant who could not distinguish cultured from real pearls simply by looking at them. The other types of cultured pearls, built around the beads of glass, could be seen to be fakes because they were always perfectly round, which none but the rarest natural pearls ever were. Both methods of manufacture were cheap, and both were virtually guaranteed to produce a pearl in every oyster.

The arrival of these pearls on the international market was accompanied by a change in fashion. By the 1930s the rich ladies of Europe and America were no longer wearing long ropes of pearls strung many times round their necks, as they had in the first two decades of the century. More serious was the effect of the Depression, which cut demand for all types of luxury goods in the industrialised countries. From the early 1930s prices sank rapidly. By the later 1940s they were only 10 or 20 per cent of the level of 1928–9. As a small, defiant gesture the Shaikh of Bahrain banned the import of cultured pearls into his territories – a ban which is still in force today.

The Depression had another serious consequence for the Arabian Peninsula. The industrial downturn caused a crash in rubber and sugar prices in Java and Malaya, which were two of the biggest and most prosperous sources of pilgrims to the holy cities of Mecca and Medina. The numbers of pilgrims from all sources fell from 100,000–120,000 a year in the later 1920s to 40,000 in 1931 and 20,000 in 1933, which saw the smallest pilgrimage of the decade. This produced a large drop in income for the merchants and people of the Hijaz and a disastrous cut in the budget of King Abdel-Aziz's government, which had been dependent mainly on a head tax levied on the pilgrims. In 1931 the government declared a moratorium on all its outstanding debts and sequestered the fuel stocks of the foreign trading companies in Jeddah. It began paying its officials in drafts on the customs receipts, which the officials sold at a large discount to the Jeddah merchants.

With the two biggest sources of their income reduced to a fraction of their former levels, the ordinary people of the Arabian Peninsula became even poorer than they had been in the 1920s. Fahd Algosaibi told me in 1978 that he remembered being on a pearling boat when it was forced to take shelter at Darin, near the Qatif oasis, during a storm: 'The next day the whole shore and the sea turned black,' he said. 'Believe me, it literally turned black – with women wading out to the depth of their chins to beg for scraps of food from our boat.'

Most of those directly engaged in pearling continued at first to work in the fisheries. Even though prices had collapsed and the incomes of many divers were reduced below subsistence level, there was very little else to do. Those who left pearling went to look for work with the oil company in Bahrain, which made a discovery in 1932, or with the exploration teams in Kuwait or Saudi Arabia. Those who failed stayed with their captains as servants or went back to the desert. Some died of starvation. The number of boats in pearling was reduced slowly. There was a good catch and a slight recovery of prices in 1937. A few years later, at the beginning of the Second World War, the merchants hoped that there would be a revival, with the same surge in demand that there had been during the First World War, when people in Europe had bought pearls for hoarding. Further hopes were raised in 1945, when there was another good catch and a small rise in prices caused by the low level of stocks and the destruction of Japan. On both occasions the merchants' and divers' hopes were disappointed. By the later 1940s pearling employed only a tenth of the numbers it had employed in the early decades of this century. Within a few years the industry was dead.

There is no question that it was the introduction of Japanese cultured pearls and the Depression that caused the suffering of the Arabian population during the 1930s. Yet these were not the main factors in the decline of the numbers engaged in pearling. The industry faded away because the oil companies that arrived in the Gulf in the 1930s and 1940s offered easier and more rewarding employment. Even if there had been a recovery in pearl prices after 1945, pearling would never have competed with the attractions of the oil industry.

It is tempting to see a stark contrast between the 1920s and the 1930s with, in the first period, the pearl industry giving a hard but adequate living to the people of the Gulf, while in the 1930s the Depression and the introduction of cultured pearls caused an appalling decade of unemployment and starvation. In fact very few old Arabians say they remember much difference between life in the 1920s and the 1930s. Some of the oil men who arrived in the late 1930s remember being told that there used to be hundreds more dhows and how many more people used to go to sea during the summer, but these comments were never accompanied by any lament about how good and prosperous times had been when the pearl industry had been at its peak. There was no dramatic difference between a life of subsistence for all in the 1920s, and a harsher life in the 1930s, when the incomes of a few dropped below subsistence level. To confuse recollections, there were some people –

those employed by the oil companies – who were better off in the 1930s than they had been before.

The arrival of the oil companies in the 1930s held out the hope of better times. Saudi Arabia and all the Gulf states signed concession agreements during the inter-war years, and in due course the oil companies made discoveries – in Bahrain in 1932, Kuwait and Saudi Arabia in 1938 and Qatar in January 1940.[1] Bahrain began regular exports in 1934 and Saudi Arabia in 1939. But within months of the first tanker loading at Ras Tanura, attended by King Abdel-Aziz on 1 May, the Second World War began. Salvation seemed to fade away before the rulers' and people's eyes. In Bahrain production continued, but in all the other states operations were scaled down or halted. In Saudi Arabia there was some exploration and development work, but exports stopped. In Kuwait and Qatar all operations were abandoned and the oil company personnel were withdrawn to Iran. The new discovery wells in Qatar were first plugged and later stripped and destroyed. The British decided that they did not have the spare steel to continue with work in remote and as yet unproductive oil fields. They preferred to concentrate their resources in Iran and Iraq.

For the people of Saudi Arabia and the Gulf states the war meant much worse deprivation than the 1930s. The direct results of the fighting were minimal. One night in October 1940 an Italian aircraft from the Dodecanese flew across Arabia to bomb the new American oil-company town at Dhahran and the Bahrain refinery at Sitra, which blazed with lights. Some very slight damage was done to Dhahran, but the bombs intended for Sitra fell in the desert. Matters became more

1. The companies that won concessions were as follows: in Bahrain Standard Oil of California; in Kuwait the Kuwait Oil Company, owned by Anglo-Iranian (later BP) and Gulf; in Qatar Anglo-Iranian; and in Saudi Arabia Standard Oil of California, which named its local operation CASOC – the California Arabian Standard Oil Company. After the award of the concessions other companies entered into partnerships with the concessionaires. In Bahrain Texaco joined Socal to form the Bahrain Petroleum Company (BAPCO). In Saudi Arabia Socal was joined first by Texaco and then by Standard Oil of New Jersey (now Exxon) and Mobil, forming Aramco – the Arabian American Oil Company. In Qatar Anglo-Iranian promptly transferred its concession to the owners of the Iraq Petroleum Company, in accordance with an agreement which the owners had made in the 1920s. Anglo-Iranian had equal shares in IPC with Shell, Compagnie Française des Petroles (Total) and a Mobil–Standard Oil of New Jersey partnership. The production operation was called the Qatar Petroleum Company.

serious at the end of the following year when Japan entered the war. The Japanese rapidly overran the rice-growing areas of South East Asia, which had provided much of Arabia's food, and extended submarine warfare to the Indian Ocean. Ships carrying food were sunk between India and the Gulf. There were food shortages in Saudi Arabia and the Gulf states.

The state that suffered worst was Qatar. It was not only poorer than its neighbours, but had to contend with an embargo on trade with Bahrain imposed by the Shaikh of Bahrain as a result of a long-running territorial quarrel over Zubara. This was a deserted town on the north-western coast of the Qatar peninsula, claimed by the Bahraini ruling family. The condition of the Qataris became so wretched that pearl boats were broken up to be used as fire wood. Some people sailed away in search of a better living in India, Africa or other parts of the Gulf, others moved to the Eastern Province of Saudi Arabia in hope of finding work with Aramco. According to the most pessimistic estimates, during the years of the Depression and the war Qatar's population declined from about 25,000 to 10,000.

To alleviate the distress in all the Middle Eastern countries the British and American governments organised a system of subsidies and food allocations. The Saudi government qualified for both food and a cash subsidy, which was intended originally to compensate for the loss of pilgrim traffic caused by the war. From 1941 to 1943 the cash was provided by the British, who paid more than $50 million. The Americans at first declined to contribute, arguing that Saudi Arabia was in Britain's sphere of influence. This policy changed in 1943, when the Kingdom was made eligible for Lend-Lease assistance.

Food allocations for Saudi Arabia and all the other states came under government authorities in India and Egypt. The Gulf states and the Saudi Eastern Province were supplied by the Ministry of Food in Delhi; Jeddah, the Levant, Iraq and Iran were supplied by the Middle East Supply Centre (MESC) in Cairo. Between them these authorities controlled all major commodities transactions in the Middle East and south Asia. They allocated specific quantities of cloth, grain, rice, tea, sugar and one or two other basic foodstuffs to each of the countries under their control. These supplies, subsidised by the British and American governments, were sold or given to the Middle Eastern governments. In Qatar and the Trucial States the supplies were sent directly to the rulers; elsewhere it was arranged that the supplies should be sent via the established importers. As a condition of their being allowed to buy supplies, the merchants were required to sell to their usual retail clients and to restrict their profits to 15 per cent. It was asked that governments should try to control retail prices in their territories.

From the start the system was subject to abuse. Large quantities of food were taken out of the local governments' control to be sold at black market prices by merchants and officials. The working of the system in Saudi Arabia was further damaged by the government's practice of settling some of its debts in wheat and rice. Merchants were told to go to Jubail, where the Eastern Province imports were stored, and collect whatever quantity of foodstuffs the government decided they were owed. For practical purposes there was no price control in Saudi Arabia.

In Bahrain controls were relatively effective. The population was issued with ration cards and was encouraged to come forward and report cases of hoarding and overcharging. This did not prevent the growth of black markets, but it did mean that the population got some of its foodstuffs at the subsidised price. The merchants withheld food from the retailers to smuggle to neighbouring states where the price controls were not effective or sell on the local black market. The tea importers explained the 'leakage' from their warehouses by saying that tea had fallen out of damaged chests or that rats were eating it. At the same time they took to showing the government invoices and shipping documents in which the purchase prices were grossly inflated. The Bahrain authorities, composed of the Ruler, Belgrave and a small British, Indian and Bahraini civil service, were not deceived. The invoices were found to be implausibly high and not to be consistent from one merchant to another. Nor did rats seem a reasonable explanation for the leakage.

The Bahrain government gradually took over responsibility for buying and distributing all foodstuffs, and continued this system for several years after the war. It used merchants with offices in India to purchase the food for a commission of $1\frac{1}{2}$ per cent, and then sold it through authorised retailers or its own shops. Sales were made only to ration-card holders. Inevitably the merchants complained bitterly about the new system and petitioned the Ruler to have it disbanded. The Ruler was not sympathetic.

The reaction of ordinary people was one of gratitude to the government. Several years after the war it was discovered by Belgrave's wife,

Marjorie, that many little girls at school, from black families descended
from slaves, were named *Bataka* – Ration Card.

Bahrain's response to the food-supply problems of wartime was typical
of the island. It dealt with the Depression and the war much better than
any of its neighbours. Between 1928 and 1932 its government's revenues, drawn mainly from customs dues and an income tax levied on the
divers, pullers and captains in the pearl industry, dropped from £82,000
to £50,000. This was insufficient to cover the cost of administration. To
meet the shortfall the shaikhs agreed with Belgrave, after some argument, that their own allowances should be reduced and that the salaries
of government officials should be cut by 10 per cent. At the same time,
work on new projects was slowed down, a small sum was withdrawn
from the reserve fund, and customs duties on non-essentials were
increased from 5 to 10 per cent.

The orderliness of Bahrain's policies stemmed in large measure from
Charles Belgrave, the Shaikh's adviser. Belgrave obtained his post after
replying to an advertisement which he had seen in the personal column
of *The Times* while having breakfast in a flat in Chelsea on Monday, 10
August 1925. The advertisement read: 'Young gentleman aged 22/28,
Public School and/or University education, required for service in an
Eastern State. Good salary and prospects for suitable man, who must be
physically fit; highest references; proficiency in languages an advantage. Write with full details to Box S. 501, The Times, London EC4.'

Once installed in Bahrain, Belgrave set about running the government in a totally unselfconscious British manner. From 1934 his work
was helped enormously by oil revenues, which increased the government's income to £334,000 in 1938 and £421,000 in 1943. With these
funds the government was able to carry out a serious development
programme. In the late 1920s and early 1930s it had opened six new
schools and introduced education for girls, under the direction of Mrs
Belgrave. In 1937, the year after the Shaikh paid an official visit to
Britain,[2] the government embarked on a programme for the eradication

2. The Shaikh had been invited to London to be awarded the insignia of a Knight
Commander of the Order of the Indian Empire. The British authorities arranged for
him a tour of the various attractions of the day, which included: the Trooping of the
Colour, Hendon Flying Display, a visit to the *Queen Mary* at Southampton and a
Huntley & Palmer biscuit factory at Reading, dog racing at Wembley, the sports day at

of malaria, which affected about 20 per cent of the population. After careful explanations to the people of the villages, officials began clearing the choked water channels and stagnant pools of the date gardens, and breaking the big earthenware water jars kept in people's homes. By the mid-1950s less than 1 per cent of the population suffered from malaria. Other projects carried out in the 1930s and 1940s included some small electricity power stations and a causeway and swing-bridge connecting Manama with the island of Muharraq.

Belgrave's approach to the tasks of government and the style he stamped permanently on the Bahrain administration, are shown in some of the minor events and routines he described in his book.[3] Every morning he used to ride to the fort for the police parade, taking a different route through the town each day so that he could check that the municipal authorities had cleared the streets and emptied the dust-bins. He taught the police bandsmen by whistling to them or playing gramophone records; one of the tunes they were taught by whistling was 'Marching through Georgia'.

Belgrave's wife had a similar down-to-earth approach. Soon after introducing girls' education she began organising an annual exhibition of girls' needlework, held in a palace room lent for the occasion by the Shaikh. A similar event, organised partly by the Belgraves, in the later 1940s was a garden fête in aid of the Church of England church fund. The Bahrain Petroleum Company managing director's garden, where the fête was held, had smooth green lawns, hedges of pink, white and red oleanders, flowerbeds of stocks, carnations, tobacco plant and larkspur. In the shade of the trees beyond the flower garden were sideshows and tea tables. Stalls run by Bahrainis and Indians sold homemade sweets and cakes, flowers, fresh vegetables, embroidery and needlework, and various items given by shopkeepers in the souk. The 'bring and buy' one year had a suit of armour, which Belgrave says proved very difficult to sell. Under a palm grove the police band, which by this time had a professional director, played Strauss waltzes and Sousa marches. There were donkey rides, on donkeys borrowed from the Manama municipality, competitions for judging the weight of a cake

Belgrave's son's prep school at Brighton, and Madame Tussauds. 'Ah yes,' said the Shaikh when he saw the waxwork of Henry VIII, 'the King who chopped off the heads of his wives when they bored him.'

3. See *Personal Column*, Hutchinson, 1960. The title of the book refers to the advertisement in *The Times*.

and the number of peas in a bottle, a baby show, and dancing on the lawn by the girls of the BAPCO school. All this would have been inconceivable in Saudi Arabia or any other Gulf state.

Under the regime of Belgrave and the political agents Bahrain became very British. Bill Mulligan, an Aramco employee who arrived in Dhahran in 1946, described the island to me as being almost a British colony: 'It had churches – there weren't any of those in Saudi Arabia – clubs, an American mission, a hospital. There was a small European community of people who *weren't* in oil, and a small community of Arabs who knew English. People wore topees in Bahrain, they dressed for dinner – in "whites", with a black cummerbund and black shoes. There was a very pronounced colonial-Indian class-conscious flavour about the place – a lot of Indians and Indian vocab – *dhobi*, *coolie* – all the workmen were *coolies*. Aramco started importing some of these attitudes, and the vocab, which was a problem. Americans who went over there would come back and have the natives calling them *Sahib* – "You call me *Sahib* boy." This was very un-American and un-Arabian.'

With its oil and the strong British presence, Bahrain was much more sophisticated and prosperous than its neighbours. For the oil men who began arriving in the Gulf in large numbers in the later 1940s, it was an oasis in an otherwise totally underdeveloped part of Arabia; it was the place one went to relax, enjoy oneself and buy the minor luxuries of life.

In Saudi Arabia, Kuwait and Qatar real changes began at the end of the Second World War. The Saudi concessionaire, the California Arabian Standard Oil Company, had discovered the Dammam field in 1938. The field was huge by normal US standards and quite acceptable by Middle Eastern standards; so straight away CASOC realised that if it maintained a reasonable rate of discoveries over the rest of its concession area it could not help but become a big exporter. Then in 1940 the company struck Abqaiq. As it appraised its new find in the middle war years of 1942–3 it saw that all its hopes were justified. The field was gradually proved to contain some 12 billion barrels of recoverable reserves, which made it one of the half-dozen biggest fields on earth – bigger than any field that has ever been discovered in North or South America.

Abqaiq and other discoveries had their effect on the policy of the US government. Hoping to counter British influence in a country where there was an all-American concessionaire, and already aware of its own country's slowly declining reserves, the US government reconsidered its attitude towards Saudi Arabia. One consequence was the extension of Lend-Lease aid to the Kingdom in 1943; another was a new policy of encouraging the fast development of the Saudi fields. Saudi reserves were seen as a new source of supply reasonably close to both the Japanese and European theatres of war. Materials were made available for the construction of a large refinery at Ras Tanura, which was built by Bechtel between 1943 and 1946. The labour force was composed mainly of Italian settlers and prisoners of war, sent by the British from Ethiopia.

During 1945 the development of the oil fields in both Saudi Arabia and Kuwait gathered momentum; in 1946 exports were quietly resumed in Saudi Arabia and inaugurated with pomp and ceremony in Kuwait. In the following year drilling began again in Qatar and in December 1949 the state made its first exports. There was a huge surge in demand for Middle Eastern oil. The United States in the post-war years swung rapidly from being a major exporter of oil to being a permanent net importer. At the same time Europe began drawing on huge amounts of oil for its reconstruction. To make this oil more easily and cheaply available to their European subsidiaries, the Aramco owners built the Trans-Arabian Pipeline (Tapline) between 1947 and 1950, from Dhahran to Sidon on the Lebanese Mediterranean coast.

These developments entailed a huge influx of foreigners and an enormous change in the lives of the Eastern Province Saudis, Kuwaitis and Qataris. The population of the Eastern Province was increased by immigration from the Hijaz, Bahrain and the other states of the lower Gulf – roughly the reverse of what had happened in the 1920s and 1930s. In Qatar almost everyone who had any significant income at all in the later 1940s drew it from the oil company; for five days of the week the entire life of Doha seemed to drain away to Dukan, the oil-company town on the other side of the peninsula.

The oil companies had thousands of simple jobs to offer – digging trenches for pipelines, mixing cement, unloading stores, truck driving, building accommodation and warehouses. At a slightly more sophisticated level men became warehouse clerks, construction-equipment drivers, electricians. A large number of the early employees of Aramco were former pearlers. Like the bedouin of the desert, these people were found to be stronger than the farmers of Hasa and Qatif, and they had the big additional advantage of being used to working as a team. They were less fatalistic than the farmers; they had had to deal with changes in tides and winds and they had learned to be disciplined in their work. Many of them also had a rudimentary knowledge of diesel engines. For those divers and pullers who were in debt to their captains, Aramco arranged a fair repayments system. The debtors were given 'guardians', with whom both parties agreed the size of the debt and a repayment schedule. This permitted the captains to take only a percentage of the divers' monthly pay, rather than all of it.

Much of Aramco's work, including all the more menial jobs, was done by Shias. In its early years Aramco found itself working in predominantly Shia areas, so Shias came to make up an unusually large proportion of its workforce. Once the Aramco–Shia connection had been established it stayed; Shias still account for a majority of the Saudis working in oil production.

There was never any specific policy of employing Shias. Tom Barger, who arrived in Saudi Arabia in 1937 and later became Chairman of Aramco, explained how the company worked in a conversation in 1978: 'We were a godsend to the Shia community because we were "colour-blind". We were a kind of emancipation for them. The bedouin from the desert just wouldn't touch jobs like sweeping – they would train as machine operators, but they wouldn't sweep around the lathe, and if they were told they had to do this they wouldn't train. They wouldn't do plumbing either. The Shias would work as hospital orderlies, in the laundry, they would do cooking, serving in the dining halls, gardening – of course handling water was something the Shias were used to doing in Qatif. There was no reverse-discrimination in any of this – we just employed anyone who came along. We definitely had a different attitude from the British. Looking back I'd say we assumed all the Arabs were just as trainable as anyone else. We assumed the problem was just their environment.'

There were numerous incidental consequences of Aramco's presence. The company had to sink holes for water before it drilled for oil, because it needed water as part of the normal process of drilling. Inevitably anyone involved with the rigs quickly learnt the fundamentals of drilling, and very soon there were Saudis with their own cable-tool rigs drilling for water.

As the people of the Eastern Province took regular jobs, new towns were formed. The oil company first based itself at Jubail but soon moved to establish an entirely new settlement at Dhahran, which was higher, less humid in summer and near its first discovery.

Dammam began to develop as the main port of the region. In 1946 it was a community of about two or three thousand people, with two thin lines of coral-block houses and dhows pulled up on the shore. The building of a pier in the late 1940s and the terminus of the railroad which Aramco constructed from the coast to Riyadh in 1950–51 transformed the town. In the early 1950s Saud, the son and successor of Abdullah bin Jiluwi as governor of the Eastern Province, moved his capital to Dammam from Hofuf.

A slightly different transformation took place a few miles along the coast at Alkhobar. In the 1930s Alkhobar had been just a dozen *barasti* and a coral stone mosque. By 1951 a banker described it as: 'A mud village by the sea – one dusty street of little shops, mostly food stores, with several exchange dealers and a few consumer goods shops.' The Aramco employees began using Alkhobar for buying foreign currencies and air-tickets before they left the Kingdom – though when they drove the five miles from Dhahran they took spades with them in case their cars stuck in the sand. The first banks in the Eastern Province were set up in Alkhobar and the more modern-minded merchants established themselves there. While Dammam developed as a Saudi town, Alkhobar became a centre for the expatriate community and foreign businessmen.

Aramco was the foundation for virtually all of the new businesses established in the Eastern Province. In the early 1940s William Eltiste, one of the company's American employees, took an interest in helping Saudis to establish small manufacturing and trading businesses. Eltiste not only gave advice, he helped with the maintenance of machinery and on one or two occasions invested some of his own capital in ventures. One of the first enterprises he backed was a small ice-making plant. In the mid-1940s Eltiste and his colleagues turned the operation into a formal organisation within Aramco, called first the Arab Industrial Development Department, and later, for reasons of tact, the Local Industrial Development Department. It goes without saying that Aramco was very aware of the benefits of AIDD in impressing the Saudi government. The new organisation helped to foster relations between concessionaire and government which over the next thirty years were probably better than those enjoyed by oil companies in other Middle Eastern producers.

AIDD gradually evolved several clearly defined types of activity. It undertook feasibility studies, provided technical assistance and occasionally guaranteed bank loans. It also arranged for Aramco to 'base load' new companies. This involved the Department giving guarantees that Aramco would buy certain quantities of the new enterprises' products or services, provided they reached a specified standard. AIDD became the instrument through which Aramco pursued a policy of 'divestiture'. The intention was to encourage Saudis to take over all the non-oil support activities which the company had been obliged to enter when it arrived in the Kingdom. If Aramco found itself consuming a large quantity of a particular product, or could see that it was going to be forced to enter a new non-oil operation, AIDD would write a report on the operation and distribute it among the local merchant community.

Not everyone who took up AIDD's suggestions and received its backing was successful. The Department often points out that there were a number of aspiring entrepreneurs whom it helped, but whose businesses did not take off and who have hardly been heard of since. Among those who were successful, the men with the biggest operations today are Suliman Olayan and Ahmed Hamad Algosaibi, whose businesses are described in later chapters. Others include the contractors Ali Tamimi and Abdullah Fuad, Abdel-Hadi Qatani, who owns a large trading business, and Abdullah Matrood, a Shia entrepreneur, who received help with his automatic bakery in Alkhobar. Mohammad Moajil was helped with the establishment of his drilling company, Sa'ad Moajil had Aramco as his main customer in the early days of his food-importing business, Mohammad Dossary carried out a number of oil company contracts and established a hospital specifically for Aramco.

There was a set pattern to the careers of many of the new Eastern Province businessmen. They received their education in Bahrain in the 1920s and 1930s, moved across to Saudi Arabia and took their first jobs with the oil company. Aramco gave them an insight into the modern industrial world which inspired them to go into business on their own as the building of the oil industry began in earnest after the war. This was exactly the course followed by Ahmed Hamad Algosaibi and Suliman Olayan.

A person who had a similar career was Abdullah Abdel-Ghaffar Alireza, a member of the Ali Akbar branch of the family and the son of one of the most widely travelled of the Arab pearl merchants.

Abdullah's story is a classic illustration of how Arabians were forced to adapt to new types of business as the pearl industry declined and the oil company became the main employers in the region. Abdullah received the usual good education of the Alirezas, being taught first in Bahrain and then at St Xavier's, the Jesuit school in Bombay. He returned to Bahrain for a few months at the beginning of the 1930s, but he and his father decided that there would be no point in his entering the pearl business, which was already showing signs of decline. Instead Abdullah went to Jeddah and embarked on a professional career of his own. First he worked as a private secretary for Karl Twitchell, the geologist whose reports encouraged Standard Oil of California to pay 35,000 gold sovereigns for the Saudi oil concession in May 1933. When he employed Abdullah, however, Twitchell was engaged in investigating the gold-mining potential of the Kingdom. In 1935 Abdullah moved to Standard Oil as a translator, and it was in this capacity that he interpreted for King Abdel-Aziz when he visited Dhahran and Ras Tanura to see the first shipment of Saudi crude in 1939. This small service to the Saudi royal family is commemorated in a photograph which now hangs in Abdullah's apartment in Kuwait.

Having gained some experience of the workings of a Western business at Standard Oil, Abdullah served for a time in a junior position in King Abdel-Aziz's government and then moved to Tehran, where he established a business of his own. By a stroke of good luck, while he was in Iran he met Shaikh Fahd Salem al Sabah, a member of the Kuwaiti ruling family who was to become the driving force in the state's development in the 1950s and the arbiter of many a fortune made out of land. The two men became friends and in 1949 Abdullah moved his business to Kuwait. Once established in yet another new home, he had the further good fortune to become a friend of the Ruler, Shaikh Abdullah Salem, and his son, Sa'ad, who since 1978 has been the Kuwaiti Deputy Ruler. Abdullah was periodically consulted on business matters by the old Ruler, he carried out odd assignments for him and travelled with him – as he sometimes does today with Shaikh Sa'ad. With these connections it was not surprising that Abdullah prospered in real estate. Early on he saw the potential of Salmiya, now one of the smartest residential suburbs, but then still a dusty area of a few villas and palaces to the east of Kuwait City. His success in real estate now makes him one of the richest of all the Alirezas. Since the 1950s Abdullah's company, known as the Rezayat Group, has developed a relatively

low-profile Kuwaiti trading business, a substantial international investment operation, which is backed by offices in Paris, London and
Boston, and a host of industrial and service operations in the Saudi
Eastern Province, run by his son Teymour. The main customer for
these enterprises in Saudi Arabia is Aramco.

The story of Saudi Arabia and the Gulf states since the oil companies
established themselves and development started in the late 1940s and
early 1950s is modern history. The evolution of all the states in this
recent period has been described in chapters 2, 3 and 4. In the past
thirty years Arabia has been utterly transformed, but its experiences in
the first half of this century still partly condition the attitudes and
aspirations of the Arabians. Dr Ghazi Algosaibi, the Saudi Minister of
Industry, once remarked in a newspaper interview: 'Unless you bear in
mind this yearning of our people for a better life after three thousand
years of sub-human existence you will not understand what is going on
in Arabia today.'

Even though Arabia may now seem less picturesque than in the days
of pearling, its people live lives that are not only more prosperous, but
more dignified and happier. One might expect old men to look back on
the past with nostalgia, but to a surprising degree old Arabians do not.
The attitudes of the old to the change that has overtaken them are
summed up in the statements of two Qataris in 1977.[4]

A pearl diver: 'Times have changed. We are happier now. There was
no peace at sea; the work was depressing and dirty. We drank water
while our sweat was dripping into it. The food wasn't clean. The clothes
we wore were also dirty from sweat . . . Now we must wear nice and
clean clothes to compensate for what we missed in the past . . . I never
went to school. So I didn't know what was good for me. In the case of
my sons they will know better because of their education. I wish I could
be young again and had the same opportunity as my sons. I would study
to become a doctor or a director, the number one boss, second only to a
minister.'

A merchant in the souk: 'We had nothing really until God opened the
door to prosperity and the oil companies came. Then people started to
work in the companies. They would start off as labourers, then learn a

4. See *Arabian Time Machine* by Helga Graham, Heinemann, 1978.

bit, and progress to driver, then learn a bit more and become a mechanic, then learn English, so they would become clerks, and so gradually our standard of living began to rise, until we reached our present level . . . Now, praise be to God, our Ruler has made everything easy. We now have embassies in every country, and these embassies are there above all to look after sick people. In my opinion we were living in darkness in the past, and our condition has changed from darkness to light.'

11

Algosaibi: The Story of an Old Family

One year in the late nineteenth century a man named Abdullah moved from the poverty-stricken mud village of Gassab to the equally wretched village of Herreimlah. The two communities were quite close to each other, 150 miles north-west of Riyadh. In Herreimlah the man became known as Abdullah Gosaibi – Abdullah, the little man of Gassab. He became an associate of the amir (governor) of the village, and was charged with the task of collecting the religious tax, Zakat, from those farmers in the area who acknowledged the amir's authority. Yusuf Mohammad, Abdullah's grandson and the oldest of his living descendants, believes the rate of tax levied was about one sheep for five camels. The tax financed the amir's household, and Abdullah himself lived off a small percentage of what he collected. This is all that anybody knows about Abdullah. The Algosaibi family today finds it difficult to date his movements to within fifty years; its members are not even sure of the name of Abdullah's father.

Slightly more is known about the early careers of Abdullah's three sons, Mohammad, Hassan and Ibrahim. They worked in the Nejd as camel drivers. They did not own any camels themselves; they helped to organise small caravans, supervised the grazing of camels, loaded camels. The decisive event of their lives was a terrible drought which struck the Nejd in the 1880s. Mohammad Almana, King Abdel-Aziz's interpreter half a century later, said in a conversation in 1980 that all the best people – those with courage and initiative – left the area: 'Then there was nothing but poverty and stones.' Villagers from Gassab went to Hail in the northern Nejd, to southern Iraq, where there is a big Nejdi community around Zubair, and to Asir in the south-west of the Peninsula. All of these places now have families with the name Algosaibi. Mohammad, Hassan and Ibrahim moved from Herreimlah to the Gulf coast in about 1885. They continued to work with camels,

Algosaibi Family Tree – Much Shortened

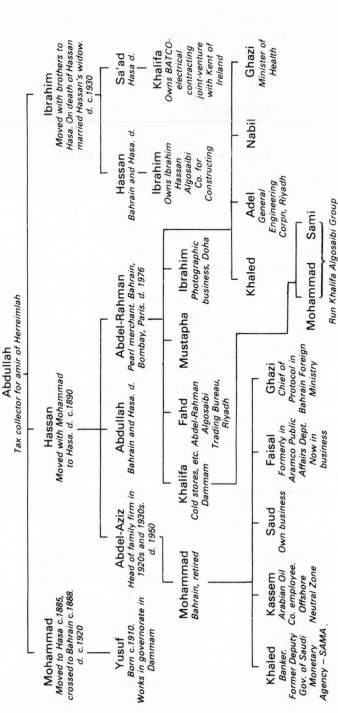

Abdullah
Tax collector for amir of Herreimlah

Hassan
Moved with Mohammad to Hasa. d. c.1890

Ibrahim
Moved with brothers to Hasa. On death of Hassan married Hassan's widow. d. c.1930

Mohammad
Moved to Hasa c.1885, crossed to Bahrain c.1888. d. c.1920

Yusuf
Born c.1910. Works in governorate in Dammam

Abdel-Aziz
Head of family firm in 1920s and 1930s. d. c.1950

Abdullah
Bahrain and Hasa. d.

Abdel-Rahman
Pearl merchant. Bahrain, Bombay, Paris. d. 1976

Hassan
Bahrain and Hasa. d.

Sa'ad
Hasa d.

Khalifa
Owns BATCO-electrical contracting joint-venture with Kent of Ireland

Ghazi
Minister of Health

Mohammad
Bahrain, retired

Khalifa
Cold stores, etc. Abdel-Rahman Algosaibi Dammam

Fahd
Abdel-Rahman Algosaibi Trading Bureau, Riyadh

Mustapha

Ibrahim
Photographic business, Doha

Ibrahim
Owns Ibrahim Hassan Algosaibi Co. for Constructing

Khaled

Adel
General Engineering Corpn, Riyadh

Nabil

Khaled
Banker. Former Deputy Gov. of Saudi Monetary Agency – SAMA.

Kassem
Arabian Oil Co. employee. Offshore Neutral Zone.

Saud
Own business

Faisal
Formerly in Aramco Public Affairs Dept. Now in business

Ghazi
Chief of Protocol in Bahrain Foreign Ministry

Mohammad

Sami
Run Khalifa Algosaibi Group

NOTES

1. The Algosaibi family does not belong to a tribe and therefore has no ancient lineage. Its members are from the class known as *bayasarah* – freemen farmers who worked in the date gardens but normally did not own land. To this day the men of the Algosaibi family do not marry women from tribal families. The name Algosaibi comes from the village of Gassab – which can be translated as 'reeds' or 'cane'. The British authorities in Bahrain, who disliked the family, used to believe that they had descended from a butcher, this being an alternative meaning of gassab. However, it is suggested by Arabians that if the family had taken its name from a butcher, it would have adopted another name as it began its rise to prominence.

2. As of about 1910 the Bahrain and Bombay trading firm and the Hasa date gardens were owned in partnership by Mohammad, the three sons of Hassan – Abdel-Aziz, Abdullah and Abdel-Rahman – and Ibrahim. In about 1920 Mohammad died and his son, Yusuf, the only child, being still a

and two brothers not shown in the family tree) were still children, and they say now that the date gardens they received were not as good as they might have been and were not well looked after on their behalf by their cousins. The Mohammad branch of the family tree today could not be described as even moderately well-off by Saudi standards.

Some time after Mohammad's death, Ibrahim's share of the business was given to his sons – Hassan and Sa'ad (whose mother was the dead Hassan's widow), and two much younger sons, Abdullah and Yusuf, who at the time were only children and are not shown in this family tree. The assets given to Abdullah and Yusuf were considerably less valuable than the assets given to their older brothers, and were eventually used as the basis of separate businesses of their own. For most of the 1920s and 1930s, therefore, the major Algosaibi business in Bahrain, Hasa and Bombay was transporting goods from the anchorage at Uqair to Hofuf in the Hasa oasis.

The story of how Mohammad soon broke away from this menial employment was told to me by his son Yusuf, who is now an old man working in the governor's palace in Dammam: 'Mohammad was the only literate brother. He said to the others that it really was not much of a living with camels. He had heard about the prosperity of Bahrain – there was already some British influence there, and the pearling – and he decided that he would do better if he went there. He left the camels with his brothers and went to Bahrain, where he met a big merchant. This man was Abdel-Rahman bin Idan, who came from Hasa. He was looking for a clerk – he had been asking his friends to see if they could find a clerk for him. Of course my father was literate, and he was discovered by the friends of bin Idan, who was one of the biggest merchants in pearls. My father was put in charge of financing the pearl dhows.

'After a time bin Idan told my father that he could use some of his money to establish a separate business – a business for my father on his own. Gradually my father became rich and separated from the merchant – but he continued to look after his accounts because bin Idan did not have any sons of his own. My father's business was the same as bin Idan's – he lent money to the captains of the pearl dhows. He soon became richer than bin Idan himself.'

Not long after Mohammad arrived in Bahrain, the second of the three Algosaibi brothers, Hassan, died while on a pilgrimage to Mecca. In accordance with the common custom, Ibrahim, the third brother, married Hassan's widow, and named his eldest son Hassan in his brother's memory. The thought behind marriages of this type was that they provided security for the widows and kept families united. Within a few years, in about 1898, the dead Hassan's sons, Abdel-Aziz, Abdullah and Abdel-Rahman, were sent to Bahrain to join their uncle in trade. One by one they were then despatched by Mohammad to India to learn English, buy foodstuffs and deal with the Bombay pearl merchants. They mixed with the other Arabian families that had established businesses there; Mohammad Almana, the interpreter, whose father was a horse dealer, remembers meeting the young Abdel-Rahman in the garrison town of Poona in 1914. The profits of the Algosaibi offices in Bombay and Bahrain were sent back to Hasa, where Ibrahim bought extensive date gardens.

It seems that Ibrahim was no less enterprising than the other members of his family. In about 1906 he met the Amir of Nejd, Abdel-Aziz bin Saud, while he was travelling on a pilgrimage to Mecca. How exactly the paths of the two men crossed is not known. One suggestion is that the Algosaibi caravan went through Riyadh and was obliged to pay the Amir for an escort and safe passage; another is that to the west of Riyadh, in the territory of the Utaiba tribe, the caravan encountered one of the Amir's raiding parties. In any event Ibrahim and Ibn Saud became friends – a relationship made possible by Ibrahim's Nejdi ancestry. Ibrahim admired the Amir, whom the people of central Nejd, wherever they lived, were beginning to see as representing firm government, security and their own supremacy over other Arabians. Like the rest of the coastal population Ibrahim despised the Turks, who were then still the nominal rulers of the Hasa province. Under the Turks anarchy prevailed. Yusuf Mohammad remembers being told by Ibrahim: 'You would go to your gardens and find that the bedouin had come in the night and stolen the dates off the trees. The Turks never bothered about this and they could not prevent it. The troops in the garrison were useless.'

Ibrahim became the leader of a Nejdi fifth column in Hasa. It happened that because he was a Nejdi he was much consulted by the Turks on desert politics and used by them in dealings with the bedouin. The Turks entrusted the pay and provisions of the Hofuf garrison to Algosaibi caravans; this was the only way they could guarantee their safe passage between the anchorage at Uqair and the oasis. Ibrahim used his frequent excursions from the oasis to pass information to the agents of Ibn Saud. If there was ever any chance of him or his messengers being searched, his descendants today say that he used to roll up his letters and hide them in cartridge cases.

In 1913 Ibn Saud decided to take Hasa. He had a mixture of motives. He wanted to demonstrate his strength to the British, and he coveted the taxes from the Hasa date gardens and the customs dues of Uqair, Darin and Jubail. According to the tradition of the Algosaibi family, he sent a note to Ibrahim telling him of his intentions and asking him to have materials for the attack hidden in a palm garden. Ibrahim took wooden poles, ladders and ropes through the city gates on the pretext of building a house outside the walls. This was not normally permitted by the Turks, but as his descendants say today, 'Ibrahim had influence.' Ibn Saud meanwhile assembled a force of 1,500 – mostly townsmen with some bedouin – and advanced until he was five hours' march from Hofuf. After giving a rousing speech to prepare them for the battle, he picked 300 men and scaled the city walls by night – according to the Algosaibis using the materials hidden in the palm groves by Ibrahim. There was some minor fighting in which twelve were killed. The Turks retreated to a fort in the city and surrendered the next day. Within a fortnight Uqair, Qatif and the rest of the Hasa province had fallen.

The conquest of Hasa is now represented in Saudi Arabia as a liberation by Ibn Saud of fellow Arabs from the weak and venal rule of the Turks. At the time it was not certain that the Hassawis were so pleased to be liberated. Most of the region's population were Shias, who became even more second-class citizens under the rule of the Sauds and Abdullah bin Jiluwi than they had been under the Turks. When he realised that Ibn Saud was intent on conquering Hasa, the Shaikh of Seihat, a Shia village near Qatif, made a desperate appeal to the Agency in Bahrain to be taken under British protection. The appeal came through Yusuf Kanoo, the richest Bahraini merchant, who worked as an interpreter for the Bahrain Agency. Kanoo wrote to the Political Agent on 18 April 1913:

Dear Major Trevor,
Shaikh Hassan bin Nasser, Sheikh of Seihat, has spoken to me privately to see you that he wishes to be under the protection of the British with his people under him who are 1,500, his object being that if he gets any trouble from the Turks, or bedous or others, the British will help him. I told him that I would see you and let him know verbally the result . . . of course you know best.

The British saw immediately that it was Ibn Saud whom the shaikh feared, and turned down the request. After the inevitable conquest of Seihat and all the other towns and villages of the area, the main benefit of Saudi rule for all the Hassawis was the curbing of bedouin raids.

There are also doubts surrounding the details of the role of the Algosaibi family in the conquest of Hasa. Nobody questions that Ibrahim was the leader of the pro-Saudi faction in Hofuf, but it is only members of the Algosaibi family who recount the story of his providing materials for Ibn Saud. In the British records there is no mention of the family's connection with the attack.

What is not challenged is that the fall of Hasa marked the beginning of a very close relationship between the Algosaibi family and Ibn Saud's government. Members of the family became some of the most valued servants of the monarch – though they never married into the royal family or wielded any influence in politics, as did the Sudairis and other leading tribal families of the Nejd.

The role of the Algosaibis was to be Ibn Saud's representatives in Bahrain. The family had begun to carry out odd assignments for the ruler of the Nejd through their offices in Bahrain and Bombay in 1908, but it was only after Ibn Saud established a presence on the coast that their work became important. By this time the Algosaibi business was being run mainly by the sons of Hassan and Ibrahim, normally referred to as 'the five brothers' – Abdel-Aziz, Abdullah, Abdel-Rahman, Hassan and Sa'ad.

The brothers were used to arrange shelter and transport for all visitors to Ibn Saud, whether he was in Hofuf, which he visited occasionally, or Riyadh. The Sultan, as Ibn Saud became soon after taking Hasa, would send them messages telling them to provide accommodation for particular people or parties in their houses, either in Bahrain or Hofuf, and entertain them until they were sent word that the Sultan was ready to receive them. At different times the family entertained or transported St John Philby, the explorer, Major Frank Holmes, the eccentric New Zealand concession hunter who was the first person to be convinced that there was oil in Arabia, a succession of British political agents, and the British delegation that attended the Uqair Conference in 1922. Outside the Algosaibi house on the Bahrain sea front there were always moored several motor-driven dhows.

The Algosaibis were the channel for diplomatic communications between Ibn Saud and the British. During the First World War the British sent their subsidy to Ibn Saud – £5,000 a month – by paying the money in cash to the Algosaibis. The family handled supplies of arms and ammunition for the Sultan. (It was British policy to encourage Ibn Saud to attack the Rashid family of Hail, who were supporters of the Turks.) Other communications were letters and verbal messages, embellished with the Algosaibis' own comments. Members of the family used to give to the British their personal interpretations of Ibn Saud's views – always in accordance with the known wishes of the Sultan. Much of their effort went into trying to worry the British about the parlous state of Ibn Saud's finances, in the hope that the subsidy payments would be increased. This was done with a careful air of casualness. One of the brothers – normally Abdel-Aziz or Abdullah – would call on the Political Agent with a routine piece of news, and then contrive to be sidetracked into communicating 'confidential' financial or political intelligence. The agents generally concluded that Ibn Saud had intended the intelligence to be passed to them, and they relayed it to the Residency in Bushire as if it had been official.

The main part of the Algosaibis' work involved buying supplies. The family's office in India supplied the business in Bahrain and Hasa with the usual assortment of staple foodstuffs and materials – rice, tea, sugar, cotton cloth, spices and timber. For Ibn Saud the family's purchases were more varied. Letters that survive include orders for: rice – to be bought in Basra for Ibn Saud in Riyadh and the reprovisioning of Hasa and Qatif (December 1915); lead, iron bars, paint and salt (September 1917); copper sheets and plates, iron sheets and bars, white tin, a telephone, safes for cash, lamps and lanterns, iron horseshoes and nails (August 1918). In 1920 the Algosaibis were instructed to buy and install a light buoy in Uqair harbour. The letters from Bombay which acknowledge these orders were written on a fairly cheap cream writing paper, with a blue heading: 'Abdel-Aziz Hassan Algosaibi, Mangaldas Road, Opposite G.T. Hospital. Cables Mowafik, Bombay'.

The Algosaibis often had to wait months or years for payment from Ibn Saud. At times they were asked to advance money to the Sultan; in 1914 Yusuf bin Ahmed Kanoo reported to the Political Agent that he had heard that the family had advanced 20,000 rupees ($6,000). During the First World War and the following two or three years Ibn Saud periodically authorised the family to reimburse itself by keeping part of the subsidy payments it forwarded from the British. Later, when the subsidy payments ceased, the brothers recompensed themselves for the credit they gave by increasing their profit margins; it was not normally revealed to Ibn Saud's court what price they had had to pay for the items they bought. At no point did the Sultan ever pay the family directly for its services. Its reward was entirely in its profit margins and the prestige it gained.

One of the most important assignments the family received in the early years of its service was the request from Ibn Saud that Abdullah should accompany his son, the fourteen-year-old Prince Faisal, on an official visit to Europe in the autumn of 1919. The visit was arranged by the British, who wanted to reward Ibn Saud for his friendship during the war. For the Arabian party it provided an extraordinary exposure to a totally alien culture. The young prince rode in a donkey cart in Ireland, inspected a captured German submarine and took tea on the roof garden of Selfridges, the Oxford Street department store. He was taken to a performance of Gilbert and Sullivan's *Mikado*, and to the Royal Ordinance Depot, the Zoo, the Greenwich Observatory and the Royal Metal Exchange. At Buckingham Palace he exchanged swords with George V; in Snowdonia his party was invited to try some mountain walking and encountered a Welsh snowstorm. When the long programme of activities in Britain was finished, the Saudi party was taken across the Channel for a tour of the trenches and shattered villages of the Western Front.

What Prince Faisal made of his visit is not recorded, though he behaved throughout with perfect calm and good manners. Abdullah Algosaibi, for his part, was considerably impressed by what he had seen. He had travelled less than his brothers, Abdel-Aziz and Abdel-Rahman. The visit was still fresh in his memory in 1923, when Major R.E. Cheesman visited Arabia with an official letter for Ibn Saud and found himself staying with the Algosaibis in Hofuf. Cheesman afterwards wrote of Abdullah in a book entitled *In Unknown Arabia*:[1]

> The Savoy Hotel had impressed him more than the Carlton chiefly on account of the dancing. The London policemen took first place among all the marvels he had seen. He jumped into the middle of the room and gave an exhibition, holding up his hand and gazing intently and fiercely at the opposite wall as an imaginary string of motor busses bore down on him and pulled up, till he majestically waved them on. 'And you will hardly believe me', he said to his audience, 'but the policeman never shouts, he never even speaks.'

Cheesman then reminded Abdullah that they had met during the London visit:

> . . . he sent off for a box of treasures from his home containing photographs of himself, picture postcards, and illustrated newspapers with photographs of the Nejd mission to England. What he wanted to find were the Carlton Hotel menus signed by the guests at the various parties. I could not remember signing one, but he burrowed among his papers, showing me menu after menu, until almost at the bottom there appeared

1. *In Unknown Arabia* by R.E. Cheesman, Macmillan, 1926, pp. 134 and 143.

one with my signature. His delight knew no bounds. As he put it, we had been friends for five years, and I learned next day that he had been to tell the governor [Bin Jiluwi] about it . . . His collection of works of art was an amusing collection of picture postcards of towns and coal mines, with some appalling coloured cards of women in undress, luckily all perpetrated in Brussels, which he had been given during a tour of the continental battlefields. I blushed when these were passed round in such an assembly, but regained my composure when I saw that the cards were being looked at sideways and upside down and examined as landscapes.

Cheesman spoke Arabic, so there seems to be no possibility that he misunderstood the townsmen's reaction. The explanation of their extraordinary behaviour must have been that the men of Hasa, who were very much isolated from the world outside Arabia and totally unfamiliar with photographs or postcards – or European landscapes for that matter – were simply unable to recognise nude, or almost nude, women, with unfamiliar hair, dress and make-up, outside their own cultural context. It is unlikely that anyone living under the upright and God-fearing rule of Abdullah bin Jiluwi had ever conceived of women posing for salacious photographs.

At the time of the postcard episode the Algosaibis were already worth about a million rupees – some hundreds of thousands of dollars. They had a virtual monopoly of the carrying trade between Bahrain and the mainland, and were reported by the British to have great influence in the Nejd and Hasa. In 1922 the Political Agent wrote: 'The Algosaibis now rank only after Yusuf Kanoo in wealth and are rapidly gaining on him.' Visitors to Hasa reported that the Algosaibi gardens contained fruit of every description and several rice fields. Their offices in the main market square of Hofuf occupied a big three-storey white building, surrounded by a colonnade and with an imposing Persian-style arched doorway. Today members of the family who were children in the 1920s say that they remember a huge house at Rifaa in Bahrain. This would accommodate up to a hundred people – twenty or so husbands and wives of different generations, children and foreign guests. The family might consume five sheep and a sack of rice for dinner.

The growing wealth and prestige of the Algosaibis made the family into a political power in Bahrain. At first the brothers' relations with the other political powers – the Khalifa family and the British – were excellent; in 1919 the Political Agent invited Abdel-Aziz Algosaibi and

Yusuf Kanoo to share his Christmas dinner. Then in the early 1920s relations between Ibn Saud and the British started to deteriorate, mainly because Ibn Saud would not abandon his quarrel with the Hashemite royal family of the Hijaz, who had been Britain's principal Arab allies during the war. The British cancelled Ibn Saud's subsidy, and Ibn Saud in return began a policy of what the Political Resident termed 'penetration' of the British protected shaikhdoms all along the Gulf. Naturally the Algosaibis became the Bahraini agents of Ibn Saud's policy. At the same time they used the deteriorating relations between the Sultan and the Gulf shaikhs to further their own interests. The British suspected that the family aspired to a diplomatic status as Nejdi consular representatives in Bahrain, charged with guarding the security of Nejdis and issuing them with passports. This would have run counter to the terms of the British treaties with the Khalifa family, which specified that the British were to conduct all relations between Bahrain and foreign powers.

The first of a series of issues that brought the Algosaibis and the British into conflict came to the fore in 1921. During the previous two years the Algosaibis and another Nejdi merchant had been paying customs dues of only $2\frac{1}{2}$ per cent on goods trans-shipped through Bahrain to the mainland, whereas all other merchants had been paying 5 per cent. Eventually the Political Agent decided to end this unfair situation, which had arisen through a misunderstanding of the orders of the Shaikh, and set $2\frac{1}{2}$ per cent as the duty for all merchants in the mainland trade. He also announced that in future mainland merchants should be free to appoint as their agents, or use as their suppliers in Bahrain, whomever they liked – and not feel obliged to use the Algosaibis. He wrote to Ibn Saud to tell him that the changes could only be to the benefit of the Nejd. When Abdel-Aziz Algosaibi heard of this he visited the Agent, 'blustered and threatened to raise the anger of Bin Saud . . . he became very disgruntled.'

Some time later, in early 1923, there occurred a strange instance of Algosaibi high-handedness involving the persecution of a Shia. At the time of the incident Abdel-Aziz Algosaibi was in India and Abdel-Rahman in Paris, leaving Abdullah in charge of the office in Bahrain. Abdullah used his temporary position as the official agent of Ibn Saud to exacerbate a dispute which had come about through members of the Khalifa family bullying a Shia resident of Qatif who had owned land in Bahrain, in a thoroughly dishonest attempt to claim the land for themselves. The Shia had been ordered by Ibn Saud to go to Bahrain so that the matter could be settled. After his arrival the dispute had seemed likely to fade away – until Abdullah took it upon himself to order the man to appear before the *qadi* – the judge. In the event the case was not pressed. None the less it worried the Agent because it so obviously showed the Algosaibis, the Khalifas – then under the ageing and ineffective rule of Shaikh Isa bin Ali – and Ibn Saud to be willing to aid and abet each other in bullying Shias.[2]

Within a few weeks Abdullah became involved in a much more serious matter. In April 1923 a fight occurred outside the Algosaibi offices in the Manama souk between a Nejdi and a Persian, 'both of the cooley class'. The fight led to a general fracas. The Political Agent, Major Daly, was quite certain that the Nejdis were more to blame for the disturbance than the Persians, who were normally rather meek. He wrote to the Resident in Bushire: 'I was informed that there were a number of witnesses, including Indians, to the fact that Gosaibi appeared at the beginning of the fracas and urged the Nejdis to beat the Persians, and then retired to his office and bolted the door. It is certain that while the fracas was in progress the Nejdis continually shouted "Long Live Ibn Saud" and similar remarks.' The roots of the trouble, the Agent said, lay in 'religious fanaticism in the trying period of Ramadan' (the month of fasting).

On 10 May there was a much more serious riot. The immediate cause was trivial. A boy in the service of the Algosaibis was said to have stolen a broken watch from the Algosaibi house. Another servant of the family then told Abdullah Algosaibi that he had seen the watch for sale in a shop owned by a Persian and had demanded that it should be handed back. The Persian replied that he had bought it from the boy for 1 rupee (30 cents), having no reason to suspect that it was stolen, and had paid R 2/- for its repair. He said that he would return the watch if he was paid his out-of-pocket expenses. Abdullah, when he heard of this, went with two Nejdis and demanded the return of the watch without payment. There was an argument. Abdullah then compelled the shopkeeper to go with him to Mohammad Sherif, the chief of police. In the process his Nejdi followers roughly handled the shopkeeper. Mohammad Sherif, who was himself a member of the island's Persian community, wisely

2. The past treatment of the Shia population has become a subject of interest in Gulf politics since the various disturbances in Qatif and Bahrain in 1979, 1980 and 1981.

paid the R 2/- that was in dispute, and Abdullah left, the matter apparently being settled.

Shortly afterwards two Persians arrived at Mohammad Sherif's house bleeding profusely from dagger wounds, which they said had been inflicted by Nejdis. Mohammad Sherif summoned Abdullah and asked him to send the men responsible to the Political Agent, saying that he would do the same with the two Persians. He explained that it would be better to have the Agent settle the matter, because it might otherwise develop into something serious, beyond their own abilities to handle. Abdullah, however, suggested that he and Mohammad Sherif should first make their own enquiries. During the delay the whole souk flared up.

Abdullah and Mohammad Sherif went at once to Major Daly. The Agent reported:

. . . then Yusuf Kanoo arrived accompanied by Mr Meikle of 'Mespers' [the Mesopotamia Persia Corporation]. He stated that the affray had grown serious and suggested the use of Agency troops in the bazaar. I declined on the grounds that this might have forced the situation and led to unpredictable consequences. Having however ascertained that there was no crowd between the Agency and Messrs Mespers office, which is well away from the bazaar, and therefore no likelihood of a collision, I left orders for the guard to march there, but to take no action of any sort. I caused Yusuf Kanoo to despatch several people to the bazaar to spread the news that the troops were coming. I then proceeded to the bazaar myself by car. Gosaibi declined to accompany me, and fearing that it would give a false impression if I took with me only the leader of the Persians, I went accompanied by Yusuf Kanoo and a Qatar merchant. On arrival I found the actual fighting had ceased, doubtless as a result of news that troops had left the Agency. The bazaar was full of excited Nejdis armed with lathis, and some with swords and daggers and fire-arms. At first no Persians were to be seen, but later a few who lived on the spot came out of their buildings. I proceeded to collect sticks etc. from the crowd and to disperse them as far as possible. When it was clear that the situation was in hand and a collision was very improbable, I sent word to the guard who were at Messrs Mespers to march with me through the bazaar, and then sent them back to the Agency. Shortly after Gosaibi arrived with a crowd of Nejdis. Meanwhile Mr Mackie (Anglo-Persian Oil Company) had arrived from Yusuf Kanoo's house. He assisted me to cause the dead and wounded to be removed, which I was anxious to do early lest their presence should cause a further outbreak. We caused to be removed two dead Persians and one Nejdi, and two Persians and one Nejdi who were still just breathing. A number of wounded who could walk were sent to the hospital. During these proceedings Gosaibi was beside himself with rage against the Persians, making a fresh scene as each injured Nejdi was discovered.

That evening Major Daly signalled the Resident, Colonel Knox:

ANOTHER SERIOUS DISTURBANCE⁺ BETWEEN PERSIANS AND NEJDIS TODAY, CASUALTIES 7 OR 8 DEAD AND LARGE NUMBER INJURED. HAVE STOPPED THE DISTURBANCE FOR THE TIME BEING BUT THE MATTER HAS ASSUMED RELIGIOUS ASPECT AND HAS SERIOUS POSSIBILITIES IF THE LOCALS JOIN IN. DETAILS BY POST. IF GUNBOAT COULD VISIT HERE AS SOON AS POSSIBLE AND REMAIN TIL END OF RAMADAN IT WOULD HAVE A STEADYING INFLUENCE. DALY.

In the next two days the Nejdis remained uncontrollable. Bahrain suffered a collapse of law and order. Boatloads of armed men from Muharraq island, next to Manama, attempted to land beside the Agency but were deterred by the Agency troops drawn up on the sea front. The Bahraini Sunnis of Budiya and Rifaa attacked the Shias in the village of Ali. Houses were burnt; there were several casualties.

The fighting stopped with the arrival of two destroyers, HMS *Crocus* and HMS *Triad*. On 13 May Major Daly had time to compose his detailed report. He had been able to think about the allocation of blame and punitive action:

In discussing the situation with Shaikh Sulman [a leading member of the Khalifa family] he expressed the opinion that the arrest of Gosaibi would be a good thing and wanted me to carry it out. When asked why none of the shaikhs would remonstrate with Gosaibi, let alone arrest him, he admitted that as Ibn Saud's agent they were afraid to deal with him . . . It was apparent that he wished me to order the arrest, thus enabling the shaikhs to excuse themselves to Ibn Saud that it had been done under pressure from the Agency. In my opinion such action, since at that time there was no gun boat, was best left alone. In an interview with Shaikh· Hamad [Shaikh Isa's son and heir apparent] the latter expressed the opinion that Gosaibi had planned the outbreak and had been preparing the Nejdis for some days for it. My own opinion is that if he did not actually prepare the outbreak, his action in regard to the watch episode, which undoubtedly started the disturbance, was equally culpable.

During the weeks that followed, the British discussed what steps they should take. Without hesitation they resolved that Shaikh Isa should be replaced by Shaikh Hamad, a change that had been pending for some time. Towards the end of May Colonel Knox came to Bahrain to explain the decision to an assembly of notables. It proved more difficult to agree how to deal with Abdullah. After long correspondence it was decided to send him to Ibn Saud with a letter describing his own misconduct. Ibn Saud, of course, stood by his agent, blamed the Persians, alleged police bias, and pointed out (correctly) that almost all the police in Bahrain were Persians. He sent an envoy to the Resident to argue Abdullah's case. This led to a further period of inter-British consultation, with letters going from the Agency in Bahrain to the Residency in Bushire, from there to the Government of India offices in Delhi and Simla, and in a few cases to London. The Secretary of State for India, the Duke of Devonshire, was obliged to turn his attention to the matter. Finally it was decided that Abdullah should be allowed to return to Bahrain, it having been tacitly accepted by all parties that he should 'lie low' and confine himself to purely commercial activities. Col. Knox elaborated on the decision to Ibn Saud's envoy and reported his conversation in a letter to Major Daly: 'I used a homely simile to the envoy to comfort him, telling him that if Abdullah only followed out our advice and instructions he would speedily find out that he would be able to couch a camel in the PA's drawing room, while Abdullah by the former methods, would find it impossible to introduce a mouse wrapped in a napkin into a corner of the PA's compound.'

The issue had revolved very much around saving face on all sides. Abdullah did not normally reside in Bahrain and had had no special reason for wanting to return there. When Abdel-Aziz Algosaibi came back from India he advised his impetuous brother to stay on the mainland for a time. Major Daly did not see Abdel-Aziz's arrival as being liable to lead to much of an improvement in the situation. He wrote a 'personality report' on Abdel-Aziz to Knox:

> . . . probably the second biggest grain merchant here now. In partner-
> ship with his brother [Abdel-Rahman] he is engaged in the pearl trade
> and owns pearling boats. He has also of late years acquired a great deal of
> house property etc. in Bahrain . . . he is far from being a peaceable
> person and his various activities, combined with a very overbearing
> manner, frequently bring him into conflict with other persons of impor-

tance in the place. Also he is an oppressive pearl trader and frequently has cases with his divers. The shaikhs dislike him intensely and he has in the past bullied them a good deal and made them part with valuable land etc. cheap solely because they feared his power to make trouble for them with Ibn Saud . . .

From this low point relations between the Algosaibis and the British began to improve. In October 1923 Major Daly reported: 'Abdel-Aziz is keeping very quiet and trying to get over the bad impression made on us by his brother . . . As long as he continues to act as a purely private agent of the Sultan here and refrains from interference he cannot do much harm and might be allowed to continue as such, without further need to definitely define his status.' By 1925 the Agency was again using the Algosaibis as a channel for sending letters to Ibn Saud. Yet relations were never entirely easy and periodically members of the family would encroach on the domains of politics and Bahrain–mainland community disputes. In the later 1920s they were involved with Bin Jiluwi's oppression of the Shias of Qatif and Hasa, who once again applied to the British for help. In October 1930 the Political Agent reported an instance of political interference: 'On my return here I found that a prominent merchant, Mohammad Yateem [who was playing a leading role in the Kuwaiti oil-concession negotiations], recently ran over a Nejdi in his car and was at once summoned by the Gosaibis who severely reprimanded him for having injured a subject of HM King Ibn Saud. He was later prosecuted by the police, but their action caused much comment.' Mohammad Yateem had his licence suspended for twelve months. The sentence says much for the more orderly way in which the government of Bahrain was being conducted by this time, under Shaikh Hamad and Charles Belgrave.

Despite their difficult relations with the British, the Algosaibis prospered greatly in the 1920s. They became probably the richest family in Arabia. In 1931 the Agent in Bahrain wrote: '. . . the firm is reported to be worth 50 lakhs of rupees [$1.5 million] and their property in Bahrain cannot be worth less than 14–15 lakhs [about $460,000] at normal prices.' At one point Belgrave had to ask the family not to buy any more land in Bahrain.

Each brother had his own role in the family business. Abdel-Aziz, the head of the family, ran the Bombay–Bahrain importing operation. Abdullah and Hassan looked after varying items of business and rotated between Bahrain, Qatif, Hasa, Riyadh, Jubail and India. Abdel-Rahman was the family's main pearl buyer, assisted by Hassan, and the only member of the family engaged in selling pearls. He travelled regularly to Bombay and Europe, partly to sell pearls and partly to carry out assignments for King Abdel-Aziz. Sa'ad remained almost permanently in Hasa. The characters of the brothers were summed up in a British report of 1931:

(a) *Abdel-Aziz*: is a simple and wise man and is the mainstay of the firm. He passes as being pious. He seldom interferes in things which do not concern him and he is liked and respected by Ibn Saud. [Either Abdel-Aziz or the Political Agent must have mellowed since Daly sent his personality report in 1923. The reference to Abdel-Aziz 'passing' as being pious is not particularly insulting because the British scarcely ever gave anyone credit for being genuinely pious.]

(b) *Abdullah*: is very intelligent and sharp but is a very mean and low character. Interferes in everything and is inclined to be boastful. He is not liked by Ibn Saud. ['Interference' was the worst possible sin in the eyes of all political agents. Before this report, in the early 1920s, Abdullah had been close to Ibn Saud.]

(c) *Hassan*: is very foolish and gruff. He dashes in where the others would fear to tread and is of as low a character as Abdullah. He is hot tempered and on receiving unwelcome correspondence has been known to tear it to pieces and eat the fragments.

(d) *Sa'ad*: I have never met him but he is said to be a good mixer. Also of low character like his brothers Hassan and Abdullah. He always remains in Hasa.

(e) *Abdel-Rahman*: is more enlightened with more education and has a wonderful flair for pearl dealing. He knows some French and English and normally conducts the firm's business in Paris, where he casts aside the garments of orthodoxy and sallies abroad in a dinner jacket 'et melon'. He is sensible but very conceited.

The British had reservations about Abdel-Rahman – as they did about all the more sophisticated Arabians – because he was not a groveller and dealt with them as equals. Others said he was grasping and liked to make a show, but they acknowledged him as one of the great figures of Arabia in the 1920s and 1930s. Mohammad Almana, King Abdel-Aziz's interpreter, told me in 1980: 'He was charming – courteous, hospitable, magnificently dressed – he arrived at the mosque in Bombay in splendour. He married several wives, in Hofuf, Bombay and Medina; often he had three or four wives at the same time – different wives in different places.' Tom Barger, one of the early Standard Oil employees in Saudi Arabia was equally complimentary in a conversation in 1978: 'I much respected Abdel-Rahman, he was absolutely honest. He was a good-looking man, tall and spare in build; he didn't develop a paunch with affluence. He was dignified but not reserved – I just enjoyed him, when I was talking to him I never felt I had to keep my guard up. On the other hand Abdullah was a miserable sod. I remember I once wanted to establish the principle of people paying for medical treatment and I sent him a bill; but Abdullah wouldn't pay.'

Abdel-Rahman's sons recount how when he was going to India to sell pearls he used to insist on all the other Arabs on the voyage eating on his account. His knowledge of pearls had come not from his uncle, Mohammad, but from an old merchant of Bahraini extraction. He had realised at an early age that the only real source of wealth in the Gulf was pearls, and that the best way to become rich would be to deal directly with pearls. He had the advantages of finding it easy to work with foreign cultures and learning languages quickly; he spoke excellent Urdu as well as moderate English and French. He became the main Bahrain buyer for the Paris merchants Rosenthal, Pack and Habib. When he went to Paris himself he was entrusted by the Gulf rulers with pearls to sell on their behalf.

It was a terrible blow to Abdel-Rahman, Hassan and the other Algosaibis when the pearl industry began to crumble at the beginning of the 1930s. Like all the pearl merchants Abdel-Rahman had a great emotional attachment to pearls. They were not only beautiful; they carried with them ancient traditions in the ways they were displayed (on red twill), graded, bought and sold. The element of pure chance in the discovery of a big pearl gave the trade a special romance, which the new cultured pearls lacked totally.

As well as causing personal distress, the decline of pearling soon had an effect on the Algosaibis' finances. Albert Habib, Victor Rosenthal and Saul Pack went bankrupt, all owing Abdel-Rahman large sums of money which he was forced to write off. Albert Habib, the Turkish Jew, suffered a stroke and partial paralysis as a result of the strains of bankruptcy. Abdel-Rahman felt obliged to support him and pay his medical bills.

The pearling disasters coincided with a deterioration in the Algosaibis' relations with King Abdel-Aziz. The family's financial problems did not cause the deterioration, but in due course they made it worse. The British monitored the situation closely. They not only found the family a nuisance in Bahrain and hoped to see its power diminished, they were perennially interested in the King's finances, and the Algosaibis were the King's biggest source of loans and credit. The British spent a great deal of time keeping count of the level of the King's debt to the family. In February 1931 the legation in Jeddah discovered that the King owed the Algosaibis about £8,000 ($32,000) and that the family badly needed the money. Sixteen months later the debts remained unpaid. The Bahrain Political Agent, Captain Prior, wrote to Bushire:

I have the honour to say that matters have apparently come to a head between Ibn Saud and the powerful Gosaibi family. In a conversation with the adviser [Belgrave] before a third person, Abdullah Gosaibi, who is notoriously hot-headed, stated that all the brothers had combined and signed a letter to Ibn Saud saying that they would not supply him with any goods on credit unless he made some arrangements for settling their outstanding debts, which amount to some 17 lakhs of rupees [$510,000]. Abdullah Gosaibi expressed himself with unusual heat and stated that they had even given an ultimatum to their Royal master to the effect that, if their demands were not met, they would remove their families from Nejd to Bahrain and apply to be registered as Bahraini subjects . . . Abdel-Aziz went to Jeddah with the thinly veiled intention of extracting some money from Ibn Saud, and it is obvious from other information that I have received that he has completely failed . . .

The Gosaibis are undoubtedly pledged to the hilt with Ibn Saud and can ill afford to break with him, for any repudiation or delay in settling his debt of 17 lakhs, coming on top of the sum they have lost in the insolvency of Victor Rosenthal, may have a disastrous effect on them, and render it difficult for them to pay the instalments due to the pearl dealers in Bahrain. However foolish Abdullah may be, Abdel-Aziz, the senior partner in the firm, has great intelligence, and I do not doubt that he will find some means of bringing Ibn Saud to terms, even though it may take time, though his task will be facilitated when the firms who are taking their place discover the difficulty in obtaining payment from their august client.

Abdel-Aziz was not given the time he needed. The impetuous

Hassan, who was in Bombay, began sending a stream of cables to the King, demanding payment. Saudis who were at the court at the time say that the King grew more and more disgusted as each telegram was read to him. Eventually, in early 1933, he summoned Abdel-Aziz and Abdel-Rahman to Taif. He was heard to tell his minister, Abdullah Suliman, to go and sit with the two merchants and settle the account. He instructed the minister to concentrate on bargaining with Abdel-Aziz, saying that he would be 'the more reasonable'. Those present have told me that they felt that the King really meant that Abdel-Aziz would be the weaker of the two brothers, or that he wished to spare Abdel-Rahman from the force of Suliman's bad temper. Certainly it was known that the King was very fond of Abdel-Rahman and it was noted that Abdel-Rahman was lavishly entertained whenever he came to court. Whatever the reasons it was Abdel-Aziz who bore the brunt of the bargaining and who was forced to agree a figure to settle the account.

The British believed that the Algosaibis' misfortune stemmed mainly from the enmity between them and the Syrian faction in the King's government. The family made no secret to anyone of its dislike of the Syrians, and the Syrians were thought to be trying to undermine the family's influence with the King. Saudis who were with the King in the 1930s take a more Arabian view of the situation. They recall that Suliman himself did not like the Syrians, and they suggest that the Syrians, as foreigners, would never have dared to volunteer opinions to the King on a Nejdi family. From 1933 onwards it was Suliman who was made responsible for dealing with the Algosaibis, and he who decided to use the family less. The Algosaibis themselves now say that it was Suliman who caused the cooling of their relations with the court.

The decline of the Algosaibis in the years that followed was a slow, drawn-out process. Sometimes it seemed that the family was about to recover its position. Abdel-Rahman continued to carry out foreign business assignments for the King, and the family's operation in Bahrain arranged the provisioning of the King's army in Yemen during the war of 1934. In the mid-1930s Abdullah provided accommodation in his compound at Jubail for the first prospectors from Standard Oil. The family's business in Hasa then arranged warehousing and transport for the oil company's equipment and geological specimens. In 1939, just before the Second World War broke out, the Algosaibis had the honour of entertaining the King. They gave a huge banquet in their house in Rifaa when he came to Bahrain on a state visit.

These successes only partly hid the weaknesses of the Algosaibi business. In the later 1930s the five brothers seemed to be looking backwards to the old world of pearling, and not to be able to visualise the new world that was beginning to emerge with the arrival of the oil companies. They did not fully grasp the scope for selling consumer durable goods that would stem from rising living standards in Bahrain, and later in Saudi Arabia. Nor did they see the contracting opportunities that would come from the companies.

Dr Ghazi Algosaibi, the Saudi Minister of Health and eighth son of Abdel-Rahman, says that the brothers were 'confused'. Together with the losses that came from the decline of the pearling business, this led to disagreement and recriminations. In 1977 Dr Ghazi told me: 'The family never had any ability at administration. There had never been any budgets, or formal sharing of profits, or clearly defined responsibilities in the business. Each brother took what money he wanted out of the firm and pursued whatever schemes he wanted to pursue.' Significantly, two of the qualities of the brothers that are most clearly remembered by Arabians are their strength of character and independence.

While business prospered in the 1920s the disorganisation of the family did not matter – though even then there were occasionally quarrels between the brothers. As times became more difficult it caused the family to split. The break occurred in 1943. In that year the fourth son of Mohammad bin Abdel-Aziz was born. Abdel-Aziz, his grandfather, commemorated the family split by naming him Faisal after an Arabian sword.

The family set up a committee which valued and divided its assets, its land, houses and gardens. Each brother went his own way. Sa'ad stayed in Hofuf and Abdullah retired to Qatif. The three others remained in Bahrain. Abdel-Aziz and his sons traded in food and consumer goods and established a cinema and Bahrain's first cold store and ice-making plant. It was the sons rather than Abdel-Aziz who were responsible for the innovations. Abdel-Rahman and his sons imported cars and durable goods, and Abdel-Rahman himself continued to invest in pearls for sentimental reasons. Among the agencies that this branch of the family obtained were Chrysler, various Swiss watch manufacturers, Singer sewing machines and Pascall sweets.

Within a few years a further series of splits began. On the death of Abdel-Aziz in 1950 his sons divided his business between themselves, sold their agencies and concentrated their efforts on real estate. At the same time the elder sons of Abdel-Rahman started to go their own ways. By the mid-1950s the once mighty Algosaibi business had shattered into some twenty parts, King Abdel-Aziz was dead, the pearl trade was extinct. The sons of the five brothers who set out to make their fortunes in the modern world of oil-producing Arabia started almost from scratch.

Khalifa, the eldest son of Abdel-Rahman, once told me that in 1950 he had no capital of his own at all. He borrowed some money, moved to Jeddah, and began buying food from Egypt to supply the Saudi army. In 1960 he moved back to the Eastern Province, where he had already while in Jeddah, established the first cold store outside Aramco. From that point on Khalifa and his sons have had a chequered business career.

To his great credit Khalifa has always tried to develop unusual or modern businesses – schemes that have been slightly more ambitious or forward-looking than the conventional businesses of most other Saudis. The cold store was established at a time when virtually the only market for imported frozen or packaged foods was Aramco; it was fifteen years before the Saudis themselves began to buy this type of food.

In 1963 Khalifa began to develop a fishing company. He went to Aramco's Local Industrial Development Department, which helped with his feasibility study and provided guarantees for his loans. The rights for fishing he bought from Prince Mitaab bin Abdel-Aziz, who had been given a concession for the fishing and processing of Gulf shrimps. By 1968, which was the company's best year, Khalifa had sixteen trawlers and was selling some $5 million of shrimps. Most of his catch went to the United States under the brand name 'Ocean Reef'. Then the company began a rapid decline. Several Kuwaiti, Iranian and Bahraini companies had developed fishing fleets at the same time. The Gulf became seriously over-fished, catches fell and some of the companies went bankrupt. Since the early 1970s there have been several times when it has seemed that large-scale shrimping in the Gulf might be revived, but each upswing has been followed by over-fishing. The Khalifa Algosaibi Fishing Company has been reduced in size and now concentrates on supplying the local market. Khalifa's eldest son, Mohammad, says that the Gulf states and Saudi Arabia do not care enough about the fishing industry to make a real effort to fix fishing quotas. They feel that the prize is not worth the risk of an argument.

In the 1970s the biggest single source of the Khalifa Algosaibi Group's income has been the Kraft agency, handled by the cold store. The innovative tradition has been maintained by the manufacture of sand-lime bricks. These are strong, weight-bearing bricks, designed as a substitute for steel in building, which have not previously been produced in the Kingdom and have seldom been used there. New projects recently discussed by Khalifa's company have included bottling spring water and manufacturing Korean food for construction workers.

Khalifa's brothers have been less original. Adel runs a successful engineering business in Riyadh, and Fahd inherited the Saudi part of his father's business, known as the Abdel-Rahman Algosaibi General Trading Bureau. From a small dark office, leading off a side alley in the old part of Riyadh, Fahd runs a varied operation. He owns the Canada Dry bottling plant in Riyadh, travel agencies, a large amount of real estate, and an importing business. This embraces steel pipes, medical supplies, tents for the military, and the Singer sewing machine agency. One of Fahd's travel companies and some of his real estate represent the only remaining Algosaibi commercial presence in Bahrain.

The commercial revival of the sons of Abdel-Rahman and other members of the family has been paralleled by a renewal of their political service. In Bahrain, Ghazi, the youngest son of Mohammad Abdel-Aziz, has been appointed Director of Protocol in the Foreign Ministry. Among Bahrainis, members of his family are regarded as Saudis – but they are respected. With hindsight it seems that the British political agents in Bahrain were unduly harsh in their judgements of the family in the 1920s and 1930s. They disliked the Algosaibis because the interests of King Abdel-Aziz, which the family loyally represented, often ran directly counter to the British policy which the agents had to implement. This was a good enough reason for British hostility, but it probably led the agents to overestimate the degree to which the Algosaibis' behaviour was resented by the Bahraini ruling family and other Arabs in a society which at that time was inherently disorderly. It is significant that when Abdel-Rahman Algosaibi died in 1976 members of the ruling Khalifa family came to sit for half a day in his house.

In Saudi Arabia two of the Algosaibis have risen to the top of the government service – though neither aspired to a high official post. Khaled, the eldest son of Mohammad Abdel-Aziz, was working in the Ministry of Agriculture when King Faisal asked him to be Director of the Railroad in 1967. Then in 1973 he was appointed Deputy Governor of the central bank – the Saudi Arabian Monetary Agency – a post in which he served until 1980.

In the early 1970s Ghazi Abdel-Rahman was pursuing an academic career. He had read law at Cairo University and International Studies at the University of Southern California, where he had shared rooms with his cousin Khaled. (In 1978 Ghazi was one of the promoters of an idea for a chair in Middle Eastern studies at USC. The scheme was mishandled at the Californian end, provoked opposition from Zionists and others who feared that the Saudis were trying to 'buy' a university department, and was abandoned.) Three years after finishing at USC Ghazi moved to London to take a doctorate in international relations and then returned to be dean of the Faculty of Commerce in Riyadh. It was then that he was 'drafted into government' as he puts it, to take over his cousin's post as Director of the Railroad. In 1975, when a new government was formed after the death of King Faisal, he was appointed to the new post of Minister of Industry and Electricity, and in 1983 he was appointed Minister of Health. In these positions he has been one of half a dozen or so technocrats at the top of government. These men – ministers and heads of major government agencies – are the only people outside the royal family who have been given real authority over the day-to-day running of the Saudi administration.

Neither Khaled nor Ghazi were greatly surprised by their elevation to high office; service of the King was in the family's tradition. Although the Algosaibis' relations with the court had deteriorated in the 1930s, King Abdel-Aziz, and later King Faisal, had not lost their personal affection for members of the family. The feeling was reciprocated. At the end of his life Abdel-Rahman Algosaibi said that never a week passed when he did not have a dream of King Abdel-Aziz.

12

Ahmed Hamad Algosaibi

Ahmed Hamad Algosaibi once spent a long holiday in his own country. He took a convoy of cars and trucks, with tents, supplies of food and water, fuel, guides from the Ministry of the Interior – everything that might possibly be needed on a long journey across desert – and drove round every part of Saudi Arabia. He saw what sights there were to see, stayed with the provincial governors and was lavishly entertained. Wherever he went he found that local notables pressed him to marry their daughters; he was only able to decline these unwelcome and expensive offers by claiming that he had already taken the maximum of four wives permitted by Islam. In fact this was not strictly true: Shaikh Ahmed had, and still has, only one wife.

When he returned from his epic journey, Shaikh Ahmed went to the Interior Ministry and obtained a certificate with a list of the places he had visited, to prove that he had done it. He believes that he is the only Saudi ever to have made the tour.

His Saudi journey is typical of Shaikh Ahmed. He is a tough, bull-necked man – extrovert, unsubtle, with a straightforward pride in what he has achieved. In a nation which has taken to travel with casual ease, he is unusual in having a genuine interest in the places he visits. Few other Saudis would think of driving around their own country – they lack the explorer's instinct. They also prefer their holidays to take them to comfortable places where they can relax and enjoy themselves, and escape from the austerity of their own society. Ahmed's frequent visits abroad have a different purpose. Bit by bit he is seeing the whole world – Scandinavia, Switzerland, eastern Europe, the Far East, Africa. Some of the places he visits he looks at for a few days and then dismisses. He is not a man to search out features of subtle historical or cultural interest. But if a country appeals to him he tries whatever pastimes it has to offer. On the wall of his hotel in Alkhobar hangs a plaster model of a large blue sailfish which he caught off the coast of East Africa.

At home Shaikh Ahmed makes a point of inviting to his house almost all the Western executives who come to do business with him.

This is unusual among Saudis. One evening he will give a dinner for some Swiss insurance executives, with whose company he has a joint venture; a few days later he will invite a group from Continental Can to a wedding reception he is holding for the son of a distant cousin. Continental Can a few years ago fitted out an Algosaibi Pepsi-Cola canning plant.

Summing up Shaikh Ahmed, a Bahraini banker said to me in 1980: 'People are sometimes put off by his abrupt exterior, but underneath he's a very warm person. He's generous – he and his brothers have a concern for what goes on around them in the community. On the other hand they're not wasteful – they don't dissipate money or opportunities.' One of the more unusual good causes to which the Algosaibis have contributed is the Seihat Society for Social Services, the Shia self-help organisation established by Abdullah Matrood. Several Sunni merchants with operations in the Eastern Province have given to this organisation, but according to the Society's annual report the Algosaibis' donations have been the most generous.

Shaikh Ahmed is not closely related to the Algosaibi family of the 'five brothers'. His ancestors were among many people towards the end of the last century who were forced by drought to leave Gassab, and so were given the name Algosaibi. Like Abdullah, the founder of the other Algosaibi family, Ahmed's forefathers went first to Herreimlah. Given that both Gassab and Herreimlah a hundred years ago were very small communities, it is assumed that at some point the two families were joined by marriage or a common ancestor. Ahmed would dearly like to discover this link because it would establish him as part of a family which became famous for its service to King Abdel-Aziz, but the connection has eluded him. He is no more sure than the other Algosaibis of the names of his ancestors beyond three or four generations. What he does know is that his grandfather went to Zubair, the Nejdi town of southern Iraq, with which Ahmed's family still maintains contact. Ahmed has Iraqi tapestries hanging on the walls of his house.

From Zubair at the beginning of this century Ahmed's father, Hamad, together with his uncles, Mohammad and Ibrahim, went to

AHMED HAMAD ALGOSAIBI FAMILY TREE

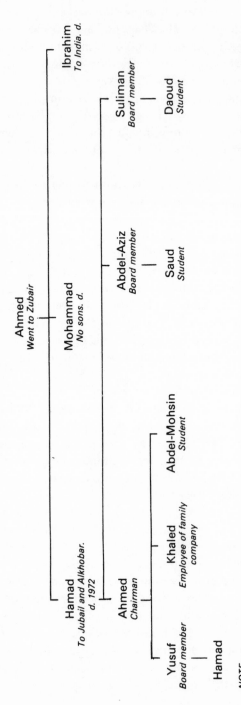

Ahmed
Went to Zubair

Hamad
*To Jubail and Alkhobar.
d. 1972*

Mohammad
No sons. d.

Ibrahim
To India. d.

Yusuf
Board member

Hamad

Ahmed
Chairman

Khaled
*Employee of family
company*

Abdel-Mohsin
Student

Abdel-Aziz
Board member

Suliman
Board member

Saud
Student

Daoud
Student

NOTE

Ahmed Hamad Algosaibi and Brothers is a partnership of Ahmed, Abdel-Aziz and Suliman. The board, under the chairmanship of Ahmed, is composed of the three brothers, with Ahmed's eldest son, Yusuf, and the firm's Palestinian general manager, Mohammad Hindi. Ahmed and Abdel-Aziz exercise overall control, with Abdel-Aziz more involved in practice.

Suliman supervises the *Pepsi-Cola,* ice and carbon dioxide businesses; Yusuf looks after the shipping and travel operations, and Mohammad Hindi manages general trading. The insurance and hotel businesses have their own managers reporting to the board.

Jubail. Here they established a general trading business, importing the usual basic commodities – foodstuffs and timber from the Malabar coast of southern India. They owned two or three pearling dhows and traded in a small way with the pearl merchants of Bahrain. As the pearl business slowly collapsed, in the early 1940s Hamad moved to the tiny coastal settlement of Alkhobar, where he developed an exchange-dealing business. He bought silver coins in Kuwait, where he dealt with the well-established firm of Muzaini, transported them down the coast by camel and sold them to Aramco for dollar bills. Aramco employees at this time insisted on receiving their pay in metal coinage.

The young Ahmed had been sent to school in Bahrain. He returned to Saudi Arabia in 1935, but soon decided that there would be no point in working for his father in the pearl and trading business. He went to the oil-company camp at Dhahran and signed on in October 1936 as number 1325, a workman in the company's storehouse.

In his office in Alkhobar in 1977 Ahmed gave me a detailed account of his early employment: 'I remember it well. My first salary was about 12 annas a day – that was three quarters of a rupee [about 22 cents]. Anyway, I recently got my discharge certificate from Aramco – I asked them for a copy – and I've got a list of my different jobs and the money I got. In 1937 I became a pumper for 1 rupee a day, then I was a tallyman for 1½ rupees and then a pier checker for 4 rupees. These last two jobs, you understand, were both much the same – they involved checking goods being unloaded from the ships. After two years the war started, so I left – Aramco was not doing much at that time. I went to work with my father in his exchange business in Alkhobar – the town was nothing in those days. You see that photograph on the wall over there – that was Alkhobar, just those *barasti* huts . . . By 1944 things were moving again, so I went back to Aramco, and they sent me to Bechtel who were building the refinery at Ras Tanura – it was just a little one. I started as a pier checker again. I was paid 125 riyals a month [about $35]. Then they promoted me to storeman, and interpreter, and senior clerk. Eventually I became a head clerk – my title was "Clerk Grade A, Maintenance and Shops". That earned me 334 riyals [$95] a month, which was a lot of money for me before I started this business. You know, when I left they gave me this certificate which I have still got. I'll read it to you, it says: "He was of good conduct and citizenship during the period of his employment." '

By 1947 the Saudi government was receiving oil revenues, money was beginning to filter through society and it was becoming obvious that there was a better living to be made in business than working for Bechtel. Ahmed and his brother Abdel-Aziz, who had been employed by Aramco as a clerk in the customs, went back to work with their father. Initially it was Ahmed who was the driving force. His first idea for modernising the business was to open a gasoline station: 'I noticed that everyone was going to Dhahran to buy gasoline, so I suggested to Aramco that they should give me the agency to sell gasoline in Dammam and Alkhobar. That's where I set up the first two stations. I got pumps at the beginning from Aramco – they lent me the pumps and tanks on credit terms. Later we had six stations and I got my own pumps from the US. Aramco used to deliver the gasoline to me; then at the end of every day I went to Aramco to settle for what I had sold. This meant that I didn't have to borrow to pay for my stocks.'

The gasoline stations led Ahmed to establish a shop to sell batteries, tyres, Esso lubricating oil and other car accessories. As he says, he 'sold anything that people seemed to need'. The breakthrough for the business came in 1950. In that year construction work began on the Dammam-Riyadh railway, under the supervision of Aramco. The contractors asked the oil company whom they could use for buying materials on their behalf, and Aramco recommended the Algosaibi business. Once again Ahmed applied himself to discovering what was needed by a foreign company and its employees, then buying it and reselling it. This was not as simple as it seemed. The skills which helped establish Ahmed as a regular purchasing agent were his knowledge of which stocks the contractors were most likely to need and his efficiency in arranging for the right materials to be shipped at the right time.

After the railway contract was finished, opportunities were few. The reign of King Saud bin Abdel-Aziz in the 1950s was a period of financial chaos, during which the government came to the verge of bankruptcy. Oil revenues remained small relative to the size of the Kingdom; there was none of the flood of money into society that Kuwait experienced at this time. For businessmen all over the Kingdom growth was slow. Ahmed Algosaibi's most important decision in the late 1950s was to diversify into Pepsi-Cola manufacturing. Aramco already had a Pepsi plant capable of producing over half a million bottles a month, but Ahmed and Abdel-Aziz had been importing their own Pepsi from Bahrain. They had found that the drink sold well. Together they went to Aramco and suggested that if they began manufacturing Pepsi,

Aramco should buy from them and close its own plant. The oil company saw this as a classic opportunity for putting into practice its divestiture philosophy; Pepsi production was an activity far outside the normal confines of the oil industry and the business of collecting the empty bottles was a nuisance. The only problem was the fear of Aramco's American employees that locally manufactured Pepsi-Cola might not be totally hygienic. Worried delegations of employees and their wives came to see the company's Purchase and Stores Department. The officers of the Department reassured the nervous 'Aramcons' – reminding them and the company's medics that it gave priority to hygiene at all times. They then agreed with Ahmed that provided his Saudi Pepsi reached the right standard the company would close its own Pepsi business. The Local Industrial Development Department helped Ahmed with the design and operation of his plant, and gradually Aramco began phasing in the new product. The Aramcons drank it, discovered that it tasted exactly the same as their own Pepsi-Cola, and found themselves as healthy as ever. No announcement was made when the Aramco plant was closed.

In the next few years Ahmed and Abdel-Aziz went into the shipping agency and stevedoring business in Dammam port. They expanded their trade in contractors' materials and machinery, importing line pipe, well casing and tugs for Aramco. They opened the first bonded warehouse for the company and the first pipe stock yard. The advantages of concentrating on Aramco business were that the company was a big and reliable market, unlike the local economy at that time. It was only in the later 1960s and early 1970s that the brothers started to look more at the developing towns of Dammam and Alkhobar. They diversified into insurance and real estate, and built the Algosaibi Hotel in Alkhobar because they saw that there were then no proper hotels in the region. They became founders and board members of every important industrial venture established in the Eastern Province before the mid-1970s: the electricity companies of Hofuf and Dhahran, the cement company in Hofuf and the Saudi Fertiliser Company (SAFCO). In the process they made Ahmed Hamad Algosaibi and Brothers into the biggest indigenous merchant group in the Eastern Province.

In 1982 the biggest activity in a company which had a turnover of more than $200 million was still trading – and half of the trading turnover was accounted for by sales to Aramco. First and foremost the company remains an importer of steel pipe and heavy mechanical equipment. The manufacturers it represents are mostly engineering firms: Sumitomo Corporation for pipe, Christensen Diamond Products for drilling bits, Fairmont Railway Motors, Mirlees Blackstone, Fiat and Borsig Gmbh for generators, diesel engines, gas turbines and compressors, Essochem for oil-field chemicals. In 1980 the brothers revived their father's currency-dealing business when they took the Saudi agency for American Express and established the Algosaibi Money Exchange Bureau.

During the last ten years it has been Abdel-Aziz who has masterminded the company's growth. Abdel-Aziz is the brother who is now recognised as having the business flair, the keen analytical mind and the talent for investment in real estate. Ahmed is best known for his concentration and his willingness to involve himself in follow-up work on projects. He has become a somewhat patriarchal figure – the company's spokesman and representative in dealings with foreign businessmen and important people in government. While Abdel-Aziz works behind the scenes, Ahmed is the man with an open door and an office full of visitors.

13

Darwish – an Arabian Contractor

In the early spring of 1941 a strange holy man appeared at a family
funeral outside the little town of Doha in Qatar. When the body had
been buried he accompanied one of the mourners home, walking backwards before him and crying. Then he continued to cry outside the
mourner's hole-in-the-wall stall in the souk, forcing the owner to retreat
inside and bolt the doors. To friends of the family he indicated that he
wanted to be allowed to cry in front of the mourner for a quarter of an
hour every day. Throughout the whole performance he spoke not a
word. He was either dumb or pretending to be dumb.

Word quickly spread through Doha that the man was an Italian –
Italians being totally unknown in Qatar but unpopular by reputation. It
was said that he had arrived from India or Central Asia. In due course
the British authorities in Bahrain heard about the man, and decided that
he sounded sinister. The Political Agent wrote to the Resident: 'He may
be an enemy spy pretending madness or trying to play a trick through
which he may make people believe him a holy man.' It was decided to
ask the oil concessionaire in Qatar to make enquiries. The company's
senior manager wrote to the Agent on 5th April outlining what he
intended to do: 'I suggest that I write to Abdullah Darwish Fakhroo,
who is the Anglo-Iranian Oil Company agent in Doha, and also in
receipt of an honorarium from us. He is intelligent and perhaps no more
of a rascal than the others, and our own agent, Mohammad Abdlatif al
Mana, is absent from Qatar at present.'

The company's faith in Abdullah was not misplaced. Abdullah took
soundings in the souk and wrote a concise, businesslike reply, in which
he itemised the various points he had discovered. There were, he said,
two men, not one; they were Iranians or Afghans, and the one who did
speak spoke a language from somewhere in Central Asia. The men had
had no connections with anyone in particular while in Doha – though

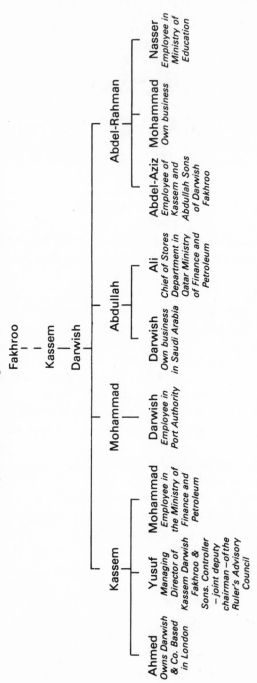

DARWISH FAMILY TREE

Not complete before the generation of Darwish bin Kassem

Fakhroo
|
Kassem
|
Darwish

Kassem

- **Ahmed** — *Owns Darwish & Co. Based in London*
- **Yusuf** — *Managing Director of Kassem Darwish Fakhroo & Sons. Controller – joint deputy chairman – of the Ruler's Advisory Council*
- **Mohammad** — *Employee in the Ministry of Finance and Petroleum*

Mohammad

- **Darwish** — *Employee in Port Authority*

Abdullah

- **Darwish** — *Own business in Saudi Arabia*
- **Ali** — *Chief of Stores Department in Qatar Ministry of Finance and Petroleum*
- **Abdel-Aziz** — *Employee of Kassem and Abdullah Sons of Darwish Fakhroo*

Abdel-Rahman

- **Mohammad** — *Own business*
- **Nasser** — *Employee in Ministry of Education*

NOTES

1. The Darwish family has common ancestors with the Fakhroo family of Bahrain. The two families have often intermarried.

2. Mohammad bin Darwish was not in business with Kassem, Abdullah and Abdel-Rahman.

3. The family tree does not show the members of the youngest generation, all of whom are still of school age or younger. Nor does it show the younger sons of the four brothers, who are either still at school or university, or have recently left university. There are three sons of Abdullah: Yusuf, Badr and Saud; and seven sons of Kassem: Darwish, Nasser, Hassan, Salman, Khalil, Abdullah and Hamad.

4. The 'mother company', Kassem and Abdullah Sons of Darwish Fakhroo, is still owned by Kassem, Abdullah and Abdel-Rahman. About half of its assets have been hived off into the three brothers' separate businesses. See Appendix 2 for details.

one of them had 'a strong inclination to seeking pleasure with tender youths'. By the time the letter was written the men had left Qatar – on their way to al Hasa and thence the Hijaz. In concluding his report Abdullah struck a reassuring note: 'I shall spare no pains to fish out further facts in regard to these two men on their return to Doha.' The oil company was delighted with the letter and thanked Abdullah warmly. The British were able to relax in the knowledge that Qatar was safe from the machinations of Mussolini's agents.

The incident of the Afghani fakir, as the matter became known, tells much about Abdullah Darwish. Unlike most of his compatriots he was a man who was able to deal with Westerners in Western terms. In 1941 it would have been unthinkable for anyone else in Doha to have written an itemised reply to the oil company's enquiry. Abdullah had a good memory for names and precise dates and spoke reasonably good English, which he practised by talking to foreigners who came to stay in his family's house. His value to the English and Americans of the oil companies was in saving them the difficulty and frustration of having always to think in Arabian terms and conduct their business at an Arabian pace.

Nothing in Abdullah's background had trained him to make this jump between cultures. He had not travelled very much, nor been educated in India.

Abdullah and his brothers, Kassem, Mohammad and Abdel-Rahman, were born between about 1905 and 1920. They were taught by the *qadi* (judge) in the 'palace' class with the younger members of the ruling family. As in every other traditional school in the Arabian Peninsula at this time, their lessons involved reading and instruction in the Koran. When the brothers were still young their father, Darwish, a small food importer of Persian origin, died in a fire in his house. The brothers were more ambitious than their father. They took over his trade and slowly began to expand it. Kassem became one of the leading pearl merchants of Qatar and the official pearl buyer of the shaikh, the venerable Abdullah bin Jasim al Thani.[1] Today he says that he has the

1. The names Jasim and Kassem are the same and interchangeable. In Qatar one normally sees the name of Shaikh Abdullah's father written as Jasim, while the eldest Darwish brother's name is written as Kassem. Abdullah bin Jasim was the shaikh featured in the *People* report of 1935 (see chapter 10).

biggest collection of pearls in the Gulf. In 1932, Kassem and Abdullah agreed with the Anglo-Iranian Oil Company that they would sell kerosene in Qatar on the company's behalf. Apart from whatever profits they were able to make, they were paid an honorarium of 100 rupees ($31) a month. When competition for the Qatar oil concession became serious a year or so later, the British authorities in Bahrain agreed to pay Abdullah a further R150 a month to pass on quietly any information he could collect on rival American oil companies contacting the Shaikh. Apart from this 'unofficial' work, for which the British felt him to be well suited, neither Abdullah nor any of his brothers was involved in the oil-concession negotiations. In the 1930s AIOC's agent in its dealings with the Shaikh was Mohammad Abdlatif al Mana, a close relation of Salih al Mana, the Shaikh's secretary. The Mana were originally from the Nejd and had long been the major merchant family of Qatar. They looked down on the Darwish, whom they regarded as being still Persians.

The rise of the Darwish at the expense of the al Mana began soon after the signing of the oil concession in 1935. When Petroleum Development Qatar[2] prepared to start drilling in 1939, the Darwish brothers were given contracts for a few minor buildings in the company camp at Dukan. The scale of expertise required was very small; one of the early Darwish contracts was described simply as 'stone and mud work', worth R 20,000 ($6,000).

More important for the family was a loose business relationship which Abdullah entered in the later 1930s with the Shaikh's second son and chosen heir, Hamad bin Abdullah al Thani. The two men were similar in character. Abdullah Darwish was a big, one-eyed man with a gruff voice – tough, ruthless, a good judge of people, who could sort out those he could ignore from those who might present obstacles to his schemes and would have to be bribed or coerced. Shaikh Hamad was described by the British as 'a man of some character, though grasping and oppressive . . . a bully, avaricious, unpopular but feared'. His father, Shaikh Abdullah bin Jasim, had had a long rule during which he had done much to weld Qatar together as a state, but by the late 1930s he was

2. Owned by the Iraq Petroleum Company, composed of Anglo-Iranian (later BP), Shell, Compagnie Française des Petroles (Total), Standard Oil of New Jersey (Exxon), Mobil and the Gulbenkian family. The concession had been won by Anglo-Iranian and passed to IPC under the terms of an inter-company agreement made in the 1920s. PDQ later became the Qatar Petroleum Company.

approaching eighty and had made Hamad responsible for most of the day-to-day administration of the shaikhdom. He believed that Hamad had the strength necessary to keep his turbulent relations from fighting each other.

Abdullah and Shaikh Hamad set out to make as much money as they could from the few business opportunities that were available in Qatar in the late 1930s. They noticed immediately that Salih al Mana was levying a form of income tax, of about 10 per cent, on the Qatari employees of the oil company. These men were mostly labourers ('coolies') and drivers. Officially the tax was being levied on behalf of the Shaikh, whom Salih represented, but in practice much of the money was going into Salih's own pocket. Indeed the Shaikh, in response to queries by the British authorities in Bahrain, was never prepared to admit that any tax was being charged at all. Hamad and Abdullah became jealous of Salih and decided to levy their own income tax. Together, they were more powerful tax collectors than Salih, and they gradually squeezed their competitor out of the business.

The two men's co-operation survived through the Second World War, even though the oil company stopped its operations after its initial discovery in January 1940 and later withdrew all its employees to Iran. In March 1940 the company reported to the Political Agent in Bahrain: 'Abdullah Darwish appears at the Shaikh's conferences and takes a seat with less diffidence as though confident that his status will protect him against the charge of over-familiarity. Abdullah still caters for Hamad's illicit pleasures and shares with him the profits of his business enterprises.' Hamad at this time was a close friend of Abdullah's younger sister, Moosa, a person of considerable character and almost the only person in Qatar able to stand up to her brother.[3] A few years later it seemed that the partnership was stronger still. In 1944 one of the Agent's staff reported after a visit to Qatar: 'Abdullah bin Darwish is now the right-hand man and partner of Shaikh Hamad in practically every underhand dealing of any magnitude which takes place in Qatar.'

The biggest of the 'underhand dealings' was the smuggling of British food quotas. These quotas were assigned by the Ministry of Food in India to the Shaikh in person, it being intended that he should see that they were fairly distributed among his people. Responsibility for this

3. Today, Moosa Darwish is a stout lady of about sixty. Like her equally intelligent, well-informed and strong-willed sister, Benna, she has never married, but is known to be a significant power in the state. She sits with two telephones beside her.

task devolved automatically on to Shaikh Hamad. As businessmen Hamad and Abdullah did not fail to notice that the prices which prevailed in Qatar were very much lower than the black-market prices in Bahrain, southern Iran and Saudi Arabia. Rice, for example, fetched 45 rupees a bag internally and R120 on the black market; the equivalent prices for sugar were R65 and R450. With the co-operation of Salih al Mana, the two men moved wholeheartedly into the business of re-exporting the quotas. The British found that they received a stream of messages from the Ruler of Qatar asking for higher quotas. They were not unaware of the smuggling and decided that the messages must mean that the partnership wanted to expand its operations. They refused to meet the requests and sent a number of warnings to Shaikh Abdullah, telling him to have the smuggling stopped. Their words were totally ignored.

Eventually, in November 1944, the problem was brought forcibly to the attention of the Agent and Resident by a petition sent from a deputation of Qatari citizens. The message was translated as follows: 'Matters have come to a head and we have been reduced to a wretched state on account of the tyranny and ever-increasing oppression we are receiving at the hands of our Ruler, Shaikh Hamad. What has made matters worse is his injustice in taking away what the High British Government has kindly granted in this hard time . . . The Shaikh and Abdullah Darwish have put us in this pitiable position. We have therefore written you this letter requesting you to save this miserable nation . . .'

This grovelling missive obliged the British to act. First they decided to withdraw the Darwish brothers' travel documents and ask all neighbouring countries to refuse the brothers entry. They had an announcement to this effect broadcast over Bahrain Radio. By chance the Darwish heard the radio announcement while they were sitting in the *majlis* of Mohammad al Mana, and they were mightily disturbed. The Political Agent in Bahrain reported to Bushire that they then confined themselves to their house for two days 'on account of shame and anxiety'.

Secondly the British told Shaikh Abdullah that they would themselves take over the rationing of foodstuffs in Qatar. This was a blow to the Shaikh's prestige – as well as to his son's pocket – and Abdullah bin Jasim objected. Eventually he and the Agent compromised on a system whereby the British made periodic checks on the distribution system in Qatar.

Lastly it was decided that Qatar should be banned from exporting or re-exporting any goods whatever direct to India. The purpose of this ban was to enable the authorities to monitor Qatar's trade more closely by confining Qatari boats to the Gulf.

Despite these draconian measures some smuggling continued. In March 1945 a Kuwaiti dhow was wrecked on the coast of Sharjah with 20,000 lb of tea on board. Much to the surprise and annoyance of the British, the captain of the vessel, when questioned about his cargo, revealed that the shipper had been Abdullah Darwish. He added, with a singular lack of tact, that he had been sailing from Doha to Bandar Abbas (in southern Iran) and that Darwish had been given an export permit for the tea by the Shaikh. The incident drew a curt letter from the Agent to the Shaikh demanding that he explain why he had authorised the re-export of such a large amount of tea. Thereafter it seems that the Darwish stopped smuggling, or had the good fortune not to have their activities discovered. The travel ban was relaxed after intercession by the ruling Thani family in June 1946.

During the years 1946 and 1947 the Darwish remained a major force in Qatari trade but managed to avoid attracting the attention of the British. The concern of the Qatari establishment and the British authorities at this time was focused on the deteriorating health of Shaikh Abdullah bin Jasim and his son, Hamad, and the return of the oil company to Dukan. It was clear to all that Qatar was about to enjoy an income on a scale it had never dreamed of before. Whoever became the new ruler would determine the direction of Qatar's development and would choose which families would be rewarded by government contracts. Nobody took the succession more seriously than the Darwish brothers, whose fortunes ever since – for good and bad – have been very much influenced by the stance they took in the late 1940s.

At first the Darwish just watched and waited. It was assumed by all that Shaikh Abdullah would die before his son and that Hamad would succeed him, though a British report to the Resident in 1944 had said that Hamad would not live long because he was a diabetic and that if he did succeed he would almost certainly be shot because he was detested. If Hamad was to die in the near future there was some question as to whether the succession would then go to his son, Khalifa, who was still a youth but already seemed to have the makings of an excellent ruler, or to

Hamad's elder brother, Shaikh Ali bin Abdullah. Shaikh Ali showed none of the strong qualities of leadership that distinguished his aged father and had been the mark of all previous Thani rulers. In the report of 1944 referred to above, the Agent had recorded a conversation between one of his staff and the Ruler of Bahrain (who never had much respect for the Qataris) in which the two men had agreed that 'the only difference between Ali and a cow was that a cow gave milk.'

As it turned out Shaikh Hamad died before his father, in May 1948. Khalifa was passed over as being too young and Ali was made heir apparent; it was said that one of the conditions of his elevation was his acceptance that Khalifa would succeed him. A year later Abdullah bin Jasim finally abdicated and Ali became Ruler. Abdullah Darwish lost no time in switching his allegiance from the Hamad branch of the family, now centred on Khalifa, to Shaikh Ali. In doing this he finally eclipsed the power of Salih al Mana, who had been a long-standing confidant of Shaikh Ali. It is thought that Shaikh Ali may have associated Abdullah Darwish with Hamad's success in business and hoped that a close bond with the merchant would bring similar good fortune to himself.

It was early in the rule of Shaikh Ali that Abdullah pulled off his first big business deal directly related to the oil industry. In 1948 and 1949 the Qatar Petroleum Company was bringing on stream Qatar's first (and only) onshore oil field, at Dukan, on the Western side of the Qatar peninsula. It embarked on a large construction effort, involving a mixture of sophisticated and rather ordinary projects – degassing stations, tank farms, a pipeline across the peninsula to Umm Said, a loading terminal, stores, accommodation for Western personnel, workshops, kitchens, roads. For transporting its unskilled labour across the peninsula from Doha each week the company awarded a contract to Abdullah Darwish who operated a small fleet of 3-ton trucks. To its disappointment the company found that the transport system did not work well. Many labourers would fail to report to the trucks in Doha on Friday nights, others would send inexperienced friends as substitutes. Occasionally the drivers themselves failed to appear. The company decided that it would do better to put the entire operation in Abdullah's hands, entrusting him with recruitment as well as hiring his transport. It reasoned that even if it paid more to Abdullah in the short term, at least it would be saved the embarassment of firing its men or the cost of keeping them on its books when the construction work was finished.

The company paid Abdullah 11½ rupees per labourer per day. Abdullah provided food and water, and paid his men 3¾ rupees (by this time worth only 70 cents) per day. With a labour force of about 1,500 employed for two years Abdullah made himself well over $1 million in profits. The labourers were the poorest of Qataris, former slaves and Persians from southern Iran. None of these people had lived above subsistence level before oil, and they did not seem discontented with their lot. After a life of fishing and pearl diving any regular income with free food was a novelty. More unpopular at the time was the way the labour contract made Abdullah the arbiter of the employment of virtually every worker in Qatar. Anyone who wanted to be sure of employment had to stay on good terms with the Darwish. The contract led to the Darwish agents deducting 'registration fees' and other extra costs from the labourers' wages. Meanwhile members of the Thani family had slaves working as drivers of the trucks which the Darwish were leasing to the oil company under a totally separate contract. Whenever the shaikhs wanted to expand their incomes they ordered their slaves to strike.

While he was organising the company's labour Abdullah tied up most of the other contracts that QPC was able to offer to Qataris. He became a friend of the company's field manager, a Texan known as 'Boots' Langham – a man who was interested in 'results' and not over-fussy about how they were achieved. In Abdullah, Langham found someone who understood exactly what was needed and could produce it without constantly turning to the oil company for help. Whenever Langham wanted something built or had any local problem he went to Abdullah.

The Darwish family business won contracts for accommodation and office buildings, a dining hall and a staff club. For a quarter of a rupee per gallon it arranged a water supply for the oil-company camp. Abdullah had some of his dhows equipped with galvanised tanks, which were filled from the sweet water springs off the coast of Bahrain. Inevitably all the company's 'fresh' water had a slightly salty taste. At Dukan, Abdullah established a canteen for oil-company employees.

The bigger contracts were carried out in a partnership with the Lebanese Contracting and Trading Company – CAT. This was arranged in 1953 by the oil company, which wanted to bring together the local influence of Abdullah and the technical expertise of CAT, which had carried out pipeline ditching contracts in Iraq and Syria.[4] It was agreed that in return for his 60 per cent share of profits Abdullah would put in all of the finance required by the partnership – CAT's contribution was to be its own engineers and experience. The new company dominated the civil construction market in Qatar for the next fifteen years. Its contracts included the first hospital in the state, built in 1954–6, installation work on the early desalination plants and power stations, the country's road system, parts of the Umm Said oil-loading terminal, a plaster of paris plant, several palaces for members of the Thani family, and the Oasis Hotel – which was built to accommodate the crews of the airlines represented by Darwish. Until the mid-1960s no Qatari established an engineering partnership to challenge the company. Anyone who considered the idea concluded (rightly) that Qatar was a one-company-sized market, and that it was filled very neatly by Darwish-CAT.

The company's strength was considerably reinforced by Abdullah's position as the Ruler's Petroleum Representative. There had been a clause in the original concession agreement of 1935 stating that the Shaikh had a right to appoint to QPC his own representative who was to be paid a salary by the company. In the early years the position was held jointly by Shaikh Hamad and Salih al Mana, but on the accession of Shaikh Ali, Abdullah had had himself appointed to the job. He mastered the technicalities of the oil business far more thoroughly than his predecessors had done. In the early 1950s he negotiated with QPC the 50–50 company–government profit split, which in all the Middle Eastern producers at this time was introduced to replace the old fixed royalty arrangements. A little later he agreed the terms of the new offshore concession awarded to Shell. He handled both of these negotiations almost alone.

4. CAT was established in Lebanon in 1941. The founders were Abdullah Khoury, Shukri Shammas, Raïf Fawaz and a partnership of Emil Bustani and Kamal Abdel-Rahman, who had previously set up a small engineering firm of their own. All were former employees of the Iraq Petroleum Company, which had brought the oil fields of Kirkuk, in northern Iraq, on stream before the Second World War. In the post-war years CAT became famous as an oil-company contractor throughout the Middle East. Kamal Abdel-Rahman broke away in 1952 to found his own highly successful rival firm, the Consolidated Contracting Company, CCC. After the death of Bustani in an air crash in 1963 and the death of Khoury in 1964, CAT lost much of its dynamism. (Bustani had been the driving force in the firm.) The company entered a partnership with the British mechanical engineers, Motherwell Bridge, forming Mothercat, though it later bought out the Motherwell Bridge holding. The CAT operation now is divided between two companies – CAT itself, which is a civil contractor, and Mothercat, a mechanical contractor. Most of the Arabian and Palestinian engineers in the Gulf today are CAT-trained.

Abdullah came to know the concession agreement virtually by heart. He took an interest in every detail of it. Hector Thompson, who ran QPC's government relations in the early 1950s, told me in 1979 how Abdullah appeared from the company's point of view: 'His job seemed to consist of formulating one demand after another, week after week for chiselling more money out of us . . . I remember one day he brought up the question of our providing quarantine facilities at Doha port; for a long time we couldn't understand what he meant – we thought he was saying "canteen" facilities, but eventually he showed us the clause in the concession. What he wanted was that IPC should establish quarantine facilities and pay for them in perpetuity. Of course we didn't agree. After weeks of argument I expect that we said that we would make a contribution, or something like that – this was the sort of solution we used to reach.' Ranald Boyle, who held much the same post as Thompson a year or so later and became Political Agent in Doha in the 1960s, described Abdullah's technique for softening up the company's employees: 'I used to dread picking up the telephone and discovering that it was Abdullah. There would be this terrible, grating, doom-laden voice: "Abdullah hina, ta'al hina" – "Abdullah here, come here". He didn't give you time to ask what it was all about. Sometimes when you arrived you discovered that it was just a joke. He'd be full of smiles. "Ah, Mr Boyle," he'd say, "I thought you'd like to come for a cup of coffee." '

In essence Abdullah's policy was to hold the initiative in his dealings with the oil company by maintaining a permanent state of mild tension. If there was no important issue to discuss he would find something small to which he could object. Once he protested at the activities of the European Club, claiming that tombola was gambling. On other occasions he was handed perfect opportunities for protests by the company itself. In 1951 a junior clerk in the commissariat sent a note to Shaikh Ali saying that the company would not supply him with more lemonade until he had sent back his empty bottles. Abdullah's fury at the incident had no sooner subsided than the commissariat followed up its coup by sending the Ruler a bill for 1 lb of tea. The incidents tell much about the traditional low status of shaikhs and the self-confidence of the oil companies in the 1950s.

The company employees were exasperated by Abdullah, but most say that they developed a sneaking regard for him. George Rentz, the head of Aramco's Arabian Research Division, who dealt with Abdullah when he moved to Saudi Arabia in the later 1950s, described him to me as 'an engaging conversationalist with a salty sense of humour and a hearty laugh'. In the same vein George McGeachie of QPC said: 'I liked Abdullah. He was a generous, expansive character who was honest by his own lights. You had to take him or leave him – he was not the kind of person to be dissected and judged quality by quality.'

At the time when most of the oil men were dealing with Abdullah, he had become ruler of Qatar in all but name. His house in the early 1950s was as big as Shaikh Ali's palace, the chandelier in the main hall was so vast that visitors had to bend to get under it. On feast days Abdullah's *majlis* was the best attended in Doha. Nobody could set up a business in Qatar without his blessing, and no foreign company could sell anything in any quantity in the state without employing Abdullah as its agent. If Abdullah discovered that the oil company or the government's civil engineering department would be needing a particular item of equipment he would take the agencies for all the leading manufacturers.

Abdullah's influence ran throughout the Qatar administration. The way he was able to profit from practically every significant transaction that took place in the state is illustrated by a letter of 1949 written by the newly appointed Political Agent in Doha (Wilton) to the Agent in Bahrain (Jakins). The background to the letter was complicated. It had been reported from Doha early in the year that about 12 per cent of the customs receipts was going into the pockets of Mohammad Uthman, the Director of Customs, who happened to be married to one of Abdullah Darwish's sisters. There was nothing wrong with this in principle; the directorship of the Qatari customs was (and still is) unofficially hereditary in the Uthman family, and like other government posts in the 1940s and 1950s, it was granted to the holder as a concession. The director was expected to enrich himself from the post. The problem that had arisen at this point in the tenure of Mohammad Uthman was that the Shaikh felt that the share of the customs that was being passed on to himself was not as big as it should have been. Commenting on Shaikh Ali's decision to appoint a servant to check Uthman's records, the Agent in Doha had written that the Shaikh's worries were probably justified, because Mohammad Uthman's 'style of living would arouse the suspicions of a babe in arms'. Somewhat to his surprise a few months later the Agent was told by Abdullah Darwish that it was his intention to reorganise the entire customs system. This news, in October 1949, prompted a renewal of correspondence between the two agents, in the course of which Wilton in Qatar examined the Darwish method in detail:

Dear Jakins,

It is amusing to think of Abdullah Darwish wishing to reorganise the customs administration, and difficult to see in what way any reorganisation would be an improvement on the present system from his point of view.

Mohammad Uthman, his brother-in-law, arrives each month by a process into which it is difficult to enquire closely, at a sum which he describes as the customs receipts for the month. This represents the Shaikh's entitlement. Even this, however, is not handed over to the Shaikh in person. It is transferred to Abdullah Darwish, on whom the Shaikh then draws for the payment of bills, sundry purchases and the discharge of other current expenses. The actual cash thus never passes through the Shaikh's hands, nor is there any system of accounting, and the Darwish are in most cases both buyer and seller of the purchases which he makes.

The sums which I gave in my letter of 3rd October as having been extracted from the customs by the Shaikh in fact represent merely his drawings on the Darwish for the period in question, and much of the money involved will in any case have found its way straight back into their pockets.

Yours sincerely,
A.J. Wilton

Such all-pervading control of the government machinery by the Darwish did not come about through the ceaseless pushing of Abdullah alone. The three Darwish brothers who worked together in business, Kassem, Abdullah and Abdel-Rahman, had their individual roles – perhaps not formally defined, but agreed tacitly within the family. Abdullah was the man who clinched the deals; he was the person to whom foreigners or Qataris went when they wanted quick, decisive action. He was not a courtier – he totally dominated the Shaikh – but he was shrewd enough to make himself always available at any time of day or night should Shaikh Ali want to discuss some minor anxiety.

Kassem was a patriarchal figure. He was (and is) very devout. When he hears the *muezzin* (call to prayer) he does not pray, like most people, in the room where he happens to be at the time – he goes to the mosque. Kassem has always made it his business to greet important visitors on behalf of the family and to undertake any subtle, diplomatic manipulation that might be needed to prepare the ground for a deal. Shaikh Ali and the other senior members of the Thani family entrusted Kassem with diplomatic missions. He helped to arrange the important marriage between Shaikh Ahmed, the son and successor of Shaikh Ali bin Abdullah, and Miriam, the daughter of Shaikh Rashid of Dubai.[5]

The youngest brother, Abdel-Rahman, was the eyes and ears of the Darwish family. In 1947 and 1948, when he was a young man, he was sent to work for QPC, who made him a supervisor in the commissariat. The arrangement was advantageous to all parties. The company was pleased to have an establishment Qatari on its pay roll, while the Darwish brothers gained a further detailed insight into the requirements of the oil industry. When he left QPC, Abdel-Rahman became the family's representative at court. At banquets he would be seen sitting close to Shaikh Ali, giving delicacies to favoured guests. He made travel arrangements, supervised protocol and provided girls and other entertainments for the ruling family. He was something of a playboy himself. It was said at the time that if Kassem Darwish had prayed for his family's fortune and Abdullah had made it, Abdel-Rahman spent it.

The Ruler, Shaikh Ali, did not object to the Darwish supremacy, but other members of the Thani family were less happy with the situation. Most of them received stipends from the state's oil revenues, but the amounts were not great and none of them was nearly as rich as Abdullah. They resented the way the English and Americans referred to Abdullah as 'the Prime Minister', they were jealous of his business and his influence over Shaikh Ali, and they were angry at the seeming impossibility of their competing with him. None of this Abdullah noticed. His great flaw was that he never observed how others reacted to him. In the mid-1950s there appeared a Thani opposition to the Darwish, of which Abdullah as almost completely unaware. One of the leaders of the opposition was Shaikh Nasser bin Khaled, a humorous, dignified person, who has since become Minister of Commerce and one of Qatar's most successful businessmen.

Matters came to a head rather suddenly. On a visit to Beirut in 1956 Abdullah had a quarrel with Khalifa, one of the sons of Shaikh Ali. The matter in dispute was a car, which Khalifa was demanding Abdullah gave him as a present. It is said that Khalifa fired a shot at Abdullah – though the Darwish family will neither confirm nor deny this.[5] Abdullah returned straight away to Doha, confronted Shaikh Ali and demanded that he guarantee his safety in Qatar. He said that if Shaikh Ali could not guarantee his safety he would leave the country. To Abdullah's surprise, the Ruler said that there was nothing he could do. Abdullah was forced to go into self-imposed exile.

It was not difficult for Abdullah to find a new home. With an eye to the growing power of the Saud family, and perhaps to the possibility of his having one day to leave Qatar, he had developed a friendship with Saud bin Jiluwi, the Governor of the Saudi Eastern Province. The connection had begun in 1939, when Abdullah had passed through Hofuf with Shaikh Abdullah bin Jasim and Hamad bin Abdullah on the way to Mecca for the pilgrimage. In 1950 the two men had met again when Abdullah had carried a message from the Ruler of Qatar to King Abdel-Aziz. On this occasion Abdullah's nephews say that the King asked Abdullah in the normal way 'What can I give you?' – it being the custom in Arabia for rulers to give presents to messengers. Abdullah had said 'Nothing', but had requested that the King should ask his sons to give him help should he ever have need of it. The story goes that the King then gave Abdullah a letter. Whether or not Abdullah came under the protection of the Saudi royal family in this way, he travelled often to the Saudi Eastern Province in the early 1950s. When he was forced to go into exile it was natural for him to settle in Dammam.

The Darwish remained the biggest and most powerful merchant family in Qatar for fifteen years after the departure of Abdullah. From the mid-1950s until the later 1960s the government spent little on construction, and so provided few opportunities for competitors to break into the market. In capital and consumer goods the Darwish brands were supreme. Until British Leyland ran foul of the Arab Boycott in the late 1960s, Austin outsold all other cars in Qatar; GEC dominated the electrical goods market; the Darwish canteen at Dukan accounted for most of the Western clothes, perfumes and consumer foods sold in the state.

The first signs of competition came in the late 1950s. A minor trader named Ali bin Ali formed a contracting partnership with Shaikh Nasser

5. Khalifa bin Ali had something of a reputation in Qatar as a gun enthusiast, until he began to go blind a few years ago. In 1973 he had the misfortune at Heathrow airport to be taken for a possible hijacker and searched. He was found to be carrying a loaded, gold-plated Walther PPK – the 'Bond gun' – valued at £3,000.

bin Khaled and began bidding on his own for small QPC supply contracts. At about the same time Jasim Jaidah, a member of one of the old pearl-trading families who ran a business on behalf of his father, began to diversify out of foodstuffs into machinery and construction materials. In the 1960s Omar al Mana began the revival of his family's fortunes with his enterprising marketing of Peugeot cars – though he was much helped in this by the boycott of Austin. Ahmed Manai, who had previously owned a small shop selling car accessories and spare parts, took several of the GM car lines. For the Darwish the problem was not just that Abdullah was no longer in charge of their business; the Qatari market was slowly becoming too big to be controlled by a single company.

Competitors were encouraged by Shaikh Khalifa bin Hamad, the son of Abdullah Darwish's original business associate and the intended successor of Shaikh Ali. In 1960 Shaikh Ali had been obliged by members of his family and the British authorities to go into retirement, but instead of handing the succession to Shaikh Khalifa, as it was believed he had promised to do when he had been made heir apparent in 1948, he had had his own son, Ahmed, appointed to the position. Khalifa was later made Deputy-Ruler and Prime Minister, but still felt bitter about the decision. In part it was said he blamed the Darwish. There had been some question at the time of Shaikh Hamad's death as to how fairly Abdullah Darwish had divided the business the two men had run together. Furthermore, Khalifa was said to believe that the Darwish had encouraged Shaikh Ali to ignore his promise that Khalifa should become ruler. It was reasoned that, having transferred their allegiance to the Ali branch of the Thani family with unseemly haste in 1949 and having backed that branch unswervingly for a decade, the Darwish would be anxious not to see one of Hamad's successors come to power.

The Darwish therefore suffered a setback when Shaikh Khalifa bin Hamad seized power in February 1972. Shaikh Ahmed bin Ali had proved himself as incompetent as his father and more extravagant, and Khalifa had been running the day-to-day administration of the state for most of the previous ten years. Since his coup Khalifa has proved to be one of the hardest-working and most able rulers in the Gulf. The younger members of the Darwish, the sons of Kassem and Abdullah, have tried to gain his favour for their family, making it clear that they do not see themselves as having been responsible for the past misdeeds of

Abdullah – but they have not been particularly successful. Ironically, while Abdullah is out of favour, his former associate, Shaikh Hamad – Khalifa's father – has been reinstated by the government public relations machine as a virtuous national hero.

In September 1973, a year and a half after Khalifa's succession, the Darwish company was partially split. Some of its businesses – including the Oasis Hotel, Darwish Engineering (which was created when the Darwish-CAT partnership was dissolved in 1967) and the Darwish Travel Bureau – remained with what the family calls the 'mother company'. This is Kassem and Abdullah Sons of Darwish Fakhroo, owned by the three brothers and based in Doha. Other assets were transferred to the brothers' private businesses (see appendix 2). Kassem, whose company is managed by his son, Yusuf, took most of the consumer-durables trading business; and Abdel-Rahman, who spends much of his time in Abu Dhabi, took the Fiat agency and Qatar Cold Stores. Abdullah was given the Modern Home Department store in Doha.

Even if it had not fragmented, the Darwish business would no longer be the biggest in Qatar; by consensus that honour now belongs to Ahmed Manai, the General Motors agent. The Darwish are thought to rank somewhere among the next half-dozen merchant houses.

For most of his self-imposed exile Abdullah has been more successful with his own business in Dammam than his brothers have been with the family company in Qatar. On several occasions in the 1960s and early 1970s Abdullah managed to expand his fortune by cornering the market in different foodstuffs and building materials. Throughout his time in Saudi Arabia he has maintained his friendship with the family of Bin Jiluwi. Every day he visits the palace of Abdel-Mohsin, the present Governor of the Eastern Province. He sits in the Governor's *majlis*, picking his toenails, shouting his jokes and adding his comments to whatever subject happens to be under discussion. He stopped being actively involved in trade in the mid-1970s, when his doctors advised him that he should lose weight and take life more easily. His managers look after his interests in Qatar and his airline agencies in Dammam; he has closed his commodities operation.

In retirement he has become reflective: 'I have tried my best and I have succeeded, thank God,' he told me in his deep voice when we met early in 1980. 'I start business when I am ten years old, and I enjoy it. I have done many interesting things. The Coronation was very nice.[6] We were in the Abbey for six hours. I enjoy the British custom. We had tea at the Buckingham Palace the next day and lunch at a girls' school. I remember Belgrave – I think he made an excellent job in Bahrain. The British did a lot of good in the Gulf . . . My age now more than sixty-five. I got property in Beirut, I got some shares. So I say "Why trouble myself?", and every year in the last ten years my health gets better. Now there are some young people doing business. But I will tell you something: they are eating grass that already sprung up, they are not the people who watered the ground.'

6. Abdullah was a member of the party that accompanied Shaikh Ali when the rulers of the Gulf states were invited to the Coronation in London in June 1953. When the service at Brown's Hotel in Mayfair proved inadequate in some minor detail, he was seen in the corridor outside his room bellowing for 'Brown'.

14

Kanoo – the Rise of a Modern Company

I wish to have on record my acknowledgement of the good work Yusuf bin Ahmed Kanoo has done for the Agency during the whole of the eighteen months that I have been Political Agent here . . . I have found him absolutely trustworthy and reliable in all the many tasks, confidential and otherwise, with which I have entrusted him. He has great tact and is most successful in carrying through missions, as he has considerable influence with all classes in Bahrain from the shaikhs down.[1]

It was the practice of the British political agents in Bahrain early in this century to write end-of-posting reports on the chief personalities of the island and the main problems they had encountered during their stay. Apart from leaving a record in the files, the agents' intention was to provide detailed briefings for their immediate successors. In 1910 Captain Mackenzie, who wrote the comments on Yusuf Kanoo, was drawing partly on the reports of the two agents who had occupied the post during the previous ten years. Both of these men had spoken highly of Yusuf, who had worked for them as interpreter, right-hand man and go-between in matters concerning the Agency and the Shaikh. It was left to Mackenzie to recommend Yusuf as a useful man to all who might succeed him at the Agency.

Yusuf Kanoo was one of the few men of his generation in Arabia who knew his date of birth. He had been born in Bahrain in 1874. His father Ahmed was a small landowner and trader in foodstuffs – not a very substantial man but a well-regarded member of the community. It was remembered many years later that in 1903 and 1904, when Bahrain had been struck in succession by bubonic plague and cholera, Ahmed had

---

1. All quotations concerning Yusuf's political activities in this chapter are drawn from the file R/15/2/241, headed 'Yusuf bin Ahmed Kanoo', at the India Office Library in London.

helped wash and bury the bodies of the victims. One of the dead was his own second son, Mohammad. Yusuf, when he was a boy, helped with the menial tasks of his father's business. From an early age it was realised by those who knew him that he possessed unusual intelligence; by the time he was eight he had learnt to recite the Koran by heart. When he was twenty he started travelling to India for trade, and four years later, in 1898, he began part-time work for the first British representative in Bahrain, Haji Ahmed bin Abdel-Rasool. It was not until six years later that a full scale Political Agency was established on the island.

Yusuf became the source of most of the political agents' knowledge of local gossip. He would make enquiries in the souk on the agents' behalf and occasionally give the agents advice. Inevitably he came to be seen by the Bahraini population as a representative of the agents – a position which gave him enormous local influence. People asked him to arbitrate in disputes. The Sheikh of Seihat, on the mainland near Qatif, wrote to Yusuf asking him to intercede with the Agent when he wanted his village to be taken under British protection in 1913 (see chapter 11). A year later the Shaikh of Qatar, Abdullah bin Jasim, sent a rambling and plaintive letter to Yusuf asking his help in settling a quarrel which had erupted among the turbulent members of his family. After the usual greetings the Shaikh wrote:

> Recently you advised me that you have ideas related to my interests and I have been awaiting your arrival. Now, there has been an argument with my cousins and my brother, Khalifa. I do not agree with what they are doing – they are oppressing people and do not respect women, my followers or foreigners . . . Such actions cannot continue. When I try to bring a wrongdoer to justice they stand against me. All the time I am trying my utmost to ease the situation and make their deeds less bad, hoping that God will guide them to the right path . . . but they are not willing to change their bad ways. Perhaps you might hear from certain people that I may change my residence from here [Doha] to another place. This, please understand, is not true and is not my intention. I therefore seek your advice and request your opinion as I cannot take action in this matter without hearing from you . . . Please give me your opinion, which I will keep as a secret between you and me.
>
> Greetings,
> Abdullah bin Jasim

Had Yusuf been an unambitious man he might have contented himself with pursuing his religious learning, helping the political agents and living the life of a respected pillar of the Bahrain establishment. His position might have been not unlike that of the *qadi*, the chief religious teacher and judge. He looked as if he would have been well cast in this role. He was described as a small man, short-sighted, with one glass eye and black spectacles. He cultivated a small, round black beard and always wore a white *dishdasha* and a white *mishlah* (cloak).

In fact, Yusuf was a man with a lust for power, fame and wealth. As soon as he found himself in a position of influence he began to concentrate his efforts on developing more lucrative business activities and making himself a power in Bahraini politics.

In 1913 Yusuf acquired his first modern agency – for the newly formed Anglo-Persian Oil Company. A year or so later, during the First World War he signed a contract to represent the Bombay and Persia Steam Navigation Company, which later became the Mogul Line. Soon afterwards he accepted an agency for the rival Persian Gulf Steam Navigation Company – a decision which led to his first serious skirmish with the British. To his surprise and disappointment, shortly after the deal he was informed by Turner Morrison, the owner of the Bombay and Persia company, that it was not the company's policy to have its agency held by anyone who represented other shipping lines. Yusuf promptly went to the Political Agent to ask if he would use official influence to persuade Turner Morrison to abandon its objections, but was told curtly that he should remember that he had become Turner Morrison's agent first, and that he should consider his position and make a choice of one line or the other. On reflection Yusuf decided to relinquish his new agency, the Persian Gulf Steam Navigation Company, which was much smaller than the other line. He was not pleased by this setback, but managed to compensate himself soon after the end of the war by taking an agency for Frank C. Strick, which had established itself in Basra in the wake of the British occupation of Mesopotamia. The company exported dates, barley and other grains grown in the valleys of the Tigris and Euphrates, and imported more sophisticated goods, such as electric generators, from Bombay. Inevitably Yusuf became one of the first Bahrainis to own a motor car and install electric light in his house.

Among the population of Bahrain Yusuf was best known as a banker. His customers were the pearl merchants who wanted somewhere safe to keep their money between the pearl market in the autumn and April and May of the following year, when they would draw on their funds to lend to the dhow captains. The captains in turn advanced the money to their divers. As the pearling season progressed the merchants would make further drawings to finance their purchases of pearls from the captains. At times Yusuf held nearly 2 million rupees ($540,000) – sealed in 2,000-rupee bags and stored two bags to a box. His special value to the merchants was that he had offices in both Bombay and Bahrain. Merchants who went to Bombay to arrange the sale of their pearls in October and November could leave their money with Yusuf in India and make their drawings a few months later from his Bahrain office. Those who ran food and timber-importing businesses would pay into their accounts in Bahrain and make their drawings in India, either from Yusuf's own offices or from various Bombay merchants with whom Yusuf held accounts. Relatively little money had to be moved physically from India to Bahrain and when it did move, its passage was made simpler by the system of the R2,000 sealed bags and boxes, which was in use throughout the subcontinent.

For Yusuf the benefit of the operation was partly prestige. It was the custom in Gulf society at the time for the most eminent and best-trusted citizens to act as bankers for the rest of the community. Equally important was that Yusuf was able to use some of the money placed in his charge to trade to his own advantage and make loans to other merchants during the winter. Sometimes he charged interest, at other times he lent the money interest-free; what he did depended on local custom and the status of the borrower. The most important of Yusuf's clients, Abdel-Aziz bin Saud, the Sultan of Nejd, was never charged interest, even though he borrowed from Yusuf almost as much money as he received in credits from the Algosaibi family. By the end of 1917 Abdel-Aziz owed Yusuf R46,000, equivalent to $14,000. Again, the advantage for Yusuf in these transactions was prestige. If Yusuf was known to be favoured by Abdel-Aziz, he reasoned correctly that he would gain further advantages in his dealings with the rest of society.

When Yusuf began to grow rich, in about 1910, he formed a well-judged political friendship with Abdullah bin Isa al Khalifa, the youngest and most able son of the Shaikh. At this time the Shaikh, Isa bin Ali, was already ageing and beginning to lose his grip on the affairs of the island. The power vacuum he left came to be filled by an increasing number of political factions, each representing a particular community or interest group. Yusuf and the Shaikh's son formed their own faction, known as the Reform Party, through which they tried to dispose of the affairs of Bahrain in co-operation – exploiting Yusuf's connection with the Agency and Abdullah's influence with his father. The Reform Party, despite its name, was not designed to further or protect the interests of anyone except its founders; it was just a convenient label for Yusuf and Abdullah. It avoided giving itself any clear political objectives which might have brought it into conflict with any of the other political factions on the island. Indeed, Yusuf managed to win the goodwill of the leaders of all the other factions. He regularly visited the head of the Merchants Party, an old Nejdi named Muqbil al Dhukir, gradually being regarded almost as a son by the old man. He would pass bits of news to Muqbil and make a show of asking him for advice. To the head of the Arab or Local Dignitaries Party, Abdullah Dossari, Yusuf lent large sums of money. Shaikh Jasim bin Mahza, the Qadi, who led the Conservative Party, became Yusuf's spiritual father. Yusuf would visit him every Friday morning to give him his Zakat – the religious income tax that is paid by all devout Muslims.

As the internal politics of Bahrain became more turbulent new parties appeared – representing the Persians, the Shias and the Indians. These too had to be taken into account by the Reform Party – though they did not demand the same subtlety that Yusuf had had to use in dealing with the leaders of the Sunni establishment parties. After consideration Yusuf and Abdullah bin Isa decided to ignore the Persians and the Shias. Neither was powerful, and the Shias were frightened of Yusuf and of all members of the ruling family. The Indians meanwhile were dealt with by blackmail. They were richer and more powerful than the Persians and Shias, but their leader, Gangaram Tikamdas, was known to be corrupt. Tikamdas controlled the Shaikh's customs house and had recently been caught cheating him, by some of the merchant community. He was therefore obliged to agree to a package deal, in which the merchants managed to combine politics with a most satisfactory business arrangement. In return for a pledge that his embezzlement would not be exposed, the frightened Tikamdas agreed to give Yusuf his community's political support. He also gave Yusuf, Abdel-Aziz Algosaibi and Yusuf Fakhroo (another prominent merchant of the day) exemption from taxes on most of their imports.

During the period from 1910 to 1920 Yusuf Kanoo was involved in almost every event of importance that took place in Bahrain. He helped

Mohammad Ali Alireza establish a Fallah school on the island. He was an early supporter of the idea of a Manama municipality – though he later reversed his position on this issue. Whenever there were disturbances or communal murders, Yusuf was involved in calming the situation. It was noted, however, that he did not like sitting on the committees of enquiry that were set up on such occasions; the feeling at the Political Agency and among members of the Bahraini establishment was that Yusuf was anxious never to be seen on the unpopular side in an important community dispute.

The British authorities had no objection to Yusuf's political career in itself, even though they occasionally complained about his lack of 'public spirit'. Several of the political agents during this period, including one who was sick for most of his posting, continued to rely on Yusuf in their dealings with the ruling family and the other factions on the island. What the British did not like was the way Yusuf used his work for the Agency to further his political and business interests. One of the agents wrote that Yusuf's rise from being a young man in quite a small way of business to being one of the most 'respectable and respected' merchants in Bahrain was 'almost entirely due to his connection with the Agency'.

The more perceptive of the British officials could see clearly that Yusuf was almost bound to exploit his position in the way he did. In May 1911 Major Knox had discussed the background to Yusuf's behaviour in a report he had written for his successor at the Agency:

> . . . to my mind the position is unsatisfactory. Yusuf Kanoo works for nothing and there is no probability that the government will grant him pay. It cannot possibly pay him to do this unless he gains in influence and prestige, and to a certain extent at the expense of the PA. It is a great relief to me to learn, as I did yesterday, that Colonel Cox [the Political Resident] has independently arrived at the same opinion. There would be no object in quarrelling with Yusuf Kanoo but it would be distinctly advisable if his constant employment were discontinued.

There was an obvious difference in philosophy between the British and Yusuf. The British, concerned with the principle of conflict of interest, did not feel it right that a man should use his employment in their service to further his private business and political interests. Yusuf took exactly the opposite view; to him it seemed that his work at the Agency provided a good opportunity for making money which it would have been utterly illogical for him not to have taken. By Arabian standards there was nothing improper about this attitude. The Algosaibi family at this time was using its connection with Abdel-Aziz bin Saud to further its own political influence and wealth in Bahrain, and there is no record of Abdel-Aziz ever objecting. Nor is there much evidence that Yusuf's own countrymen were shocked by the ruthless manner in which he exploited his position; had any of them found themselves in the same position they would undoubtedly have acted in the same way.

The British became much more annoyed as time passed to discover that Yusuf was actively playing them off against the Shaikh. In the early years of his employment he had used his Agency connection to pose as someone exercising a decisive influence on events; later, in the words of Major Dickson, who was Agent in 1919 and 1920, he decided to 'force the pace'. Successive agents described his methods:

> Yusuf, of course is a past master of intrigue; he is rich, is looked up to by the common people and wields great power. His policy as he has confessed to me on several occasions is 'Divide et Impera', in other words keep the PA and the Ruler in a state of enmity and manage them . . . I regard Yusuf Kanoo as a dangerous person and I write this note in the hope that it may be of use to future political agents. (Dickson, 1920)

> I am afraid that the disturbed relations that have existed between the Agency and [the trading company] Messrs Gray Paul after all are to be traced to Yusuf Kanoo's influence . . . The practice of his accompanying the PA on visits to Shaikh Isa is particularly bad. (Captain Lorimer, 1912)
> [In the margin Dickson later printed his comment in blue crayon: 'A vast number of difficulties were deliberately caused by him.']

> I told him straight that the reason his services had not been in request lately was that no PA would trust him to play the game. (Captain Loch, 1918)

In practice rifts such as occurred in Captain Loch's posting were temporary. However much they disliked him, there were always occasions when the British found it necessary to use Yusuf again. The government of India also felt obliged to reward Yusuf periodically for his services by giving him medals. These awards invariably caused further ill-feeling between Yusuf and the Agent, who had the thankless task of bestowing them. The British regarded medals as something which a gentleman should receive with pride and modesty. Yusuf, on the other hand, saw them as a form of payment – his rightful due as a servant of the government. His attitude was that of one who had performed a useful service for a shaikh and who expected a grant of land or a concession in return. Having a high opinion of himself and of the services he had rendered, he felt on each occasion that he should be receiving a better medal than that which the authorities were actually giving him. Rather ineptly he would also put it about in the souk that he was about to receive the medal for which he was hoping, and so lost face when it was discovered that he had been over-optimistic. He gradually worked himself into such a state of anguish that the political agents found that a considerable part of their dealings with him were revolving around his complaints about his decorations.

In 1911, when Yusuf was awarded the Kaisar-i-Hind, he gave a speech to the group of friends and dignitaries that had been assembled for the presentation. In it he thanked the Indian government for the award, but qualified his thanks by adding the words 'although it is only of the second class'. Six years later, when Yusuf discovered that he was to be given the title Khan Sahib, he telegraphed the Resident to ask for something better. When he failed he begged to be given the sanad in private, which the British eventually agreed to do. In order to distract attention from the irregularity of this procedure it was decided by the authorities that the Agent should write to Yusuf saying that had it not been for 'this dreadful war, which has cast such a shadow over the world', they would have liked to bestow the title with more ceremony.

Much to the horror of the British, Yusuf adopted the same ungrateful attitude when he was told in 1919 that he was to be given the MBE (Member of the Order of the British Empire). He begged that it should not be given in public, claiming that it was too degrading for him and that it was a clerk's decoration. The Political Agent was later forced to admit that during the war several clerks in the Gulf had been awarded the MBE. Yusuf accepted the medal, but was quite clear about what he would have liked instead. This was the CIE, Companion of the Most Eminent Order of the Indian Empire – the most important decoration awarded in the Gulf to anyone other than the shaikhs. From 1919 onwards he mounted a campaign for the CIE, which within six months, according to Major Dickson, had become a 'positive obsession'. 'At times,' the Agent wrote, 'his goings on were so strange that I began to wonder whether there was not a strain of lunacy in him.' When Yusuf was eventually given the CIE he began to turn his attention to even grander decorations. At this point the patience of the British authorities ran out. It was made clear to Yusuf that nothing more would be forthcoming. The Agent in Bahrain at the time remarked: '. . . I do not think he should get any further decorations from government. He always scoffs at them and belittles them.'

The British were not displeased in 1920 to discover that Yusuf's political career had reached a crisis. As in many such cases, the causes of Yusuf's problems were numerous and individually not very important. What mattered was their cumulative effect. The establishment of a branch of the Eastern Bank (now Standard and Chartered), which provided a more efficient service than Yusuf's banking operation, was followed by a quarrel between Yusuf and Abdullah bin Isa and the break up of the Reform Party. At about the same time the leaders of the Merchants and Persians parties died and were succeeded by Abdel-Aziz Algosaibi, the agent of Abdel-Aziz bin Saud, and Mohammad Sherif, the chief of the island's police. Neither of these men was in the least afraid of Yusuf, and both were rich and ambitious. Abdel-Aziz Algosaibi's influence was steadily enhanced by the rising prestige of Abdel-Aziz bin Saud, who after the First World War emerged as the most powerful ruler in the Arabian Peninsula. Within a short time Yusuf suffered a serious loss of face over his failure to be appointed president of the board of governors of Bahrain's first modern school. This was established in the wake of Abdullah bin Isa's official visit to Britain in 1919. Yusuf was duly offered membership of the board but felt unable to accept. Having recently been 'humiliated' by being given his MBE, he had become anxious to find a way of restoring his prestige and had let it be known that he was to be offered the presidency. In his disappointment he said that he would refuse to accept a place on the board unless he was given six votes to each of the other members' one. Inevitably his proposal was rejected, and Yusuf made some sarcastic remarks about Shaikh Abdullah bin Isa. The latter retaliated by publicly withdrawing his large subscription to the school fund. Yusuf eventually agreed to accept a place on the normal terms, but by this time the incident had led to another embarrassment and a further deterioration in his relations with Abdullah bin Isa.

More serious problems were to come. In 1919 the post of Political Agent had been taken by Major Dickson, a man who developed very strong likes and dislikes. Dickson brought with him to serve as his personal assistant and emissary to the Ruler, an Iraqi whom he had previously employed when he had been serving in Mesopotamia. He also instituted a Political Agent's *majlis*, 'at which', he wrote, 'all were welcome, and discussions of people's and merchants' difficulties were encouraged.' Both of these developments Yusuf saw as disasters; they struck at the very roots of his special access to the Agency and his influence with the Agent. To make matters worse Dickson conceived one of his powerful dislikes for Yusuf. His assessment of Yusuf, written at the end of 1920, was as thorough a piece of character assassination as any Political Agent ever undertook on anyone in the Gulf:

> Outwardly cheerful to an embarrassing extent. Poses as being religious. Perpetually makes fulsome compliments – a humbug and actor. Always talking about his great services to the Government and the unjust way he has been treated. His special grievance is that he has not been given the CIE. In short, to one meeting him casually he gives the impression of being rather a nice mannered fool. Behind this rather unprepossessing exterior will be found the true Yusuf Kanoo. A splendid businessman . . . unscrupulous and cruel, woe betide the unfortunate whom he gets into his power . . . A money lender, he is not above blackmail methods. He possesses no friends. All fear him. Extremely self-willed, he is revengeful beyond the ordinary run of Arabs. 'To crush my enemy, I am prepared to sacrifice three-quarters of my wealth', I have heard him say.[2]

After Dickson's posting and the other disasters of 1920 Yusuf was never as powerful again. Until the end of the First World War his influence had increased fairly steadily. Although some of the British agents had distrusted him, and rivals had appeared in Bahraini politics, he had been possibly the most active and powerful political figure on the island. From the early 1920s onwards he became no more than one

---

2. In case the views of Yusuf held by Dickson and the other political agents had been in some way biased by their own backgrounds and the age in which they lived, in 1982 I asked someone who had known Yusuf in the early 1930s for his opinion of the man. His reply was as follows: 'I'd say he was a man with a hairy heel – unscrupulous, a slight touch of the Mafia . . . Oh yes, he was a grand, splendid figure – he looked very holy and as far as I was concerned he was very pleasant and helpful. But really he was a very big frog in a very small pool, and he meant to stay it come hell or high water.'

important figure among many. In wealth he was overtaken by the Algosaibi family; in politics his influence was reduced not only by his own misjudgements but by a series of political changes that took place in the 1920s. In the summer of 1923, after the Nejdi–Persian riots inspired by Abdullah Algosaibi, the British arranged the replacement of Shaikh Isa by his son, Shaikh Hamad. Yusuf was closely concerned in the events that led up to the abdication – he was one of the Bahrainis who went to Shaikh Isa to suggest that he should make way for his son; but the long-term consequences of the change did not enhance his own power, or that of any of the island's other political figures outside the ruling family. Hamad bin Isa quickly set about resuscitating the authority of his position, and was soon to be assisted in this task by Belgrave, who arrived in 1926. Under the new regime political parties in the formal sense became unimportant, though each community retained its acknowledged leaders. One of Hamad's early moves was to stop the abuse whereby Yusuf Kanoo, Abdel-Aziz Algosaibi and Yusuf Fakhroo had been given partial exemption from import taxes by Gangaram Tikamdas. The merchants were still bold enough to get together a petition for the abolition of the tax, which was one of the main sources of funds for the Shaikh and the Manama municipality, but Hamad ignored it.

The British political agents in the 1920s seem to have been much influenced in their attitudes to Yusuf by Dickson's damning character sketch. Dickson blighted Yusuf's chances of re-establishing his special role at the Agency. Yusuf often met the political agents, and in the later 1920s and the early 1930s he played a valuable role on the British behalf in the opening rounds of negotiations for the Qatar oil concession. His work was appreciated, but it was no longer essential and was of no use in internal Bahraini politics. In British eyes Yusuf gradually became a quieter, humbler, better person.

In 1930 Yusuf's business began a rapid decline. As the collapse of the pearling business began, the amount of money coming into the Gulf economy from outside fell, and merchants in all imported goods experienced a drop in sales. Several of the pearl merchants and many of the dhow captains and small traders in commodities went bankrupt. Yusuf's own business was hit by a fall in income from his agencies. More important, the amounts of money handled by his bank decreased, and many of those to whom he had lent money declared that they were unable to repay him. Some gave him pearls instead of cash, the expectation of the parties being that sooner or later the price of pearls would rise by enough to cover the amounts of the debts. In fact pearl prices continued their decline. Yusuf was obliged virtually to write off the loans he had made. This in turn meant that he had difficulty in repaying people from whom he had himself borrowed money. The one small bright feature, in what became a very gloomy period for Yusuf, was his acquisition of the agency for the Dutch-owned Silver Java Pacific Line, which carried sugar to the Arabian Peninsula from the East Indies. The agreement, arranged partly by Yusuf's nephews, Jasim and Ali, was significant as the Kanoo family's first contact with Dutch shipowners. This connection was to become important after the Second World War. It also happens that Ahmed bin Ali, the present head of the Kanoo family, remembers a visit to a Silver Java Pacific steamer as the first occasion on which he tasted a cold fizzy drink.

By 1934 Yusuf's financial problems had become very serious. The Political Agent in Bahrain, who was worried that the bankruptcy of Yusuf would pull down many other people, filed regular reports on the state of his debts. From these it seems that in early 1934 Yusuf must have owed about R500,000 ($150,000). In March of the previous year he had mortgaged some property to the Eastern Bank for R75,000 at an annual rate of interest of 9 per cent, but when his loan had fallen due at the end of the year he had been unable to repay it. He owed a further R20,000 to the Anglo-Persian Oil Company, which insisted on having the debt secured on some more Kanoo property. Hilal Mutairi, a successful Kuwaiti merchant and friend of Yusuf, was owed R180,000. To finance his debts Yusuf resorted to the standard combination of further borrowings and sales of assets. APOC turned down his request for a new loan of R160,000, but the government, which began to receive oil revenues in 1934, lent him R20,000 and bought a small piece of land for about five times its real worth. Hilal Mutairi helped Yusuf by buying from him a large building in the centre of Manama for R250,000. Over the next six years Yusuf was obliged to make a series of further sales, disposing of the greater part of his land and buildings. Many of the assets he sold had been left to him by his father and had great senti-mental value.

It became a point of honour for Yusuf to repay all the money he had borrowed. Other merchants in the 1930s went bankrupt, but Yusuf was too proud and too conscious of what other people thought of him to default on his debts. He therefore handed over the day-to-day running of his business to his nephews and concentrated his own efforts on improving his financial position. He was even forced to go into the pearl business in a small way. For several months of the year he would travel to India to deal in the pearls that he had had to accept in lieu of repayment of his loans. Gradually Yusuf repaid almost all of the money he owed the government, and for the balance handed over another small plot of land. His debt to the oil company rose and fell according to the level of his stocks, the amount of credit he was given and the amount of money he was able to persuade the company to lend him. At one point his debt rose to R135,000, but by the end of the decade it had fallen to R26,000.

Among the Bahrain merchants Yusuf's efforts to repay his debts were admired. They are remembered in Bahrain to this day and in the Kanoo family are talked about in almost heroic terms.

Unfortunately Yusuf's struggle was not completely successful. The Kanoos found themselves in another financial crisis in the early 1940s. Yusuf visited Belgrave on several occasions, described his financial plight and pleaded for further help from the government. On each occasion he put pressure on Belgrave by telling him that unless he were given loans he would have no choice but to go bankrupt. In view of Yusuf's prestige in Bahrain and the advice and financial help he had once given to the rulers of other Arabian states, Belgrave and Shaikh Hamad decided that his bankruptcy would be politically unacceptable. Although Belgrave resented the pressure put on him in his interviews with Yusuf, it was decided that Yusuf would have to be helped. This time the government could afford to be more generous than it had been in 1934: Bahrain was entering the affluent age when Arabian rulers would feel an obligation to use their new wealth from oil to support the finances of their more important subjects. Shaikh Hamad and his government bought more property from Yusuf at above market prices and gave him a succession of loans totalling R50,000 ($15,000) without demanding interest or security. In due course these loans too were repaid, either by Yusuf or his successors. The Kanoo family today stresses – and it seems to be generally accepted in Bahrain – that eventually none of Yusuf's debts went unpaid.

In what seems to have been one of the last attempts made by Yusuf himself to generate some business that would enable him to repay his debts, he travelled to Iraq in 1942. While exploring the possibility of some commodities deals, he requested an interview with the British ambassador in Baghdad. The ambassador wrote to Bahrain enquiring who Yusuf was and asking whether it would be wise to grant his request. The reply he received said much about the sorry state into which Yusuf had fallen, his chequered career with the British authorities in Bahrain, and British attitudes in dealing with Arabs:

> Yusuf Kanoo is doyen of the mercantile community here. Rendered valuable services to British Government during last war and was made CIE. Has now lost former wealth and has many debts. Has become querulous and disgruntled and period of usefulness is over. During his days of prosperity however, he was the valued associate of many high British officials and should still, I think, be treated with courtesy.

Three years after this telegram was sent Yusuf Kanoo died, on 21 December 1945. The British Political Agent wrote to the Resident on 6th January 1946:

> My Dear Sir Geoffrey,
>   Haji Yusuf Kanoo died on 21st December. You will doubtless let me know if the jewels of the various orders of which he was a member are returnable.
> > Yours sincerely, A.C. Galloway

The great-nephews of Yusuf, who now run the company he founded, all began work with the most menial jobs. Ahmed and Mohammad were summoned back from the American University of Beirut (AUB) in 1941, before they had taken their final exams. Their father was worried by the fighting between the Allies and the Vichy French in Syria. Back in Bahrain they were employed refuelling the few aircraft which called at the island. After the war their younger brothers, Abdullah and Mubarak, returned from the AUB with degrees and took similar jobs. Abdullah became a checker and Mubarak an assistant to one of the family's clerks. Abdel-Aziz, who was educated in Britain, took his first job in London, at the British Overseas Airways Corporation terminal in Buckingham Palace Road.

The young Kanoos set out to transform their company. Within a few years of their return Ahmed and Mohammad had learnt about every aspect of the business and had taken over the day-to-day management from their fathers. Ahmed, a small man with the canny, calculating look of a person who planned his actions several moves ahead, concentrated on the financial side of the business. Mohammad was more interested in running operations on the ground. 'A real ball of fire', was how one of the family's earliest English employees described him to me in 1978: 'Probably not somebody who cared very much about accounts.' While Mohammad looked after the company in Bahrain, Ahmed was free to travel. A British Political Agent who served in Bahrain a few years later says that Mohammad was more traditional than Ahmed: 'He handled the local things – staff, keeping in with the Ruler, "listening" to what was going on. Meanwhile Ahmed was the man who went to London, made new contacts, came up with new ideas. Oddly enough I seem to remember that it was Mohammad who used to disappear during Ramadan [the month of fasting], while Ahmed used to return to Bahrain as a sort of penance.'

The company the brothers inherited in the late 1940s was a tiny, run-down affair, representing four dry cargo shipping lines, the Anglo-Iranian Oil Company and Nash motor cars. It had about 90,000 rupees ($28,000) of assets, and two clerks, one Indian and one Bahraini, both of whom worked for the Kanoos for over thirty years and died in the family's service. Ahmed and Mohammad and their brothers decided that their company's future would lie in providing services rather than importing. This had been the essence of the family's business under Yusuf and it seemed to be the right direction for the company in the post-war years, when Bahrain's neighbours were becoming oil producers. The major problem – which made the brothers' decision a bold one – was that the competition in this area came not from other Bahraini merchants but from the Bahraini branch of a British company, Gray Mackenzie. To overcome this obstacle the idea of Ahmed and Mohammad was to travel to Europe to meet the companies they represented on their home ground and ask them in what ways they would like to see their service improved. Then the Kanoos would sometimes ask the companies for help in putting the new ideas into practice.

The first foreign journey, undertaken by Ahmed in 1948, was to Oslo and New York. Ahmed had introductions from the Bahrain Petroleum Company (BAPCO) to a Norwegian shipping company and Mobil, both of which had tankers calling at the Bahrain terminal of Sitra. With little difficulty Ahmed was able to persuade both companies to contract the Kanoos as their agents in place of the rather half-hearted shipping

KANOO FAMILY TREE

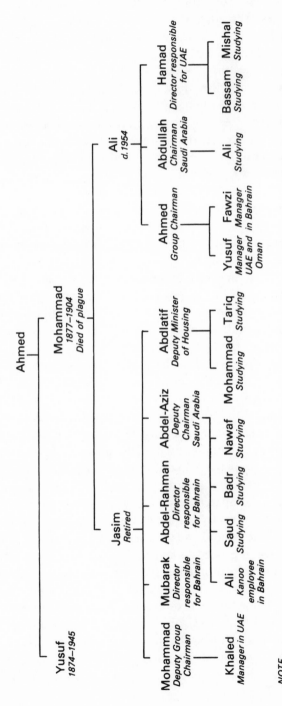

NOTE

There are two companies known as Yusuf bin Ahmed Kanoo. One operates in Bahrain, the UAE and Oman and has its shares distributed in equal numbers between all the brothers and cousins of the 'older' generation except Abdlatif. The other Kanoo company operates in Saudi Arabia and is owned formally by Abdullah and Abdel-Aziz, who are Saudi citizens.

Informally, the family regards the Saudi company as having the same ownership as the Bahrain-based company. The main board of the Kanoo group sits in Bahrain. Its members, in order of seniority, are: Ahmed (Chairman), Mohammad (Deputy Chairman), Abdullah, Mubarak, Abdel-Rahman, Abdel-Aziz, and Hamad.

department of BAPCO. On his way back from New York, Ahmed stopped in London and bought eight second-hand Thames barges and an ex-Royal Air Force rescue launch to tow them. The whole deal, arranged through a friendly former employee of Gray Mackenzie, cost £4,000. The barges were small, but they gave the Kanoos at least the appearance of being able to compete with Gray Mackenzie. 'In those days', Ahmed told me in Bahrain in 1977, 'there was no proper port in Bahrain – that wasn't completed until 1961. All the ships were unloaded offshore and we used to bring the cargoes to land by dhow. This was all right for cement and general cargo but not for cars. When we got the barges the great advantage was that they were much stronger than dhows and purpose built. Gray Mackenzie had had barges for a long time and we could see that if we didn't get barges too we would lose our agencies. I remember soon after they arrived Mr Orde, who was one of the Gray Mackenzie managers, was standing on the pier with Abdullah watching the ships being discharged. He thought the barges were very small – they were just 50 tons – and he made some remark to Abdullah about "what can you unload in tea cups?" I don't remember quite what Abdullah said in reply, but I think maybe he just laughed and said "Well, we'll see how these tea cups will do." '

In the next two years the Kanoos made further innovations. They agreed to take on the agency for the Norwich Union, which became the first insurance company to have a representative in the Gulf. The family had been approached on Norwich Union's behalf by Charles Belgrave, whose brother-in-law was one of the company's directors. At about the same time the family negotiated a ticket agency for the British Overseas Airways Corporation, which then ran a flying-boat service in short hops from London to Karachi. Ahmed told me that at first BOAC was not very interested in attracting Bahraini passengers: 'Most of the seats were taken by servicemen – this was both on the east-bound flight and on the return flight a few days later. The service operated once a week. But sometimes the airline had some empty seats and it didn't mind selling these to a few merchants who wanted to go to India. The flying boats went to Karachi, but from there anyone could take the train for about three days to Bombay . . . What happened was that these merchants would normally come to us because we did the refuelling and we had good relations with BOAC. They'd ask us for an introduction to BOAC, which we would give them for nothing, and then they would buy their tickets at the BOAC offices – not from us. Because of this Mubarak had the idea to set up a travel office in about 1949 or 1950, and African and Eastern suggested we ought to get an IATA licence – without this we couldn't earn any commission from selling tickets.[3] Once we had the licence we got all our commission backdated, but even then we didn't make much money for a time. There was still a shortage of seats and most of the traffic was servicemen until 1953 when they introduced skymasters as well as flying boats . . . I think you could say that this was our first big breakthrough, because it was the basis of our whole travel operation and all our general sales agencies.'

Another important deal came a year or so after the travel office. In the early 1950s the Kanoos were already agents for several dry-cargo lines in Bahrain and Dammam, but all of the tanker work in Saudi Arabia was handled by Aramco.[4] Ahmed and Mohammad were told by some friends in Aramco of the oil company's policy of divestiture. They were advised that if they wanted to get into the tanker agency business in Saudi Arabia, the company would be happy to close its own agency department and give the work to them – which was exactly the procedure it adopted a few years later when Ahmed Hamad Algosaibi went into Pepsi-Cola manufacturing.

In the early 1950s the Korean War was in progress and most of the tankers loading at Bahrain and Saudi Arabia were taking refined products – mainly gasoline and aviation spirit – to the American forces in the Far East. The tanker owners were leasing their vessels to the US Navy, which organised its chartering through an organisation known as the Military Sea Transportation Services (MSTS), a section of the Navy Transportation Department. To help him with an introduction to MSTS Ahmed turned to the American admiral on Bahrain. Since the Second World War there had been a very small, low-profile US Navy base on the island and the young Kanoos had made a point of cultivating the goodwill of its commander. The admiral willingly gave Ahmed a letter of recommendation to a senior naval officer in Washington, and with this in his pocket Ahmed travelled once more to the United States in October 1951. He found the Navy Department and the tanker companies only too anxious to do business with him. In effect MSTS told the

3. IATA is the International Air Transport Association. African and Eastern is a British trading company.
4. Shipping agents are the representatives of ship owners in foreign ports. They arrange the unloading of ships, clear goods through customs, provide food, water and fuel, arrange medical treatment and crew changes if necessary, and hold crews' mail.

tanker owners that Aramco was pulling out of the agency business and that Kanoo was available – a bold and unambiguous message which almost threw the owners into the Kanoos' arms. By the end of his visit Ahmed had signed up all of the tanker companies that had a direct operating relationship with the US Navy.

As a result of the US deals, Abdullah, Ahmed's brother, established a Kanoo business in Saudi Arabia in 1951 and became a Saudi citizen in the following year. In 1955 Abdullah's experience of working with Americans made him the obvious man to accompany the Bahraini Ruler's son and heir apparent, Shaikh Isa bin Sulman, on a visit to the United States.

The last of the series of initiatives that established the foundations of the modern Kanoo business provided a classic example of the Kanoos' flair for enlisting the help of their principals. Again it was Ahmed who described to me what happened: 'We had always had a close relationship with the Dutch – mainly with the Holland Persian Gulf Line. I remember there was a great friend who was managing director of this line – Corbijn Van Willenswaard. We often used to go to Amsterdam or Rotterdam to visit him. Other companies were the Nedlloyd Line, Java Pacific and the Royal Inter-Ocean Lines – they're now all merged into the Royal Nedlloyd Line . . . These Dutch companies wanted to get round the Gray Mackenzie monopoly, because it meant that otherwise their ships had to queue up when they arrived here and wait their turn. So to help us they seconded several of their people to us from their inspectorate in Basra – these arrangements lasted for about twenty years. The Holland Persian Gulf Line also introduced us to a company in Holland that built barges, and over a period of time we bought quite a number of much bigger barges. The shipping line transported these barges to Bahrain free for us. They found that if we had better barges we could unload their ships faster – much faster than if they waited for Gray Mackenzie or the dhows . . .'

By the mid-1950s the Kanoos had become serious competition for Gray Mackenzie. On the surface the two companies' rivalry was kept at a rather gentlemanly level; before the arrival of the Dutch barges Gray Mackenzie would even hire its own barges to the Kanoos. This happened if the Kanoos had several of their ships calling at the same time. Later a more awkward edge developed in the companies' relations with each other. The good-neighbourliness stopped, the British company became more reluctant to share its equipment, and all the time in subtle and indirect ways the Kanoos and their managers did everything they could to exploit Gray Mackenzie's weaknesses. The Kanoos were less complacent than Gray Mackenzie, and less casual in dealing with their customers. Ahmed Kanoo mentions that his family was much more approachable than the Gray Mackenzie managers.[5] As soon as they noticed that senior Gray Mackenzie managers often were too busy to see customers and were referring them to clerks, the Kanoos made a point of seeing that they were always available to visitors in person. This is essential for success in business in all Arab countries. They continually canvassed importers, asking them to nominate a Kanoo line to carry their cargo, and whenever their intelligence network told them that a particularly big cargo was going to be shipped to Bahrain they would notify their shipping lines so that they could approach the exporter. With luck they would be able to arrange for an importer to put in its letters of credit the words 'to be shipped with Kanoo shipping agencies'. 'The Kanoos', as one of their longest-serving managers put it to me, 'never hesitated to play the nationalist – "local Arab" – card if there was any chance of it being useful.' To have this card in the rather troubled times of the 1950s and early 1960s was an enormous advantage. It was important as much with the oil companies, which were always anxious to cultivate local goodwill, as with the Bahraini and Saudi population.

Looking back on the battle, Gray Mackenzie's managers agree with most of the Kanoos' assessment. They add that they think that the Political Agency wanted to promote local firms and that this led the Kanoos to foster assiduously good relations between themselves and the Agent and his staff. They also say that the Kanoos were great copiers of Gray Mackenzie. They employed a mainly foreign staff because that was what the British company had, and when Gray Mackenzie introduced any new piece of equipment, the Kanoos would do the same, on the reasoning that if their competition was bothering to buy 80-foot barges, for example, there must be some advantage in them. All parties agree that much of the Kanoos' expansion did not involve a direct loss on Gray Mackenzie's part; in most cases the Kanoos were taking for themselves the major share of the growth of the market. As new lines began sailings to the Gulf they went more often to Kanoo than to Gray Mackenzie. An important and almost inevitable Kanoo acquisition was the Kuwait Shipping Company.

5. See Suliman Olayan's experience of Gray Mackenzie in the 1950s in chapter 16.

By 1961, when the Bahraini port at Mina Sulman was opened – an event which allowed both companies to disperse their barge fleets to other places in the Gulf – the Kanoos reckoned that they were winning their battle. If they were not actually bigger than Gray Mackenzie at this stage they could see that they were set to overtake their rival in the future. From the later 1960s it seems that relations between the two companies became more harmonious again. When Gray Mackenzie was obliged by a new edict to close its offices in Saudi Arabia it recommended its shipping lines to switch to Kanoo. In the 1970s it changed the emphasis in its Gulf operations from plain agency work to large-scale contracting, mainly in port management. Obviously nobody outside the Gray Mackenzie board is likely to know exactly what considerations prompted the change, but the Kanoos like to think that one of the factors might have been the board members' realisation that the Kanoos had beaten their company at its own business.

In a sense the rivalry with Gray Mackenzie sums up the development of the Yusuf bin Ahmed Kanoo companies in Saudi Arabia and Bahrain in the 1950s, 1960s and 1970s. Whereas other merchant houses steadily diversified, the Kanoos had to focus their efforts on doing the work they already did better. Because they succeeded in this their operations steadily expanded, both in the number of companies they represented and in geographical area. During the 1960s and 1970s the Kanoo companies established branches throughout Saudi Arabia and in Abu Dhabi, Dubai and Oman. By the late 1970s the Kanoos represented most of the major oil companies' tankers calling at Bahrain and Ras Tanura, the Saudi loading terminal. They also held agencies for several European and Japanese tanker owners and a large number of dry-cargo lines, including P & O and Royal Nedlloyd. The family reckoned that it accounted for over half of the agency business involving regular-sailing dry-cargo vessels (as opposed to charters) in both Bahrain and the Eastern Province. Between them the Kanoo companies acted as general sales agents for more than a dozen airlines, which was probably more than any other travel agency in the world. They ran aircraft-handling services at the airports, stevedoring and tug services at the ports and oil-loading terminals, a slipway company in Bahrain, and an insurance business, representing Norwich Union. All of these activities had developed from operations which had been established in embryonic form thirty years earlier.

The family's only radical diversifications in this period have been into heavy-equipment importing and service and industrial joint-ventures – mostly in Saudi Arabia. The import operation, involving construction machinery and practically all materials needed for oil production, grew out of the family's desire in the 1950s and 1960s to avoid competing with the merchants whose cargoes they were unloading at the ports. At the time they found that the business in which none of the other Bahraini merchants was engaged was heavy equipment, and so the Kanoos made it their own. By the later 1970s they estimated that their heavy-equipment sales were running at $100 million a year.

Taking into account all of the Kanoos' activities, there was no question that the group was by far the biggest Bahraini-owned merchant house, in both turnover and profits. It was one of the few merchant companies with a genuinely decentralised management: in response to the recommendations of successive consultants, the family members had surrendered much of their day-to-day decision-making to the managers of their company's different departments. The Kanoo company in Saudi Arabia and the branches in the UAE and Oman operated completely independently of the Bahrain headquarters. In all centres of Kanoo operations, stock control and accounting were monitored by computers – which, unlike a few other computers in the Arabian Peninsula, had been installed not as status symbols but as operational necessities.

A generation after his death, Yusuf's influence lives on in the Kanoo family. He may not have been a benign force in Bahraini politics – in British eyes at least – but he was obviously a devoted family man. This more human side of his character seems to have stemmed from a desire to compensate for the lonely life he had lived during the early years of this century. His brother, Mohammad, had died young, and he had had no family of his own. Yusuf therefore dedicated himself with great seriousness to the upbringing of his nephews and great-nephews. In the process he made a deep impression on them. All of the older members of the family today remember him with reverence.

When Mohammad had been stricken by plague in 1904, Yusuf had taken his two sons Jasim and Ali, into his own household, in accordance with the common custom in Arabia at the time. He was anxious that they should have the best possible education. Long before it became usual for Bahraini merchants to send their children abroad to school, he sent Jasim and Ali to learn English in Aligarh, near Delhi. Later Yusuf became the guiding influence in the lives of Jasim's and Ali's own sons. Even though he was desperately short of money in the 1930s, he insisted that these too should have a foreign education. When he went to Bombay during the pearl season one year he took the young Ahmed bin Ali with him and put him into the Fallah school founded by Mohammad Ali Alireza. By coincidence Ahmed, who had been in the same class in Bahrain as Suliman Olayan, found himself at the Fallah at the same time as Ahmed Yusuf Zainal Alireza, the present managing director of Haji Abdullah Alireza & Co. For the later stages of their education the young Kanoos were sent to Beirut, Cairo and London.

One of the principles that Yusuf instilled most forcibly into his adopted sons and grandsons was the need for them to act together. When they were children the sons of Ali and Jasim say that they were all brought up to think of each other as brothers; for a long time they were not even aware which of them were real brothers and which cousins. The eight children were taught what they refer to as a 'chain of respect' for each other according to age. In the event of disputes among them they were told to respect the decisions of the majority.

A curious incidental effect of this upbringing is that the Kanoos today are all rather similar in manner and character. They look very much like each other: they all wear black-rimmed spectacles and they all have long, lugubrious faces and long noses. Each of them has an air of serious, confident, comfortable prosperity. Ahmed and Abdullah, the two men who have led the family since Mohammad became chronically sick in the early 1970s, are rather strict, cautious people. Outwardly they are cold and formal, but when they are with people they trust they relax. They have even been known to become quite humorous. This is a side of the Kanoo character which is seen more by employees than by people outside the company.

Many of the ideas which Yusuf taught the present generation of Kanoos when they were young were formalised some years after his death in a remarkable document always referred to within the family as 'the Deed'. This was drafted in 1954 in Arabic and English; it was endorsed by the Ruler, Shaikh Sulman bin Hamad, and copies were lodged in the vaults of the Manama branch of the British Bank of the Middle East. The document was brief but enlightened for its time. Its true legal authority probably did not extend beyond transferring owner-ship of the business from Jasim and Ali to their sons; Ali rightly believed at the time that he did not have much longer to live and both he and his brother thought that it would be sensible to have the well-educated younger generation in control of the business as soon as possible. The most important parts of the Deed contained advice for the younger generation on how it should manage the business and use its income. The document stated that there should be a board of directors with Ahmed (the eldest brother) as Chairman and Mohammad as Deputy Chairman, and that Ahmed should have a veto – though in practice this has never been used. The Deed also stated that the business should become a private shareholding company, as opposed to a partnership, as soon as it became practicable to make the transformation. The purpose of this clause was to ensure the continuity of the company. With regard to the use of the money generated by the company, it was stated that all male and female children of the family should be properly educated and that no one should ever be allowed to fall into poverty.

On the basis of the Deed's instructions the family has decided that all brothers and cousins who are involved in the company should have equal shares. In practice this means that the company is owned by all the members of the present older generation except Abdlatif, who decided, when he finished his education as an engineer, that he wanted to go into government. He sold his shares to his brothers, took a small amount of property, and in due course became Deputy Minister of Housing. Although his children will not inherit shares and may one day receive a smaller income from the company, Abdlatif's departure has not so far involved any financial disadvantage for his family. All of the brothers and cousins, including Abdlatif, receive the same salary from the company; their wives are paid allowances, their children get salaries or 'pocket money' according to whether they work for the company or are still at school, and all members of the family have their housing, education, food and travel expenses paid by the company. All of the profits are ploughed back into the company.

The well-organised cohesion of the Kanoos has been one of the great strengths of the family during the last thirty years. In other merchant families brothers have split or have had their sons set up independent businesses, but in the Kanoo family the only major disruption has been the break with Abdlatif. Looking back at the end of his career with the company, one of the Kanoos' longest-serving expatriate managers, Cyril Jones, told me in 1980 that he had often considered the reasons for the company's success and had decided that family cohesion had been the most important single factor. He added: 'A very striking point is their acceptance of the authority of Ahmed – and, of course, Ahmed has taken on the mantle of leadership with great responsibility. He visits the houses of all members of the family every evening . . . They have also been helped by a remarkable stroke of luck which I think the family has probably never fully appreciated: the two people who ran the firm in the early days were Ahmed and Mohammad, and it is very fortunate that these were the heads of the two sides of the family.'

The Kanoos' other great strength, according to Cyril Jones, has been their long-serving European management. The family took the brave decision to recruit expatriates at an early stage in its post-war development; the first foreigners came on to its payroll in 1948 or 1949, long before any other Bahraini merchant thought of employing Europeans. From that time on they played a crucial role in enabling the Kanoos to compete with Gray Mackenzie.

At first sight the Yusuf bin Ahmed Kanoo headquarters in Bahrain seems to be dominated by the influence of Western management. The offices of the directors and senior managers are comfortable, thickly carpeted and shut away from the rest of the company's staff. Outside are smartly dressed, attractive English secretaries. Visitors are served rather watery instant coffee as a matter of course. In most other merchants' offices the norm is Turkish or Arabian coffee, but in the Kanoo Building in Bahrain it would probably be difficult to get either of these even if one asked for them.

Appearances are deceptive. Kanoo is not a totally Westernised company, and its owners have never set out formally to 'modernise' it in the way that the owners of a few other Arabian merchant houses have done with their businesses. The company has been developed in a purely practical and piecemeal way, with changes being introduced as and when necessary. The product is a blend of management that is part Western and part Arabian.

The pragmatic approach shows in the types of people the Kanoos have employed. They have not taken on many young, business school-trained technocrats who might have tried to impose their own methods on the company: their Western employees have been mostly slightly older men with practical experience in one of the company's spheres of operation. One hardly ever hears a Kanoo employee theorise about management.

The Kanoos do not treat their employees in the traditional Arab way as servants, but nor do they lead them to expect that they will be allowed to exercise the same authority at work and live the same independent lives as they would in their own countries. The course they have steered between these two extremes has been a paternalistic one, but it seems to have been a success. The Kanoo employees have a reputation for being pleased with their jobs and staying long with the company – although their salaries may be slightly lower than the salaries of employees of other merchant houses.

The family's methods in working with its employees have been described to me by Abdel-Aziz Kanoo, who is younger and more informal than Ahmed and Abdullah. 'To keep the best of the old ways of management, which means making the family accessible and having our doors open, we have to put in more hours. But I think we have succeeded. *Anyone* can walk in and see the Chairman or one of the directors with a family problem. Often employees are more prepared to accept the authority of a family member than of their own boss. People even come to our houses – from the watchmen upwards. It's surprising how much the directors of the company benefit from this – not least in the management's loyalty and its length of service. I think this is a very Arab approach to employees. We see employment like a Catholic marriage – we take our employees into the family.

'The members of the family supervise everyone very closely. If we ask an employee to do something we will make a note of it and check a few days later whether it has been done or whether there are problems. For the employees the important thing is a good house to satisfy their wives: this is the key to the happiness and good work of the husbands – a good house in a good area and good furniture. We keep the houses in Saudi Arabia close together and encourage competition in gardens, tennis tournaments and so forth. If we keep the wives busy then the husbands will be happy. We encourage reciprocal entertainment, among employees and between the employees and the Kanoos; and we give the employees tickets home twice a year.'

Much of Abdel-Aziz's view was confirmed to me by a former Kanoo middle manager, who used to work in the equipment sales department in Bahrain: 'They are a very closely knit family and they exercise tight control over their company. Ahmed knows everything that's going on – the departments produce monthly reports that are circulated to all members of the family, so they're all well informed right down to quite small details. Really you work not for the company but for the family – you're treated almost as a member of the family. And the Kanoos do treat their staff extremely well. They are very generous to them, and they are very approachable on personal matters . . . In other companies you hear that they're sometimes fifteen days late with salaries, but the Kanoos pay you automatically through your bank. With the Kanoos you know that you'll always be paid on time.'

15

The Family Corporation

'I never make appointments before I go to Saudi Arabia. If I send a telex from New York I just deal with some Indian clerk who always feels that it's wisest to say that his master is busy on the day I want. So I just drop in . . . I say "Hello Shaikh Ahmed, I know you're terribly busy now but I'm here for some time and I wondered if you could see me in the next day or so." Of course, more often than not it turns out that Shaikh Ahmed isn't that busy, so I go in and have a glass or two of tea, and while I'm arranging my appointment I do half the business I want to do anyway. I also get to see Shaikh Ahmed twice and I get to know him better – which is very important in the Middle East. I'd say one makes much more progress by seeing somebody for a few minutes on several occasions during a visit than by setting up a long formal appointment in advance – which is quite likely to be cancelled at the last minute of course. Just dropping in is more in line with the ordinary pace of life in Saudi Arabia.' Barrett Petty, Vice-President, Morgan Guaranty, in a conversation with me at lunch in the Saudi International Bank in 1981.

Anyone who has spent any time in the offices of Arabian businessmen will have noticed that in all the older establishments the doors stay open. People who have business with a member of the family will come into his office, exchange a muttered greeting and then take a seat next to the wall. At any moment in the day the widest variety of people may be present: foreign salesmen, relations, junior clerks seeking the merchant's judgement on some minor problem. A few of these people will drink a glass or two of tea, or a cup of coffee, and then get up and leave. They either will have decided to discuss their business at some other time, or will have come for purely social reasons. In the Arab world simply to call on somebody is regarded as good manners. Those who stay in the merchant's office will chat among themselves until each person is summoned in turn for a private conversation.

This conduct of business in the *majlis* style is held to show that an honest man has nothing to hide. The presence of spectators acts in a way as a censor of business morals. The open door also enables the merchant to watch what is going on outside: if his offices are arranged in a semi-open-plan fashion, he will be able to see everyone who comes in, observe any arguments among his staff, notice who appears to be the most efficient or the hardest worker. A Western manager might not want to be worried by all the details of the functioning of his company around him, but for an Arabian the feeling that he is in complete control of events is important.

The merchants' concern with control seems to stem from the bazaar trader's desire to avoid dishonesty among his employees. This is obviously an important and sensible objective in unsophisticated businesses in which nobody ever has to think about delegating responsibility to enable different departments to operate more efficiently. In modern times the habit means that the owner of a company not only initiates all new projects, authorises all expenditure and signs all cheques; he has every minor decision referred to him. During the course of research for this book, a conversation I was having with Mohammad Hindi, the general manager of Ahmed Hamad Algosaibi and Brothers in Alkhobar, was interrupted on three separate occasions. First a rather nervous Indian mechanic came in to be interviewed about a job in the company's garage. Fifteen minutes later the conversation was broken off for half an hour when two New York carpet salesmen arrived to make a pitch for having their carpets fitted in the Algosaibi Hotel, which was then undergoing one of its periodic refurbishments. Their product was much more expensive than the competing brands, but the salesmen explained that theirs was a stronger, better class of carpet. They told Hindi that comparing the price of their carpets with the price of other companies' carpets just wasn't comparing 'apples with apples'. Hindi, who was no expert on carpets, tried rubbing his shoes on the samples and feeling them with his thumb. He said he would talk to Shaikh Ahmed about the matter and told the salesmen to come back the next day. Half an hour after the carpet salesmen had gone, Hindi was finally summoned away to attend a meeting with a team of executives from Continental Can, who had come to Alkhobar to discuss a joint-venture Pepsi-Cola canning plant worth several million dollars.

Even in merchant companies with turnovers of $100 million, partners can involve themselves in the most trivial matters. In the middle of an important meeting a merchant may summon his English or Indian male secretary, and tell him to write a simple telex confirming some purchase which has nothing to do with the meeting in progress and to come back in twenty minutes to have the wording approved. Then the secretary will be ordered to return to tell the merchant when the telex has been sent. The tendency is for merchants to treat their middle-rank employees as schoolmasters might treat their dimmer pupils. Rather than looking at their performance as a whole and complimenting or criticising them in this broad context, the merchants go through the employees' work in detail, modifying or overriding their decisions point by point. The result is that demoralised employees get into the habit of avoiding responsibility and referring all matters to the top. For their part the merchants become used to not discussing their decisions with their managers.

If a merchant director makes a wrong decision it becomes very difficult for even the most trusted senior employees to get him or his brothers to change it. Because the managers normally have so little authority, any admission by a partner that he is wrong and the manager right will involve a serious loss of face. From the manager's point of view the situation will not be helped by the extreme cohesiveness of Arabian families, which will cause the brothers and uncles to back the family member who has made the mistake, regardless of the consequences. The manager's best chance of putting matters right is to find a way of enabling the family to save face. A good technique is to argue that circumstances have changed in some way – which may involve developing quite an elaborate story – and that in the new circumstances presumably Abdullah or Mohammad 'will be wanting to change' the previous policy and take a different course instead.

In this very personal and *ad hoc* scheme of management, nobody tries to plan a company's development, produce formal budgets or work out a system of departmental responsibilities. Companies evolve from month to month in response to the various opportunities and problems that arise and the amount of cash they have available.

Company finance is rudimentary. Many companies in the $100 million annual turnover bracket still have only one bank account. The firm's contracting subsidiary, its trading department and its property-development department all draw the money they need from a central pool: this keeps all the company's funds under the direct control of the partners. It also means that the specialist Western managers running the different departments have to keep reporting to the partners. Sometimes managers will be given the funds they need for several different purposes, such as salaries, rents and materials purchases in one large cheque, which means that when they go to the bank and cash it, they will find themselves with hundreds of thousands of dollars in their possession. The partners will be much more willing to trust an employee with these sums than to surrender control by allowing the employee's department to open a bank account of its own, so that it can pay its expenses by cheque.

Occasionally the pool from which all the cash is drawn will run dry for a week or so. Then salaries cannot be paid, stocks are run down, contractors find themselves having to delay purchasing equipment. An American executive once told me that he remembered spending a morning with the managing director of a large and famous Saudi merchant house and seeing a member of that company's contracting subsidiary come in four times to collect funds to buy some cars that the subsidiary needed. At 8.30 a.m. he was given 25,000 riyals, which was all that was available at that time. By 10 a.m. the managing director had had his staff collect another SR 40,000; and during the rest of the morning a further SR 40,000 was found.

The obvious solution to these problems, apart from permitting separate departmental bank accounts, would be for the merchants to arrange overdraft facilities and ask their bank managers for these to be increased as and when required. Many of the Arabian real estate developers during the boom of the mid-1970s were only too anxious to borrow as much as they could, but the conventional merchant companies have traditionally been rather cautious in borrowing money. There is still a feeling among the older and middle-aged generations of merchants that financial self-sufficiency is a virtue and that borrowing is slightly shameful. The Jeddah firm of Haji Hussein Alireza, the world's biggest importer of Mazda cars, does not borrow from the banks at all. The Kanoos, remembering the misfortunes of Yusuf in the 1930s, keep their borrowing to a minimum. Almost all of their expansion since 1974, including a huge increase in numbers of staff and an expansion of office accommodation, has come out of profits; the family's managers say that the firm would have been able to grow faster if they had been authorised to borrow more.

Most merchants have a similar rudimentary approach to taking on new business. They are very prone to grasp every opportunity that is offered to them, without regard to the type of business they have been doing in the past or the resources they might tie up in the new operation. Managers sometimes say that they cannot even be sure which products they will be handling six months ahead. With admirable frankness, a director of a quite sophisticated merchant house described to me how in 1978 his company had reacted to the various opportunities presented by the boom of the previous four years: 'A lot of business I suppose we took on just because it was the first to come up – with somebody walking through the door and suggesting it, so to speak. We didn't necessarily take the best business: to some extent we took things to stop somebody else getting them first.'

The director could have added that once a new product had been taken on his company would be extremely reluctant to give it up. Arabian merchants have very little concern with 'opportunity cost'. It does not seem to occur to them that if they surrender an agency they might quickly make up their 'loss' several times over by giving more of their attention to some other product. One hardly ever hears of companies saying that they are 'getting out of' a line of business that is proving unprofitable or yielding disappointing profits. To do so would not only look like a public admission of failure, it would seem to the merchant to involve the gratuitous abandonment of something of value, equivalent almost to throwing away money.

Underlying both the merchants' reluctance to borrow and their lack of awareness of opportunity cost, is an innate conservatism. They are attached to an old commercial morality and are reluctant to embrace new concepts of Western accounting which they are told will help them increase their profits and turnover. Occasionally the contrast between old and new views can be stark and simple. A merchant may ignore warehouse rental and interest charges (if he has borrowed to finance a batch of imports), because neither of these costs were part of the old business world of the souk which he knew in his youth. He will reckon that he has made a profit on a series of transactions, while his Western or Indian accountants will tell him that he has actually made a loss.

More often the differences between old and new are rather subtle and have a mainly moral character. There are frequently minor arguments over the terms of contracts and payment dates. These were described to me in 1976 during a visit to Oman by Michael Squibbs, a New Zealand manager of the Sultan family's company: 'People like Haji Ali [the chief executive of W.J. Towell] just don't have the same view as a Western accountant about what has been agreed in a particular deal and what is therefore right, or fair. This might apply to credit terms, where there is a question of whether payment is due or not – whether the credit extends from the date of billing or the date of delivery. Ali will always take the view that it is what both parties understood to be the case that counts, or what has been done in the past, not what is technically correct from an accountant's point of view.' Extending this line of reasoning Squibbs added: '. . . In a Western company you might find that an accountant one day would tell the owner that to increase his profits he should close a particular department and make half a dozen people redundant. Someone like Ali would never dream of doing such a thing: it would seem to him to be grossly immoral.' These comments would go for the owners of all the traditionally managed merchant companies, and for the owners of most of the modern ones. They are echoed by the remarks of Abdel-Aziz Kanoo, quoted at the end of the last chapter.

It seems that although the merchants will ruthlessly exploit 'the market' for every riyal they can extract from it, in purely human matters they work on a paternal morality. This is probably because a family feeling enters the picture. In a society which does not have a long-established tradition of large companies or an accepted framework for employer–manager relations, it is probably natural for the merchants to look upon their employees as extensions of their own families. This instinct will be reinforced by the fact that traditionally Arabian businesses have been family concerns, run entirely by a group of relations. Forty years ago most of their 'employees' were slaves, living as part of the merchants' households. The way a family treated its dependants was nearly as important to its reputation as the honesty of its dealings with other merchants in the souk.

An interesting sidelight on the connection between family reputation and business is shown by a remark made to me by Mahmoud Yusuf Alireza, one of the directors of Haji Abdullah Alireza & Co. Mahmoud was commenting on the traditional preference of Arabian merchants for doing business as partnerships, and his own family's reluctant conversion to the idea of a shareholding company: 'Had they been alive when we made the change the older generation would never have agreed. They would have felt that the principle of us being liable for only the capital of each shareholder would have been against the proper way of doing business. For them business was confidence, trust and loyalty.'

The thought of a family limiting its liability to the rest of society would not have seemed honourable.'

The most striking feature of the hundreds of merchant businesses that are still run in the traditional way is that they are extremely profitable. This stems directly from their old-fashioned character with its concentration of all decision-making in the hands of the owners. The companies do not have the expense of running special departments for planning, market research, personnel or corporate finance. Their costs are low and their profits high. This is acknowledged as readily by the few companies that have developed a decentralised specialist management as it is by the traditional houses. In the late 1970s a senior manager of Yusuf Ahmed Alghanim and Sons confessed that he suspected that the Behbehani company, the Kuwaiti agent for Buick, was making more money than his own company. He then added, half enviously: 'The owners are very much on the floor – they virtually sell the cars themselves.'

What happens to the profits of a merchant business varies from company to company. They may go to just two or three very rich partners or be spread among fifty or sixty relations. Even though the merchant houses are always referred to as 'family businesses', they are not necessarily owned by all the members of the large extended family whose name is attached to the business. There are even cases where close relations living in the same family compound draw incomes of very different sizes from entirely separate companies. The pattern can appear to be completely random; in practice it is determined by a combination of the Islamic laws of inheritance and informal family custom.

Most Arabian merchant businesses are founded by an individual or two brothers. If the founders have a younger brother to whom they are close, the custom is for them to take him into their business when he finishes school. This is especially so if all three brothers share the same mother. Older brothers and first cousins, however, are extremely unlikely to be included in the business. If these people or their descendants suddenly fall on hard times the owners of the company will certainly help them. They may also give them periodic presents regardless of whether times are hard or not, but they will not give them any regular income. In many families, Algosaibi being an example, one can discover quite poor men who are brothers, nephews or first cousins of men with tens of millions of dollars.

When the founders of a business die their assets will always be shared between all of their dependants and descendants – wives, sons and daughters. Under Shariah law, a man cannot leave his business to just two or three particularly able sons and give his other dependants minor pieces of land or sums of cash. Nor, in theory, can he disinherit a son with whom he has quarrelled. The consequence is that after a generation or two a business may have as many as twenty or thirty partners. Of these perhaps three will be interested in working full time in the business. Half of the others will still be at school, one or two will be pursuing professional careers using the qualifications they have gained at university in Europe or America, and the rest will have established their own businesses or decided not to do any serious work at all. (They might dabble in a little property speculation.) In most families the cousins or brothers working outside the business will be entitled to the same amount of income as those who are actively engaged in its management – assuming that they have the same stake in the partnership. Abdel-Aziz Quraishi, the Governor of the Saudi Arabian Monetary Agency, and several of the senior Alirezas have spent most of their careers in government, but they still draw their full share of income from their families' companies. (They may of course have gone unpaid in their government posts.) Only in the most modern-minded businesses, with the most enthusiastic owners, are the brothers that run the business paid a separate management fee.

In virtually all merchant houses – whether they be partnerships or private companies – the managers and other owners take their incomes informally and piecemeal during the course of the year. Merchant houses do not normally hold annual general meetings as Western companies do. The eldest brother does not sit at the head of the table, read out an auditor's report and declare a dividend.

In the best-organised families, such as Kanoo, there is a system whereby the owners, their wives and their children draw on a special account within the company for all their living expenses. The bigger and richer the business, the more generous is the definition of expenses: it may include just household expenses, travel and education, or it may extend to the cost of running an aircraft. In other families members will dig into the partnership funds not only for their living expenses but for personal capital spending as well. This may involve almost any type of investment: buying a house at home or abroad, local land speculation, or personal investments on foreign stock markets. A partner may draw money to indulge in some piece of business which he has previously suggested to his brothers that they should do together, but which they have rejected.

In some families, if one brother takes out $1 million, the others will all take the same at the end of the year. Alternatively the year's accounts may show a figure for the profit of the business, and beside it list the sums already extracted by each member of the family. The whole family will know how much each brother has taken but will probably not be worried by whatever disparities there may be. Underlying this is the traditional belief of many poor but religious societies that each man should take according to his need.

The whole system works well enough in modern Arabian families as long as their business is profitable and the partners are not too numerous. If there are just two or three far-sighted brothers with reasonably sober lifestyles, the system makes huge sums available to be ploughed back to expand the business. The difficulties arise if the company goes through a bad period in which the drawings of one brother are felt by his partners to be damaging its day-to-day operations. Alternatively, there may be endemic problems if there are large numbers of partners or shareholders who have no particular interest in their company's activities and see the company mainly as a convenient source of private income. There are some companies, regularly milked by twenty or more owners, that are permanently short of cash.

Arguments over each other's drawings have been known to lead brothers and cousins to break away from their family's business. Much more often there are separations caused by one or two brothers wanting to go into business on their own, using their share in the family firm as their initial capital. If the business is a private company, the dissidents can simply sell their shares to their relations and take the proceeds as cash. However, if the business is a partnership – which it is much more likely to be – a separation is more difficult to arrange. A partner who wants to break away from a family business is entitled to his share of the actual assets of the business. If his brothers or cousins are lucky he may settle for some land or a series of cash payments; if not he may demand some of the partnership's agencies or one of its contracting subsidiaries. Whatever happens his departure is likely to lead to a restructuring of the business that remains.

Separations of this type have been very common in Arabian family businesses. The risk of disruption after the breakaway of a partner is acknowledged in Arabia to be the biggest disadvantage of running a business as a partnership. Traditionally, it has also been a powerful disincentive to diversification from trading into industrial operations, which are capital-intensive and difficult to divide.

It is not surprising that families are always terrified of divisions occurring in their ranks. They become particularly apprehensive if one of their members seems likely to die. It is the death of a partner which is often the occasion for the fragmentation of a business. If two or three of his heirs have recently returned from an education in the West and are not willing to accept the old-fashioned management of their elders, a large part of the existing business may be hived off at one time. Sometimes the whole unfortunate process can be gone through quite amicably. On other occasions there are such serious disagreements within families that the courts have to be asked to decide which assets belong to whom. This can lead to appalling distress and bitterness, and rifts in families lasting for a generation or more.

To avoid this possibility, the Almoayyed family in Bahrain built its large office block in such a way that it could be divided without argument. The building consisted of two large towers, which were by far the tallest in Bahrain at the time they were constructed in the 1960s, and a much lower structure running between them. When the brothers, Yusuf Khalil and Abdel-Rahman Khalil, split their business some years later, one established himself in the northern tower while the other took the southern.

Since the mid-1970s the merchants have been under slowly increasing pressure to change the way they run their businesses. As the boom years have passed, the growth rates of all parts of the Arabian market have slackened. Now merchants with new agencies are no longer accommodated painlessly by the growth of the market, leaving everybody else's business intact. The biggest partnerships have noticed that their small rivals are providing quite serious competition. They may be selling just a few products, but they are imaginative and energetic, and in their own particular areas they may be providing a better service than the established giants. The Kanoos refer to these small competitors as 'warning lights'. They admit that in the shipping and travel businesses their dominance of the market is not what it was.

The warning lights are causing the big companies to consider how they might strengthen the marketing of the products they represent. The most widespread reaction has been a trimming of profit margins. A few companies are experimenting with Western-style advertising campaigns; many more are building (or talking about building) proper service facilities to support their consumer-durable agencies.

In the most modern-minded companies owners and managers are for the first time trying to work out serious strategies for their companies' development over five or ten years. The days of merchants taking every bit of business that is offered to them are coming to an end. The new emphasis is on deciding sets of commercial priorities – products and regions on which they are going to concentrate their efforts. In 1978 the Kanoos conducted an internal study of their whole business to see if it was really worth their while marketing their full range of products and services in each of the Gulf countries in which they had branches. A year later Juffali decided to give up its agency for Volkswagen. When it did this it was working on a plan for a huge development of its IBM office-equipment sales business. In effect the company was deciding to leave small-car sales to the Japanese and put more of its time and effort into a high technology operation.

Most of the big merchant companies are developing specialist contracting and service companies. These embrace such activities as oil-rig maintenance, rock blasting and construction-camp catering. The merchants have decided that as the regional economy expands it is becoming economic for them to market sophisticated services locally, instead of turning always to companies based in Europe or America. It has also occurred to them that local service companies are less vulnerable to competition than import businesses. They require fairly large sums of capital, reasonable long-term commitment, and foreign technical expertise. These factors make them unlikely to be copied by small competitors.

The same logic, on a bigger scale, lies behind the merchants' investment in industrial ventures. These involve their turning themselves from importers into manufacturers of the products they sell. The Kanoos, for example, are now manufacturing drilling muds in Saudi Arabia and marine paints in Dubai – two products in which their company has had long-established sales operations. Abdullah and Teymour Alireza, owners of the Rezayat Group, have steel-pipe fabrication yards in the Eastern Province. Consortia of merchants and members of the Saudi ruling family own numerous factories, with products that range from bottled mineral water – notably Safa water from springs near Mecca – through an enormous variety of building materials, to phosphate fertilisers.

In almost every case the new industries have higher capital and running costs than the same industries in Europe, America or Japan. But they are not necessarily uncompetitive with imports. In general it is reckoned that they can compete if they are not too technologically complex or if the product they are marketing is bulky and expensive for competitors to ship from an industrialised country. Almost all Arabian plants benefit from cheap loans, at 2 or 4 per cent, provided by state industrial development banks. A few of the plants that are found to be marginally uncompetitive even after receiving cheap loans are protected by tariffs. Normally, before giving protection, the Arabian governments insist that a plant should be able to supply most of local demand.

An extension of the industrial-investment strategy has led a few merchants to buy shares in their suppliers abroad, on the reasoning that this will give them better access to those companies' products and technical expertise. One of the best-known cases has been Kutayba Alghanim's takeover of Kirby Industries of Houston, Texas; another was Majid Futtaim's investment in Tower Scaffolding, a British company based in Bristol. The Futtaim Group and Tower had established a scaffolding joint-venture in Dubai some time before Majid made his purchase.

All of the recent developments have pushed the merchants' businesses towards a watershed. The diversifications have called for specialist management knowledge and a grasp of the engineering involved. They have also needed large sums of capital, which the merchants have wanted to consider carefully before committing. If they have financed their investments partly with loans, their banks have asked to see detailed appraisals of the projects. Both the new projects and the steadily increasing size of the old trading operations have involved an enormous growth in the sheer volume of work that the merchants have had to handle. Some of them have found themselves mentally and physically exhausted. The *majlis* system of management and the exercise of total control are becoming impracticable.

The merchants' problems are well known to Western companies. Successful private firms run by just one or two members of a family, assisted by a few long-serving, loyal managers, who become friends of their employers, eventually reach the same watershed. Other watershed companies are rather bigger, but have to break out of their regional or national environment, on the principle that they must not stop growing if they are to remain profitable. These companies will already be employing larger managements than the family firms, and will have turnovers of anything between $50 million and $250 million, depending on the type of their business. If they are starting to invest or sell their products in other regions or export markets, their senior managers will find themselves faced not only with more work and a need to take specialist decisions, but with all the administrative difficulties of setting up operations that are distant from their headquarters.

Both the successful family firm and the bigger company will find that crossing the watershed involves a big increase in the scale of their management. They have to decentralise, employ many more staff, and open a large number of new departments. Most of these involve service functions, such as personnel and market research, which do not directly yield income. In a family firm the whole style of management has to change. Relations between owners and staff become more distant and impersonal.

There are any number of merchant companies in Arabia which fit into one or other watershed category, or combine elements of both. Yet there are only a few families which have resolutely and definitely crossed the watershed. These include Juffali, Olayan, Kanoo, Alghanim, Futtaim and Jameel.[1] A few families, including the Zahids, were in the process of crossing the watershed in the late 1970s and early 1980s. Many others know that they ought to be thinking about crossing it but are postponing the evil day or just nibbling at the idea. They are holding back because they hate the thought of having to delegate and because they can see two important disadvantages in the new system.

1. The Jameel family, whose company now has the biggest turnover of any Arabian merchant group apart from Juffali, was in a very small way of business until the early 1970s. Its members, who are Hijazis, had no great traditional prestige, royal connections or real estate. Abdul-Latif, the father of the family, had had the Toyota agency for a decade but was selling only about 1,000 cars a year. The business took off when his very able sons, Yusuf and Mohammad, returned to the Kingdom from university at the beginning of the 1970s. Over a decade they have increased Toyota sales to 130,000 units a year – at which level the cars account for well over 90 per cent of the company's turnover. In the early and mid-1970s the company used its profits to buy a large amount of real estate north of Jeddah. In the early 1980s this was being sold, mainly to finance a big foreign-investment operation, which was run by Yusuf out of Monte Carlo.

The first problem is financial. Every one of the companies that has crossed the watershed has incurred large extra costs and a drop in profits. To be strictly accurate, the buoyancy of the Arabian market, until 1983, was such that the 'drop' in profits in most cases showed up in the form of static profits on a rising turnover. Some of the extra costs have been heavy enough to lead companies to borrow on the international market. The Abdul-Latif Jameel company has borrowed to finance the back-up for its Toyota sales operation, and Yusuf Ahmed Alghanim and Sons has taken at least two syndicated loans to finance the credit it gives to customers. In other merchant houses major syndicated borrowings have been to finance the new operations that have caused the companies to reach the watershed, rather than to meet the costs incurred after the crossing. Parts of the Olayan Group have resorted to the market on several occasions, as has Ghaith Pharaon's company, REDEC, and W.J. Towell, which borrowed to finance a big one-off building contract it won in Riyadh.

The second problem concerns the recruitment of managers and the amount of authority they have to be given. Managers who are both technically sophisticated and able to work in an Arabian environment are not easy to find. The Indian clerks who make up much of the middle management of the traditional merchant houses cannot cope with the complexities or responsibilities of the new system. Instinctively they continue to refer even the most minor matters to their superiors. Experienced Indian graduate managers are rare in the Middle East and do not necessarily find it easy to work with Arabs. One of the few companies to have a number of Indian senior managers is Futtaim. Westerners, meanwhile, find the new management procedures familiar, but they do not stay long enough to learn about the society in which they are working. Most of them see a job in Arabia as a good way of saving a large amount of money in two or three years. At the very point at which they and their employers are striking up a rapport, which enables the employers to trust them, they leave.

The ideal employees are Egyptian, Palestinian or, even better, Arabian graduates. These men may be educated in the West but are still able to work naturally with fellow Arabs. They find it easier than Westerners to think of themselves as part of the family of their employer; they are also far better at dealing with rows and tensions among their junior Arab staff. One of the secrets of Ahmed Juffali's success is that he has had good Arab senior managers. Several com-

panies are now making great efforts to recruit Arab graduates:
Alghanim, with its liking for Western jargon, has called its scheme a
College Management Development Programme. Apart from simply
trying to encourage Arabs who have already graduated to join the firm,
it undertakes every year to finance ten non-Kuwaiti Arabs at American
universities.

The most common complaint of both the new recruits and the rest of
the management of the 'trans-watershed' companies, is that the owners,
having restructured their enterprises to allow decentralised decision-
taking, do not co-operate with the new system. Some seem subcon-
sciously to see a modern management structure as something which can
be bought. They enjoy the prestige it brings and they believe sincerely
that it is an investment which will yield financial benefits in the long
term, but they do not realise at all that it calls for a change in behaviour
on their own part. They continually check on their managers' decisions,
involve themselves in little problems and overrule their managers if they
think they know better. Other owners delegate at first, but as soon as
anything goes wrong reinvolve themselves. Mark Thomson, one of
Suliman Olayan's managers in London, once said to me that delegation
for Arabs was like giving up smoking for Westerners: it was something
which one always intended to do but could never bring oneself to do in
practice. He was able to speak confidently because the owner of his
company is probably the only Arabian businessman to have given his
managers as much independence as the managers of a big Western
company.

The classic example of an Arabian company which has experienced
all of the trans-watershed problems has been Yusuf Ahmed Alghanim
and Sons. When Yusuf's son Kutayba took over the company in 1971 he
established a large number of new service departments. These enabled
the company to launch a professional programme of market research
and run the best series of advertisements and special promotions seen
in the Arabian Peninsula. At the same time Kutayba decentralised
decision-making in his company and began employing some extremely
intelligent and able managers. All of these developments enormously
impressed everybody who visited the company – including journalists.
Their impact was strengthened by good public relations and a highly
articulate chief executive – in the person of Kutayba. On several occasions YAAS was written up in magazines as a prime example of what
could be achieved by a dynamic, young, American-educated owner

introducing Western methods to a traditional environment.

Unbeknown to the writers of these stories, the real results of Kutayba's revolution were rather chequered. The cost of the new management was so high that when market conditions became more competitive at the end of the 1970s YAAS came close to making a loss. The company's position was not helped by its having had to borrow to finance its instalment sales programme. This had been one of the key factors enabling it to hold on to its very large share of the Kuwaiti car market.

Similar problems affected the new scheme of management. Kutayba quite frequently intervened in day-to-day operations. If he had a serious clash with a senior manager he fired him. This led to an undercurrent of political intrigue, with each manager trying to isolate his rival and prevent himself being isolated – which was very much what had happened in the later days of Yusuf's regime. It was often said within the company that, for all the official decentralisation, the only person with any real authority was Kutayba. It was not until the early 1980s, by which time the new structure had been modified in the light of experience and Kuyayba was spending most of his time in the United States, that the modern Alghanim management stabilised.

Merchants who have gone to the trouble of taking their companies across the watershed are naturally anxious to perpetuate their creations. Ahmed Juffali and Kutayba Alghanim do not see their businesses simply as sources of income for their families, which may be split into several pieces in the next generation merely because two or three of the partners think that they would prefer to be in business on their own. On a purely practical level they argue that it would be almost impossible to split an operation on the scale of Juffali's Mercedes truck business. More important, they believe that they have created something of value for their countries. They are particularly proud of their contracting and industrial subsidiaries. Kutayba Alghanim is much more anxious to talk about Kirby Industries, his steel buildings company, than about selling GM cars. Kirby is already earning Kuwait foreign exchange by exporting steel buildings to Iraq, Saudi Arabia and the lower Gulf. In the longer term the company should stimulate other investments by other entrepreneurs – in machine-tool maintenance for example – which will lead Kuwait towards its goal of a self-sufficient post-oil economy.

For almost all the big merchants the first step towards perpetuating their businesses has been to change them from partnerships to private limited liability companies. This enables any of the owners who wants to leave the business to sell his shares to his relations instead of taking his assets with him. The disadvantage is that private companies are obliged to run their finances according to more formal rules than are applied to partnerships. They have to file accounts at the end of the year with the ministries of commerce and raise their paid-up capital as their turnovers increase. They may even have to have representatives of the ministries at their shareholders' meetings. These regulations involve extra paperwork and a reduction of the merchants' freedom to run their affairs as they wish. They also appear to destroy the secrecy of a family's business. In normal circumstances the regulations would worry the merchants enough to deter them from establishing private companies, no matter how much they wanted to avoid having their businesses split. In practice the rules are not enforced. The ministries insist that the merchant companies are seen to go through all the formalities, but once they have checked that the law appears to have been obeyed they turn a blind eye to the most extraordinary manoeuvres designed to circumvent the actual intentions of the law. Some families run two sets of totally different accounts – one for themselves and another for the government. There has been no known case of a ministry of commerce representative attending a merchant shareholders' meeting.

Among the firms that have turned themselves into private companies are Alghanim, Jameel, Olayan, and Kanoo. The owners of these firms do not suggest that the formation of private companies has in itself guaranteed the perpetuation of their businesses. They all say that it will stop the division of their businesses after their deaths, which is a partial answer to their problems, but it will not guard against the companies being allowed to decline through bad management. The most that the merchants can do to anticipate this danger is to try to employ a competent management in their own lifetimes and allow it as much authority as they can bring themselves to give it. This at least makes their companies partially independent of their own presence at the helm, and avoids the companies suffering a major shock on their retirement or death. In the back of their minds, however, the merchants know that in the longer term they cannot guarantee that their heirs will continue to employ good managers. Inevitably the thought occurs to them that if they were to launch their businesses as public companies at least some of the shareholders would be active and intelligent and would do all they could to ensure the appointment of good directors.

There are quite frequent rumours in Saudi Arabia and the Gulf states that one or other of the big merchant houses is thinking of going public. In Jeddah the name of Juffali is often mentioned. It is known that the Saudi government would like to see more of its people given a stake in the profits of the Kingdom's business community. All of the foreign banks' branches in Saudi Arabia have been obliged to turn themselves into local companies and offer some of their shares to the public. The National Commercial Bank, entirely owned by the Bin Mahfouz and Kaaki families, in 1981 was under pressure to follow suit. There were believed to have been discussions on the same subject between the government and one of the most successful of the Kingdom's industrial companies – the cement-pipe firm, Saudi Arabian Amiantit. In these circumstances it is not surprising that speculation sometimes attaches itself to the big merchant houses. Their owners and managers have unconsciously encouraged the process by occasionally talking to visitors about the debate on their future that they are conducting among themselves.

What is interesting is that every merchant house after considering the idea of going public has rejected it totally. They do not need to raise money from selling shares, which is what normally prompts companies to go public. Operating in countries where there is no corporation tax, they can usually finance the expansion of their businesses with retained profits. If they are investing in industrial projects they can supplement their own resources by borrowing money from the governments' industrial development banks. In these circumstances the prospect of continuity of management is seen as the only advantage to be gained from going public – and it is heavily outweighed by the disadvantages.

The problems of issuing shares centre on the lack of sophistication of the Arabian stock markets. Only Kuwait has a proper stock exchange, and even this behaves in a fashion which is eccentric by Western standards. Because the market has vast sums of capital chasing relatively few securities, shares can rise to ridiculous prices. It is commonplace for a share's 'p-e ratio' – the relationship of its market price to its earnings – to reach levels that are unheard of in Western markets. New issues can be oversubscribed up to a hundred times. There are dramatic booms and crashes. On two occasions, in 1977 and 1982, when shares on the official stock exchange collapsed after periods of absurd speculation, the Kuwaiti government intervened in the market to protect investors from making disastrous losses. It set a series of intervention prices at which it guaranteed to buy distressed stocks, and acquired substantial portions of several companies' equity.

Those merchants who have occasionally thought about offering shares to the public say that they feel that their companies would do better without these excitements. One of the obvious considerations is that gyrating share prices would not help them to raise money on the international markets on the few occasions when they need to supplement their internal funds with borrowings. Many of the most successful merchants also have the salutary experience of being directors of Arabian public companies and of having witnessed the extraordinary scenes that sometimes take place at annual general meetings. Suliman Olayan wryly remarked to me in 1980 that a stockholders' meeting could be 'a circus' in the US – 'in Saudi Arabia', he added, 'it has to be seen to be believed.' The directors and managers of Arabian public companies find that huge amounts of their time are wasted by ignorant and unsophisticated shareholders.

Last, but not least, the merchants have noticed that the stock of public companies often ends up in the hands of just a few shareholders. Quite frequently the same groups of families invest together in several different companies; the same faces can appear on five or six boards of directors. With impeccable logic the merchants reason that in this society an offer of shares in their companies might well be pointless. After a short period they would probably find that the shares were owned by a group of well-known competitors who were no more able to guarantee the future of their companies than they were themselves.

16

～₩₩～₩₩～

Suliman Olayan

'I arrived in New York on the tenth anniversary of Pearl Harbour – it was Friday, December 7th 1951. I'd been given three golden rules for things I shouldn't do, they were: don't go above 72nd Street, don't go down to Greenwich Village, and don't strike up acquaintances in bars . . . Well, first of all I spread out all of my maps of New York on the floor of my hotel room – the chambermaid thought I was engaged in some sort of a cartographic study of the city; she left them all in place . . . I went everywhere. I began by going to Greenwich Village. Then I went up to Times Square. I remember when I got there I saw smoke coming from the top of a tall building. So I said to myself, "Well, this will be interesting, I'd like to see fire-fighting in a skyscraper, let's see how it's done." So I waited. But nothing happened – no fire brigade – nothing. Then I realised that it was a Camel cigarette advertisement which used to puff smoke in those days. It was quite a famous sight, you could see it for some distance on Broadway – but it's gone now.

'Later that day I took a cab. The driver was a friendly fellow; he said, as they all do, "Where are you from?" So I told him I was from the Middle East. Then there was quite a long pause. He said, "Well, I've heard of the Middle West, but I never heard of the Middle East" . . . All the time I was very impressed by the affluence. I'd been at the Savoy in London, where there was rationing. Sugar was in short supply, I just got two little lumps with a pot of coffee. To get one cup of the right Arab sweetness I had to order three pots. So at the Waldorf Astoria I was very pleased to find that they gave me a whole bowl of sachets. I thought of taking a handful and mailing them to the Savoy.

'I was in America as part of a tour around the world. It was partly for pleasure and partly for business – I was making contact with American companies that I hoped I might represent back home in Saudi Arabia. I used to disarm the people I met by saying: "Well, I'm an Arab and a

OLAYAN FAMILY TREE

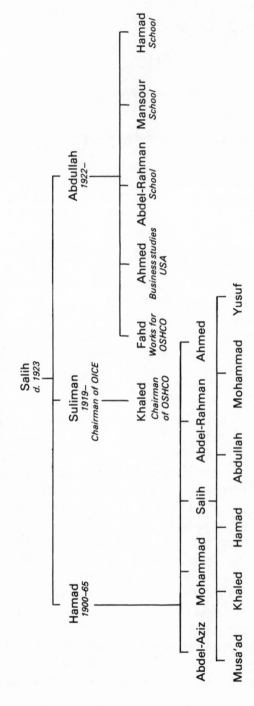

Salih
d. 1923

Hamad
1900–65

Suliman
1919–
Chairman of OICE

Abdullah
1922–

Abdel-Aziz Mohammad Salih Hamad Abdel-Rahman Ahmed

Musa'ad Khaled Hamad Abdullah Mohammad Yusuf

Khaled
Chairman of OSHCO

Fahd
Works for OSHCO

Ahmed
Business studies USA

Abdel-Rahman
School

Mansour
School

Hamad
School

NOTES

1. The Olayan family comes from Onaizah. It is part of the Dughiyrat clan of the Abdo branch of the Shammar tribe. Olayan, the man who gave his name to the family, was the great-great-grandfather of Suliman.

2. Hamad, Suliman's elder brother, worked briefly for the General Contracting Company soon after it was founded. He then left to start his own business in Kuwait. His sons are now Kuwaiti citizens, most of them working for the government.

3. Abdullah, Suliman's younger brother, used to be the general manager of General Transportation Enterprises, the Kuwaiti part of the Olayan heavy transport operation. He is now semi-retired, dealing privately in real estate and attending to family matters. Abdullah has shares in the Transporting and Trading Company Inc (TTI) and the Olayan Real Estate Company (ORECO) – see organisation chart below.

crook, and what I want is . . .." ' Suliman Olayan in a conversation with me in early 1980.

Suliman's father, Salih, was a merchant in the holy city of Medina, in the northern Hijaz. He used to travel across the Red Sea to the African coast, calling at Massawa and Suakin, the ports of Eritrea and the Sudan. In the middle of the First World War he was forcibly evicted from his home by the Turks. At that time Medina was still under the direct authority of the Ottoman Empire, unlike the southern Hijaz, which the Turks had entrusted to the ambitious and rebellious Hashemite family. The Turks decided that to alleviate the shortage of food, which plagued all parts of their crumbling empire, they would evict from Medina all those whose original homes were not in the town. Salih was a Nejdi from Onaizah, so he was told to go. He returned to Onaizah and started a small business importing foodstuffs from the Gulf. He did not travel himself; he used as correspondents the Ajaji family, which was based in the Eastern Province and Bahrain. To cement the relationship he sent his son, Hamad, to work in the family office in Bahrain as an accountant. In 1919, about four years after Salih had established the new business, his second son, Suliman, was born.

When Suliman was four his father died. For a short time he stayed with his mother in Onaizah. Then in 1925 his elder brother returned to the town to be married. When he left for Bahrain with his bride he took Suliman with him, arranged for the boy to stay in the Ajaji household and sent him to the American missionary school. Here Suliman found himself in the same class as Ahmed Kanoo. The two stayed together until their early teens. According to Suliman, Ahmed to this day reminds him that he was always top of the class and asks him what he ate to develop his prodigious memory. Suliman's standard reply is that his family was not as rich as Ahmed's and that he had to work harder because he knew that he would have to leave school earlier. Unlike Ahmed, he was not going to be sent to complete his education in India and Beirut.

When he reached the age of seventeen, in 1936, Suliman left school and went to work for the Bahrain Petroleum Company (BAPCO), which had recently brought on stream Bahrain's one and only oil field, at Awali. After just over a year he crossed to Saudi Arabia to take a job with the California Arabian Standard Oil Company (CASOC), the forerunner of Aramco. In this he was doing exactly the same as a large number of other young Saudis, including Ahmed Hamad Algosaibi, for whom the oil companies offered the only opportunities for reliable, permanent work. Suliman was given badge no. 40 and started work, in the classic fashion, as a transportation despatcher, supervising the loading of the small fleet of trucks that CASOC used to ferry supplies to its crews in the field. Soon he became a floorman in the storehouse at Dhahran, issuing, receiving and keeping running inventories of such items as hand tools and automotive parts. As he gained experience, he was assigned to the storehouse order desk and was given full responsibility for ordering stock. Unlike Ahmed Hamad Algosaibi, who went through a rapid series of job changes, Suliman spent nine solid years in the storehouse. He was fortunate in being able to stay with the company during the inactive period of the early years of the war, when many of its staff were made redundant. By 1947 he had managed to buy his own house in Alkhobar. He had also risen to the position of Senior Floorman in the Dhahran District Storehouse. The job did not sound very grand, but it had hidden advantages. 'Working for Aramco then', Suliman once told a Saudi newspaper, 'was as good as or better than a college education. As an order man I had to speak the language of the driller, the electrician, the plumber, the doctor and the cook. I learnt the name of every item in the stock, and I made sure that I understood its function. I remember once I even won a "dictionary" argument with a physician over the meaning of ruby and agate type.'

Suliman found that his job made him fluent in English. This led to his being called upon from time to time by other departments in Aramco to work as a translator and interpreter. If senior Aramco executives had to go to Riyadh for discussions with the government he was sometimes asked to accompany them. Among other work, he was involved with the establishment of an administrative organisation for the new Saudi Arabian Airlines. This was one of several non-oil projects which Aramco was undertaking on behalf of the government. In due course he met George Rentz, who had recently arrived in Dhahran and was engaged in setting up an Arabian research organisation, which was to become a highly prestigious office within the Government Relations Department. In early 1947 Rentz persuaded Suliman to join him as a full-time translator. Here Suliman was engaged partly in map-making and topographical research. It seems incredible to foreigners, but every tiny feature of the Arabian landscape has been given its own name by

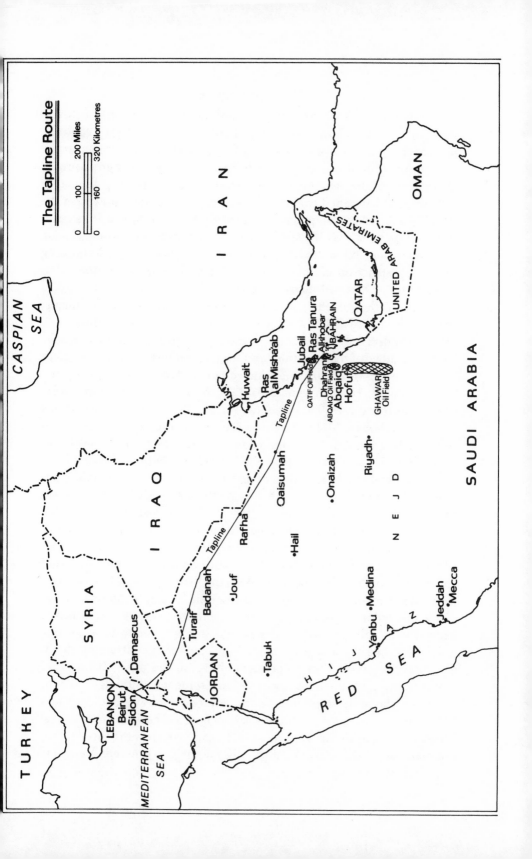

The Tapline Route

the bedouin, and a major part of Aramco's research work in its early days was involved with discovering these names so that they could be incorporated in its maps. The rest of Suliman's new job was concerned with the usual work of interpreting in negotiations with the government and other Saudis, whom Aramco was already beginning to use as suppliers. It happened that one of his assignments took him with the Local Industrial Development Department to Ras al Misha'ab, a small promontory on the Gulf coast just south of the Kuwait border. His job here was to help explain to Saudi contractors the procedures for bidding on the construction of the Trans-Arabian Pipeline – Tapline. This project was owned and managed by the Tapline company, which had exactly the same shareholders as Aramco – Standard Oil of California, Texaco, Standard Oil of New Jersey (now Exxon) and Mobil.

Suliman decided to seek some of the new contract work for himself. He told Aramco of his intention, and the company granted him a ninety days leave of absence, so that if he failed he could come back without any loss of seniority. He then went to Bahrain and arranged with Abdel-Aziz Bassam to borrow 14,000 riyals (about $4,000) to be secured on his house in Alkhobar. Abdel-Aziz Bassam was a member of a well-known and widely travelled Nejdi merchant family which had come from Onaizah, Suliman's birth place. With the $4,000 Suliman bought himself a partnership in a small building firm known as the General Contracting Company, which had been established in Alkhobar two years before. One of the founders of this enterprise had been Abdullah Olayan, Suliman's younger brother, who had previously worked as a clerk for the King's government in Riyadh.

From the time Suliman joined GCC he became the dominant partner and driving force in the company. With the firm's finances bolstered by the money he had borrowed from Abdel-Aziz Bassam, Suliman bid for and won a contract for unloading pipe from barges on to the beach at Ras al Misha'ab. The Aramco management was so pleased to have one of its most able and articulate employees going into contracting that it gave him the contract for 25 per cent above his bid price. It reasoned that it would be very useful for it to have someone 200 miles north of Dhahran who understood how Aramco worked and who could act as a link between Aramco and the local Saudi authorities. At Ras al Misha'ab, and in all the Tapline work he did over the next three years, Suliman continued to work informally for the Government Relations Department.

After agreeing the contract, Suliman, in his own words: 'hired a few people, bought two or three trucks and started work. Fortunately the type of contracting I got into didn't involve investment in materials. I had to invest in equipment. You know, trucks and food. But the payments were coming in faster, so I managed to float. After six months I told them, "Don't worry about me, I'm off and running." '[1] The unloading contract led into a contract to transport the pipe from Ras al Misha'ab to where the pipeline was being laid. Ras al Misha'ab had been carefully chosen by Tapline as the unloading point which would involve fewest ton-miles of transport between Qatif, where the pipe started, and the Jordanian border. It was here that the Saudi pipe-laying operation, under the overall management of Bechtel, was due to meet the Williams Brothers operation, working down from Sidon on the Mediterranean coast.

Over the next three years, from early 1948 to the end of 1950, the General Contracting Company carried out work in almost every phase of the Tapline project. It built camps, ran dining rooms, buried pipe and made steel and concrete 'H' supports for those sections of the pipe that were laid above ground. Its most sophisticated contract was for welding pipe. The agreement Suliman signed for this job was a unit price contract, under which he received a fixed payment per 100 metres of pipe his workmen welded. He was only paid after American inspectors had approved the work. Most of the men who were employed on this job were Bahrainis and Palestinians, whom Suliman obtained through his own labour recruiters. His ability at finding relatively skilled Arab labour, which was extremely scarce throughout the Middle East, was one of the keys to his success in the Tapline work. In the late 1940s even truck drivers in Saudi Arabia were regarded as skilled workers – when they were taught to drive they were given elementary instruction in reading, so that they could understand the dials in their cabs. At this time all contractors in Saudi Arabia were plagued by burned-out bearings and other avoidable mechanical breakdowns.

As the line progressed, Suliman became involved in the development of the Tapline towns – Qaisumah, Rafha, Badanah and Turaif – which. grew out of the desert next to the places where the Tapline company established pumping stations. These were maintenance bases and

1. Suliman Olayan to Steven Flax of *Forbes* magazine. See 'Sweet equity, Saudi style', *Forbes*, 6 July 1981.

permanent camps for Tapline employees. As soon as the first American accommodation had been built it was noticed that the bedouin would arrive. They would first pitch their tents in the areas that Tapline had laid out as town sites three or four kilometres from the pumping stations, then cover their tents with sheets of corrugated iron, and finally build walls around them. The settlements immediately turned into trading posts. Sheep and camel markets appeared, merchants established stalls to sell tent ropes and other day-to-day necessities of Arabian life, enterprising bedouin developed a thriving cross-border trade with Iraq. If tyres, for example, were found to be cheaper in Iraq, the Tapline towns would become tyre importers; if gasoline was cheaper in Saudi Arabia they would become gasoline export depots, supplying Iraqis driving small tankers across the border.

The King had foreseen that this type of development might occur when a vast piece of modern technology was introduced into the apparently empty desert. As part of the agreement with Tapline he had insisted that the company should provide the Northern Frontier governorate, then known as the Tapline governorate, with a new administration, a police force, schools, telecommunications and all the buildings associated with these institutions. The company was also required to build a road beside the pipeline, provide medical centres and drill wells for water. It was in this context that Suliman Olayan was drawn into Tapline's work in the towns. He helped the company with the difficult business of land registration, which became necessary as soon as Tapline or anyone else wanted to allocate land for building. He also helped provide funds for an electricity generating company in Badanah. In this he was joined by Mohammad Sudairi, the Northern Frontier Governor.

By the end of 1950 Suliman had reached the Jordanian border. When he got there he says he realised for the first time that over the previous three years he had walked the whole 1,000 miles from Ras al Misha'ab; every night he had slept underneath a truck. He decided that the time had come for him to leave the supervision of the work on the line to his chief Palestinian manager and return to Alkhobar. His concern was to diversify his business, so that he would not remain totally dependent on a single series of contracts linked to a project which was then almost complete.

In the Eastern Province he took a number of relatively small Aramco contracts. The General Contracting Company (GCC) carried out pipeline welding work around Qatif and Abqaiq, it built a theatre at Ras Tanura and houses in Aramco's compound at Dhahran. It established a plant to produce crushed rock to be used in building runways at Dhahran airfield. While these projects were under way Suliman established an insurance-broking company and bought Aramco's bottled-gas operation. These for the first time gave him ordinary Saudis rather than Aramco or Tapline as his customers. In the gas business he experienced considerable difficulty persuading people that there was something of value inside the steel containers he was selling. According to Suliman, the normal reaction of the bedouin, on being told that at the turn of a knob the container would produce an invisible vapour, was to say: 'By God, this is an enterprising man indeed, he is trying to sell us air.' This type of half-incredulous, half-mocking remark is very characteristic of bedouin humour. In fact, the bedouins' doubts were rapidly overcome. By 1953 the gas was selling so well that Suliman launched the operation as a public company.

Suliman's other major diversifications in the early 1950s were in consumer foods and trucking. The food operation was turned into the General Trading Company (GTC), which took such agencies as Campbell's Soups, Uncle Ben's Rice and Nescafé, which it sold partly to Aramco and partly to shopkeepers in Dammam and Alkhobar. The trucking business was bigger and more diverse. One of its first contracts was for moving cement and other materials to the construction site at Dhahran airfield. At about the same time as he won this contract, Suliman bought some tanker trucks from Aramco and began transporting gasoline and diesel fuel from Ras Tanura to the other new towns of the Eastern Province. He won a contract to supply the Tapline pumping stations with refined products as far up the line as Turaif. The trucking business also undertook common carrier haulage for Saudis. As it expanded, the workshops which maintained its trucks were financed with loans guaranteed by Aramco's Local Industrial Development Department. In 1954 LIDD guaranteed $83,000, which Suliman used to buy a bus fleet and expand his garage. Another $121,000 was guaranteed over the next two years for the further expansion of the garage and the purchase of new equipment. Later LIDD signed an even bigger guarantee for a loan to refinance the old loans.

By 1955 Suliman had transformed his business. He was no longer in contracting; his labour force had been cut from 4,000 at the peak of the Tapline operation to some 200. Gradually he was making himself less dependent on Aramco. He was coming through the first post-oil Saudi Arabian recession. Like all later recessions in the Arabian oil states, this was caused by a slowing-down of government and oil-company spending. Tapline had been finished at the end of 1950. The next year or so saw the completion of the Dammam–Riyadh railway, the first major series of oil-field installations, the expanded refinery and loading terminal at Ras Tanura, the Dhahran camp and the airfield. Through most of the reign of King Saud bin Abdel-Aziz, from 1953 to 1964, government spending on serious development was small. Many of the businesses that had sprung up during the post-war construction boom simply disappeared.

Looking back today, Suliman says that the element in his diversification in the 1950s of which he is most proud is the insurance-broking business. This arose out of an accident which occurred during the construction of Tapline. Two of GCC's workmen were killed. This led to the usual demands for compensation amounting to 27,000 riyals ($8,000) per man. Suliman was unable to pay this, so Tapline paid the money for him. The whole rather embarrassing episode made it obvious to Suliman that he would need to take out some workman's compensation insurance. He went to Bahrain and asked to see a manager in the trading house of Gray Mackenzie, which among its many other activities acted as a broker for English insurance companies. In 1978 Suliman described to me the response he received: 'It took me three days to see the man. Then, when I told him what I wanted, he replied in a grand voice that he couldn't insure me because I was an Arab, and Arabs "could not be relied upon to keep an honest payroll record" – this was the basis for writing workman's compensation insurance. So I decided there and then that I might as well go into the insurance business myself. I told the man that I would compete with his company and drive it out of business. He said that I didn't know what I was talking about – but eventually I did just what I said I would. I began in 1952 by representing the Arabian Insurance Company Limited, of Lebanon, and by 1973 I had twenty-three branches spread throughout Saudi Arabia and the Gulf.

'The other big contract I signed at this time – a contract which I think marked a completely new departure – was for hauling oil rigs in the Neutral Zone. In 1959 I went to see Aminoil and Getty[2] and proposed to them that I should buy their heavy-truck fleets, and lease them back to them. I knew that there would be several advantages for the companies in this arrangement. The most obvious point is that it would release some of their capital. It would also mean that they wouldn't have very big items of equipment lying idle for most of the year; and it would enable them to know in advance exactly what each job was going to cost them. Even so, it was a hard job selling the idea to them. Once we had agreed the deal I got to work with a consultant from the US and reduced the number of pieces into which we had to break down the rig before transporting it. We cut assembly and disassembly times by several days. But what I'm proud of was that I was able to go across the border to another country, and get two companies to trust me with a financial arrangement that was completely new in the Middle East. That I think was a turning point in accomplishment.'

It was quickly discovered that running the Getty and Aminoil rig operations out of a base in the Eastern Province was impossible. In 1959 mail took thirty days between Kuwait and Alkhobar, and telegrams a week. There were virtually no international telephone links with Saudi Arabia and the government did not allow private companies to own telexes. Suliman's employees in Kuwait found that it was easier to communicate with the company's small office in Beirut than it was with the Alkhobar operation. The Beirut office had been established about ten years earlier during the Tapline contract. Its purpose had been partly to recruit skilled Greek and Levantine labour, and partly to put Suliman in closer touch with the Tapline company, which had set up an office of its own there. Inevitably the idea occurred to Suliman and his staff soon after the Neutral Zone deal that it would make sense to develop the general administration of his companies in Beirut. This policy was put into effect from 1960.

For the next ten years Suliman travelled between Saudi Arabia and Lebanon. He sent his children to school in Beirut and took the main decisions affecting his business there. He and his few managers found that Beirut offered better air communications and more competitive banking. They could meet more often with representatives of the companies whose products they sold in Saudi Arabia. All of the Olayan

2. Aminoil and Getty ran onshore oil-production operations in the two parts of the Kuwaiti–Saudi Neutral Zone. Aminoil, owned by a consortium of American companies, was based in Kuwait and held the Kuwaiti half of the concession; Getty held the Saudi half.

ORGANISATION OF THE OLAYAN GROUP

OLAYAN INVESTMENTS COMPANY ESTABLISHMENT (OICE)
Holding company, registered Lichtenstein, offices Athens.
Manages own cash and investment portfolio

TRANSPORTING AND TRADING CO. INC. (TTI)
Registered in Liberia. Owned by: OICE
Jardine Matheson 40%
Abdullah Olayan
American Express 3%

OLAYAN FINANCING CO. (OFC)
Holds Olayan shares in industrial, contracting and service joint-ventures and private companies in Saudi Arabia.
Based in Alkhobar

OLAYAN REAL ESTATE CO. (ORECO)
Some shares held by Abdullah Olayan.
Invests in real estate in Saudi Arabia.
Based in Alkhobar

ARABIAN COMMERCIAL ENTERPRISES (ACE)
Insurance, insurance broking and travel agencies.
Owned one-third by OICE, one-third by Sedgwick Forbes (whose share was bought in 1974), and one-third by Prince Khaled bin Abdullah bin Abdel-Rahman al Saud (who bought his share in 1978).
Operates throughout Arabian Peninsula.
Based in Athens

INVESTMENT GROUP
Overseen by OICE in Athens.
Composed of: *Crescent Diversified*, registered in Virgin Islands with offices in New York – runs portfolio composed mainly of US equities; *Olayan Investments Co NV*, registered in Netherlands Antilles, offices with OICE in Athens – runs portfolio mainly of eurodollar fixed interest securities; *Olayan Properties NV*, wholly owned by OICNV (above) – runs portfolio composed mainly of US real estate

COMPETROL ESTABLISHMENT
Registered in Lichtenstein, owned 50–50 by OICE and Prince Khaled bin Abdullah bin Abdel-Rahman al Saud. Manages own portfolio and owns three investment companies: *Competrol Ltd* (in London) – manages UK and European properties and provides support for Olayan companies in Saudi Arabia; *Competrol NV* – a Netherlands Antilles subsidiary investing in US securities; *Competrol Inc* – a Delaware corporation holding US real estate

GENTROL INC.
Based in New York. Provides services for Olayan companies in Saudi Arabia.
Liaises with US companies represented by GCC and GTC

OLAYAN SAUDI HOLDING CO. (OSHCO)
Based in Alkhobar. Provides senior management and services for companies below:

GENERAL CONTRACTING CO. (GCC)
Originally a contractor. Now sells cars, trucks, construction equipment throughout Saudi Arabia

GENERAL TRADING CO. (GTC)
Sells packaged foods and cosmetics throughout Saudi Arabia

SAUDI GENERAL TRANSPORTATION CO.
in Saudi Arabia and **GENERAL TRANSPORTATION ENTERPRISES** in Kuwait.
Transport services including very heavy off-road transport. Grew out of Neutral Zone oil-rig contract. Rig activity now mainly in Empty Quarter.

PROJECTS AND DEVELOPMENT CO.
Holds OSHCO shares in contracting and engineering joint-ventures in Saudi Arabia

companies' personnel and buying operations were run from Beirut.

The people who worked closely with Suliman in the 1960s say that they came to see the company's presence in Beirut as a necessity for all the more modern parts of their business. They could, and did, operate a straightforward importing business out of Saudi Arabia, but they could not have developed the insurance-broking business there. In this sense the period in Beirut transformed the Olayan companies. Its influence on Suliman himself was more indirect. The Lebanese did not have any important effect on his thinking about business, but his presence in Beirut increased his contact with the international business community. It expanded the American connection which had begun with his work for Aramco.

It was only in the mid-1970s that most of the administration of the Olayan companies was moved back to Alkhobar – mainly because there had been a dramatic improvement in Saudi communications. In Alkhobar the administrative operations were formed into OSHCO – the Olayan Saudi Holding Company. This became the owner of GCC, GTC and the Olayan Transport Company in Saudi Arabia (see organisation chart). For three years after their arrival in 1976, the OSHCO staff worked in several very small, unpretentious office buildings in a side street; it was not until 1979, when they established themselves in a large, grand, purpose-built block, that the Olayan headquarters in Alkhobar became 'visible'. Other back-up services, including public relations and liaison with foreign principals, were moved to London and New York. The insurance-broking business, by now known as Arabian Commercial Enterprises (ACE), and the group headquarters were established in Athens.

While Suliman was considering moving part of the Beirut headquarters back to Saudi Arabia in 1973 and 1974, he was also thinking about making a fundamental change in the ownership and management of his companies.

He had long been committed to the idea that a professionally managed company was more efficient than a family-run company. Families, he argued, had a limited view of the world and could not be objective in making decisions; professional managers were more flexible and could draw on wider experience. Two major influences had drawn Suliman to these conclusions. One was his interest in the Western business world. He had been one of the first of the merchants mentioned in the last chapter to become interested in developing his business for its own sake.

At an early stage he had begun to see it as a provider of a useful economic service. The other factor in his thinking was the small size of his own family. Unlike most other Arabian merchants Suliman had never been able to rely on a large number of brothers, cousins and sons to run different branches of his business. He worked with only one of his brothers. This was Abdullah, who ran the Kuwaiti part of his transport operations and attended to all family matters concerning the Olayan relations in Kuwait and Onaizah. Suliman also had only one son, Khaled, who in the early 1970s had recently returned from university in America. The limited number of his relations had meant that professional managers had been more or less forced upon him. Even so he seemed never to have had regrets about the loss of personal control of the day-to-day operations of his business that employing managers had entailed.

It was the idea of taking partners that Suliman was considering in 1973 and 1974. He had reached his mid-fifties and he knew that sooner or later he would be retiring. In the past, he felt that his management team had not amounted to much more than a group of close aides; he now wanted to hand over his company to a bigger, completely independent management. The matter was being made all the more urgent by the growing size of his company's operations. How he solved the problem was described to me by Zahi Khouri, an American of Palestinian ancestry, who was trained as an engineer at INSEAD[3] and who was to become President of OSHCO.

'It began as a series of coincidences. For some years Mr Olayan had had a close relationship with the head of the American Express Bank. At the same time I was working for the American Express Middle East Development Company, which was the Middle East merchant banking arm of Amex – and Mr Olayan and I also happened to live in the same building in Beirut. The idea came to Mr Olayan that he might take on American Express to run the trading operations in Saudi Arabia under a formal management contract . . . We reached agreement in principle on this in early 1974, and detailed negotiations went on for about a year after that. One of the terms on which he insisted was that I should be the person seconded by American Express to run the Saudi operation – that's the importance of the personal link in the Middle East. Another

3. Institut Européen d'Administration des Affaires – the French business school at Fontainebleau.

part of the terms was that American Express should buy a small share – about 3 per cent – in TTI, which is the holding company above OSHCO in our corporate structure. This deal came into effect at about the same time as we moved the Beirut operation to Saudi Arabia. It gave the Olayan group just the basic management support for the top of the trading operation.

'What he wanted then was some institution which would provide him with a bigger reserve of manpower to help establish new service departments. If possible he wanted a company with expertise in trading *per se*. So he commissioned American Express to find him a partner. We looked at a lot of US companies, but eventually we found Jardine Matheson, the investment and trading group based in Hong Kong. It was American Express in Australia which had come up with Jardine – the head of Amex there was Nick Whitlam, the son of the Australian Prime Minister. In mid-1976 we agreed that Jardine would take 25 per cent of the stock of TTI. This was later to be increased to 40 per cent if all went well. At the same time Jardine's Chairman, David Newbigging, became the Deputy Chairman of TTI.'

In the first three or four years after the deal, the Jardine connection lived up to the expectations that Suliman and his managers had of it. The company did not send many people to Alkhobar, but those it did send were good. This has not always been the case when big companies have become partners in operations far from home – there has been a tendency for them to off-load their dead wood on to their foreign associates. The Jardine staff at OSHCO established the new service departments that Suliman had intended they should establish; in effect they took the company across the 'watershed'. They and the other OSHCO managers were given more genuine independence by Suliman than the managers of any other merchant group in Arabia; they were the only managers in a merchant company to enjoy the same authority that they would have expected in a Western company. Rather than consult Suliman on every matter, they could take important decisions themselves and tell him later.

Matters became more difficult in 1980. At the end of the previous year Suliman's son, Khaled, had become Chairman of OSHCO and had begun to play a more active role in the management. His arrival coincided with a worsening of business conditions. During the early years of the American Express–Jardine Matheson regime the turnover of OSHCO had increased dramatically. In 1980 it ran at just under $400 million, compared with $48 million in 1974, the year before the American Express management contract was signed. Profits, however, had a more chequered history. The company does not publish any figures, but it admits that 1980 was a very bad year. If it did not actually make a loss, its profits must have been minimal. It was hit by the general downturn in the Arabian market, increasing competition and high interest rates. Its managers pointed out that since it had modernised its operations and opened new service departments – which in themselves were a drain on its resources – it had had to borrow; until the mid-1970s the level of interest rates had been of little relevance to its performance.

Even before the market turned against the company, it was known that the Jardine management had been finding the process of working in a Middle Eastern business more difficult than it had anticipated. In 1981 some of the less important new service departments were closed or had their staffs reduced. There were also redundancies, resignations and rumours of resignations among the non-Jardine managers. Although 1981 was not a happy year for the company, it did at least see OSHCO return to making healthy profits – on a turnover of $430 million.

The performance of the rest of the Olayan group is less easy to assess, because the Olayan managers only talk about profits in the most general terms. In fact, Arabian Commercial Enterprises, which had a turnover in 1981 of some $170 million, is known to be highly profitable, as are most other insurance and travel businesses in Arabia. Conventional wisdom in the Peninsula says that industrial and high-technology service companies, such as those wholly or partly owned by the Olayan Financing Company, are not so profitable. However, the men who run OFC claim that now that they have gained experience in managing such companies in an Arabian environment, many of their joint-ventures are yielding bigger percentage profits on turnover than the OSHCO trading operation. In 1981 the companies in which OFC had an interest turned over $580 million.

In the long term there is no doubt that the OFC companies have more potential for growth than any other part of the Olayan group. By 1982 there were more than forty of these companies, about two-thirds of them providing high-technology services, such as aircraft-engine maintenance, and the rest in manufacturing and agricultural industries. OFC was a shareholder with Prince Abdullah Faisal (the oldest son of King Faisal) and Omar Aggad in the Saudi Plastic Products Company,

SAPPCO. This company manufactured PVC pipe on the industrial estate at Riyadh, and was rated as one of the most successful of all the new Saudi industries established in the later 1970s.

The most profitable of OFC's ventures were assumed to be the companies it had established with Bechtel, the massive San Francisco-based construction group. Among other project-management contracts won by the Olayan–Bechtel companies in the later 1970s were the new Riyadh airport, part of the Aramco gas-gathering network, two Eastern Province power stations, the sea-water injection system for the huge Ghawar oil field, and the infrastructure for the Jubail industrial city. It is intended that Jubail will eventually have a population of 350,000 and about a dozen very large oil and gas-based export industries. These will include six petrochemical plants, at least one refinery, a steel mill and a fertiliser plant.

Suliman now devotes a good part of his energies to his foreign investments. Like many other parts of his business these had their origins in his early dealings with American companies.

'When I first went to America,' he once explained to me, 'I found that my suppliers got nervous about my buying from them just on the basis of letters of credit. It was no good telling them that I had x, y or z in cash or balances in Saudi Arabia. People wanted to be able to dial 212 area code and check on it. The US in those days was terribly un-export minded.

'So, after a time I decided that I would have to get some assets in New York – something people could seize if I defaulted. During the 1950s the assets increased rather slowly. I kept adding to them year by year as the value of my imports increased, but the amounts were not big. I remember it was a banner year when I transferred $28,000. By 1958 I suppose I must have had a fair sum, because in that year I approached Sherman and Sterling, the law firm, to establish an investment vehicle for me in Curaçao. This was nothing to do with managing the funds – I just wanted to cut my tax liability.

'Then in the 1960s the US banks went international, and I moved to Beirut, so things changed. I no longer needed assets in the US to get credit on goods bought from the US. But the interest and dividends kept being reinvested, and these things just grow without one noticing them. So in the late 1960s I thought "Well, I'll bite the bullet." I decided that despite the overheads I would set up my own investment-management departments – before this I'd just used the trust departments of the banks. Of course, once a functional operation is set up it develops a will of its own. This has some advantages. You find that a bank's trust department will only look for an investment once you've given it the funds, but your own department will spot an opportunity and borrow, in the knowledge that a month or two later the funds will be coming in for it to repay the borrowing. Your own department will also compete with other departments in the group for funds: they'll say, "the markets are going up this year, you'd do better giving us the money than using it to build new warehouses." Anyway, one of the results of my establishing my own investment departments is that in the last ten years my assets have got a lot bigger.'

The allocations made to Suliman's various foreign-investment vehicles are controlled by OICE's board of directors. This body, composed of Khaled and the senior managers of the group, normally meets twice a year. It discusses plans for the group's development over one or two years and decides how to allocate its capital resources. In effect it has the job of deciding how much of the group's profits are to be ploughed back into Saudi Arabia and how much is to be invested abroad. Of the funds that are allocated to foreign investment, a large amount is handled by the OICE office in Athens; this controls a euromarkets securities portfolio of its own and manages the deployment of temporarily surplus working capital. Other sums are managed by the Competrol office in London, which runs a small European-property portfolio, and the Crescent/Gentrol office on Park Avenue, New York. Crescent's and Gentrol's Chairman from 1980 to 1982 was William Simon, the former US Treasury Secretary. In all, the three offices control about a dozen investment vehicles – the most important of which are listed in the organisational chart above. The Olayan group no longer uses any outside organisations as discretionary portfolio managers.

The Olayan investments are conservative, but actively managed – unlike the investments of the Arabian governments, which are conservative and not very actively managed. It is not Suliman's policy to acquire very large blocks of stock or to buy a bank; his managers point out that most of the banks bought by Arabs to date have been disasters. The striking characteristic of his investment operations is the very careful watch he keeps on the state of the markets. Almost every day, wherever he may be in the world, Suliman makes a longish conference call to his fund managers in New York. If there are other senior managers of the company with him, they gather in the same office and listen to the New York end of the conversation through a loudspeaker.

The classic Olayan investment strategy is to watch the movements of a category of shares for a long period and to wait until they seem to be underpriced. In the autumn of 1980, for example, it was felt that oils, one of Suliman's favourite stocks, were overpriced. After hitting highs in November, they were sold steadily to a point where Suliman regarded them as very attractive. In the summer of 1981 his managers in New York moved into the market and bought blocks of Conoco, Standard Oil of California, Standard Oil of Indiana and Texaco. In situations of this sort the normal procedure is for managers to take an initial stake of about $1 million. If the share goes up they stop investing; if it goes down they buy some more, building a position in stages.

Suliman has a preference for New York over the London and European markets. In 1981 he told Steven Flax of *Forbes*: 'I like the American stock market because there is a wonderful amount of information here. For someone who wants to research and look for situations the disclosure is excellent.' About 30 per cent of the Olayan funds invested in US equities are in bank stocks. 'Banks', Suliman remarked in the same interview, 'are not volatile. They give good dividends and normally appreciate. They are scrutinised by regulatory agencies and aren't susceptible to labour disputes or changes in prices of commodities. Their raw material is money and the finished product is money.' These views have led Competrol – owned 50/50 by Suliman and Prince Khaled bin Abdullah bin Abdel-Rahman al Saud – to buy about 1 per cent of the stock of Chase Manhattan, making it the biggest shareholder after David Rockefeller. It has similar proportions of the stock of several other US banks – Mellon Bank of Pittsburg, Southeast Bancorp of Miami, Valley National of Phoenix, First Bank Systems of Minneapolis, First Interstate and Hawaii Bancorp of Honolulu. Its two biggest holdings in financial institutions are a 19 per cent stake in Donaldson, Lufkin and Jenrette, the Wall Street investment banking firm, and nearly 8 per cent of the First Chicago Corporation, the owner of the First National Bank of Chicago.

After bank stocks the biggest slice of Suliman's US equity portfolio has been invested in oils. His most important holdings are in Mobil and Occidental. In 1980 he became a member of the board of Mobil. A further substantial percentage of the portfolio is in high-technology

companies, including Thermo Electron, a company near Boston involved in industrial-energy conservation, Whittaker, the hospital-
equipment company, United Technologies and Westinghouse.

The most closely guarded of all the Olayan group's secrets is the size
of its foreign investments. Suliman's managers are not prepared to
admit anything more specific than that his total European and American assets, including equities, debt and real estate, come to something
between $100 million and $500 million. From circumstantial evidence
and the odd remarks of Suliman and his managers, it seems that a more
accurate guess in 1982 would have been between $250 million and $300
million.

Almost any other Saudi investing in the United States on the same scale
as Suliman Olayan would be certain to arouse controversy and hostility.
In the mid-1970s both Adnan Khashoggi and Ghaith Pharaon suffered
this fate. Even though their investments were much smaller than
Suliman's, they were highly conspicuous and much less successful in
their activities. More recently Ahmed Juffali has accumulated a substantial portfolio of US assets without attracting attention. He has
managed to avoid publicity mainly because his investments are smaller
and less formally organised than Suliman's. He is also particularly
reluctant to talk to journalists.

Suliman has not only avoided controversy, his involvement in
American business has been actively welcomed. Before he was invited
to join the board of Mobil, he had been a director of the American
Express Bank. He has also joined the International Council of Morgan
Guaranty and several other American academic and business councils.
He is Chairman of the Saudi-Spanish Bank in Madrid and the Saudi-
British Bank, which is owned partly by the British Bank of the Middle
East and is one of the leading banks in Saudi Arabia.

Suliman's success has much to do with his personality. A friend once
remarked of him that he seemed less like 'a billion dollars on the foot'
than anyone he had ever met. He dislikes ostentation. He has no yachts
or private aircraft. When he flies across the Atlantic on Concorde, as he
normally does, it is because he calculates that he is using his time most
efficiently by doing so. He avoids unnecessary overheads and keeps
down the numbers of his staff in his London and New York offices. One
of the employees in the Competrol office in London once told him that
there was supposed to be a ghost in the building. 'Well that's all right,'

said Suliman, 'but I hope it's not on the payroll.'

Most of his employees and business associates staunchly maintain that behind the quiet, unassuming exterior is a business genius. They say that Suliman has no interests other than business (and his family), he works extremely hard, sleeps little and does not take holidays. He has a giant memory and an extraordinary flair for spotting an investment opportunity. In this he has recently been assisted by his very able American wife, Mary.

Two people who testify to Suliman's abilities are Carl Mueller, the Vice-Chairman of Bankers Trust, and Richard Jenrette, Chairman of Donaldson Lufkin & Jenrette. In an interview in mid-1981 Mueller remarked: 'If Suliman came in here in a hurry one afternoon and said he wanted a large sum of money and would explain later, he'd get it. He could walk into five banks here in New York and do the same thing.' Six months earlier Richard Jenrette, talking to the *New York Times*,[4] had said: 'Suliman may be the best businessman I've ever met. Anywhere. Of any nationality.'

4. See *International Herald Tribune*, 22 October 1980. The article was written by William G. Shepherd Jr of the *New York Times*.

17

卐 The Future

The Arabian merchants in the early 1980s are conscious of a change
taking place in their world. This is caused only partly by the oil glut, the
decline in OPEC production and the cut in oil prices in March 1983.
Despite the fall in its revenues and the drop in spending budgeted for
1983/4 the Saudi government is still planning in the first half of this
decade to disburse $300 billion, which is what it forecast it would spend
in the period when the Third Plan was published in 1980. Some of this
money is going into government-to-government defence deals, but
most of it at some stage will pass through the books of local businesses.
These may be giant merchant–foreign contractor partnerships or minor
import operations based in the souk. Even if the annual growth rates of
the non-oil parts of the Arabian economies are no longer in the 30 per
cent plus range reached in the mid-1970s, the Peninsula is still one of the
world's fast developing economies.

What concerns the merchants is that their lives are becoming more
complex. They are facing more competition and being forced to modernise the management of their companies. Their operations are becoming longer term. Instead of importing products and services – in effect
just representing foreign companies – they have found themselves
establishing their own local manufacturing and service companies.
Meanwhile they are being increasingly hemmed in by legislation. In the
past, as long as they had the good will of their ruler, they could do
virtually what they liked. Now there are controls on prices, profits and
commissions – albeit widely ignored. Governments have taken over part
of the foodstuffs market. There are new safety regulations, labour and
social insurance laws, and, in Kuwait, an embryonic form of corporation tax. One side-effect of the boom in legislation has been a shortage
of lawyers. Governments have been heard to complain that there is
nobody to advise them; the merchants have been obliged to open legal

departments. Many Lebanese and Western law firms and accountants have seized the opportunity to establish offices in the area.

Not the least of the merchants' problems concerns what they should do with their money. They are now turning over vastly greater sums and making vastly greater profits than they were ten years ago. Admittedly their growth has been checked in 1983 by the fall in government spending. At the same time some companies have incurred higher overheads by establishing new service departments and employing expensive Western managers. But these developments are having only a dampening effect on profits; there are not many big companies that are actually running at a loss. The problem is that the opportunities for investing profits locally are becoming fewer. Now that growth rates in the non-oil sectors of the economies are running at more reasonable levels, merchants no longer have to plough back most of their profits into ever larger quantities of stock. The real estate boom has ended; in most centres there are now surpluses of hotels, apartments and office space. The most ambitious companies have completed their investments in workshops, spare-parts stores and other back-up facilities; they have also completed most of the first wave of industrial and service projects. In due course, the new industries, if they are successful, will give rise to opportunities for further spin-off industries and services to support them. Vehicle assembly, for example, might provide an opportunity for the manufacture of spray paints. For the moment, however, there is a lull in demand for new industrial investment.

If the merchants were living in the same type of society as American millionaires in the late nineteenth and early twentieth centuries, they might found philanthropic institutions. Andrew Carnegie, J.P. Morgan, John D. Rockefeller and Henry Ford were all at least as ruthless in business as the Arabian merchants, they accumulated fortunes of a similar size, and they gave away enormous quantities of their money. The big Arabian families have given very little to charity. The nearest that any of them has come to establishing a permanent charitable trust was when Mohammad Ali Alireza founded the Fallah schools in the early part of this century. More recently, in the early 1970s, the Kanoo family established the Yusuf bin Ahmed Kanoo School of Nursing, in memory of its members' great-uncle. Its charity was partly stimulated by the then Bahraini Minister of Health, Dr Ali Fakhroo, himself a member of a prominent merchant family, who mentioned to Ahmed Kanoo that Bahraini hospitals were short of nurses. A few years after the opening of the School in 1973, the Kanoos financed an expansion programme which broadened the scope of the School's curriculum to embrace medical science in general, and raised the number of its students to 500. At this point the Health Ministry, with a budget strengthened by higher oil revenues, took responsibility for most of the School's running costs.

By coincidence, another nurses' training school, in this case in Lebanon, has been partly financed by Suliman Olayan. It is characteristic of Suliman's whole approach to business that he has arranged for his charity to be given corporately. His company has a donations committee which subjects requests for money to careful scrutiny. One of its most generous gifts has been $750,000 to Beir Zeit, the Palestinian university in the Israeli-occupied West Bank. Most of the charity given by other big merchants has been disbursed in a similar piecemeal fashion, rather than as part of a programme of finance for a particular institution.

In 1977 Faisal Marzoukh, a member of an old Kuwaiti family well known for high-quality real estate developments, gave $250,000 for new playing fields at his old college, the University of Hartford, Connecticut. The recipient in this case was slightly unusual. There have been a few other Arab gifts to Western universities, but in general the idea of giving charity to Western institutions is seen in the Arabian Peninsula as being 'sensitive'. The normal view is that although the Arabian oil states receive vast oil revenues, in terms of their ability to generate their own wealth by producing services and industrial products in the future, they are still not rich societies. It is felt that Arabian money should go first into developing Arabia's, or the Arab world's, own human resources.

The main reason why the merchants have not given charity on a bigger and more organised scale at home, is that philanthropy of the traditional Western type cannot be applied very easily to Arabian society. An obvious, though relatively unimportant, consideration is that the lack of tax in Arabia means that there are no financial advantages to be gained from establishing charitable trusts. Since the oil price rises of 1973–4 there has also been a shortage of opportunities for charity. It is difficult for a rich man to be a philanthropist when his government is intent on building one of the ultimate welfare states for its people. A specifically Arabian complication is that any merchant who tried to add to his government's work might not only be wasting his money; he would run the risk of appearing to be competing with the ruling family. In the intensely personal society of Arabia, government spending on social projects is still seen by ordinary people as a reflection of the power and generosity of the ruler. For a merchant to take part of the ruler's role for himself would cause embarrassment to all parties. The most tactful course for a determined philanthropist might be for him to build a museum of modern Arabian art, for example, and then present it to his ruler. In this way he would be doing something for the community and endorsing the supremacy of the ruler at the same time.

Confronted with such an array of sensitivities, most of the merchants have contented themselves with dispensing charity in a traditional Arabian fashion. Many of them have built mosques. The Sultan family in Oman has built the Abdel-Reza Sultan Mosque, as a memorial to its revered eldest brother, who died in 1967. The building is regarded as the most attractive modern mosque in the Sultanate. All of the rich merchants dispense charity in their *majles* on the occasion of family celebrations and during the two Eids – the feasts at the end of Ramadan and at the time of the Pilgrimage. The recipients may be old servants or retainers, distant relations or anyone else who feels his vague connection with the family entitles him to consideration.

Hussein Alireza tells a story which well illustrates the elements of demand and obligation, as well as generosity, which lie behind the disbursement of this traditional type of charity. In the late 1920s, Hussein's father, Ali, who owned one of Saudi Arabia's first motor cars, had the Kingdom's first motor accident. He ran over a boy and broke his leg. Ali's uncle, Abdullah, who at that time was Governor of Jeddah, insisted on the proper application of the law, and Ali was obliged to pay substantial compensation. The accident and compensation together established the necessary relationship between the boy, as deserving pauper, and Ali, as rich benefactor. From the time of the accident to the present, the victim, who is now quite an old man, has attended the Eid *majles* of the Hussein branch of the Alireza family to have his compensation topped up.

The most important outlet for the merchants' growing surpluses has been foreign investment. The merchants' motives have been partly commercial and partly political; in the back of all their minds is the knowledge that the Middle East is chronically unstable and that one day they might be forced into exile by revolution. The biggest merchant foreign investor is generally accepted to be Suliman Olayan; other well-known investors are the Juffalis and Abdullah Abdel-Ghaffar Alireza. The Jameels run an investment operation out of Monte Carlo, through which they put money into portfolio and direct investments, particularly in real estate and shipping. Ahmed Hamad Algosaibi in 1982 established an investment division in his company in Alkhobar and began to channel his family's foreign investments through the London office of a subsidiary company registered in the Dutch Antilles. The trend at this time was for merchants to set up formal investment operations in their corporate names; previously they had invested on an *ad hoc* and personal basis.

Until the advent of the professional investment department most of the merchants' investments were conservative; their money went mainly into bank deposits, bonds and real estate, but not gold on a very large scale.[1] More recently there has been a growing interest in equities, and even a willingness to buy majority or large minority stakes in small companies which the merchants believe will complement the development of their own companies at home. What the merchants do not seem to be interested in doing is taking over Western companies in order to develop these companies in the Western industrialised world. The famous deals of Ghaith Pharaon and Adnan Khashoggi in the mid-1970s, involving such corporations as the Bank of the Commonwealth in Detroit and the Arizona-Colorado Land and Cattle Company, are still very untypical of Arabian investors. Most Arabians are less flamboyant than these two. They have noticed that the big, well-publicised take-overs have mostly been failures. They have also been frightened by the controversy that has surrounded these deals and by the Western public's hostile reaction to Arab investment.

The one element of investment philosophy which most Arabian investors share with Khashoggi and Pharaon is the belief that America makes a safer home for their more ambitious, longer-term investments than Europe. This is not just because more Arabians speak English than French or German. In the bottom of their hearts they have a somewhat 1950s Cold War view of East–West politics, and they believe that over a thirty-year period America will offer them better political security. Their attitude was summarised unselfconsciously by Kutayba

1. For a discussion of Arabian private investment abroad in the mid-1970s, see *A Hundred Million Dollars a Day* by Michael Field, Sidgwick and Jackson, Praeger and Fayard, 1975.

Alghanim in a conversation with Kenneth Crowe in 1977: 'Our choice is America,' he said. 'If there are ten [companies of a particular type] in Europe, there are a hundred in America . . . If the whole world turns Communist, the last country will be the United States.'[2] Kutayba added that if he invested in a large share of an American rather than a European company, he would have the advantage of operating in a single big market, with a single body of commercial legislation.

As their foreign investments grow the Arabian businessmen are spending more of their time in the West. They have bought apartments and country houses, and opened liaison offices to act as links between their companies and the manufacturers they represent. Most of the offices are in London and New York, but a few of the most enterprising merchants have established offices elsewhere. The Juffalis have a liaison office in Zurich, Abdullah Alireza has offices in Paris and Boston, the Kanoos have an office in Houston.

Inevitably their presence in the West brings the merchants into contact with leading Western business figures and politicians. One or two Arabian names have become mixed up in Western political scandal. Khashoggi had connections with some of the figures of the Nixon administration; Pharaon in 1977 bought most of the stock of the National Bank of Georgia held by Bert Lance, President Carter's unfortunate director of the Office of Management and Budget. A few Arabians have adopted the lifestyles of Western millionaires and taken up Western pastimes. One, Suliman Olayan, has been invited into Western boardrooms.

Suliman has also distinguished himself by being one of the very few Arabians outside the ranks of government ministers who have been prepared to enter into Western political debate and present a pro-Arab, pro-OPEC case. He has written articles on OPEC and the Arab–Israeli conflict for *Fortune* and the *Washington Quarterly*. In October 1982, at a meeting of the US–Saudi Joint Commission in Washington DC, he made a widely reported speech in which he called for changes in three pieces of US legislation which he argued were damaging US–Saudi economic relations and leading to the Kingdom doing more business with Europe and Japan. The regulations in question concerned the exclusion of Saudi Arabia from favourable tariff treatment under the Generalised System of Preferences, the charging of withholding tax on

2. See *America for Sale* by Kenneth C. Crowe, Doubleday, 1978, p. 34.

dividends and interest earned by Saudi investors on assets in the United States, and the controversial matter of the anti-Arab Boycott legislation. At the end of his speech he addressed himself to a broader, more widely publicised issue:

> 'Fourth, [he said], 'item 9 on our agenda refers to a bilateral investment treaty. The proper atmosphere for such a treaty is damaged by the hostility of some quarters against Arab investments in the US. Congressional Committee hearings purport to examine the influence of foreign investment on US policy, but concentrate almost entirely on Arab investment, ignoring the much more significant investments by British, Dutch, German, Japanese and other investors. We object to the singling out of Arab investment and strongly urge that this discrimination be stopped.
>
> 'Our investments in the US help to create jobs, improve productivity, support capital markets, and improve the US balance of payments. In Saudi Arabia we actively encourage foreign investors to bring in capital and know-how. We see the substantial foreign investment in our country as healthy both for us and for our foreign partners . . . To us businessmen it is clear that it is the investor, not the investee, who is held hostage to the legal and political policies of the host country in which he invests.
>
> 'With all this in mind, I would encourage the American private sector delegation [at the Joint Commission meeting] to reassure those alarmed that our investments are comparatively modest and are more likely to give the US undue influence over us, rather than the reverse.'

Other Arabians endorse Suliman's views, but they hesitate to express them in the West in public. Some feel that their English is not up to the task; most are frightened by what they feel to be the undignified rough and tumble of Western debate. Almost all believe that if they were to enter the arena, pro-Israeli lobby groups would do everything in their power to discredit them. Even Suliman Olayan has not yet appeared on Western television.

However much the Arabians become involved in the Western world in their business, in all other aspects of their lives they stay anchored to Arabia. It would be quite wrong to imagine that as their countries become more developed and as they have more contact with the Western world they will automatically become more Westernised. A very few may leave their own society and plunge wholeheartedly into the world of the jet set, but most will not want to adopt a Western morality or live their social lives along Western lines. Western morals are too permissive for Arabians, and Western social life is too individualist and too far removed from the extended family to appeal to them.

In the last two or three years there has been a reaction in Arabia against imported Western culture. This is not just a product of the 'Islamic revival' or fear engendered by Khomeini's revolution in Iran. There is a feeling that some of the excesses produced by the vast and sudden inflow of oil money have been distasteful and un-Arab. This attitude was exemplified in the attacks on Adnan Khashoggi during the early stages of his divorce proceedings in America in 1979 and 1980. Saudis were also shocked by the activities of the Fassi, a Jeddah family of Moroccan origin. Two members of this family built a large and vulgar mansion in Hollywood and erected life-like, painted nude statues in their garden – an act which raised eyebrows even among the southern Californians. In 1979 their house was burnt to the ground, giving rise to gleeful speculation that the fire may have been an act of arson.

The wave of criticism of vulgar materialism has been accompanied by an awakening of Arabians' interest in their past. Old houses in Jeddah are being preserved and restored. One family, the Binzagrs, is even using its old, tall, coralstone house in a company advertisement; beneath a painting done by one of the daughters of the family the caption reads 'The House of Binzagr: your entrée to Saudi Arabia'. This type of advertisement would never have appeared in the early 1970s; then the emphasis was entirely on being as modern as possible.

Young Arabians are taking a delight in telling somewhat idealised stories of their ancestors. It is fashionable to bemoan the passing of the honest, friendly world of the souk thirty years ago, when a merchant who fell on hard times would be rescued by his fellow storekeepers. It is certainly no longer regarded as smart for an Arabian to flaunt his money or to talk about his latest business deal. There has been pressure on the senior members of the Saudi royal family to curb the activities of the most greedy of the younger princes – though in 1982 there were conflicting signs as to whether the pressure had been successful.

The climate of opinion was well summarised in an anecdote told to me at this time by Suliman Olayan. Two Saudis, he explained, had recently found themselves sitting next to each other on a flight from Europe to Jeddah. One was young and a bit brash. He struck up a conversation with his neighbour, in which he quickly managed to mention that he was returning to Saudi Arabia to complete a major business deal and that he had a large number of very important contacts in and around the government. The other Saudi was rather older and a man of some importance in the Kingdom. When there was a lull in his companion's chatter, he closed the conversation by saying: 'Well, I have come back to Jeddah to see my father. He is a taxi driver and he is in hospital.'

APPENDIX 1

The Ten Biggest Merchant Companies in 1982

The turnovers below are 'consensus' figures made up of the average of several people's guesses. Only companies that are known for importing as much as any other activity are included in the list. Exchange dealers, such as the Rajhi brothers, and contractors, such as Bin Laden and REDEC, have turnovers that are not strictly comparable with importing companies' turnovers. In the case of contractors there is the question of whether the whole value of construction and supply contracts should be included in turnover, or just the profit element. The same issue of the treatment of reimbursables occurs when one is considering companies such as Yusuf bin Ahmed Kanoo and Ahmed Hamad Algosaibi and Brothers, which have big shipping agency and airline-ticket businesses. In the figures given below for Kanoo and Algosaibi, reimbursables have been excluded. This gives them turnover figures which are rather small in comparison with what are thought to be their profits.

It goes without saying that this turnover list does not provide any indication of who are the richest Arabian businessmen. Generally it is thought that the richest people are those in banking and exchange dealing, such as Bin Mahfouz, Kaaki and Rajhi, and those with large amounts of real estate, including members of the ruling familes.

Company	Headquarters	Major source of turnover	Estimated turnover 1981
E.A. Juffali & Bros	Jeddah	Daimler Benz	$1,300 m
United Abdul-Latif Jameel Group	Jeddah	Toyota	$1,100 m
Olayan Group	Alkhobar	Machinery & Industry	$ 600 m
Futtaim Group	Dubai	Toyota	$ 500 m
Alghanim Industries & YAAS	Kuwait	General Motors	$ 400 m
Zahid Group	Jeddah	Caterpillar	$ 350 m
A.S. Bugshan & Bros	Jeddah	Komatsu	$ 300 m
Abdel-Aziz A. Suliman & Co	Jeddah	Datsun	$ 275 m
Yusuf bin Ahmed Kanoo	Bahrain	Machinery	$ 250 m
Abdel-Aziz & M.A. Jomaih	Riyadh	General Motors	$ 230 m

Notes:

Olayan: The turnover of the Olayan Group in the table is made up only of the Olayan-owned parts of OSHCO, ACE and OFC. OSHCO is owned 40 per cent by Jardine Matheson, ACE is 67 per cent Prince Khaled bin Abdullah bin Abdel-Rahman and Sedgwick Forbes, and OFC, on average, owns only about half of the shares of the companies in which it has interests. If the turnover attributable to the non-Olayan holdings in these companies were included in the figure, the total group turnover in 1981 would be $1,200 million. Technically the Olayan group headquarters is in Athens, but its operations are managed mainly from Alkhobar, which is why that town is given as its base in the table.

Abdel-Aziz Suliman: The Datsun agency in Saudi Arabia is vested in a company called Siraj Zahran, which is owned by Abdel-Aziz Suliman and three other leading merchant houses, including the Moshaikih family of Buraidah. In the table of turnovers about a quarter of the assumed turnover of Zahran is included in the Abdel-Aziz Suliman figure.

Smaller turnovers: There are several companies with turnovers of about $200 million or a bit below. These would include the following: Ahmed Hamad Algosaibi and Brothers, heavy-machinery importers, Alkhobar; Haji Hussein Alireza and Co., Mazda agents, Jeddah; Abdel-Aziz and Sa'ad Moajil food importers, Dammam; and Abdullah Abbar and Ahmed Zaini, food importers, Jeddah.

The Companies in This Book:
Operating Divisions, Agencies and Joint-Ventures

These lists are not necessarily complete. Many of the companies' smaller agencies and most recently formed joint-ventures (j-vs) are not included. In Saudi Arabia and the Gulf states in the late 1970s and early 1980s, many merchant houses were still forming several new joint-ventures every year – though not all of these were expected to emerge as significant businesses.

HAJI ABDULLAH ALIREZA AND COMPANY LTD

Owned by members of the Zainal and Abdullah branches of the Alireza family. Board members: Ahmed Yusuf Zainal, Ali Abdullah, Mohammad Yusuf Zainal and Mahmoud Yusuf Zainal. Haji Abdullah Alireza & Co. comprises the following divisions and joint-ventures.

Real Estate Division: developing Alireza Centre in Jeddah; owns large pieces of real estate in Jeddah including an area near the new airport to the north of the city, and in Dammam, Alkhobar, Rahina, Jubail, Yanbu and Khamis Mushait.

General Technical Division (GENTEC): telecommunications contracting, represents ITT and Frederick Electronics Corpn.

Insurance Division: represents Liverpool & London & Globe, and Provincial Insurance.

Maritime Division: represents dry-cargo carriers – American Export Lines, New York; DDG 'Hansa' Line, Bremen; Deutsche Ost-Afrika Linien, Hamburg; Mogul Line, Bombay; Nippon Yusen Kaisha, Tokyo; Navale et Commerciale Havraise Péninsulaire, Paris; Saudi Orient Maritime, Jeddah; Shipping Corporation of India, Bombay. Represents oil-tanker companies – Compañia Española de Petroleos, Madrid; Global Chartering; Mobil; Olympic Maritime. Services include stevedoring, barging, customs clearance etc., runs ro-ro terminal at Dammam.

Travel Division: handles general sales agencies and provides ground support at Jeddah airport for KLM and Air Algérie; runs travel agency in Jeddah.

The Golden Palm: jewellery and luxury goods retail division in Jeddah; sells jewellery by most famous jewellery houses; agencies for Saint Louis crystal, Coalport and Spode china, and watches by Vacheron et Constantin, Jaeger le Coultre, Yema and Pulsar.

Laing Wimpey Alireza: civil construction company owned by HAACO, John Laing and George Wimpey, based in Riyadh.

Saudi Maritime Company (SAMARCO): tanker-owning and chartering company owned by HAACO, Mobil, Fairfield Maxwell and Prince Mohammad bin Fahd al Saud.

Arabian Petroleum Supply Company (APSCO): owned by HAACO and Mobil; runs aircraft-refuelling operation at Jeddah airport, and represents Mobil lubricants; also has (smaller) ship-bunkering operation.

REZAYAT GROUP

Established by Abdullah Abdel-Ghaffar Alireza, who is now President of the group. Teymour, Abdullah's son, is Vice-President of the group, and President of the Saudi companies. The group is based in Kuwait but has its biggest offices in Alkhobar and Riyadh. Real estate and foreign investments are held by Abdullah and Teymour outside the context of the group. Main companies and joint-ventures in the group are as follows:

Rezayat Trading Company: there are two companies of this name, in Kuwait and Alkhobar; both are importers of consumer goods and equipment. The companies hold Alireza interests in various joint-ventures.

Rezayat Trading Establishment: based in Alkhobar, operates motels in Eastern Province, leases and runs contractors' camps, holds Alireza interests in various j-vs.

National Contracting Company (NCC): there are National Contracting Companies in Saudi Arabia, Kuwait, Abu Dhabi, Dubai and Oman. Operations include: cement unloading at Dammam port (in association with Van Ommeren Shipping and Trading and Muller Thomsen of Rotterdam); heavy transport and plant hire in Saudi Arabia, Oman and UAE; portable-building manufacture in Abu Dhabi and Dubai; and camp leasing in Abu Dhabi. NCCs also hold Alireza interests in various j-vs.

Saudi Arabian Fabricated Metals Industry (SAFAMI): partnership between NCC and Williams International of Tulsa, Oklahoma; pipe and structural steel fabrication in Eastern Province.

Saudi Arabian Engineering Co. (SAECO): j-v with Amindha NV of Holland for servicing and repair of oil-field equipment in Eastern Province.

Arabian Mechanical Engineering Co (AMEC): j-v with George Wimpey based in Alkhobar; undertakes mechanical and electrical construction contracts.

Brown and Root-Alireza (BRALCO): j-v between Brown and Root of Houston and Rezayat Trading of Alkhobar for offshore pipeline construction.

Rezayat and Williams Construction Company (RAWCON): j-v with Williams International of Tulsa for onshore pipeline construction.

Crescent Transportation Co: j-v with Sea-Land Service Inc. of New Jersey; operates container terminal at Dammam, and provides trucks to take containers to customers.

Lamnalco: long-established partnership between NCC of Kuwait and Land and Marine Engineering, a subsidiary of Bos Kalis Westminster; operates oil-loading terminals, provides offshore oil services, pilotage, maintenance of navigational aids. There are Lamnalco operations throughout the Gulf.

National Aggregate and Asphalt Co: j-v of NCC (Kuwait) and George Wimpey for production of aggregates and asphalt for road building.

Shareholdings: The Alirezas have holdings in various private and public companies in Kuwait and Saudi Arabia. The most ambitious of these, the National Pipe Company, in which Sumitomo has a shareholding, manufactures spirally-welded steel pipe in Dammam.

YUSUF AHMED ALGHANIM AND SONS AND ALGHANIM INDUSTRIES

Based in Kuwait and owned by four of the sons of Yusuf Ahmed Alghanim – Kutayba, Bassam, Salem and Omaya. Alghanim Industries is a holding company established in 1976. It owns Kirby Kuwait and Kirby USA, both of which manufacture pre-engineered steel buildings, and the major shares in two joint-ventures. These are Gulf Trading, a food-importing company established with the British firm Steel Brothers, and Alghanim Shipping, a shipping agent in which Wilhelmson of Norway holds 40 per cent. Yusuf Ahmed Alghanim and Sons is a trading company incorporating the following operating divisions.

Automotive: sales and service for General Motors (Cadillac, Oldsmobile, Pontiac, Chevrolet and Opel), Holden and Isuzu.

Commercial Equipment: sales and service for Chevrolet and Bedford trucks, Detroit Diesel Engines, Galion earth movers, Link-Belt cranes, Terex loaders and crawlers, Challenge-Cook concrete mixers, Airman compressors, Cedar Rapids asphalt and crushing plants, Millars road maintenance equipment, BP lubricants, Toyo tyres.

Engineering: agents for Hitachi and Frigidaire; installation and service of air-conditioning systems, manufacture of Blue Star water coolers.

Electronics: agents for Philips and Decca Radar; installation and service of closed-circuit TVs, sound and music systems, intercom systems.

Travel: general sales agents in Kuwait for British Airways, Gulf Air, Air India, Qantas, Cathay Pacific, Cyprus Airways; arranges tours for Kuwaitis abroad; runs air-freight, courier and packaging operations; car rental.

E.A. JUFFALI AND BROTHERS

Owned by Ibrahim, Ali and Ahmed Juffali; headquarters in Jeddah, with activities spread over all parts of the Kingdom. The partnership runs a trading business centred on trucks and heavy machinery, and holds participations in various joint-ventures, private and public companies.

Agencies: EAJB is the Saudi representative of some sixty international companies, the most important of which are: Daimler Benz – Germany, trucks and cars; Michelin – France, tyres; Barber-Greene – USA, crushing machinery and asphalt plants; FMC – USA, mobile cranes; Peiner – tower cranes; Worthington – USA, concrete mixers, batch plants and pumps; Clark – USA, forklifts; Scheid – compactors; CompAir – UK, compressors; Massey-Ferguson – Canada, tractors; Heidelberg – Germany, printing presses; Klimsch – Germany, printing products; Linotype – printing equipment; Borg-Warner – USA, York air conditioners; White Consolidated – USA, Kelvinator refrigerators; Bosch – Germany, auto accessories; Becker – car radios; Behr – car air conditioners; BICC – UK, cables, wires and electrical accessories; Dow Chemical – USA, specialist chemical products; Raychem – USA, heat-shrinkable materials; Liebherr – tower cranes, mobile cranes, concrete batch plants, excavators; L.M. Ericsson – Sweden, telecommunications equipment; Siemens – Germany, electrical generating and transmission equipment; Fluor – USA, oil and petrochemicals industry contractor; Henry C. Beck – USA, civil contractor; Ishikawajima Harima Heavy Industries (IHI) – Japan, desalination-plant contractor; Butler International – USA, pre-engineered steel buildings; IBM – USA, computers; Pool International – USA, oil drilling and workover; Munich Reinsurance – Germany; Kuehne & Nagel – Germany, freight forwarders.

National Automobile Industry: joint company with Daimler Benz assembling heavy trucks in Jeddah.

Arabian Metal Industries: manufacture of truck tipper and tanker bodies and other specialised bodies on site next to NAI.

Steel Products Co. (STEPCO): manufacture of steel wire mesh and wire fencing, with Korf Industries and other Saudi investors.

Saudi Building Systems and Saudi Building Systems Manufacturing Co.: design, manufacture and construction of pre-engineered steel buildings with Butler Manufacturing Company of USA.

Saudi Air Conditioning Manufacturing Co. and Maintenance of Air Conditioning & Refrigeration Co.: joint-ventures with Borg-Warner for manufacture of unit air conditioners and maintenance of units and air-conditioning systems.

Saudi Tractor Manufacturing Co.: joint-venture with Massey-Ferguson for manufacture of tractors.

Saudi Cement Co. and Saudi Bahraini Cement Co.: Juffali is leading shareholder in two major cement companies in the Eastern Province.

Arabian Chemical Co.: joint-venture with Dow Chemical to manufacture styrofoam roof insulation and various polyurethane compositions.

Saudi Raychem Manufacturing: joint-venture with Raychem producing polymer chemical materials including heat-shrinkable products for power utilities, telecommunications and oil industry.

Circuit Box and Fuse Manufacturing Co.: production of circuit boxes and HRC fuses.

Saudi Insulation Manufacturing Co.: manufacture of fibreglass insulation products.

Saudi Refrigerator Manufacturing Co.: joint-venture with White Consolidated manufacturing refrigerators of Kelvinator brand.

Fluor Arabia: contracting j-v providing engineering services for oil, gas and petrochemical projects. Fluor Corpn of California is partner.

Petrochemical Engineering Ltd: engineering and construction management services for petrochemical industry.

Beck Arabia: joint-venture with Henry C. Beck of Texas for civil construction.

Saudi Ericsson Communications: j-v with L.M. Ericsson providing downstream telecommunications products: specialised communications systems, private telephone exchanges and mobile telephones. Provides support services for L.M. Ericsson in the government's Telephone Expansion Project.

Arabia Electric: joint-venture with Siemens for design, supply, installation and maintenance of power distribution, communication and control systems.

IHI Saudi Arabia: joint-venture with IHI of Japan for engineering and construction of desalination and cement plants.

BICC *Saudi Arabia*: j-v with British Insulated Callender's Cables for installation of high-tension power lines.

Saudi Business Machines: wholly owned by Juffali. General agent for IBM data-processing products and distributor for IBM office products. Provides data systems and other customer-support services.

Arabian Computer Projects: Installation, facilities management, software development and data-processing turnkey services.

Pool Arabia: j-v with Pool International (a division of Ensearch Corpn of Texas) for oil drilling and workover services.

National Insurance Co.: partnership with Munich Reinsurance providing general accident and casualty insurance.

Orient Transport Co.: j-v with Kuehne & Nagel providing freight-forwarding services.

National Electric Products Co.: supply and installation of power-engineering systems.

Juffali Real Estate: development and management of commercial, industrial and residential real estate projects.

W.J. TOWELL

There are two major W.J. Towell companies – W.J. Towell and Company in Oman and W.J. Towell and Company Agencies in Kuwait. The ownership of these is explained in the notes below the family tree in chapter 8.

W.J. Towell & Co. Agencies: Kuwaiti company trading in bulk commodities, packaged consumer foods and other consumer items. Commodities include rice, sugar, barley and cement. Consumer foods agencies are: Hero (Switzerland), A&P (USA), Lindt (Switzerland), Universal Food Corpn (USA), Mitsubishi (for juices, nectars and fish) (Japan), Rotterdamsche Margarine (Holland), Lesieur Cotelle (France), Joseph Terry (UK), K.H. McClure (USA), W. Biesterfeld (Germany), Associated Exports (UK), Tims Products (India), Lotte Confectionery (Korea). Other consumer agencies are: R.J. Reynolds (USA), Hanes Garments (USA), Montagut International (France), 4711 (Germany), Cheseborough Ponds (USA), Ray-O-Vac (USA), Wilkinson Sword (UK), Delsey Suitcases (France), Thermos (UK), Addis Plasticware (UK), Parfums Lagerfeld (France), Wilk Industries (USA), Swank (USA), Evyan (USA), Molygon Cologne (Lebanon), Maschmeijer (Holland), George Kaufmann (UK), Kiwi Polish (UK), Stability Hosiery (UK), Springmills (USA), AMIEL Industries (Switzerland), Confininco (Switzerland).

W.J. Towell & Co.: Omani trading company with major real estate interests and shares in numerous joint-ventures. The company's trading divisions and shareholdings are as follows:

Automobile Division (Japanese): sales and service operation for Mazda.

Automobile Division (USA): sales and service operations for Buick cars and GMC trucks.

Autoparts Division: agents for Castrol, Lucas-CAV-Girling, Hazet Tools, NGK spark plugs, Bridgestone tyres.

Building Materials Division: agents for Twyford Sanitary Ware, Shapland and Petters, Blue Circle Products, Expandite Products, Hepworth Plastics, Crown Paints, British Cellophane Co., Dunlop Semtex Carpets.

Consumer Agencies Division: agents for Unilever (soaps etc., not food), Wilkinson Sword, Thermos, Ray-O-Vac, Britannia Biscuits.

Taylor Woodrow-Towell: joint company of Towell and Taylor Woodrow, civil contracting.

General Electric and Trading Co.: j-v with Sadiq Hassan Ali in Oman; agencies include Sanyo, Siera, Citizen Watches.

Muttrah Cold Stores: j-v with Spinney's (Overseas) Ltd; owns Muttrah Hotel and runs chain of large supermarkets known as Muttrah Cold Stores. Supermarkets stock virtually all well-known brands of consumer goods imported both by Towell and other merchants. Muttrah Cold Stores holds Oman import agencies for: Allied Manufacturing & Trading Inds (Australia), Associated Biscuits (UK), Ardmona Fruit Products (Australia), Ballantyne Export (Australia), T.W. Beach (UK), Berri Fruit Juice (Australia), Brooke Bond Liebig (UK), Dak Meat Packers (Denmark), Del Monte International (Belgium), Edgell (div. of Petersville) (Australia), Hero (Switzerland), Kraft (USA), Meatcut G.O. (Denmark), Mars (UK), Nestlé (Switzerland), R.H.M. Overseas (UK), Riviana International (USA), Ross (UK), Rowntree Mackintosh (UK), Standard Brands (USA), Stabburet (Norway), Star-Kist Foods (USA), Tate & Lyle (UK), Uplands Bacon Factory (Kenya), W. Weddel (UK), British American Tobacco (UK & USA), Cooper McDougall and Robertson (UK), Odex Racasan (UK), Procter and Gamble (UK), Scodia (France), Stevenson Mills (UK), Henri Winterman (Holland).

International Furnishing Co.: partnership with Abbas Ali Hazeem of Kuwait with showrooms in Abu Dhabi, Dubai and Oman; owns sponge factory in Dubai.

Shareholdings: Towell has important shareholdings in the Oman National Dairy Plant, National Bank of Oman, Kuwait International Finance Company, Design Consortium International (UAE company undertaking town planning and architectural work), Oman International Development Co. (investing in Omani real estate), Jotun Paint Factory in Dubai, and various investment and real estate development companies abroad.

W.J. Towell & Co Dubai Ltd: owned by Towell in Oman, but much smaller than the Towell companies in Kuwait and Oman; runs Towell Stores, a big supermarket in Dubai selling consumer items.

KHALIFA ALGOSAIBI GROUP

Owned and managed by Khalifa Abdel-Rahman Algosaibi and his sons; based in Dammam with most of its operations in the Eastern Province. Includes real estate interests and following subsidiaries and joint-ventures.

*Khalifa Algosaibi Cold Stores (*KACS*)*: major packaged-foods importer, agent for Kraft and SPC (Australian tinned fruit).

Khalifa Algosaibi Cold Stores/Jos. Hansen (Hamburg): arrangement whereby KACS sponsors Hansen in Saudi Arabia – specialists in design and installation of cold-storage facilities.

Algosaibi Grandmet Services: j-v with Grand Metropolitan for construction-camp catering and maintenance.

Khalifa Algosaibi Fishing Co.: wholly owned subsidiary for shrimp fishing, processing, packaging and sales.

Algosaibi-IFT: j-v with US company for meat and poultry processing, packaging and distribution.

Khalifa Abdel-Rahman Algosaibi Contracting: importer of construction materials and machinery; sponsorship for contractors. Principals: Mitsubishi Electric Corpn, Ishikawajimaharima Heavy Industries (IHI), Sanki Engineering, Mitsui Harbour and Urban Construction, Nippon Benkan, Guerdon Industries (USA), Building Systems and Equipment (USA), Caracola (division of Dragados Constructos – Spain), Haywood Taylor/Sumo Pumps (UK).

Algosaibi Rea: j-v for manufacture of crushed aggregates.

Construction Materials Co.: wholly owned subsidiary producing sand-lime blocks, bricks and tiles at Dammam.

Algosaibi Diving Co.: diving company for construction and maintenance of underwater oil installations.

Algosaibi-Hydrospace (Dubai): underwater maintenance, construction and inspection for oil installations; salvage.

Algosaibi-Partek; j-v with Finnish company for manufacture of pre-cast/stressed concrete components.

Algosaibi-Atlas: j-v with UK company providing cranes and lifting expertise for heavy construction.

Algosaibi-GESI: j-v with Philippines company for installation and maintenance of electrical systems.

AHMED HAMAD ALGOSAIBI AND BROTHERS

Partnership of Ahmed, Abdel-Aziz and Suliman Algosaibi; based in Alkhobar, operations mainly in the Eastern Province. Divisions, subsidiaries and joint-ventures as follows:

A.H. Algosaibi & Bros and Algosaibi Trading Co.: two companies holding agencies, mainly for construction materials and machinery manufacturers: Sumitomo Corporation – Japan, steel pipes and casing; Christensen Diamond Products – France, drilling bits; Borsig Gmbh – Germany, valves, turbines, compressors; Triangle Valve Co. – UK, valves; Pepsico Building Systems – USA, houses and office units; Mirlees Blackstone – UK, engines; Lewis & Tylor – UK, belting; Mayyat & Scott – UK, lifts; Gilbarco – UK, petrol pumps; ABC Hansen Comp – Denmark, grinding mills; Essochem – Belgium, oil-field chemicals; Refimex – Denmark, harvesters; Redman International – USA, mobile homes; Fiat Termomeccanica Nucleare e Turbogas – Italy, gas turbines; L' Electricité Industrielebelge – Belgium, electrical equipment; Fairmont Railway Motors – USA, railway equipment; Price International – Sharjah, pipe coating and insulation; Canadian Pacific Consulting Services; KMW International – USA, electric poles; Ajikawa Iron Works and Construction – Japan, steel towers for power transmission; Daikure – Japan, steel grating; Nippon Steel – Japan, steel structures; Osaka Transformers – Japan, transformers; Teamco Meteorological & Plotting Services – UK; Yakuma – Japan, boilers; Born Heaters – UK; Wollard Aircraft Equipment – USA, aircraft ground-support equipment; Meeusen Marinas – Netherlands, prefabricated floating jetties; Desteco – UK, vertical pumps.

Algosaibi Money Exchange Bureau: exchange dealing operation with American Express agency. Provides usual Amex services. Based in Alkhobar.

Algosaibi Investment Division: based in Alkhobar, works with majority-owned subsidiary, TWH, in London.

Tecmo Ltd: joint-venture with Fiat to sell, install and maintain gas turbines.

Plastic Industries: j-v with Swiss company making plastic sheets and mouldings.

Algosaibi Real Estate: real estate development in Eastern Province.

Algosaibi Service Stations: gasoline filling stations in Eastern Province.

National Bottling Co.: holds Eastern Province franchise for manufacture of Pepsi-Cola.

A.H. Algosaibi & Bros C02 Plants: production and bottling of carbon dioxide.

A.H. Algosaibi & Bros Ice Plants: ice production.

Continental Can of Saudi Arabia: j-v manufacturing cans in Alkhobar and Jeddah mainly for Pepsi-Cola.

Oil Field Chemical Co.: partnership with Essochem of Belgium producing oil-field and refinery chemicals in Dammam.

Algosaibi Hotel: hotel in Alkhobar, managed by Grand Metropolitan since 1979.

Saudi United Insurance Co.: owned 60 per cent by Algosaibis, other shareholders: Swiss Reinsurance Co., Commercial Union, Baloise Insurance (Switzerland).

Algosaibi Shipping Co: shipping agents in Dammam for dry cargo carriers.

Gulf Agency Co.: shipping agents in Dammam for tanker owners.

Algosaibi Maritime Services Co.: owned 50 per cent by Algosaibis; operates barges and tugs at Dammam.

International Offshore Services Corpn: offshore services for oil rigs.

Yusuf Algosaibi Travel Agency: Alkhobar-based travel agency run by Ahmed's son, Yusuf.

Shareholdings: The partners are founders and substantial shareholders in the following companies: Saudi Cement (other big shareholders are Juffali and Rajhi), El-Khat Printing Press, Saudi Glass Manufacturing Co., Saudi Company for Vegetable Oil and Ghee, Saudi National Pipe Co., Saudi Crowncaps Manufacturing Co., Saudi Hotel Services Co. (owning Riyadh Palace Hotel), Egyptian Saudi Hotel Co. (owning Ramada in Cairo), International Associated Cargo Carriers, International Air Cargo Corpn, International Trucking Express Co., Gulf Ro-Ro Services, Gulf Marine Transport (Kuwait), Saudi British Bank, Al-Jazira Contracting (Bahrain), Saudi Korea Stevadoring Co., Ifabank Paris.

KASSEM AND ABDULLAH SONS OF DARWISH FAKHROO

Doha-based partnership of Kassem, Abdullah and Abdel-Rahman Darwish. Acts as agent for Atlas Insurance; sponsors International Aeradio Ltd and Bos Kalis Westminster. Owns substantial property and shares, and: Darwish Engineering (civil contracting), Oasis Hotel, Qatar National Travel (baggage and aircraft handling at Doha airport – owned with partners), Darwish Travel Bureau (airline general sales agents). Before 1973 KASDF had considerable importing and retail operations, but in that year these were divided between the three brothers. The components that remained in the partnership were those which were difficult to split and had independent managements. The three brothers' operations are now as follows:

Abdullah Darwish: owns Modern Home department store in Doha and travel business in Dammam; formerly traded in commodities in Dammam.

Abdel-Rahman Darwish Fakhroo Trading Establishment owns: Darwish Automobiles and Trading Co. (Qatar agency for Fiat), Qatar Cold Stores, and a small travel agency in Doha; acts as sponsor for foreign contractors in Abu Dhabi.

Kassem Darwish Fakhroo & Sons: owned by Kassem Darwish and all of his sons, run by Yusuf bin Kassem. The partnership operates through the following divisions and joint-ventures:

> *Darwish Trading Co.* represents in Qatar: Pirelli (cables), Union Carbide, Philips, Dunlop, Friedrich (air conditioners), General Electric, Hobart.

> *Mechanical and Electrical Division*: represents and sponsors foreign contractors and manufacturers of electrical machinery: Ellis (UK mechanical contractor), Otis, Kingson International (US manufacturers of kitchens, laundries, etc.), P. Lynch (Irish electrical contractor joined with Darwish in j-v).

> *Construction and Engineering Division*: runs heavy-duty trucks.

> *Commercial Division*: sells furniture and fittings for houses.

> *Gulf Automobiles*: sales operation for Volkswagen and Audi in Qatar.

> *Gulf Housing*: j-v with McInnerny of Ireland for production of pre-fab houses.

YUSUF BIN AHMED KANOO

There are two Yusuf bin Ahmed Kanoo companies – one based in Dammam with branches throughout the Eastern Province and in other parts of Saudi Arabia, and the other based in Bahrain with branches in the UAE and Oman. The group headquarters is in Bahrain. The two companies run much the same sorts of operations, as follows:

Shipping: shipping agencies for dry cargo companies and tanker owners, forwarding, crew changes, lighterage, tugs, stevedoring (in Bahrain and at Dammam through Saudi Korea Stevedoring Co.), container terminals and facilities for Ro-Ro and LASH, bunkering services (through associate company: Saudi Arabian Bunkering Services at Ras Tanura), agency facilities for tankers at Arab Shipbuilding and Repair Yard (Bahrain supertanker dry-dock), small ship repairs at Bahrain Ship Repair and Engineering Co. (BASREC – 51 per cent Kanoo, 49 per cent Bahraini public). Dry-cargo lines represented include: Royal Nedlloyd, Hoegh (Oslo), Maersk (of A.P. Moeller – Copenhagen), Johnson (Stockholm), Navale et Commerciale Havraise Péninsulaire. Tanker owners represented include: Standard Oil of California, Texaco, Caltex, Exxon. Not all of these companies are represented in both Saudi Arabia and Bahrain.

Travel: general sales agents for airlines, package holidays, hotel reservations. General sales agencies, including off-line agencies, are: British Airways, Air India, Qantas, SAS, Lufthansa, Swissair, Austrian Airlines, Iraqi Airways, Middle East Airlines, Singapore Airlines, Cyprus Airways, Gulf Air, Pakistan International Airlines, Egyptair. Not all airlines are represented in both Bahrain and Saudi Arabia.

Aircraft Handling: through Asgul in Bahrain (51 per cent Kanoo, 49 per cent Gulf Air), and International Travel Agency at Dhahran (wholly owned Kanoo). At Bahrain airport Asgul has monopoly.

Insurance: represent Norwich Union in Bahrain and Saudi Arabia.

Importing: very wide range of heavy equipment, including: construction equipment, fork-lift trucks, generators, engines, drilling machines, pumps, compressors, oil-field and refinery chemicals, special cements, steel pipe, ropes, chains, paints, etc. Companies represented include: British Steel Corpn, Grove Cranes, Hyster (fork-lift trucks), Massey Ferguson, Perkins, Benford, Tremix (Sweden). Not all companies represented in Bahrain and Saudi Arabia. The company also imports a small quantity of consumer goods, its major principal being British American Tobacco.

Business Services: helps foreign companies with government documentation, visas, accommodation, personnel handling, pre-qualification for bidding for government contracts, local purchasing, air cargo, couriers to meet and assist visitors, leasing computer time.

Kanoo companies also have interests in the following joint-ventures and associated companies:

Aeradio Technical Services: j-v in Bahrain for maintenance and repair of gyro-compasses, radar and radio; sales of marine-safety equipment.

International Paint (Gulf) Ltd: manufacture of marine and industrial paints in Dubai.

Ocean Inchcape (Saudi Arabia) Ltd: offshore maintenance services.

King Wilkinson (Saudi Arabia) Ltd: project engineering, consultancy and design.

Foster Wheeler Saudi Arabia Co. Ltd: major process-plant construction.

Technical Industrial and Marine Contracting Co.: construction and maintenance services and marine works.

Otis Saudi: self-elevating oil-well workover platforms.

Greyhound Services Saudi Arabia: construction-camp management.

Saudi Arabian Transport Organisation: lighterage, marine transport, trucking.

Trans-Arabian Transport Co.: sea trailer/container inland trucking.

Baroid (Saudi Arabia) Ltd: production of drilling muds and drilling chemicals.

Cable and Wireless Saudi Arabia Ltd: installation and operation of telecommunications systems.

Moran/Brown-Olds (Saudi Arabia) Ltd: design and construction of civil work.

Oil Transport Company (Saudi Arabia) Ltd: marine transport of crude oil and products.

Saudi Arabia Logistics and Construction Co.: construction and maintenance of factories.

O'Neill Industries (Saudi Arabia) Ltd: in situ concrete building systems.

Saudi Arabian Maintenance Co.: Maintenance of buildings and their service systems.

OLAYAN GROUP

Ownership and organisation of group described in chart in Chapter 16. Following is list of operating companies in Saudi Arabia. Joint-ventures and associated companies (beginning with ALUPCO, below) come under the authority of the Olayan Financing Company (OFC).

General Contracting Company: sells and services cars, construction equipment, electrical engines. Agencies: Atlas Copco, Aveling-Barford, Blaw Knox, Clark International Marketing (cranes only – Juffali has loaders), Cummins Diesel, Creusot Loire, International Harvester, Rexnord, Stetter, Warner & Swasey, British Leyland, Chrysler (Eastern Province only), Crane Freuhauf, Eaton Yale and Towne, FMC, Paccar (Kenworth trucks), Hosking, Kirloskar, United Technologies, Hobart Bros, Nippon Electric, Pirelli General Cable Works, RTE, Geosource, ITT Grinell, Airtek.

General Trading Company: import and distribution of packaged foods. Agencies: American Tobacco, Armour Dial, Borden, Boyle Midway, Bristol Myers, Campbells Soups, Carnation, R.T. French, General Foods (Tang, Maxwell House), Hunt-Wesson, Kimberly-Clark, Lesieur Cotelle, Nissah Water, Real Fresh (Australia), Robertsons, Societé des Eaux Minerales (Sohat water – Lebanon), Solo, Sterling Drug, H. Swisher, 3M, Tulip Meat Packers, Tuborg, Unigate (Australia), Welch Foods, Eric Embourg Peltz, Pepperidge Farm, QUF Industries (Australia), Rockingham Poultry Marketing, Watties, Rowntree Mackintosh, Callard and Bowser, Wrigley, Cheseborough Ponds. GTC also manages the Industrial Converting Company, which manufactures Kimberly Clark paper products in Saudi Arabia.

Transportation Group: composed of General Transportation Enterprises in Kuwait and the Saudi General Transportation Company in Dammam (both under the same management), with several specialist j-vs. Very heavy on- and off-highway transport.

Projects and Development Company: holds and administers OSHCO group's j-vs in contracting and ancillary services. Partners include: Held and Franke (Germany), Interbeton (HBG Group, Holland), Rijn Schelde Verolme (Holland), Lord International (USA), Owens Corning Fiberglass (USA), FMC (USA), Protection SA (Greece), Mitsubishi (Japan). The Projects and Development Company also handles sales of commodities required by national projects.

Olayan Real Estate Company (ORECO): holds extensive tracts of land and properties in Eastern Central and Western Provinces, including most of buildings used by OSHCO companies.

Arabian Commercial Enterprises (ACE): insurance brokers, insurance agencies, owner of Al Nisr Insurance Co. of Lebanon and the Saudi Arabian Insurance Co. (registered in Bermuda), cargo surveyor, travel agent. Major insurance clients: Aramco, Arco, Bechtel, Getty Oil, Haji Hussein Alireza, Jomaih, Jeddah Oil Refinery, Jeddah Port, Mobil, Petromin, Philipp Holzmann, Saudia, Saudi Fertiliser Co, SCECO. Major categories of work are: Contractors' All Risks, Property Damage, and (on smaller scale), Marine Hull and Marine Cargo. Insurance agencies: New Hampshire Insurance Co., Libano-Suisse Insurance Co., Al Nisr Insurance Co., Taisho Marine and Fire Insurance Co., Legal and General, Sun Insurance Co., Saudi Arabian Insurance Co. Airline general sales agents for: Saudia, Austrian Airlines, Olympic, Swissair, Pan-American.

Aluminium Products Co. (ALUPCO): Olayan Financing Co. (OFC) has shares in this company, with Omar Aggad and General Hashim Hashim. Extrudes and fabricates aluminium products at Dammam. Technical help from Alusuisse.

Al Bustan: owns high quality family housing and office complex near Alkhobar.

Arabian Metals Co. (AMCO): wholly owned by OFC. Runs metal fabricating and oil-field machine shop.

Saudi Plastic Products Company (SAPPCO): majority owned by OFC, Omar Aggad and Prince Abdullah Faisal. Produces PVC pipe in Riyadh.

Arabian Plastic Manufacturing Co. (APLACO): owned 70 per cent by SAPPCO and rest by George Fischer of Switzerland and Anger Brothers. Manufactures PVC pipe parts.

Christensen Saudi Arabia: j-v leasing and servicing down-hole tools for drilling.

CONAM Services: now wholly owned by OFC – formerly American owned. Operates and maintains desalination plants.

Drilling Equipment and Chemical Co. (DRECCO): wholly Saudi owned. Supplies oil-drilling equipment and chemicals. Agencies include Hughes Tool, Halliburton, Gray Tool, Hydril, National Supply Co., Ciments Belges, R. Belleli, Bingham Willamette, Kawasaki Steel, Plicoflex, Wagi International S.p.a.

Saudi Chemical Co. (SCC): j-v with Nitro Nobel of Sweden and Prince Khaled bin Abdullah bin Abdel-Rahman. Factories in Riyadh and Dammam manufacturing explosive for rock blasting. Company carries out blasting for customers.

Gulf Explosives Co.: part owned by SCC. Imports and manufactures explosives in Ras al Khaimah for use in UAE.

Saudi Agricultural Development Co. (SADCO): j-v with Prince Khaled bin Abdullah bin Abdel-Rahman; egg production at Kharj.

Saudi Poultry Company: part owned by SADCO, operates hatchery at Kharj – partly to supply laying hens for SADCO.

Intermarine Saudi Arabia: operates maintenance craft for offshore oil rigs, oil-well testing facilities.

Saudi Tug Services: j-v with McAllister Brothers of New York and Deutsche Schachtbau und Tiefbohr; owns and operates heavy-duty tugs for berthing supertankers.

Saudi Arabian Bechtel Co. (SABCO): j-v with Bechtel. Projects have included: Ghazlan I and II power stations in Eastern Province, sea-water injection plant for Ghawar oil field, gas and NGL pipelines.

Arabian Bechtel Co. Ltd (ABCL): new j-v in which Prince Mohammad Fahd has a small share; managing Jubail industrial city infrastructure and Riyadh airport projects.

Saudi Arabian Bechtel Equipment Co. (SABECO): heavy equipment leasing.

Saudi Arabian Staats Co. (SASCO): j-v with Staats International Inc. of Boston, interior architectural design.

Saudi Graphco: j-v with Graphco France for manufacture of industrial and medical recording charts and diazo paper.

Saudi Polyester Products Co. (TANCO): j-v with Nitro Nobel and Blmqvist Vekstads of Sweden; manufactures polyester water-storage tanks and distribution systems.

Test Saudi Arabia: association with consulting engineers, Technical Studies Bureau, to provide planning, design, architectural and engineering services.

Thermo Electron Saudi Arabia (TESA): j-v with Thermo-Electron Corp of Boston, developing energy-saving systems.

Urban and Rural Development Co. (URDCO): wholly Saudi-owned company; providing farm management and irrigation services; operates nurseries; landscaping.

United Technologies Saudi Arabia (UTSA): j-v with United Technologies and other Saudi interests; distributes, services and maintains products of United Technologies, including Pratt and Whitney aero engines and Otis elevators.

VETCO Saudi Arabia: j-v with Vetco of USA, monitors oil wells and pipes.

Barclays Jardine Olayan (BARJAROL): j-v of Barclays Bank, Jardine Matheson and OFC, incorporated in Caymen Islands; lends funds to Near East Equipment Sale Co., which provides equipment sale financing on instalment lease basis for Saudi companies.

Deutsche Schachtbau und Tiefbohrgesellschaft Saudi Arabia: j-v for drilling deep oil and water wells, and workover activities.

Span Arabia: j-v with Span International of Arizona for computerised surveying.

Kashaaf Development Co. (KDC): wholly owned by OFC; formed to participate with Petromin (state oil and mining co.) and foreign companies in mining projects.

Olayan Saudi Investment Co. (OSICO): wholly owned subsidiary of OFC, formed to trade equity shares in Saudi public companies.

Saudi Welding Industries (SWI): produces welding electrodes on Dammam industrial estate.

Aluminium Manufacturing Co (ALUMACO): subsidiary of ALUPCO, based in Jeddah. Fabricates aluminium products for Western region.

Saudi Arabian Plastic Products Co. (Dammam): affiliate of SAPPCO, manufacturing high-density polyethylene pipes in Dammam.

Sappco-Texaco Insulation Products (SAPTEX): j-v between SAPPCO and Texaco for manufacture of polyurethane panel board.

Champion Arabia: j-v with Champion Chemicals of Houston for manufacture of oil-field and industrial chemicals at Dammam.

Evergreen Saudi Arabian Aviation (ESAA): j-v with Evergreen International Aviation of Oregon. Helicopter and fixed-wing services for personal transport, handling of materials, surveying, power-line maintenance and emergency air-lift operations. Based in Jeddah.

Health Water Bottling Co. (NISSAH): produces and markets Nissah mineral water. Plant at al Hajir in Wadi Nissah, 50 km south of Riyadh.

Carton Products Co.: wholly Saudi-owned company based in Riyadh. Manufactures egg trays.

Mining Services Co. of Saudi Arabia (MINSERCO): j-v with Granges International of Sweden. Provides consulting services for mining companies.

PDM Saudi Arabia: j-v between AMCO and Pittsburgh-Des Moines of USA. Designs and installs processing, refinery and other storage tanks; carries out structural plate and bridge work.

Prefabricated Building Co. Ltd (MABCO): owned by a group of Saudi businessmen and Paraisten Kalkki Oy (Partek) and Oy Yleinen Insinooritoismo (YIT) of Finland. Factories in Riyadh and Dammam manufacture precast and pre-stressed concrete structures.

Saudi Security Services Co. (SSS): represents Burns International Security and Freeport Security. Provides guards and firefighting services, security programmes and systems.

Eastern Contracting Co. (ECCO): Saudi-owned company specialising in labour-camp management and catering.

Investment and Trading Co. (ITC): Saudi-owned company based in Riyadh investing in commercial, agricultural and industrial projects, land ownership and development, and construction.

APPENDIX 3

Note on Arab Names

In the Arab world men are normally addressed by their first names. They are called 'Mr Ahmed' or 'Shaikh Abdullah'. On the same principle foreigners are often addressed as 'Mr Michael' or 'Mr John'.

In conversation, if the identity of the person being referred to is not likely to be confused with other members of his family, the first name will be followed by the family name. In talking of the chief executive of Haji Abdullah Alireza & Co., for example, one often speaks of 'Shaikh Ahmed' or 'Shaikh Ahmed Alireza'. However, if one is talking of a member of the family who has the same name as a cousin, uncle or nephew, one might distinguish him by giving the names of his father and grandfather after his own name. Among the directors of HAACO there used to be Mohammad Abdullah Alireza, the Chairman, and Mohammad Yusuf Zainal Alireza, a director and younger brother of Shaikh Ahmed.

To complicate matters slightly, there are a few names which are double-barrelled. Examples of these are Mohammad Ali and Ali Akbar. In the case of Mohammad Ali Zainal Alireza, Mohammad Ali is a single name; but in other circumstances it could refer to somebody called Mohammad, whose father was called Ali. All of the hyphenated names beginning with Abdel-, such as Abdel-Aziz and Abdel-Rahman, are single names.

Often the word *bin* or *ibn* (son of) can be put before the father's name. Mohammad bin Abdullah means exactly the same as Mohammad Abdullah. *Bin* or *Ibn* can also be put in front of the name of a distinguished ancestor who has given his name to a family; in this case the word only means 'son of' in the sense of 'successor of'. For example, the founder of the modern Saudi Kingdom was Abdel-Aziz bin Abdel-Rahman (Abdel-Rahman being the name of his father), but he was normally known as King Abdel-Aziz, Abdel-Aziz bin Saud or Ibn Saud. Saud was the father of his eighteenth-century ancestor, Mohammad bin Saud, who began his family's rise to fame. King Abdel-Aziz's eighth son, the present Saudi monarch, is known as King Fahd bin Abdel-Aziz al Saud.

Al normally means 'the', but if it is put in front of a family name it means 'the family'. Families of great prestige, such as Algosaibi and Alghanim, have incorporated the *al* into their family name. This procedure is widely copied by lesser men hoping to enhance their own status.

Arab family names can come from a variety of sources. One of the most common is the father of a famous ancestor, as in the Saud and Alireza families. Before modern times few Arabians needed family names. A man might go through life known simply as Abdullah bin Mohammad, and his son would be Khaled bin Abdullah. However, when a person distinguished himself his children would want to perpetuate and publicise their relationship with him for the sake of their own and their descendants' prestige. The grandfather's name would then become established as a family name. For example, Zainal bin Alireza and Abdullah bin Alireza were both famous men of Jeddah, and from the 1930s on their descendants have used Alireza as a family name.

Other common sources of family names are the occupations of ancestors, tribes, villages and provinces. Geographical names from Arabia are Hijazi and Yamani, given to people whose ancestors are from the Hijaz and Yemen.

The word *Haji* in front of a man's name denotes somebody who has been on the pilgrimage, the Haj, to Mecca. In day-to-day conversation it is used rather selectively, normally being applied only to people who are known to be specially devout.

Shaikh in Saudi Arabia is a term applied to religious leaders, judges (*qadis*), the elders of tribes and other important people. Generally speaking, the lower down the Arabian social scale one is the more people in one's life one addresses as 'Shaikh'. For example, one never hears the Saudi establishment referring to Ahmed Zaki Yamani, the oil minister, as 'Shaikh' but the junior staff of his ministry invariably use the term. When foreigners talk of him they normally confuse the system by referring to 'Shaikh Yamani' – putting 'Shaikh' before his surname rather than before his first name.

In the Gulf states 'Shaikh' is again applied to religious leaders and *qadis*, but otherwise only members of ruling families are given the title. In Saudi Arabia members of al Saud are known as 'Prince' (*Amir*).

The whole system of these titles in the Arabian Peninsula is much less formal than foreigners normally imagine it to be. The Arabians themselves attach little importance to titles and are casual in their use.

Many Arab first names have quite colourful meanings: Faisal means Sword; Fahd, Panther. Other names have a religious meaning: Abdullah means Servant (*abd*) of God (Allah). The hyphenated names, such as Abdel-Rahman, refer to some of the many names by which God may be called: Abdel-Rahman means Servant of the (Abdel-) Merciful (Rahman), Abdel-Rahime is Servant of the Compassionate.

APPENDIX 4

SAUD FAMILY TREE – MUCH SHORTENED

Includes members of family mentioned in text and a few other important princes

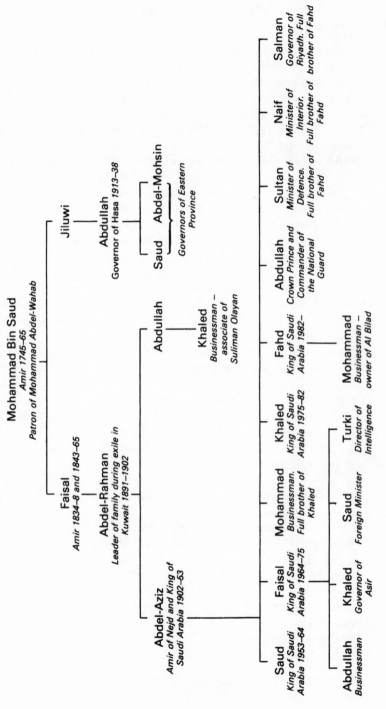

Index